TAKING DOWN FENCES:

How Liberalism and Single-Issue Politics
Are Destroying America

TAKING DOWN FENCES:

How Liberalism and Single-Issue Politics Are Destroying America

JAMES H. WALSH

LIBERTY HILL PUBLISHING

Liberty Hill Press
2301 Lucien Way #415
Maitland, FL 32751
407.339.4217
www.libertyhillpublishing.com

Printed in the United States of America

Paperback ISBN-13: 978-1-6628-1624-6
Dust Jacket ISBN-13: 978-1-6628-1625-3
Ebook ISBN-13: 978-1-6628-1626-0

CONTENTS

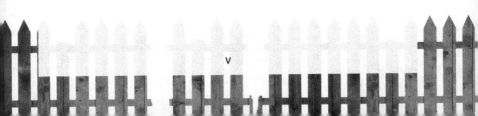

INTRODUCTION

"If you want to know why a fence was put up, take it down." I am not sure when I first heard that aphorism, or in what context, but it has served as a useful personal reality check for many years. The original saying, generally attributed to G. K. Chesterton, was a bit different than the version that plays in my mind but with identical connotations.

America is taking down too many fences, too quickly, and in the process the country is being bankrupted, morally, culturally, and financially. Like Rome in its final years, the United States is rapidly dismantling governance and value systems that were the foundations for the creation of what has been the wealthiest, most free, creative, democratic, and powerful nation in history. The principles of hard work, self-reliance, and risk-taking which fueled this enormous growth and prosperity, however, are rapidly being displaced by reliance on government largesse; obsessions with class, gender, and race; preoccupation with the assumed but unproven benefits of multiculturalism, globalism, and diversity; an indifference to social norms developed over years of trial and error; and rigid adherence to political correctness that paralyzes rational thought and decision-making. For decades, our education systems have been under attack, dumbed down, leaving us with an essentially under-educated and uninformed population, not familiar with our form of government or how the constitutional federal republic under which they live differs from the communist, socialist, and other systems that have subjugated societies and wrecked economies throughout history.

The founders understood education was key to the success of the new form of government they had created. So do the purveyors of socialism and communism calling themselves "Progressives." They have labored since the cultural revolution of the 1960s to undermine the country's educational systems and now largely have succeeded. As described by one commentator:

> Not even knowledge is prevalent in the postmodern university, if by knowledge we mean an integration of the disciplines into a coherent reality. Instead, we witness a fragmented world of deconstruction and trivial pursuits where the black perspective, the gay perspective, or the female perspective takes the place of a single reality. Each perspective is weighted by a political agenda (typically to the left), and professors, many of them having come of age with the protests of the 1960s, unload politics into the classroom.[1]

Unable to place anything in historical perspective and intimidated into silence by charges of racism, bigotry, misogyny, homophobia, and more, Americans are easy prey for the toxic ideologies of the radical left. America's shared culture and value systems are under attack by the single-issue advocates for race, gender, abortion, LBGTQ rights, open borders, single payer national health insurance, and a *mélange* of other causes du jour. "Victimhood" has become a sought-after status. Activists agitate not just for the tolerance of behaviors deemed unacceptable for centuries, but for their elevation to celebrated status. As a consequence, traditional values are being abandoned; young and old Americans alike rally to cries for "social justice," apparently without realizing that social justice is exactly what Marx, Stalin, Castro, Che Guevara, and the other "heroes" of socialism and communism promised as they enslaved their countries and destroyed their social, cultural, governmental, and financial institutions; and candidates of major political parties openly campaign as socialists or Progressives. American states and cities defy national laws and establish "sanctuaries" for aliens who have broken our laws, and state and local law enforcement agencies are prohibited from cooperating with federal authorities to arrest dangerous criminals in the country illegally, even those who have committed crimes in the United States. Our borders are largely open and unprotected despite the very real threat of international terrorism, drug and human trafficking, gang violence, and the spread of disease. Our resolve to lead and protect the free nations of the world and to promote the spread of democracy has waned to dangerously low levels. Political discourse has been reduced to unrelenting, bitter, partisan attacks and sound-bite sloganeering.

"If you want to know why a fence was put up, take it down." As America divorces from its traditional moorings and spirals into a confused state of unprincipled decision-making, we are entering one of the most dangerous periods of our country's history. Like Rome, America cannot survive if it has no consensus about what it is and what it stands for. What America is experiencing, however, may be the natural and inevitable result of too much success. As nations become wealthier and more secure, their citizens have the time and means to engage in social and political experimentation. They repeat the mistakes of history, either because they lack a knowledge of history or choose to ignore it, and without those reference points, the false promises of progressivism, socialism, and communism become too addictive for many to resist.

Social justice, equality, fairness, and similar abstract ideals sound and "feel" equitable. The always-missed question, however, is what is the best way to achieve social justice, equality, and fairness? History teaches that it is not communism, socialism, fascism, or progressivism, all of which inevitably shrink economies and create less, not more, wealth and opportunities. This country's market-based economic system, even as constrained by an increasingly intrusive and regulatory federal government, has created the greatest economic engine the world has ever experienced, generating vast prosperity and a path out of poverty for tens of millions. No system ever has benefitted a greater number of people, not just here, but around the world, a fact lost on the disciples of progressivism who daily denounce the supposed unfairness of market-based economies.

To be sure, when Progressives speak of fairness and equality, they are not advocating fairness and equality for everyone. These are code words intended to mean "we will put everyone, except us, the ruling aristocracy, who have done and sacrificed so much for you, into the same 'fair' circumstances. Rest assured, there will be social justice—all of you will be equally poor." Much like every leftist government, the elite and privileged classes prosper while the masses endure to the extent they can.

The great promise of America never has been equal outcomes, only equal opportunities, but it is a promise that has managed to create greater security, wealth, and freedom for more people than any other governing principle ever conceived. While Progressives belittle the enormous benefits market-based economies have brought to the world, they need look only to Venezuela, Nicaragua, Cuba, Russia, and North Korea for modern examples of the destruction, misery, and suffering "progressive" systems bring wherever and whenever they are tried.

In their calls for income equality and social justice, Progressives also mistake or overlook the obvious. As Thomas Sowell repeatedly has observed, except for a relatively small portion of the population, poverty is not a static condition in this country; it is significantly age-related. People are "poor" when young and in school, move up the economic ranks as they enter the workforce, and start back down the economic chain when they retire. It is a dynamic process, and Americans once recognized that the American economic system provided the best opportunity for their financial success, and if not immediately for them, then for their children, grandchildren, or great-grandchildren. If by pandering to the young, the undereducated, and the unsuspecting with promises of "social justice," "income equality," free education, free health care, and a guaranteed government wage and retirement income, Progressives are successful in assuming control of our government, this long cycle of hope, prosperity, and achievement will be interrupted, and America will join the ranks of failed socialist states.

That certainly is not meant to imply that the miracle of the American economy has freed everyone from poverty. It has not. No form of government ever can or does, but our market-based economy, paired with a constitutional government that respects the rule of law, protects private property, and defends the freedoms and liberties of its citizens, has come so much closer than any other system only the truly ignorant, the entirely self-absorbed, or the dangerously anarchistic would even question it. America offers what no other mode of government ever has—opportunity for everyone, regardless of skin color, gender, ethnicity, or religious belief. It is why so many want to come here. When collective regimes build borders walls, it is to keep people in, not out.

The commentaries and opinion pieces in this book are not a call to turn back the clock or to reinstate social or cultural norms that have caused unnecessary harm or injury. Some fences needed to be taken down, but thoughtfully and with full appreciation for the costs and consequences. They are intended, however, to be a wake-up call. The Progressives' threats are real, and to fix America we will have to rebuild fences where they should be rebuilt. We will have to strengthen America's education systems. We will have to free Americans from the tyranny of political correctness and race, gender, and identity politics. We will have to restore the sense of self-reliance and confidence that motivated the development of the United States into the world's greatest economic, political, and military power and made it an inspiration across the globe. We, in short, will have to return America to a state of rationality, where decisions are made based on facts and respect for the principles that promote the functioning of an open, free, and civil society.

CHAPTER 1

SOCIALISM

How and when did socialism become mainstream politics in America? Have people gone completely mad? The United States is the freest, most prosperous nation on Earth. It has relieved more poverty, fed more people, been responsible for more technical, medical, and scientific breakthroughs, and created the greatest wealth for the greatest number of people in the history of mankind. It is not an exaggeration to say that Western democracy owes its continued existence to the United States.

Socialism has killed and impoverished more people, created greater misery and suffering, and more completely stifled innovation than any economic system ever developed. It inevitably results in dictatorships because once the government owns the means of production, the classic definition of socialism, there no longer is any need for those in power to placate or respond to private interests. Communism, socialism's first cousin, is no better. In theory, under communism, the "people" own the means of production rather than the government, but that is a meaningless semantic exercise. Whether called socialism or communism, the results always are the same: poverty; loss of personal freedoms; and subjugation. Think Cuba, North Korea, Russia, China, Nicaragua, and Venezuela.

We can now add "progressivism" to the list. In a prescient article a few years ago,[2] Susan Stamper Brown addressed this question to Rep. Allen West (R-Fla.) during a town hall meeting: "What percentage of the American legislature do you think are card-carrying Marxists or international socialists?" His response, that he believed seventy-eight to eighty-one members of the Democratic Party were communists, all members of the Democratic Congressional Progressive Caucus (DCPC), set off a firestorm of accusations of "McCarthyism" by Democrats. While acknowledging there might not be that many "card-carrying" communists in the DCPC, Brown noted the close ties between the DCPC and both the Communist Party USA and the Democratic Socialists of America and warned that the DCPC was doing "its part to further the goals of the modern communists and socialists" within the Democratic Party. In support of those claims, she cited communications by the Communist Party USA acknowledging that the DCPC was an "important lever" to move the American political debate to the left, and a way for communists to run for political office within the auspices of the Democratic Party—in essence, disguising the fact that communists and socialists were running for office as Democrats and effectively turning the Democratic Party into the Communist/Socialist Party of America. The same communication praised President Obama's election as an opportunity to build something big, a "large, influential and effective Communist Party USA."[3]

Whether called progressivism, socialism, or communism, unquestionably the failures of our education systems account for some of the hard tacks to the left by Democrats. Graduates from our schools for the last several decades often have not studied history. Many have never taken a course in civics. They do not understand our form of government or what distinguishes it from other systems. They have no understanding of the Constitution and little knowledge of the many sacrifices their country has made around the world to relieve poverty, advance civil rights, and protect individual liberties and freedoms. Instead, liberal faculties at all levels of education proselytize students, citing the sins of slavery and American "imperialism," and rail against wealth, the wealthy, and "White privilege," while calling for "social" and "racial" justice and extolling the supposed virtues and fairness of communism and socialism. Every difference in our society is exploited to create division, anger, and envy; race, class, age, and gender all are fair game. "Victimhood" is celebrated, virtually worshipped, to a point where even the privileged seek "victim" status. How else do you explain Elizabeth Warren pretending for years to be Native American, or Jussie Smollett faking his own mugging? Single-issue voters with no apparent regard for the overall well-being of the country dominate political debate.

The Democratic Party has become little more than a big tent where single-issue voters, the disaffected, the malcontented, progressives, communists, socialists, and anarchists can assemble without any unifying or shared principles or theories of governance other than *moral relativism,* which I address in more detail later in this book. Governing principles are not needed because the goal is power, not governance, and once they assume power, they will govern as socialists always do—with a heavy hand and jackboots. Assembling and collecting votes is what matters. Within this milieu, it should come as no surprise that organized, disciplined, and focused operatives like members of the American Communist and Socialist Parties have so easily been able to hijack the Democratic Party. I use the terms *Democrats* and *Progressives* interchangeably in this book for that reason; they now are essentially one and the same. A few "traditional" Democrats undoubtedly remain in the Party, but Progressives are in control.

Most students have no idea what communism and socialism are. They only know they were excited about Bernie Sander's promises of "free" health care and education during the 2016 election cycle. They also were told that the governments in parts of Europe and Scandinavia are examples of "successful" socialism, when, in fact, those countries are simply large "welfare" states, many of which are struggling financially. Despite the major socialist programs embedded in their economies, similar to programs in the United States but on a grander scale, they are not socialist governments. Medicaid, SNAP, and many other government programs in our country are "socialist programs," but we maintain as a market-based republic because the essential means of production remain in private hands. While the Scandinavian and Nordic countries in particular, and continental Europe to a lesser extent, have created even larger welfare states than the United States, for the most part, they remain "parliamentary democracies" with the primary means of production privately held.

It is difficult to believe we are only seventy-five years removed from D-Day when countless thousands sacrificed their lives to protect democracy and provide future generations of Americans with the privileges and freedoms they enjoy today. Squandering freedoms so many sacrificed so much to achieve, and which most of the rest of the world covets, seems inexplicable until you consider how under-educated most Americans are today. In other chapters of this book, I address the systematic weakening of education that has occurred in the United States over the last sixty years and will not address it further here, except to say that unless and until we correct the educational deficiencies in this country, Progressives will have increasingly larger audiences receptive to their messages of class warfare, hate, envy, and anger.

We are even closer in time to Tiananmen Square. It is shocking to contemplate that only thirty years after the massacres of hundreds, perhaps as many as 2,600 students, by a communist government, young people are advocating for socialism in America, particularly with the even more recent example of Venezuela squarely in front of them.

Bernie came back for a second bite of the apple in 2020, announcing he again was running for president as a *Democratic Socialist*. He was the clear frontrunner for the Democratic nomination for months until Progressives became concerned with his electability. They then essentially did the same thing Hillary and the DNC did in 2016—kicked Bernie to the curb, this time in favor of fellow septuagenarian, Joe Biden, who Progressives hope would look more "mainstream" to voters. Problem is, Joe has been completely co-opted by the Progressives in control of the Democratic Party. He also clearly is having cognitive issues, which forced his handlers to keep him tucked away out of public view once he became the Democratic presidential nominee. The COVID-19 outbreak allowed that strategy to work. Now that Joe has been sworn in as president. I suspect Americans soon will learn more about the Twenty-Fifth Amendment than anyone cares to know.

The original announcement that Bernie was running a second time stirred great excitement among many Progressives, particularly the young, even though if he had been elected, he would have been seventy-nine years old at the time, older than Ronald Reagan was when he left the White House. Bernie raised $6 million within the first twenty-four hours after announcing his candidacy and $25.3 million in the third quarter of 2019. Once again "Medicare for all" was a central plank of his platform, along with "free" education for everyone. As he put it, "If our friends in Scandinavia can provide quality health care to all of their people as a matter of right, for far less than we spend, then you tell me why we can't do it."[4]

Actually, it was pretty simple to respond to Bernie—although I suspect he and his socialist friends already knew the answer—by simply considering and answering two questions: how have our "friends" in Scandinavia done; and is there any reason why we cannot legitimately compare Scandinavia and the United States for purposes of assessing the likelihood of success if we try to turn this country into the same kind of massive welfare state?

The answers, it turns out, are, "not so well," and "yes, unless you are willing to compare apples and oranges."

Bernie and the other prophets of socialism—all those Progressive candidates who ran as Democrats and scrambled to emulate or outdo Bernie—were scamming America big time. Unfortunately, many voters, particularly the young, were gullible enough to allow themselves to be duped. For example, it is a complete fantasy, as Progressives, including Bernie, surely know, to suggest the claimed "successes" of large-scale welfare programs in the Scandinavia countries means a similar approach would be a superior economic system for the United States or, for that matter, anywhere outside of the unique circumstances of Scandinavia. If Bernie and his happy band of Progressive mimes were even a little truthful, they would acknowledge that the Scandinavian countries they profess to admire so much have been able to offer the social programs they do only because of confiscatory tax rates, small, homogeneous populations, and, at most, modest defense costs because the United States provides their international security.

Using the Scandinavian countries as examples, Sweden has only about 10.4 million people; Norway, 5.4 million; and

Denmark, 5.8 million. California alone has nearly 40 million people, more than all of Scandinavia combined, even if you also include the other Nordic countries and their territories. Over 330 million people live in the United States in total.[5]

As you might expect, it's expensive to live in Scandinavia, very expensive. Income tax rates not only are considerably higher than those in the United States but also much "flatter," meaning most people are taxed at the upper levels, not just larger wage earners. Income taxes in Scandinavia, in other words, are significantly regressive and impose a greater burden on those less able to pay. And like most of Europe, Scandinavian countries utilize another seriously regressive tax, the so-called value-added tax (VAT). The VAT is similar to a sales tax except it is levied on every entity in the line of distribution—manufacturer, distributor, retailer, and consumer. The VAT end-market rates—those paid by consumers—are shockingly high, generally 25 percent. Add payroll taxes, social security contributions made by employers, extraordinarily high gasoline taxes—over $3 per gallon—in addition to state and local taxes, and the tax burdens on Scandinavians are staggering. The results are predictable—flight of the brightest, most capable, and most successful individuals to more tax-friendly countries.

Even with taxes approaching confiscatory levels, however, the Scandinavian states would have to reduce their social welfare programs or raise taxes to even higher levels, if they had to pay for a legitimate national defense. Denmark spends only about 1.2 percent of GDP on defense; Norway, 1.64 percent; and Sweden, 1.03 percent. Although some of these countries are now calling for increased defense spending in light of a more restive and adventurous Russian Federation, the truth is that every dollar spent on defense reduces their ability to fund domestic social programs, and populations that have grown complacent after years of dependency on government largesse are not likely to be in a hurry to trade "butter" for "guns."

Defense spending aside, the costs of globalization and immigration also are beginning to place significant pressures on the welfare state regimes of the Scandinavian countries. For example, Sweden has taken in tens of thousands of refugees over the last decade. The reality of extending generous public benefits to thousands of new residents already has led to a significant tightening of immigration policies and caused serious political upheaval.[6] As the Swedes are discovering, it is one thing to provide social benefits to relatively small numbers of working or retired citizens who have contributed to the system for years, quite another to try to extend the same types of benefits to large numbers of noncitizens who have contributed nothing at all.

As expensive as the large welfare state may be, when viewed in context, the performance of the Scandinavian states—sometimes referred to as "third-way socialism" by those promoting the "Scandinavian model" as a viable alternative economic system somewhere between capitalism and socialism—has been "unexceptional," according to most observers, including Nima Sanandaji.[7] That is not something you heard from Bernie or other Progressives. More importantly, Sanandaji, an Iranian-Swede and widely published president of the European Center for Entrepreneurship and Policy Reform, makes a compelling argument that the claim the Scandinavian welfare state would work in countries with different populations, cultures, and circumstances is based on a completely "flawed" analysis. He points to the fact that Scandinavian Americans enjoy considerably higher living standards in the United States than do their cousins living under the supposedly "utopian" Scandinavian model as an easy indicator of just that.[8]

That last statement again is not something you heard from Bernie and his Progressive friends. They like to pick and choose the issues they promote— "Scandinavians are providing health care at less cost than we are"—without ever addressing the "bigger picture" topics, such as, "even if we assume the Scandinavians are offering health care for somewhat less than we are, what are the costs elsewhere in their economies?" Another way to put this would be: "Overall, how does what the Scandinavian countries offer their citizens measure up to what the United States offers its citizens?" Turns out not so well.[9]

As Mr. Sanandaji notes, culture matters, and the Scandinavian countries share cultural features that have helped them survive the destructive social and economic forces of the large welfare states they created. These include small, largely homogeneous populations; non-governmental social institutions particularly adapted to the modern world: strong work ethics; civic participation; social cohesion; individual responsibility; and family values.

That once would have described the United States as well. The development of these cultural characteristics in Scandinavia, however, *predated* the rise of the large welfare states by more than 100 years, during a period when free markets, low taxes, and generous regulations allowed capitalism and entrepreneurship to flourish throughout Scandinavia.[10] Free markets, low taxes, entrepreneurship, and self-reliance, in other words, gave rise to the cultural characteristics that so far have allowed the Scandinavian countries to endure the most corrosive effects of the welfare state "socialism" Bernie Sanders and many Progressives are promoting as a "kinder, gentler, fairer" alternative to the market-based economy of the United States. And they are doing so, as Sanandaji points out, at a time when the Scandinavians increasingly are recognizing their welfare states are as "unaffordable" as they are "unexceptional," and are scrambling to return to their free-market roots by cutting taxes, reducing welfare benefits, and introducing market reforms.[11] Not surprisingly, the "brain drain" I referred to earlier, the flight of high earners, business leaders, innovators, entrepreneurs, and investors, voting, as they say, "with their feet," has become an escalating problem for Scandinavia.[12]

It should not be surprising that the Scandinavian countries are scrambling to return to more market-based economies. Much the same thing happened in China. Beginning in the 1970s, the economic disasters created by socialism and central planning caused a desperate China to permit the privatization of some state-owned companies, introduce free markets into segments of the economy, particularly consumer markets, and liberalize foreign trade.[13] The market-based reforms eased some of the financial pressures that were bankrupting China but have done little to loosen the Communist Party's iron grip on the Chinese people or promote individual freedoms and liberties.

China was clever about how it introduced "market reforms." The Chinese government promotes the theme of "one China, two systems" to justify the economic freedoms it extends to some citizens but not others. It uses "Special Administrative Regions," like Hong Kong and Macau, as well as "Special Economic Zones," like Shanghai, to attract foreign investment and allow, but only in those areas, the market-based reforms needed to overcome the stagnation created by the failed socialist policies of Mao Zedong.

However, China maintains dictatorial control over the lives of its citizens on the mainland, and in Hong Kong and Macau, protected for the moment by treaties between China and the

UK and Portugal respectively, there is considerable unease among residents about what will happen when the treaties expire. The recent unrest in Hong Kong, which started over a law that would have allowed Hong Kong citizens accused of a crime to be extradited to China for trial, was a reflection of those concerns. Unlike Hong Kong, where legal traditions inherited from years of British rule persist, there is no presumption of innocence for the criminally accused on mainland China. If the accused cannot prove their innocence, they are guilty. Public shaming remains common,[14] and it is not unusual for accused individuals to be executed without their families being notified.[15] In China, these simply are prerogatives of absolute government and demonstrate what happens when the rule of law, the presumption of innocence, freedom of speech, protection of private property, and other constitutional protections are degraded or disregarded. As the axiom goes, "power corrupts; absolute power corrupts absolutely."

There is no private ownership of land anywhere in mainland China. The government owns all land and leases "usage" rights to homeowners and developers, usually current or former Party officials, or those with strong ties to the Communist government—cronyism at its worst. Increasingly, the Chinese are housed in massive clusters of towering condominium buildings in urban centers, usually in living quarters of 800 square feet or less, intended to accommodate family units consisting of parents, children, grandparents, and sometimes others. Because the cost of housing in most Chinese cities is high, it is not uncommon for even married adult children to live with parents. The Chinese never entertain in their homes—they are far too small, crowded, and cluttered to even consider doing so. They meet instead in restaurants or public tea houses.

Millions of people continue to be forced to move from rural areas to cities where they can be stockpiled in condominium complexes, ostensibly to help relieve rural poverty, but fueled by the government's desire to consolidate farmland as China tries to become more self-sufficient in domestic food production.[16] An enduring image of the "new" China is a metropolis with drying wash hanging from thousands of new apartment building balconies on "wash days." There are no clothes dryers in China either.

With an estimated one-sixth of China's land contaminated by toxic, industrial run-off and much of its underground water supply polluted, arable land is scarce.[17] Garbage floats in major rivers and harbors, and dense smog envelopes much of the landscape. There is no such thing as potable tap water anywhere in the country, not even in high-end "Western" hotels in major cities. Medical care is so deficient an abiding mantra in China is to avoid going into a hospital at any cost; no one ever comes out.

China's per capita income is a fraction of that in more advanced countries. The World Bank, for example, uses $1.90 a day as the international poverty line—what $1.90 a day would buy in the United States in 2011 prices, which is deemed sufficient to provide individuals in China with a food intake of 1000 calories a day and certain other "basics." China's internal poverty standard, RMB 2,300 per year, is less than $330 a year. Nearly 380 million people, more than the entire population of the United States, live *below* the "upper-middle-income international poverty line" of $5.50 a day.[18] China's GNI, the gross national income per capita, stands at $14, 358, trailing a number of "developing" countries and below the average for OECD countries by orders of magnitude.[19]

After the collapse of the old Soviet Union, Russia also tried to turn to a more market-based economy to rescue an empire bankrupted by its communist government and the arms race with the United States. It allowed the sale of some previously state-owned and operated enterprises to private interests. Impeded by rampant corruption, however, Russia has struggled to make the transition—progress has been halting, at best—and the Russian Federation remains mired in economic stagnation.

There should be a message in all of this. Socialist or communist governments, or welfare state regimes, for that matter, that get into economic trouble, meaning all of them, eventually look for relief in free-market solutions. The measures never fully work because the governments refuse to relinquish enough of their central planning mentalities to allow market economics to function at anything close to maximum efficiency. Whatever market-based policies they adopt, however, serve them better than the incentive-crushing economic principles of socialism. Logically, governments concerned with the welfare of their citizens would embrace market economics more completely, but citizen welfare is not what this is all about. It is about power, and once acquired power is so compellingly seductive few can surrender even a portion of it peacefully.

This is the vision Progressives are offering for America. They do not say that, of course, but neither did the Chinese, the Russians, the North Koreans, the Cubans, or the Venezuelans. Advocates always believe they can make socialism, a political and economic disaster that never has produced anything but misery, suffering, and poverty, suddenly start creating prosperity, social justice, and happiness. No one ever can for the simple reason that once socialism destroys the motivations and incentives that fuel all human progress and achievement and wrecks the economy, as it inevitably does, there is no money to raise standards of living, protect the environment, address poverty, provide adequate health care, or do anything of consequence. History provides no examples of civilizations

populated by people altruistic enough to sacrifice their interests to support those unable or unwilling to contribute. And
like the fabled anthropomorphic egg, Humpty Dumpty, once
broken, all the king's horses and all the king's men never can
put the economy together again. At the very least, if they aspire
to govern America, Progressives should be honest enough to
try to explain why history provides no examples of successful
socialism and how their version will be different.

Whether "classic," as in China before its market reforms,
or a welfare state hybrid, as the Scandinavia countries are
claimed to be, socialism in any form has never been a sustainable economic or political model. There is no reason to
believe even the Scandinavian welfare state, which is a far
milder dose of central planning than the grim takeover of the
economy Progressives plan for America—just read the Green
New Deal if you do not believe it—and now showing "cracks"
even in countries ideally constituted to give it the best chance
for success, would be anything other than an economic, political, and social catastrophe in the heavily populated, distinctly
non-homogenous, United States. Even tired old socialists like
Bernie Sanders should be able to understand the dramatic
differences between the cultures, sizes, and circumstances of
the Scandinavian countries and the United States. It should
be equally obvious that globalization and immigration already
are changing the cultural and demographic characteristics that
allowed the Scandinavian welfare states to develop in the first
place and are rapidly making them unaffordable, unworkable,
and obsolete.

I suppose you have to excuse Bernie for not acknowledging
either that the Scandinavian countries are welfare states—
nothing particularly flattering or glamourous about peddling
a vision of the United States as a welfare state—or that rapidly occurring changes in demographics and culture suggest

the Scandinavian model may have little remaining shelf life unless dramatic, market-based economic reforms are implemented. Bernie and his acolytes have few places they can look for "successes" in the dark history of socialism. Rebranding the Scandinavian welfare states as some type of "third-way" socialism and pretending all is well in Scandinavia is about as close as they can come. Forget the fact that the "fit" is not good for the United States—the "Scandinavian model" at least provides something less virulent and easier to talk about than the prosperity-sucking proposals contained in the Green New Deal or what is happening under socialist regimes in places like Cuba, North Korea, Russia, China, Nicaragua, and Venezuela.

Venezuela is the latest victim of socialism. It went from the richest country in South America to a humanitarian basket case in a time-period almost too short to comprehend. As with all socialist takeovers, the scenario was predictable. Key industries were nationalized. Speech was restricted. Political enemies, real and imagined, were imprisoned or intimidated. The press was censored. In short order, the country's currency was destroyed, and people were starving in the streets. In the span of a few years, the prosperous Venezuelan people lost everything.

That is the familiar and unwavering legacy of socialism, and it is why its supporters have to look for examples of success in more benign forms of political and economic organization, such as the "welfare states" of the Scandinavian countries, even to talk about this political psychosis. The real thing is so unremittingly horrific, despicable, and extreme that only the truly evil, the truly witless, or the truly uninformed would even consider it.

For many in the country, I suspect the slide toward socialism has more to do with gauzy notions of "social justice" and "income inequality" than any type of reasoned political or economic thought. Progressives have managed to make both concepts potent weapons in their assault on American democracy. The concepts are useful to them, however, only to the extent they can be taken far from their traditional roots and meanings.

In Progressive-speak "social justice" has been re-interpreted to mean the "uniform distribution by the state of all of society's advantages and disadvantages."[20] Equality in all things is good, inequality in anything is bad, and the state decides who gets what. As the late professor, philosopher, author, and intellect, Michael Novak, himself once a progressive socialist,[21] pointed out, however, you turn "social justice" from a doctrine intended to protect and promote individual freedoms and democracy into one that promotes socialism the moment you eliminate "fairness" and "equity" from the definition of equality and place the state in charge of distributing society's "advantages" and "disadvantages. Traditional concepts of "social justice" had nothing to do with giving everyone the same amounts of everything; "social justice" was achieved when people received proportionately to their contributions and efforts.

Novak cited an encyclical of Pope Leo XIII from 1891 denouncing the notion that equality has any role in social justice precisely because equality is unnatural and inconsistent with the differences between humans in terms of capacity, health, strength, and skills. These differences, far from being disadvantageous to either individuals or societies, are beneficial because societies require diverse skills and services to function. The understanding that a variety of skills is needed by society, in fact, is what influenced the development of an American economic system designed to take advantage of the diverse range of skills and talents of its citizens.[22] Nevertheless, unequal human gifts necessarily produce unequal individuals and potentially unequal outcomes, particularly after adjustments are made for effort and enterprise. Even among people of more or less equal skills, training, and experience, some will work harder, longer, and with more discipline, diligence, and care than others.

As described by Novak, until hijacked by Progressives, social justice was realized when individuals organized and associated to share complementary but unequal skills for the benefit of people outside the group, on terms acceptable to the group. Think of it as individuals coming together to start a restaurant or other small business. The value of individual contributions is determined by the group without input or interference from the government. Democracy and individual freedoms are promoted and strengthened by the private nature of the compact, not obliterated, as is the case when the state alone determines advantages and disadvantages and how they will be distributed and shared. Importantly, it is not a zero-sum game with winners and losers. Everyone within the group benefits and equality is determined by principles of fairness and equity acceptable to the group, not through remote decisions by central planners with no ability to assess "fairness" in any way other than arbitrarily.

It is an esoteric discussion, but boils down to this: in democracies, people with differing skills and abilities come together voluntarily to create something none of them are capable of achieving alone. They do so because they have identified a demand or need. They decide upon the relative values of each other's contributions based on criteria acceptable to them, not driven by government doctrine. Social justice as defined by Progressives, by contrast, is achieved when the government tells people what they will do and with whom, and everyone is rewarded equally without regard to the value of individual efforts or contributions.

And therein lies the controversy. Are we prepared to give up our freedom to choose what we do, with whom, and on what basis and allow the state to make those determinations without regard to fairness, equity, merit, or contribution? Do we have the will, in other words, to protect our freedoms and liberties, realizing that individuals are in a far better position than even the most competent and well-intentioned government bureaucrats to determine their self-interests and what is fair and equal in the circumstances of their cooperation and collaboration?

It should not be a difficult calculus. Is it fair and equitable for more skilled, talented, creative, and committed workers to take the same pay as the indolent and unwilling? If someone's natural talents, skills, and capacities are unsuited for a certain type of work, should they receive the same as the workers whose skills are essential to bringing the project to fruition? Is it somehow unjust, for example, to pay more for the skills and knowledge of a brain surgeon who spends years in schools, internships, and residencies than for the unskilled services of a construction laborer who did not finish high school and whose training is brief and "on the job?" If so, by what measure is that "social justice" for the more skilled, trained, and able workers? Why should benefits be allocated equally among people who have participated unequally? How is it even remotely possible for the state to make those decisions more correctly or fairly than the individuals involved?

Social justice never has meant, and never can mean, that the benefits of society should be distributed equally regardless of merit, effort, or contribution. Incentives matter. They always have and always will, and should the moment come when they do not, that is when all human purpose, achievement, and progress will end, the leftist "revolution" will have succeeded, and freedom and democracy will vanish.

Income inequality is the second part of this issue. Charges of "income inequality" are one of the ways Progressives pander to the naïve and turn Americans against each other. It is classic Marxism, promoting themes of class conflict and "exploitation" of workers by wealthy capitalists but with a twist: race and ethnicity now define the "oppressed," the "proletariat."

Our technology-driven economy has created the largest number of billionaires ever to exist in the world—over 2,700 currently—and many more millionaires. Once upon a time, that would have served as an inspiration, a reminder of the vast opportunities available to everyone in a country with free markets, reasonable tax rates, the rule of law, protection of private property, and respect for human rights. As I said in the *Introduction* to this book, whether someone had the immediate means for taking advantage of those opportunities or not, they did not begrudge the successes of others because they knew they were working within a system that would provide, if not immediately to them, then to their children, grandchildren, or great-grandchildren, more opportunities than any other economic or political system possibly could. They were proud of their country. They believed in American exceptionalism because they had witnessed it firsthand through two World Wars. They understood, while not perfect, the United States represented what everyone else in the world was trying to emulate but could not. They had witnessed the failures of socialism and communism around the world and the widespread misery, suffering, and poverty these systems caused. They understood intuitively that the prosperity generated by the market-based economy of this country, even if not equally shared, would benefit more people, *more fairly*, than any of the economies of countries impoverished by progressivism, socialism, and communism.

No longer. The Progressives' answer is state-run everything. They are not trying to take the United States in the direction of Sweden, Denmark, or any other Scandinavian, Nordic, or European country. Their aim is far more ambitious and dangerous—state-controlled education, health care, energy, and, ultimately, state-controlled everything.

And to what end? It cannot be because governments somehow are fairer or wiser or better able to allocate resources and opportunities. It never is the goal of any government to level the playing field for everyone; all have favored groups and causes. That is the reason the dispassionate decisions produced by market-based economies come so much closer than other systems to getting it right.

Socialism and communism are not fair systems despite their theoretical underpinnings. Those in charge prosper while everyone else suffers. The communist party leaders in Russia all had their dachas, private cars, access to luxuries, and other privileges while the proletariat suffered shortages in basic necessities, including food, clothing, medicine, and housing. Just like the Hollywood elite in this country, who preach environmental protection but live in multiple, large-footprint homes, drive energy-guzzling SUV's, and operate luxury yachts and private airplanes, sacrifice is something for everyone else, not for those in control. "Social justice" and "income equality" in the Progressive meanings of the terms, are achieved when more people look more "equal" because everyone has less, much less, except, of course, the autocrats running things, who continue to enjoy their lives of privilege and affluence.

Something else I alluded to in the Introduction: Progressives like to talk about *wealth* and *class* as if they are static concepts—some people are forever wealthy, others forever poor—a distorted worldview that Thomas Sowell has debunked often.[23] While no one denies that some are trapped in poverty, wealth and poverty tend to move dynamically with age and experience, as Sowell has documented. Those young and in school tend to be "poor," but rise in wealth and status as they enter the workforce and progress through their chosen fields before returning to a "poorer" status when they retire.[24]

I am not downplaying the plight of those trapped in poverty; there certainly are too many. But socialism has never been the answer to breaking the cycle of poverty. Too often unrecognized is the fact that the American market-based economy has lifted more people out of poverty than any economic system ever devised. Has it reached everyone? Of course not. No system ever has or will. Has it helped more, many more, than progressivism, communism, socialism, and any other collective system you can name? You know the answer.

I can hear the backlash already. "You don't understand. We are protecting the people left behind, the marginalized populations. These people are worried about food, shelter, and medical care. They don't have 'opportunities.' They are exploited and defenseless. You do not understand the plight of the poor, people of color, the disabled, and the sick."

Protecting them? How? By dismantling governance and economic systems that have created the greatest good for the greatest numbers in favor of an economic and political calamity responsible for impoverishing and depriving billions of life, liberty, and property?

Progressives never seem to understand that you cannot help more people by creating less wealth. Shrinking economies cannot sustain even existing social programs or initiatives, much less expand them or create new ones. It is completely delusional to expect socialism to provide more support to more people than the market-based economy of the United States. Do Progressives not understand why people are flocking to our borders? It is not for political asylum, but for economic opportunities and a level of prosperity that simply does not exist anywhere else in the world.

As one commentator described the muddled economic theory of socialism:

> Today's socialist dreamers think and act as if they just arrived from an alternate universe. A $19 trillion national debt means that the federal government hasn't spent enough to solve our problems. Stealing money that belongs to others through taxation is perfectly alright if you spend it on good things. People become much more honest, fair, competent, and compassionate once they get elected to office. If you force employers to pay someone more than their services are worth, they will hire them anyway and just eat the difference. Regulations always do good because their advocates mean well. Civilizations rise and become great because they punish success and subsidize failure, then they collapse when they embrace freedom and free enterprise. Each person is entitled to whatever he wants other people to pay for, like free college and birth control.[25]

Unfortunately, years of promoting class, race, and gender envy have put us in a position where the shopworn battle cry of socialism, "exploitation of the common man by the wealthy and privileged," has blinded many, particularly the young, to the boundless opportunities the United States offers every person regardless of race, ethnicity, age, or gender. Despite the seemingly unmistakable teachings of history, "true believers" simply do not accept socialism or communism as failed systems. To them, the failures of socialism and communism have been in execution, not theory. Because they are smarter, more benevolent, empathetic, compassionate, and insightful, they can make work what never has worked before. After all, today when you pull the curtain aside, you do not find the Great Oz, but supercomputers, technologies, and "understandings" of our planet and universe not even imaginable years ago, so how hard can it be to create and run paradise on Earth? Unfortunately, none of this is a joke, and too many in this country have become overly complacent; they simply do not believe socialism or communism ever could supplant democracy in the United States.

I do not share their confidence, even less so after the November 2020 elections. Billions of dollars are being spent yearly to destabilize our government. Many of our educational systems are a joke, dumbed down to a point where they no longer are effective. Just as the waves of immigrants inundating Scandinavia and Western Europe are rapidly changing the cultures of the Nordic countries and Western Europe, so too is the steady and largely uncontrolled influx of immigrants into the US erasing any sense of unity or notions of shared goals, ideals, or understandings of the "common good." We are "balkanizing," as the steady incursion of illegal immigrants with no aspirations to become Americans and with values, ideas, and cultural and religious convictions inconsistent with our Constitution, laws, and foundational principles continues. Environmentalists promote radical policies that would cripple the economy, undermine national security, starve millions, and set back human progress by hundreds of years. Police forces across the country are under attack. Progressives push to disarm America even as Silicon Valley and Hollywood get rich from selling games, movies, and music that promote gun violence, disrespect for women, and the pleasures of hedonism. Instant gratification has become a national norm, personal communications nearly obsolete. No one talks to each other anymore; they communicate by text message, Twitter, or Instagram. Emojis substitute for emotion, canned GIFs for creativity. No one is accountable for anything or to anyone. Narcissism abounds. Our culture, our history, our institutions, including the office of the president of the United States, are denigrated and attacked. The notion of American exceptionalism, virtually undeniable if measured on any fair and balanced basis, is ridiculed.

If you want to take over a government without firing a shot, first destroy its education systems. An undereducated populace loses the ability to engage in the critical thinking needed to question information and authority. Then co-opt the media and subvert the culture by undermining any sense of unity, "oneness," or shared values and dividing the country along race, gender, and class lines. Attack families, churches, and other institutions that teach and promote public and private ethics and morality. Make government the arbiter of "equality" and "fairness." Intimidate and silence opposing views by labeling anything not fitting the desired narrative as racist, bigoted, sexist, discriminatory, homophobic, xenophobic, Islamophobic, or any other stigmatizing term that can be ginned up. Underfund and deplete the military and the police. Create doubts about the continuing relevance of the Constitution. Make the country apologetic for its history by fixating on the errors and ignoring the achievements. Expand welfare programs and policies that make people increasingly dependent on government. Pack the court system, particularly the Supreme Court, with party apparatchiks and then use the courts to redefine and limit individual rights and freedoms. Assume control over health care, education, energy, and other major aspects of the economy that provide the government with even greater opportunities to "reward" supporters and punish critics. Cripple private-sector businesses with burdensome regulations and confiscatory taxes to pay for increasingly expansive and expensive social and environmental programs. As the economy falters, implement rescue plans that nationalize additional systems and industries. As civil unrest increases, declare an emergency and impose martial law.

These are the forces that have been chipping away at the fabric and resolve of the United States for decades. The rioting following George Floyd's death and the results of the 2020 elections illustrate just how much headway Progressives have made in their quest to change our form of government and way of life. There were no realistic expectations that anyone could have defeated the US militarily, but promoting revolution by weakening the structure of the country from within, slowly and incrementally, one cause at a time, are time-tested, classic Marxist-Leninist tactics. It prepares the proletariat for the coming "revolutionary combats."[26]

It can happen quickly. It took only a few years for socialism to take Venezuela from being Latin America's richest country to economic ruin. Brazil is on the same trajectory. Keep in mind, Venezuela has the world's largest oil reserves, but the effort to "transform" the country through "twenty-first-century socialism"—basically the same thing Progressives are promising in America—started under Hugo Chavez, imploded under Chavez's hand-picked successor, Nicolas Maduro. Venezuela, quite literally, "ran out of other people's money." Progressives are trying to do the same thing here.

The latest, and the most candid manifestation of how Progressives have overwhelmed the Democratic Party, if people are paying attention, is the Green New Deal manifesto.

The Green New Deal, or "Green Dream," as Nancy Pelosi described it, may seem, as President Trump noted, more of a "high school term paper that got a low mark" than any type of serious political proposal, but it speaks volumes about the Progressives' vision for this country. It is a political manifesto, make no mistake about that, and given the chance, Progressives will turn this country upside down trying to achieve their ambitions for a complete makeover of American society, politics, culture, and economy. These people are not proud of America. They despise the United States and everything it represents. They view themselves as revolutionaries, the "resistance." They do not want to improve America; they want to destroy it and remake it in the image of their socialist heroes: Che Guevara; Fidel Castro; Karl Marx; Friedrich Engels; Vladimir Lenin; and Mao Zedong. Their platform includes the elimination of fossil fuels, airplanes, cars, and flatulent cows. Every building in America would be redone to comply with some bureaucrat's vision of "energy efficiency." They would guarantee jobs with vacations for everyone and government wages to those unwilling to work. They promise "free" government-run health care and higher education. Do you like your doctors and private schools? Too bad; they will be gone. Senator Elizabeth Warren has made clear that universal day-care funded through taxes on the wealthy also is part of the "vision." Borders would be opened, the military stripped of purpose and resources, and police departments deprecated.

The government essentially would own everything, run everything, and control everything. What you eat, where and how you live, what type of transportation you use, what doctors you see, how much you are paid—everything would be dictated by the government; central planning at its finest. Because people of color and other "marginalized populations" are a special focus of the Green Dream, reparations for the descendants of slaves and Native Americans can be expected. To get a glimpse of what that might look like, look no further than Zimbabwe and South Africa.

While not nearly on the scale of what it would look like in America, approximately twenty years ago, Zimbabwe started taking land from White farmers and giving it to those considered to be the victims of apartheid. The results were looted and abandoned farms, massive food shortages, and enormous deficits as Zimbabwe was forced to buy and import food it once grew or raised. Today, even drinking water is in short supply—the government lacks the money to pay for chemicals to treat it.[27]

Despite witnessing that experience, the ruling party in South Africa, the African National Congress (ANC), subsequently started its own land reform initiative that would allow the government to take land from White farmers, without compensation, also to benefit those the government decides were victims of apartheid.

The potential cost of reparations in the United States as presently estimated? Up to $14 *trillion.*[28] How it would work is difficult to imagine with many millions in the country who are not descendants of slave owners, others who came to this country generations after slavery was abolished, many Black Americans who are not descendants of slaves, and others who are descendants of free Black slave owners or the slaves they owned.

You should not expect proponents of the Green Dream to have any greater concerns about destroying the country or its economy than did Castro in Cuba, Maduro in Venezuela, Kim Jong Un in North Korea, Idi Amin in Uganda, Pol Pot in Cambodia, or any of the other revolutionaries who ruthlessly impoverished their countries and turned them into armed prison camps. The Green Dream agenda would leave America bankrupt and defenseless, and without the protection of the United States, the other democracies of the world soon would be at the mercy of the expansionist powers around the world now constrained only by the threat of the US military.

Keep in mind that a primary architect of the Green Dream was Alexandria-Ocasio Cortez, whose economic acumen prompted her to help block Amazon from locating a new head-quarters building in New York City. Her reasoning: the "tax breaks" offered to Amazon would be better "spent" repairing infra-structure, like subway stations. She presumably did not understand that future "tax breaks" do not represent money existing in the New York state treasury available to be spent on infrastructure or anything else, while Amazon re-locating to New York would have brought billions of actual dollars to the city. If she did, then political grandstanding was more important to her than honesty or generating jobs and revenues.

Whether intentional or not, the authors of the Green Dream did a very clever thing—they obscured the fact they were pro-posing the most extreme and radical changes to the social and economic compact between the citizens of the United States and their government ever proposed by any major political party. They did so by tying their agenda to the climate change narrative. Even the name, *Green New Deal,* suggests the environment is the focus of the manifesto. Effectively, proposals for extreme political, social, and economic change were linked to climate issues in a way that appears to make everything part of a unified, "save the planet" initiative. The hope is that no one will notice what is being proposed is revolution, not protection of the environment.

Sadly, we live in a world of sound-bite campaigning and single-issue voters, often with short attention spans. Many who voted in the 2020 elections never understood, or cared, that the "Green Dream" was a political manifesto announcing an immediate intent to turn the country hard left to socialism, not a climate change document. Even for those who noticed, nesting the most radical features of the Green Dream comfortably within the climate change rhetoric dampened the stridency of the socialists' call to arms and made it more difficult to recognize the existential threat to our freedoms and democracy Progressives represent.

In another chapter of this book, I address how labels are being used by activists everywhere to covertly broaden their agendas. The technique is simple enough. First, create the label and apply it to behavior almost everyone will agree is appropriate— "rape" as "sexual violence," for example. Condition people to respond to the label "sexual violence" in the desired manner, usually emotionally and angrily. Next, begin associating other, less noxious forms of behavior with the label, broadening its meaning until even angry words between a man and a woman are viewed as "sexual violence" and evoke the same emotions as rape.

That is what is happening here. Create the label, Green New Deal, link it to protecting the environment, and then gradually introduce the socialist dogma embedded within the manifesto until the dogma itself becomes an inseparable part of what Americans understand is needed to save the planet.

The process to make this happen began almost immediately. Several leading presidential hopefuls at the time, including Elizabeth Warren, Kamala Harris, Cory Booker, and Bernie Sanders, immediately endorsed the plan. Prominent Progressives then began "walking it back," describing it as an "aspirational" document, and assuring people there was "nothing to worry about, that "any changes would be incremental and slow." Anything endorsed by Bernie, of course, is accepted by his legions of young, uninformed, detail-challenged followers without reflection or analysis.

The media also did its part, defending the Green Dream as a "plan to reduce greenhouse gases," and denying it would do any of the things President Trump warned about during a rally in El Paso, Texas.[29] One prominent, liberal commentator took a slightly different tack. He lamented the fact that Republicans, and even some Democrats, had ridiculed the Green Dream as the nonsense it is. It was a shame, he wrote, that America had lost the ability to "think big" and equated the Green Dream to the space program's effort to reach the moon.

The space program? The space program was a competition with the Russians. It was democracy versus communism, and democracy won. It was a bipartisan effort that pulled the country together on a common cause almost everyone supported. It had no implications for our form of government except to strengthen it. The Green Dream is intended to tear the country apart, to completely change our form of government. Responsible Americans object to the Green Dream not because the ideas are too big but because they are too loopy, too extreme, too un-American, and too destructive of ideals and incentives that drive human accomplishment and promote human dignity—in a phrase, "too socialist." The more observant also object to the Green Dream because they recognize it as the political manifesto it is, completely at odds with our Constitution, our form of government, our freedoms, and our way of life.

The notion that the ideas in the Green Dream somehow are too big is laughable. The ideas are the shopworn pulp-fiction of socialism and communism. They are high sounding only to those who are ignorant of the appalling suffering these ideas have inflicted on humanity wherever they have been tried, who do not care, or who believe the world is better off having less rather than more.

This game will continue to be played. Progressives will endorse the Green New Deal or a plan similar to it. They will portray it as largely aspirational and something to be implemented incrementally and slowly, but also something that must be done if we are to stop global climate change and "save the planet." The media will cast the plan as largely environmentally focused and downplay the radical nature of its core proposals for remaking America. Now that Progressives control the White House, expect them to claim a "mandate" to implement the Green Dream. Personally, I find nothing about destroying America and our way of life slowly and incrementally that makes the Green Dream any less extreme, radical, or objectionable.

The Green New Deal is socialism in its most pernicious form—think Cuba, North Korea, Russia, China, Nicaragua, and Venezuela—and the results would be the same: shortages of everything, including food and water, shelter, energy, healthcare, medicine, and transportation—everything except poverty. We used to talk about being bombed back to the Stone Age. This would legislate us back to the Stone Age. Like government-run anything, inefficiencies would abound and costs would rise. None of it would be "incremental" or "slow." Bernie Sanders, for example, has made no secret of the fact that he considers himself a "big steps" guy, "progress" on the Green New Deal's main planks has been "too slow," and the time for "action" was yesterday. There will be no restraint because none of these pinheads have even paused to consider what being wrong will do to the country or its economy. They want control and believe in November 2020 the American public was gullible enough to give it to them. They sense that their decades-long efforts to dumb down education, fan the flames of race, gender, and class envies, and infiltrate mainstream American politics finally have paid dividends and positioned them to extinguish freedoms and liberties won by the blood and sacrifices of millions over generations.

Progressives now are firmly in charge of the Democratic Party. They may not be able to eliminate airplanes in the ten-year deadline established by the Green Deal manifesto—after all, if California cannot build a high-speed train between Los Angeles and San Francisco within a reasonable time frame or for a reasonable price, building networks of trains to substitute for airplanes hardly seems practicable. But they certainly can destroy and take over the health care system; pack the Supreme Court; eliminate or sharply restrict the use of fossil fuels; hand out billions to those unwilling to work; ban the eating of meats and other unfavored foods; destroy private sector education by making all public education "free;" offer trillions of dollars in "reparations" to Native Americans and those they deem injured by racism, including, presumably, "systemic" or "structural" racism;" and, in general, create seismic upheavals in the social and economic fabric of the United States capable of bankrupting and destroying the country as least as rapidly as socialism destroyed Venezuela.

Taking down fences? This may be the biggest fence of all, and we do not have to take it down to know why it was put up—history has dozens of examples of the horrors of socialism, progressivism, and communism for those willing to listen. Let's hope most of us eventually do. The future of the Republic depends on it.

CHAPTER 2

S—HOLE NATIONS

"S—hole nations." When President Trump used the phrase during an ostensibly "private" meeting with lawmakers to discuss immigration policy, it caused a furor across the country, particularly in Washington. The Progressive nation was quickly in full song, decrying the "blatant racism" and "vulgarity" of the President's comments.

"Colorful" language in the Oval Office certainly did not originate with Donald Trump any more than sexual dalliances started with Bill Clinton. The Watergate tapes, for example, provide graphic proof of the coarseness of many of the conversations in the Nixon White House, and Lyndon Johnson was notorious for his scatological behavior and language.

I am confident every beat reporter ever assigned to Haiti or some of the African nations President Trump was accused of insulting has referred to those countries as "S—holes" or something equally graphic, not because the reporters were racists, but because it is difficult to find a better descriptor for countries where the governments are hopelessly corrupt, most of the population lives in abject poverty, civil rights are nonexistent, and people are routinely imprisoned, abused, and sometimes murdered by those in charge. They are, in every sense of the word, nonfunctioning "S—holes!"

It always is amusing when people pretend to be offended by someone's use of language they not only routinely encounter, but oftentimes use themselves. Ever been on a men's golf outing? A hunting trip? A "boy's night out?" A Friday night poker game? Name the occasion, but when men get together the language usually turns feisty and the jokes crude. In my experience, it happens regardless of age, race, ethnicity, religious belief, background, occupation, political persuasion, or socioeconomic standing. While I cannot confirm from personal experience, I am told women's outings can be just as boorish.

So, are these episodes the equivalent of "Freudian slips," revealing deeply seated racism, bigotry, and homophobia, or do they simply reflect a side of human nature that allows us to occasionally "let down," deviate from the norms, and engage in banal conversations that may be tasteless and sometimes worse, but are completely meaningless outside the contexts in which they occur? Put differently, are these simply testosterone or estrogen-fueled efforts to be "one of the guys" or "girls," or evidence of bias and prejudice? If it happens routinely across races, cultures, genders, ages, and socioeconomic groups, is everyone a bigot, racist, or homophobe, or is something else going on?

A moment's reflection suggests something else is going on. Every day, people pay handsomely to attend comedy clubs where the acts could not be cruder, go to movies that could not be more explicit, attend concerts and buy CDs and DVDs where the lyrics of the music are salacious and often disrespectful of women or others, attend theaters and concert halls to see shows and productions that essentially are pornographic, and seek out erotic literature at rates that put it on best-seller lists.

Unless you think all of these people are irredeemable deviants and degenerates, pretending to be shocked and calling the President vulgar and a racist when he occasionally resorts to profanity to make a point can only be called what it is: politics at its basest and hypocrisy at its worst.

I can hear the protests from Progressives already. "There are no such things as 'meaningless' or 'banal' conversations about race, gender, national origin, or LBGTQ rights, and the fact you do not recognize that confirms you are at least insensitive, but more likely a racist, bigot, and homophobe." In their cancel culture public world, no comment is too trivial to be ignored, and context excuses nothing.

Quite frankly, if in those meetings with Congressional leaders regarding immigration, Donald Trump had said, "You know, I love Haiti; it is a beautiful, idyllic place, and the people have a sweet, laid-back disposition and character; I think we need to allow more Haitians into the US," the media would have reported it as: "President Displays Plantation Mentality; Calls for the Importation of Slaves from Haiti."

There is nothing the President can say or do that political opponents and the mainstream media will not immediately interpret as "racist," "bigoted," and "homophobic." Those are Progressive talking points, and the Trump-hating media will not stray from them. They have learned a simple truth— we live in a sound-bite, social media-driven world. People do not check facts, nor are they inclined to engage in any type of introspection about what is reported or said. Say it often enough and loudly enough, and it will be believed.

The Democracy Integrity Project may explain why the daily attacks against the President appear to be so consistent and coordinated. Paul Sperry of RealClearInvestigations.com did the investigation and wrote the story, which Rush Limbaugh publicized on his radio show and web page in mid-March,

2019. As reported, The Democracy Integrity Project (TDIP) is an elaborate media-influencing operation that daily churns out questionable reports and "research" for the media, congressional staffers, and sometimes federal investigators to drive and shape negative media coverage and publicity against the President. The goal is his impeachment. Led by a former Clinton administration volunteer and top-staffer to California Democratic Sen. Diane Feinstein, it allegedly employs Glenn Simpson and Christopher Steele, two key figures in the discredited Fusion GPS "dossier" compiled for the Clinton campaign and DNC during the 2016 election cycle, and a key part of the impeachment efforts against the President. Financial supporters for TDIP are said to include liberal activist actor/director Rob Reiner and George Soros, the billionaire anarchist with ties to Antifa, the violent domestic terrorist group committed to the forcible overthrow of the United States government.[30]

Paul Sperry's story is well worth reading. It shows just how ruthless Progressives can be and the extremes to which they will go in their efforts to replace American democracy with socialism and Marxism. They want to change this country into one you will not recognize. The promises always are the same: give up your liberties, your freedom of choice, control over your life, and we will reward you with free education, free health care, free everything. So too are the outcomes: broken promises, poverty, shortages, suffering, and misery. In the incentive-killing throes of socialism or communism, there is no money to fulfill promises. Those in charge live comfortably, but no one else does. Think Venezuela. Think Al Gore, who makes millions from his extreme climate change rhetoric while jet-setting around the world and living in an energy-guzzling home.[31]

This is not to say the President could not be his own worst enemy at times; he often was. Even his most ardent supporters would have liked to see him act more "presidential." However, with a vast array of extraordinarily well-financed political enemies constantly scheming against him, and the mainstream media complicit to a degree never before seen in American politics, the President's oftentimes intemperate tweets surely can be excused. What choice did he have? There was no fair opportunity to respond through a virulently anti-Trump news media.

In many respects, the treatment of the President and the contempt and hatred displayed by his opposition is not unlike the criticism heaped on Abraham Lincoln. Lincoln won the lowest percentage of the popular vote in the history of American presidential elections, well under 40 percent, and was widely ridiculed as a weak, bad-mannered imbecile who had made America the laughingstock of the world, particularly in Europe.[32] His Emancipation Proclamation in 1862, done by Executive Order, was widely viewed by both the North and the South as a criminal usurpation of power and a "death blow" to the young nation, if not to democracy itself.[33] Sound familiar?

Isn't it interesting how two presidents, each widely reviled and considered embarrassments to the country by their opposition, managed to do so much for minority groups?

In a later chapter of this book, I focus on the "weaponization" of the terms *racist* and *bigot* and how it has become a key strategy in the Progressive's assault on American democracy. The feigned outrage over President Trump's "S—holes" comment is part of the same tactics. Parse every word, every sentence, not for what was said, but for the "hidden" meanings that must have been intended. In this instance, so the narrative goes, President Trump could not have been referring to the corruption and living conditions in the countries when he called them "S—holes;" he labeled them "S—holes" because the countries are governed by Black people and their populations are mostly Black. It is a never-ending game of "gotcha, and the more sensational it can be made to sound, the quicker it will go viral on social media.

It also is safe—charges of "racism" and "bigotry" never have to be defended because everyone instinctively recoils from being labeled a racist or bigot. Much like charges of "communist" during the McCarthy era, the accusations are lethal to reputation and impossible to defend.

When the target of a "racism" charge is someone as universally hated by Progressives as Donald Trump, the hue and cry escalate quickly. A lynch-mob mentality develops. The critics may understand that they too have made similar comments, but theirs were innocent misstatements at best, momentary failures of judgment at worst, while everyone knows Trump intended his remarks to be racist. No perspective is brought to bear because no one is looking for perspective; it is simply another chance to attack a political enemy regardless of the effect on the office of the president or the country.

During the President's first State of the Union Address, in January 2018, Democrats spent the evening refusing to stand and applaud even for simple things all Americans should have been able to celebrate. They did it again in 2019. It would have been comical if it had not been so un-American. At an organic level, it demonstrated undeniably that it was not possible for Progressives to acknowledge any achievement by Donald Trump no matter how beneficial for the country. They politicized everything, most of all the mundane, and were uninterested in the welfare of the country—their obsession with ousting the President and regaining power would not let them focus on anything else.

Shortly after the State of the Union address, I was listening to an NPR broadcast that reported, "In his State of the Union Address, President Trump told viewers unemployment in the US overall was the lowest in the last forty years, and unemployment levels among Asians, Hispanics, and African Americans were at all-time lows," or words to that purport and effect. However, the show's host, after acknowledging the truth of these claims, quickly added, "but the President did not attempt to explain why African American men continue to be unemployed at twice the rate of other groups." Nor, he might have added, did Barrack Obama. If at any point in Barrack Obama's presidency, economic results like those the Trump administration posted in its first year had been achieved, Progressives would have lobbied to have term limits on the president removed regardless of the unemployment rates for African American men.

The better response to NPR's snarky comment, however, would have been to call attention to the fact that because of flawed public-school systems controlled by powerful, Democratic teachers' unions, skill levels are often lower among African American men. Or that illegal immigrants are taking many lower-skilled jobs. Or that seven out of ten Black children grow up in single-parent homes. Or that public housing projects are forcing young Black men into environments where "street cred" is acquired through gang membership and the value of education is derided. Or that well-meaning, but misguided and inefficient government welfare programs are destroying the incentive to work, trapping millions in poverty. In very sharp contrast, when Black Americans obtain a college degree, their earnings are essentially the same as White college graduates. Walt Williams wrote about it often, and his explanation for the higher unemployment rates for African-American men pulled no punches.[34]

Good luck, however, trying to engage Progressives in actual substantive discussions. It's much easier simply to attribute everything to "racism," "discrimination," "exploitation," "White privilege," or any other explanation that fits with a political agenda dependent on racial, ethnic, and gender divisiveness and envy. It has the added benefit of shifting blame and responsibility away from constituencies Progressive prefer to portray as victims.

During the same NPR broadcast, an elderly Black gentleman, a proud survivor of earlier, true periods of racism in the United States, was interviewed. He had participated in the 1968 sanitation worker's strike in Memphis, Tennessee, shortly before the assassination of Dr. Martin Luther King, and marched wearing a badge that said, "I am a man." He was wearing the same badge during the NPR broadcast. The host asked him what it meant, and the elderly gentleman explained that he and his Black co-workers had been treated like *boys* before the strike, but afterward were treated as *men*. He understandably was proud of that and what the strike had accomplished for Black workers' rights.

The host, after a few moments fawning over his guest's courage and fortitude, asked why it still was necessary for him to wear the symbolic badge, obviously trolling for claims of ongoing discrimination and racism. Instead, the elderly gentleman patiently explained that he now wore the badge to show young Black workers, who never had experienced racism or discrimination in their lifetimes, that they owed their good jobs and discrimination-free workplaces to what his generation had done. After an awkward pause, and a sputtered "thanks" for providing a "historic perspective which I did not know," the host quickly ended the interview.

That is a difficult story for Progressives to deal with. It simply doesn't fit well with their narrative of a deeply racist America that continues to exploit Black Americans and other minorities, barely abated from the discrimination prevalent in the deep South during the 1950s and 1960s.

Socialists and communists worldwide always have used race, class, gender, and "exploitation of the common man," themes to stir civil unrest and political upheaval, and Progressives in America are no exception. Rallying minorities with charges of racism and bigotry are among the Progressives' most powerful and often-used weapons in their unrelenting efforts to turn America to socialism, and they have little interest in seeing any type of improvement in race relations. The Obama administration, arguably the most racially divisive administration since the end of the Jim Crowe era, did its part, callously pitting Black and White Americans against each other and interrupting years of steady progress in healing the racial divides. Progressives will continue to exploit that shameful aspect of the Obama legacy for as long as they can.

Please do not misunderstand. No one is suggesting that racism and bigotry had disappeared from America before Obama, but for the Obama administration and today's Progressives to deny the incredible progress that had been made is irresponsible. Equally undeniable is the fact that President Obama significantly worsened race relations during his eight years in office. Don't expect current-day race merchants and Progressives to do anything to change that. Why? As popularized in the movie, *All the President's Men*, if you want to understand the true source of a problem, "follow the money." In this case, add *power* to the equation.

There is money to be made from racial unrest, particularly by the leaders and organizers who emerge to take charge. If there is no turmoil, there is no need for leaders and organizers. If there is no need for leaders and organizers, the privileges of leaderships—money, entourages, cars, airplanes, attention, and influence—all disappear. If circumstances appear to be improving, donations, support, and interest may wane, so maintaining a crisis at a fever pitch is crucial. Because there are no long-term profits or benefits in resolving the issues that divide White and Black Americans, no legitimate efforts are made to do so. Instead, the consistent message sent to Black communities by their leaders is straight forward: you continue to be "victims" of White exploitation, racism, and bigotry and are not responsible for any aspect of your condition.

For Progressives, however, the real goal, power, is far more intoxicating than money. The election of Barack Obama in 2008 was instantly recognized by American communists and socialists as a breakthrough moment in their struggle to infiltrate mainstream American politics, and they moved quickly to take advantage. By the end of the Obama presidency, with American courts significantly packed with Progressive judges and race relations in shambles after years of divisive rhetoric from the White House, the stage was set for the establishment of a new order in America. All that was required to complete the transition was the election of Hillary Clinton.

Bernie Sanders was the first to recognize the opportunity Obama's election created for the spread of socialism in America, and he tried to preempt Hillary by openly running for president as a "Democratic Socialist." He might have been successful but for the fact he was running against one of the most ruthless political machines in the history of American politics. While not yet quite ready to come out of the closet and openly declare as socialists, the Clinton campaign was able to co-opt the Democratic National Committee, rig the nomination process, shuffle Bernie aside, and get in line for delivery of what obviously was considered its rightful prize.[35]

As much as they hate Donald Trump, many Progressives idolize Hillary Clinton, perhaps the most flawed and conflicted candidate ever to run for high office in the United States. Her flagrant abuses of power and epic failures of judgment are repeatedly ignored by liberals and the press, however, because in the Progressives' world the ends always justified the means. Isn't that exactly what Harry Reid said when he admitted lying about Mitt Romney's taxes? And isn't that essentially what Chuck Schumer and every Progressive endorsed when they refused to extend due process and the presumption of innocence to Brett Kavanaugh during the hearings on his nomination to the Supreme Court? They are waging a battle for the hearts and minds of the people, a battle to forever change a Constitution and form of government Progressives despise, and all "means" are acceptable.

Hillary, as president, would have moved the country giant steps closer to the Progressives' Holy Grail of single-payer public health insurance, solidifying the government's control over another enormous segment of the American economy. She also would have finished the job of packing the federal courts with Progressive judges willing to ignore the law and dictate social and economic policy from the bench, virtually ensuring the demise of the Constitution within a short span of years. Continuing Obama's methodical downgrading of the US military would have been another priority, and by making sure borders remained open to everyone, friend or foe, needy immigrant or international terrorist, any remaining vestiges of common US ideals or shared goals, values, or culture would have disappeared quickly. Citizenship for illegal immigrants would have locked in Progressive voting majorities for decades, perhaps forever.

Open borders are only one of the ploys Progressives are using to try to stack the voting ranks with individuals they consider more vulnerable to socialism's deceptive message. Conversations already are occurring, for example, about extending the right to vote to sixteen-year-olds. The justification? Since sixteen-year-olds are allowed to drive cars in most states, which "entrusts" them with the power of "life and death" over others, and since they live in this country and are subject to its laws, they should be able to vote.

I am not sure "idiotic *non sequitur*" is exactly the correct characterization, but the syllogistic fallacies should be self-evident. Even though still within the custodial care of their parents and not yet old enough to drink or even buy cigarettes in several states and many localities—most have never held a job, paid taxes, or made a decision more consequential than whether to play "Call of Duty" or "Madden 20"—Progressives feel sixteen-year-olds should be allowed to vote because they are allowed to drive.

I believe the current voting age, eighteen, is too young, much less sixteen. In most localities, eighteen-year-olds cannot legally buy beer or cigarettes either. Why should we treat the right to vote more casually than the right to drink or buy cigarettes? If eighteen-year-olds do not have the intelligence and maturity to make appropriate decisions about drinking or smoking, by what possible measure do they have the wisdom to decide who should be running their cities, counties, states, or country? Life experiences matter, as does having the maturity and judgment to make informed, careful decisions. As any doctor would attest, the portion of the human brain that controls judgment and awareness of long-term consequences continues to change and develop until approximately twenty-five years of age; eighteen-year-olds have a long-ways to go and sixteen-year-olds even further. Perhaps Ralph Northam, the governor of Virginia, should have used that excuse to defend his use of blackface during his medical school years: "My brain was not developed enough to understand the long-term consequences." I address Governor Northam in more detail in a subsequent chapter of this book.

Progressives favor lowering the voting age because they understand the younger the voter, the less they know and the more easily swayed they are by emotions; teachers, most of whom are registered Democrats; propaganda messaging; and social media. Another chapter in this book talks about the panic created in a group of California school children by claims in the Green New Deal manifesto that the planet essentially will end in twelve years if dire steps are not taken immediately to reverse climate change. Other high-school students have been organizing "stay away from school" days to protest what they view as insufficient action on climate change and to urge immediate passage of the Green New Deal.[36] The young simply do not have the life experiences, education, information, or perspective to think about or sort through these types of claims in rational ways, but Progressives never have been shy about taking advantage of anyone, children included.

These are not the only Progressive plans for ensuring and protecting voting majorities for the Democratic Party—statehood for Puerto Rico and voting rights for residents of the District of Columbia; doing away with the Electoral College; increasing the size of the Supreme Court and changing the methods by which justices are selected; and allocating Senate seats based on population all are on the agenda.

These are major structural and constitutional changes to the country, not inconsequential tinkering or fine-tuning. The Electoral College, for example, is fundamental to our republican form of government. Without it, a handful of large states would largely control national elections, and the rest of the country could stay home on election days. In 2016, Donald Trump won the popular vote in thirty of the fifty states but lost the overall popular vote by 2.9 million votes because of Hillary Clinton's nearly 4 million-vote-margin in California. Without the Electoral College, in other words, one state, California, would have frustrated the will of a majority of the rest of the country.

Despite Progressive hand-wringing over President Trump not winning a majority of the popular vote in 2016, it is not uncommon for an American president to be elected while winning a plurality or less of the vote. It has happened in twenty-four elections, including both times Bill Clinton was elected. Abraham Lincoln, at less than 40 percent, still holds the record in American presidential elections for winning the lowest percentage of the popular vote.

None of that should be surprising. The United States is a republic with a Constitution that protects against the abasement of minority rights and liberties that occurs too easily in direct democracies. Madison wrote about it extensively in *The Federalist No. 10.* The Electoral College is the constitutional guarantee to citizens of smaller states that their voices will remain relevant in the election of American presidents and that the principles of federalism on which the nation was founded will be preserved. The same thinking can be seen in the composition of the United States Senate, where each state has the same number of senators, regardless of population, to make sure the viewpoints of citizens from smaller states remain important to the Legislative Branch. As I noted earlier, that is something Progressives also would like to change— they want to allocate senate seats by state populations, truly making residents of smaller states irrelevant in national political decisions. Densely populated urban areas monitored, controlled, and manipulated by Progressive party "bosses" vote predictably and reliably, and if Senate seats are tied to population figures, expect the Senate to more closely resemble the current California delegation to the US House of Representative than anything even faintly reminiscent of the Senate as it has existed since the country's founding. Democrats currently outnumber Republicans 145-7 in California's House delegation. Controlling the Supreme Court and electing American presidents by popular vote are two additional keys to the Progressives' plans for ensuring their control of our government is unassailable and the establishment of their "new order" inevitable. Expect them to pull out all stops to make both happen.

The Electoral College remains a major barrier, a fence if you will, to the Progressives' efforts to solidify control over the country. It is the reason they are so anxious to tear it down. It also is the reason Progressive candidates for president in 2020 began calling for a complete overhaul of our voting system. Before he dropped out of the race, for example, Andrew Yang advocated for the United States adopting "ranked-choice voting." In a ranked-choice system, a voter does not simply cast a vote for the candidate of his or her choice. Instead, voters are asked to list all candidates in order of "preference." The votes for everyone's first choice are then tallied. If a "first choice" candidate receives a majority of the votes, they win. If not, the candidate receiving the fewest number of votes is eliminated, and the second choices of those whose candidate was eliminated become their new "first choice." If with the addition of these votes, a candidate receives 50% or more of the vote, they win. Otherwise, the process is repeated until some candidate receives a majority of the votes.

Although a primary benefit of ranked-choice voting is that it supposedly results in candidates winning elections by voting majorities, ranked-choice voting does not always produce winners by a majority vote either. This can happen, for example, when individual voters do not rank all candidates, and the only candidates for whom they have indicated preferences have been eliminated while others remain in the running. The ballots of those voters no longer count in the election— their ballots have "exhausted." If there are enough voters in that circumstance, the eventual winner will not end up with a majority of the vote.[37]

What ranked-choice voting typically produces are *artificial* majorities because votes for second, third, and fourth-tier candidates are re-allocated and these lower-ranked candidates become the default "first choices" for voters who may not support them. Remember, the ranking feature of this method of voting does not come into play unless the first tally has *not* produced a majority winner.

How can a subsequent "majority" created by re-allocating votes be considered anything other than "artificial?" The fact voters have listed additional candidates does not mean they support anyone other than their first choice or that they consider any of the remaining candidates to be better than the others. A voter might not even be familiar with candidates other than their first choice.

Voters will rank candidates for different reasons. A few may have a preferred order of candidates. But many more will do it because "that is the way the system works" or they are told it is what they are supposed to do. Others will simply not understand the options possible, such as not voting for all candidates. But regardless of the reasons, it makes no sense to attribute "voter support" to candidates listed as second, third, or fourth "choices." Should we assume, for example, that if Trump voters listed Hillary Clinton as a second, third, or fourth "preference" on a ranked-choice ballot they did so because they supported her and would have been satisfied to have her as president?

Ranked-choice voting also is at odds with the "one person, one vote" constitutional principle Democrats have long claimed to advocate because ranked-choice voting gives more votes to some than others.[38] To illustrate, if voter A's first choice on the ballot is the top choice after the ballots are initially tallied, voter A may never vote again. Conversely, if voter B's first choice is a candidate eliminated after the initial tally, voter B's votes for other ranked candidates will continue to be counted. Voter A will not vote again if his or her first-choice candidate makes it through the election process, while voter B may end up with a series of votes for lower-ranked candidates as higher-ranked choices are eliminated.[39] If a voter lists only one candidate and that candidate is eliminated, the vote counts not at all.

What ranked choice-voting unquestionably does is introduce significant unclarity and complexity into the voting process. And while it may have carnival barker appeal—"Come try your luck, spin the wheel and let's see who ends up as president—" it can produce some very unexpected results. Most elections, including presidential elections, have third-party candidates on the ballot. In the 2016 presidential election, for example, Gary Johnson and Jill Stein were the best known of several fringe candidates who collectively attracted almost 8 million votes. In 1992, Ross Perot received almost 19% of the popular vote in his third-party run against Bill Clinton and George H.W. Bush. Depending on the level of support for the various candidates on the ballot, voters might have to vote *against* the candidate they support to make a win more likely—they could lessen their preferred candidate's chances of winning by making him or her their top choice.[40] At times, the equivalent of a Monte Carlo simulation would be necessary for voters to try to figure out how they should cast their ballots.[41] With this level of complexity, efforts to "game" the system would become a national pastime.

The potential pros and cons of ranked-choice voting aside, Progressives want it because they believe ranked-choice voting weakens arguments for retaining the Electoral College and moves them steps closer to being able to elect presidents directly. If "consensus majorities" result from this new and "fun" way to vote, why continue a historical artifact like the Electoral College? With amnesty and potential citizenship for millions of illegal immigrants, statehood for Puerto Rico, voting rights for the residents of the District of Columbia and 16-year-olds, and the host of other "changes" on the Progressives' agenda, they are confident majorities too over-whelming ever to be defeated soon will be in place, particularly if their "new" cohorts of voters can be kept poor, undereducated, and dependent on government. Even so, because these new legions of Progressive warriors will not be evenly distributed across the country, eliminating the Electoral College remains a priority. It is something that may be appealing to those unconcerned with living under majority edicts in which they have no voice, but most of us are more comfortable when government over-reach and abuse are constrained by the checks and balances of the Constitution, and the governing majority is forced to pay attention to our views.

There is another reason the Electoral College remains important to our form of government. Election laws differ state by state. California, for example, allows *ballot harvesting*. For those unfamiliar with this newest effort to weaken voter integrity laws, ballot harvesting is when political operatives, campaign workers, and volunteers are allowed to collect ballots from voters and deliver them to the polling stations or election offices.[42] Combined with the early distribution of ballots, sometimes months in advance of an election, and the practice of sending mail-in ballots to every registered voter, whether requested or not, ballot harvesting obviously can be a fertile source of ballot fraud.

The registered voter lists in most states are hopelessly outdated and contain names of convicted felons, the dead, the underaged, those who have changed addresses or moved from the state, and others ineligible to vote for a variety of reasons. Millions of extra or unclaimed ballots end up in circulation. Even when a ballot gets to the address of a living, properly registered, eligible voter, there is no way to tell who fills it out or whether the voter's decision was influenced or coerced by the person or persons collecting it or someone else, perhaps "friends," family members, community organizers, or those with something other than the integrity of the electoral process in mind.[43] It also is easy enough for harvesters to destroy ballots they know do not support the candidate or candidates they prefer, or which are collected from areas unlikely to support those candidates.

A voting booth is private. You are alone. No matter what others may have done to try to influence your vote before you enter that booth, once inside, your vote becomes a matter solely between you and your conscience. The secrecy of your ballot may be in jeopardy when you are asked to vote at home or in some community setting but never in a voting booth. No one knows how you voted unless you tell them.

Think about it. Ballots are sent out weeks or months before an election. Political operatives and campaign workers show up at peoples' homes, go to church socials, or attend community meetings and essentially conduct pep rallies for the candidate or candidates of choice. They offer to collect and deliver ballots to election offices or provide "assistance" in completing ballots to those who may be uninterested, undecided, disabled, elderly, illiterate, or deemed in need of help. I know of nothing that would prevent a ballot harvester from collecting blank ballots from those willing to provide them and delivering completed ballots to election offices; the security measures for mail-in and absentee ballots are anything but "secure." Even those who insist on filling out their own ballots can be "checked"—if a vote has not been cast for every position on the ballot, or if "wrong" choices have been made, the harvester can correct the "mistakes."

Legalizing ballot harvesting is certainly not the only way California has weakened protections against ballot fraud. The Progressives who dominate state politics systematically have expanded voting rights for noncitizens, inmates, and felons; instituted motor vehicle voter registration procedures; preregistered sixteen and seventeen-year-olds; enacted laws mandating the automatic mailing of absentee ballots to every voter whether or not requested; approved "conditional ballots;" authorized voters who miss voter registration deadlines to register at polling places on the day of an election; and allowed ballots to be accepted for up to a week *after* an election, along with "second chances" for rejected ballots.[44] Anything that can be done to encourage ballot fraud has been done, except for extending amnesty to those who engage in it.

If you flood California with ballots weeks before an election, allow activists to knock on doors, talk to voters, and collect ballots, and permit ballots to be sent in after the polls have closed and preliminary election results announced, ballot harvesting becomes a lethal weapon in the hands of those looking to rig elections. And that is exactly what seems to have happened in California in the 2018 midterms. Several races appeared to be Republican victories until "late" ballots swung them to Democrats

No state's laws should have so much potential impact on federal elections?[45] As the most populous state in the nation, California has 17 more seats in the US House of Representatives than the next largest state, Texas, a total of 53 seats, easily enough to swing the balance of power in Washington.

The following information, all from an article by Victor Davis Hanson, does little to dispel the uneasy feeling that California has created the fertile crescent of ballot fraud by serially reducing the security of its voting procedures. [46]

Although it has a population of 40 million, only 150,000 households, 150,000, pay approximately 50 percent of the state's income tax revenue. State income tax rates in California are the highest in the nation at 13.3 percent. Because so few pay income taxes in California, voters do not hesitate to increase tax rates. California's gasoline tax rates are the second-highest in the nation, and its sales tax is the highest. A bill recently introduced in California would levy a 40 percent tax on relatively modest inheritances.

Approximately, a quarter of all homeless people in the nation live in California. As Mr. Hanson notes, so do about one-third of all Americans on public assistance. Fully 20 percent of the state's residents live below the poverty line, and about one-third of Californians are enrolled in Medi-Cal, a health program for low-income residents. Twenty-seven percent of California residents were not born in the United States.

Fertile crescent or not, it did not take Progressive governors long to spread California-like voting procedures across the nation for the 2020 elections, using COVID-19 as the excuse and the emergency powers they declared in response to the pandemic as the means. Under the rubric, "the safest way to vote in a pandemic is by mail," voters were encouraged not to vote in-person. Several states adopted "no excuse" absentee balloting. Others declared that all voting in 2020 would be by mail and ordered ballots sent to all registered voters weeks in advance of election day. Where necessary, governors used their emergency powers to override state laws prohibiting voting by mail.

The biggest problem for Progressives was making sure there were not more votes than registered voters, particularly in places like Philadelphia. Huge dumps of ballots for Joe Biden allegedly materialized late on election night, after vote-counting supposedly had been suspended, and it appeared the President was winning the state handily. Lawsuits filed on behalf of the President alleged that the late ballots favored Biden by statistically impossible margins. It is something that should concern all Americans.

I have wandered a long way from the original subject of this chapter, something I suspect will happen with regularity during the course of this book. Hopefully, the deviations will be more thought-provoking than distracting. This chapter started by taking a look at the artificial attacks and criticisms Progressives heaped on the President as they relentlessly tried to discredit him. It ended with a look at some of the equally artificial means Progressives are using in their efforts to remake the country. Let's leave it there.

CHAPTER 3

TREASON

The Hanoi Summit

When do actions by a political party move from politics to treason? Do acts by politicians intended to undermine a president's efforts to denuclearize a dangerous enemy, for example, constitute treason against the United States?

The spectacle of the Michael Cohen hearings before the House Oversight Committee in the early part of 2019 was an event that leads naturally to that question. Michael Cohen, a long-time personal lawyer for President Trump, was convicted of a variety of financial crimes uncovered during the Mueller investigation, including bank and tax fraud. None implicated the President, but after being fired as the President's lawyer in the aftermath of his legal problems, Cohen turned against him, providing information about various allegations of wrong-doing. As has been the case with almost all such claims, most proved to be nonevents, fictions created by those trying to damage the President.

The Cohen hearings, obviously timed and staged to draw attention away from President Trump's summit in Hanoi, Vietnam, with Kim Jong Un, the North Korean dictator, were a ridiculous parody in which Oversight Committee members engaged in questioning about long discredited claptrap. These included questions about a nonexistent "golden shower" tape referenced in the Christopher Steele dossier, an equally fictional tape of President Trump allegedly striking Melania Trump in an elevator, and an imaginary presidential "love child." Even Michael Cohen, obviously scripted by his Democratic handlers to inflict as much embarrassment and harm on the President as possible, rejected much of this nonsense out of hand and defended the President by saying he was not the type of man who ever would strike his wife. A glimmer of decency from an otherwise discredited and disgraced witness?

The fact Michael Cohen was testifying before a congressional committee was contemptible enough. He already was a convicted perjurer and liar who went to jail for lying to Congress, among other things. What was the justification for providing him with an opportunity to lie again, this time before a national audience? The obvious answers were that this was not a serious Congressional investigation and truth was not the objective. The Oversight Committee did not care whether or not Michael Cohen told the truth, as long as he was willing to say things that would embarrass the President. How else can you explain members of Congress asking questions about "golden showers," "presidential domestic violence," and a "love child"—things they knew never happened? It all was simply a measure of how low Progressives were willing to go in their zeal to damage the Trump presidency.

So, Cohen burnished his book and movie prospects and perhaps met the level of cooperation expected of felons trying to reduce their sentences. The chattering classes and media heard what they wanted to hear and gained something to keep them enraged and engaged at cocktail parties. And the public was entertained with stories of salacious behavior that never occurred. Meanwhile, the media diligently focused on the Oversight Committee hearings, largely ignoring the president's summit with Kim Jong Un. From the perspective of Progressives, mission accomplished.

To add to the insanity of it all, Michael Cohen testified during the House Oversight Committee hearings that President Trump never wanted to win the presidency and never expected to win either the Republican primary or the general election but was using the opportunity to run for president as a public-relations exercise to build the Trump brand. Really? What then was the possible justification for claiming someone not interested in winning colluded with the Russians trying to win?

Politics once stopped at the "water's edge," as Republican Senator Arthur Vandenberg of Michigan famously said in 1947. At the time, he was working with the administration of Democratic President Harry Truman to build bipartisan support for the Marshall Plan, NATO, and other mutual defense initiatives with the North Atlantic allies of the United States. Senator Vandenberg was chairman of the Senate Foreign Intelligence Committee, the president *pro tempore* of the Senate, and a Republican presidential candidate, but he, along with even the most partisan members of Congress, understood the safety and welfare of the country depended on presenting a united front when dealing with America's enemies. The stakes simply were too high to use foreign policy as a domestic political pawn.

But Progressives hated President Trump far more than they loved the United States and were willing to do almost anything to deny him and the country any type of domestic or international success. While the Vietnam summit with Kim Jong Un was only one manifestation of the "Trump Derangement Syndrome" that had stripped Progressives of reason and rationality, it illustrated with great clarity the degree to which Progressives were willing to compromise the interests of the country in their unrelenting quest to change the results of the 2016 election. Politics obviously no longer stopped at the water's edge or anywhere else. Another plank had been stripped from the fence.

No one expected unqualified success in Vietnam. Kim Jong Un is an entrenched dictator, the third in his family to rule North Korea with an iron fist. His grandfather, Kim ill Sung, was responsible for the start of the Korean War, and he, along with Kim Jong II, Kim Jong Un's father, and Kim Jong Un, have combined over decades to impoverish and decimate North Korea.

North Korea is a proxy state of China, and without China, it likely would have starved itself out of existence long ago. With China, it has managed to build an aggressive nuclear program. Ever since Dwight Eisenhower threatened North Korea with nuclear destruction during the Korean War, North Korea has made it a national priority to develop the means of countermanding the US nuclear threat.[47] It already has missiles that can reach the shores of US allies like Japan and Israel and is feverishly developing ballistic missiles capable of delivering nuclear warheads to the continental United States. Recent tests suggest North Korea already may have that ability. Whether it does or not, I think it fair to say that North Korea and Iran, both controlled by unpredictable, apocalyptic regimes, pose the greatest existential nuclear threat in the world.

President Trump's summit with Kim Jong Un to discuss the denuclearization of the Korean peninsula, while of critical importance, had muted expectations. American presidents had "kicked this can down the road" for decades, resulting in the intractable mess Donald Trump inherited. During the Obama years, for example, North Korea regularly tested missiles and nuclear warheads without meaningful protest or other response from the Obama administration.

While no one anticipated dramatic progress at the Hanoi summit, President Trump's first summit with Kim Jong Un in Singapore in 2018 resulted in North Korea suspending its nuclear and missile testing, a significant accomplishment in and of itself, and several tension-lessening, intermediate steps were possible in Hanoi. These included finally officially ending the Korean War and solidifying a diplomatic process that might lead to agreement long term. Nonetheless, before leaving for Vietnam, President Trump was careful to lower expectations about the outcomes possible from the Hanoi summit, recognizing that decades of distrust between the United States and North Korea was not likely to evaporate overnight. China also was the 600-pound gorilla in the room and would have significant influence over the success or failure of the negotiations. In many ways, this summit with China's proxy state was a proxy showdown between the United States and China.

Before the summit, the US media ridiculed the President's efforts to meet with North Korea, warning him not to give away too much for the sake of a deal. Contrast that reaction with the fawning press coverage Obama received when his administration participated with the other P5+1 powers in negotiating the disastrous Iranian nuclear deal, where Obama did give away too much. In exchange for almost nothing, Obama lifted the economic sanctions that were devastating the Iranian economy and forcing the Islamic Republic to the negotiating table. Iran regained access to approximately $150 billion in assets that had been frozen by the US as part of those sanctions and also received nearly $2 billion in untraceable cash that was loaded onto pallets by the Obama administration and flown to Iran. These were dollars Iran could and would use to challenge American interests in the Middle East and kill Americans. The Obama apologists who deny this presumably do not understand that money is fungible. As later discovered,

Iran never signed the nuclear deal but got its billions in assets and cash from the Obama administration anyway.[48]

No such support was offered for President Trump's efforts with North Korea, only derision and a continuous cacophony of warnings by the media predicting "disaster." The media apparently favored sitting back and doing nothing while North Korea finalized its ability to attack the United States—better that than giving the President any credit for doing something prior presidents never tried—and they continued to insist the President would give up too much.[49]

In truth, there was nothing President Trump could have given North Korea that would not have been considered too much by the media. If Kim Jung Un had agreed to completely denuclearize the Korean peninsula, the President would have been criticized for "destabilizing" the region. But leaving nothing to chance, to ensure the summit would not be successful, the House Oversight Committee, led by Rep. Elijah E. Cummings, (D, MD), scheduled the public testimony of Michael Cohen to coincide with the opening of the President's meetings with Kim Jong Un.

It was a deliberate, calculated tactic to derail the summit with North Korea, and it did just that. Based on the media show it was seeing in the US, North Korea had to believe President Trump was vulnerable and would need to reach a deal, any deal, to offset the negative effects of the Cohen hearings. Consequently, it went "all in," demanding a complete lifting of US sanctions in return for North Korea dismantling its nuclear site in Yongbyon. Unwilling to lift the sanctions against North Korea in return for partial denuclearization, the President walked away.

Predictably, when what no one expected to happen did not happen, the summit was tabbed an enormous "Trump failure." Some even suggested the President's lack of preparation caused the breakdown in the negotiations, once again confirming the "damned if he does, damned if he doesn't" approach the media takes when covering the President. Everything he does or says is turned against him in some manner.[50]

I ask again, when citizens and officials of the United States, including the media, provide "aid and comfort to the enemy" and intentionally scuttle the negotiating position of their president with a hostile foreign power, can you call it anything other than *treason?*

It is difficult to find any way to excuse the shameless showboating by the House Oversight Committee. Would delaying the hearings a few days, a week, or a month have made any difference? Doesn't common decency dictate that if you are orchestrating a "show" hearing, not for any serious public business but simply to try to smear a president you dislike, the object of your attack should at least be in country and available to respond instead of thousands of miles away and focused on making America safer? The Democratic Party, now a fetid swamp of socialists, communists, and malcontents, lacked even that modicum of civility and decency and preferred to risk a nuclear North Korea rather than give Donald Trump a fair opportunity to do his job. Whatever happened to the common-sense and strategically important notion that "politics stop at the water's edge?" What Progressives were doing was more than treacherous—they were waging war against a lawfully elected president, aiding and abetting enemies of the United States, and putting the country and the Constitution in grave peril.

It was all part of the "tear-down," "cancel culture" Progressives have built. Anyone who thinks differently than they do, by definition, needs to be destroyed as quickly and brutally as possible. No second chances, no debates, no attempts at reason or persuasion, no resolving differences at the ballot box—personal and professional destruction are the only options. Just as in war, dehumanizing the enemy permits more extreme and ruthless measures. It's the reason the mainstream media can write so collectively and dismissively about "Trump supporters." None are different. All are the same—Bible-thumping, gun-toting, homophobic, ignorant, White supremacists who are not welcome in the Progressive's version of "America."

The Progressive's strategy regarding the President's meeting with Kim Jong Un easily could have goaded a weaker or less-committed individual into giving away too much just to get a deal. Better to be accused of giving away too much than be skewered for coming home empty-handed. Like the triumphs of ancient Rome, where victorious generals displayed the spoils of war to the masses, presidents are expected to return from foreign missions with a "prize," and few can resist bringing something, regardless of the cost. Obama could not walk away in Iran, even though it meant giving away the proverbial "farm" and despite knowing he would have faced little criticism from an adoring media regardless of what he did. By being strong enough to walk away in North Korea, however, President Trump did something of great significance, even though it was completely overlooked by his unhinged critics— he put down a marker for both North Korea and China. Each learned there would be no "gimmes" in this very high-stakes confrontation.

And make no mistake—this is a high-stakes game. It is not just about the denuclearization of North Korea, but also about the relationship and trade between China and the United States. Will China stop stealing US technology and intellectual property? How will the tariff issues between these world economic powers be resolved? What will be the future of Taiwan? Who will have access to or control over the South China Seas? No less may be at stake than who ultimately will control artificial intelligence, advanced microchips, robotics, driverless cars, and a host of innovations, some of them not yet even on the drawing board.

It was a stage too big for Barack Obama and his Progressive caucus. Thankfully, it was not too big for Donald Trump. The President's trade war with China was crippling the Chinese economy, while the US economy was flourishing until the arrival of COVID-19. Not coincidentally, the United States was able to announce in December 2019 an agreement on Phase One of a massive trade deal with China. Media coverage was muted, proving again that Progressives and their media courtesans were so invested in trying to tear down the Trump presidency, they were incapable of acknowledging even its most notable successes. They would rather have seen America's economy, national security, and prosperity irretrievably compromised than concede any success by the Trump administration.

Investigations

Interference with the Hanoi summit is an example of how recklessly Progressives will ignore the interests of their country, but it was far from an isolated incident. Progressives intentionally interfered with the President's ability to govern from the day he took office, challenging the legitimacy of his election, and urging Americans to reject him as their president. For the first time in our nation's history, a peaceful transition of power, a distinguishing feature in a truly free and democratic nation, was not allowed to happen. Not since the Civil War had there been such a challenge to the unity of the country. The attacks were unrelenting, vehement, and, in true "whack-a-mole" fashion, constantly changing.

Ironically, even before his election, the media was abuzz with stories questioning whether Donald Trump would accept the results of an election they were certain he would lose. After his election, the media narrative changed. They began to question whether the President posed a threat to the peaceful transition of power if he lost in 2020. It demonstrated again how amazingly consistent and predictable Progressives are in their political tactics, a long-standing and reliable one being, "divert attention from yourself by accusing others of doing what you have done or intend to do." To bring it full circle, well before the 2020 election, Hillary Clinton publicly encouraged Joe Biden never to concede victory, presumable even if he lost.

None of this was "normal" politics. There never has been a president in the history of the Republic who endured the level of abuse and unrelenting attempts to prevent him from governing as Donald Trump, not even Abraham Lincoln. It was a mobilization by Progressives to stop the President by any means, fair or unfair, legal or illegal. More accurately, it was a lynch mob of Progressive politicians, voters, reporters, academics, celebrities, "deep-state" government officials, billionaire socialists and anarchists, and other Progressive "elites" determined to topple the Trump presidency. Like all lynch mobs, reason and rationality were not part of the equation, and nothing short of driving the President from office would satisfy them. Progressives did not believe they could defeat Donald Trump at the polls—at least not before COVID-19—and they intended to prevent him from governing by smothering his administration under an avalanche of gratuitous accusations, investigations, recriminations, fake news, and impeachment efforts.

There was nothing the President could do that the media would not attack, even if the Obama administration had done essentially the same thing. Immigration policy is an example. Obama became known as the great "deporter-in-chief" because of the millions of illegal immigrants he deported during his first term in office, the most in history by any reasonable measure, all without a murmur of protest from the public or the media. Obama also detained illegal immigrant families, again without criticism from the media or anyone else. The media was nearly manic when the Trump administration adopted similar policies.

Obama was hailed as a hero by the media for ordering the killing of Osama Bin Laden. President Trump was accused of war-mongering for ordering the drone strike that killed Iranian General Qassem Soleimani. Soleimani was responsible for the death of thousands, including hundreds of Americans, and was the mastermind of Iran's terror efforts in the Middle East.

In the eyes of the media, Obama could do no wrong, Trump could do no right, and everything was reported from those perspectives. As Glenn Beck has said, the media is on "auto-accept" for anything the left says or does—it reflexively adopts the left's narrative as credible and never questions it.

Progressives had been trying to find grounds to impeach the President even before he took office. While headlines in the *Washington Post* on Inauguration Day, January 20, 2017, announced, "The Campaign to Impeach President Trump Has Begun," the campaign to impeach the newly sworn-in President began much earlier, virtually as soon as it became evident he was a viable candidate and likely to win the Republican nomination for president. Well before election day, in the highest levels of the nation's top law enforcement and intelligence agencies, Progressive operatives were putting "insurance plans" in place to unseat a Trump presidency quickly should it ever come into being. Ultimately, they plotted with the Clinton campaign and the Democratic National Committee (DNC) to use unverified, unreliable, and false information to obtain warrants from a FISA court to surveil a Trump campaign they were certain must be violating the law in some respect. This information, compiled by a political consulting firm, Fusion GPS, and a former British intelligence officer, Christopher Steele, who made no secret of his contempt and hatred for Donald Trump, included claims that the Trump campaign was colluding with Russia to interfere in the 2016 US presidential elections. Ironically, the information used to mislead the FISA court, which came to be known as the "Steele dossier," largely was information obtained from foreign sources, including Russian sources. Put just slightly differently, the Clinton campaign and DNC colluded with foreign sources, including Russian sources, to fabricate information they intended to use to discredit their chief political rival, Donald Trump, on grounds that he colluded with Russian to interfere with the 2016 presidential election. A sympathetic FBI and Justice Department, despite knowing early in the process that the Steele dossier was unfounded garbage paid for by the Clinton campaign, were more than willing to use it, confident they would find something illegal if they could get an inside look at the Trump organization.

The Russian collusion hoax, of course, is what led to the appointment of former FBI head, Robert Mueller, as special counsel to investigate the allegations of collusion between the Trump campaign and Russia. Despite two years of exhaustive investigation by Mueller and his team of Trump-haters, not to mention investigations by the House and Senate Intelligence Committees, the House Oversight Committee, and the Senate

Judiciary Committee's Subcommittee on Crime and Terrorism, no evidence of collusion ever was found.

Many believe the only reason the Mueller investigation was started was to draw attention away from the collusion to influence the 2016 presidential election that did occur—the Clinton campaign's bogus Christopher Steele dossier and the FBI's decision to use it against the President. The dossier was one of the shabbiest efforts in the history of presidential politics, endorsed by one of the shabbiest politicians in our history, to discredit an opposing presidential candidate. Despite that, an investigation of Hillary Clinton and the DNC was never opened or even suggested. The "Teflon" lady simply added another sordid chapter to her already checkered history of deception, self-dealing, and treachery: Whitewater; Travelgate; Vince Foster's mysterious death; Filegate; Benghazi; the Clinton Foundation; and the private email server to name just some of them. As a "soldier of the cause," the mainstream media protects Hillary Clinton zealously. So does the "deep state" embedded within the Department of Justice, the Federal Bureau of Investigation, and other federal law enforcement and intelligence agencies. How else can you explain the FBI's "Russian collusion" investigation against the Trump campaign, or top Justice Department officials having discussions about using the Twenty-fifth Amendment to remove an American president from office?[51]

As I earlier said, as have many others, if you want to know what Progressives are up to, take a look at what they are accusing others of doing. It is one of the reasons the Mueller investigation was so important—it deflected attention from the collusion between the Clinton campaign and the DNC, foreign sources, and US law enforcement and intelligence agencies to influence the 2016 presidential election and shifted it to the falsely accused Trump campaign. There was no better way to control the situation than "getting out front" and making sure the investigative committees were stacked with loyalists who could be depended upon to keep the investigation from straying into areas that might be troubling for Progressives.

The Mueller probe spent more than $45 million trying to find evidence of collusion between the Trump campaign and Russia, but inexplicably, not one dime looking into the efforts of the Clinton campaign, the DNC, FBI, and DOJ to derail the presidential campaign of Donald Trump. I suspect even the Clintons and the DNC were surprised that Progressive hacks within the FBI would so readily utilize the sham Steele dossier to unleash one of the most powerful anti-espionage and anti-terrorist tools available to law enforcement, secret FISA surveillance warrants, against a rival political campaign.

To fully comprehend the enormity of what happened, it is necessary to understand the FISA apparatus, one of the most intrusive—some say most un-American—anti-espionage, anti-terrorism tools available to the law enforcement and intelligence communities.

The Foreign Intelligence Surveillance Act of 1978 (FISA) is a federal statute first introduced by Democratic Senator Ted Kennedy in 1977 and signed into law the next year by Democratic President Jimmy Carter. It was intended to allow United States law enforcement and intelligence agencies to apply to a secret court established by the Act (FISA court) for authority to engage in surreptitious electronic surveillance, as well as physical searches, of persons engaged in espionage or international terrorism against the United States on behalf of foreign powers. It is not supposed to be used intentionally against US citizens. The eleven judges of the FISA court are selected by the chief justice of the United States from among the ranks of sitting federal district court judges to serve seven-year FISA terms. The role of the FISA court is to review applications from the FBI and other law enforcement and intelligence agencies requesting permission to conduct surveillance of suspected spies and terrorists to determine whether the agency has established sufficient legal grounds to justify the surveillance authority it is requesting. However, an abiding criticism of the FISA system is that the court is little more than a "rubber stamp" for the government and provides negligible oversight of the process. Almost no applications for FISA warrants are denied.

Think about it for a moment. A statute designed to allow secret spying on suspected international terrorists and spies working for foreign governments was turned against a domestic presidential campaign. If your first impulse was not, "this could never happen in America," you either have grown immutably cynical or do not understand our history, the Constitution, or the roles the rule of law and traditions of civilian governance have played in the growth and success of the United States. It was an unfathomable decision and one that should have set off red flags everywhere—at the FBI, in the Justice Department, with the FISA court, everywhere. Surveilling a presidential campaign and doing so based on unverified information provided by an opposing political campaign? The FBI intentionally deceiving the FISA court to obtain authority to spy on a domestic political candidate? Every time you state what happened, the more incredible it sounds.

In true Alice in Wonderland fashion, however, the story gets "curiouser and curiouser." The initial attempt by the "Never-Trumpers" within the FBI to gain permission to surveil the Trump campaign was rejected internally as lacking probable cause. That forced them to turn to the Steele dossier to support their claims. By using what they knew was unverified information, and at least had to suspect was completely bogus, they were able to gain permission to seek warrants from the FISA court.

The Never-Trumpers in the FBI deepened the subterfuge by pretending Donald Trump was not the target of their surveillance requests. The surveillance applications instead targeted Carter Page, a petroleum industry consultant who served for a time as a foreign policy advisor to the Trump campaign. But the surveillance conducted by the FBI was designed to try to show the Trump campaign, with the knowledge of the candidate, colluded with the Russians. How else can you explain the decision not to inform Donald Trump that the FBI believed someone in his campaign might be illegally involved with foreign powers, as would be customary in this type of investigation? That is exactly what happened, for example, when a staff member for Senator Diane Feinstein was investigated for possible involvement with Chinese intelligence organizations while Feinstein was chair of the Senate's Select Committee on Intelligence. Feinstein, a Democrat, was informed so she could take steps internally to protect sensitive information from being compromised. Trump never was.

When the initial surveillance efforts produced nothing of consequence, the FBI doubled-down, using the dossier to obtain additional warrants. In total, the FBI made four separate applications to the FISA court for permission to surveil the Trump campaign. The court never was told that the dossier being used to support the applications had come from the Clinton campaign and DNC, that information in the dossier had not been verified, or that the FBI knew at least some of the information was untrue. Lending substance to the criticism that the FISA court is largely a "rubber stamp" for US law enforcement and intelligence: for months after the court learned it had been duped by the FBI, lied to, it inexplicably took no disciplinary measures against anyone involved. Not until December 2019 did the court even ask the FBI for an explanation.

The report of DOJ Inspector General Michael Horowitz, an Obama appointee, regarding the FBI's handling of the FISA applications, provides a chilling picture of unfathomable lapses by the FBI in its rush to spy on the Trump Campaign. Actually, to the extent it suggests some degree of "inadvertence," *lapses* is far too mild a term to describe the FBI's behavior. What the Horowitz report describes is malfeasance, and the intentionality of many of those involved is unmistakable. The inspector general admitted as much when in testimony before the House Judiciary Committee, he conceded that he understood why people would question whether it was even possible for so many flaws in the FBI's application process to have resulted from simple incompetence. It's a good point. No one possibly could be that stupid, poorly trained, careless, mindless, irresponsible, reckless, indifferent, sloppy—you get the point. If they were, we have much larger problems within our chief law enforcement and intelligence agencies. The more likely explanation: the FBI, at the behest of a cabal of "Never-Trumpers" embedded within its ranks, went rogue.

Curiously, however, Horowitz maintained, in carefully guarded language, that he had not found documentary or testimonial evidence of political bias or improper motivation influencing the decision to open the investigations.[52] The inspector general seems to be saying little more than, "no one admitted or said in a document they were motivated by political bias," but the statement is peculiar nonetheless. No one ever admits to being biased, least of all rogue government officials bent on ousting a president, but conduct speaks volumes. Had the inspector general forgotten that he found the FBI withheld exculpatory evidence regarding the Trump campaign from the FISA court? Had he forgotten that he found an FBI agent altered some of the information submitted to the FISA court? Had he forgotten that people like Peter Strzok, deputy assistant director of the FBI's Counter-Intelligence Section, and Lisa Page, an FBI lawyer with whom Strzok allegedly was romantically involved, were on high-level teams within the FBI, providing information and making recommendations that influenced the course of the investigation?

Remember Strzok and Page? They were the FBI officials who engaged in the infamous text exchange in which she asks, "[Trump is] not ever going to become president, right? Right?" Strzok responds, "No. No, he won't. We'll stop it." It also became clear the same pair, using the FBI counter-intelligence team Strzok headed, were feverishly searching for a pretext to accelerate the probe of the Trump campaign and obtain FISA surveillance warrants.[53] Strzok and Page were "true believers," committed to stopping Trump at any cost, and were certain the ends would justify the means. Even if the Steele dossier was nonsense, if they could get permission to spy on the Trump Campaign, they were sure a treasure trove of crimes and violations would be uncovered, perhaps even including collusion with the Russians.

I have no idea how Horowitz could have found that in applying to the FISA court for permission to spy against the Trump campaign, the FBI withheld exculpatory evidence, altered evidence, and relied on a completely unverified dossier supplied by the Clinton campaign and the DNC, parts of which the FBI knew to be false, and not found bias. Wasn't the Strzok/Page text exchange evidence enough? Horowitz also found egregious, inexplicable disregard of internal FBI safeguards and procedures in connection with the FISA application process, and he knew the Trump campaign had not been informed the FBI was investigating a member of the campaign for possible collusion with the Russians. The better question might be: "Where was the evidence suggesting a lack of bias?

All Americans should be outraged and alarmed. This is what happens in banana republics, not the United States. Military strongmen, secret police, intelligence agencies, and other state "operatives" manipulate and control domestic politics and influence the outcome of elections. They pick "winners" and "losers." Is that what we have become? A banana republic? It is not a rhetorical or frivolous question.

In truth, the inspector general seems to have placed undue reliance for his "no bias" conclusions on the fact there were supervisors he believed to be unbiased to whom Strzok, Page, and the others involved in the Russian collusion hoax reported, and it was those supervisors who ultimately were responsible for making final decisions about whether the investigation would be opened and how it would be conducted.

It is a singularly narrow view. Those in charge necessarily rely on information, advice, and recommendations from the people working for them, the "boots on the ground," so to speak. If the advice received by decision-makers is tainted by political bias, can decisions based on that advice be considered any less tainted or biased? If, for example, Foreman A, a line supervisor, recommends against promoting an employee because of racial, ethnic, or gender bias, is the decision any less problematic because Foreman A's unbiased supervisor, technically responsible for the decision to promote or not, accepts and acts upon the recommendation? And as one call-in guest on a Rush Limbaugh radio program pointed out, to believe the long list of FBI oversights, transgressions, policy violations, and lawlessness in connection with the FISA applications and investigation of "Russian collusion" occurred coincidentally, but always against the interests of the Trump campaign, is akin to believing that if a coin is flipped twenty-eight times and comes up "heads" each time, it simply is the "luck of the draw."

There is another indication of bias within the FBI and the DOJ that people tend to overlook. Clearly, at some point well before the November 2018 midterm elections, the Mueller team, the FBI, and the DOJ knew Carter Page and the Trump campaign had not colluded with the Russians. That information was not shared with voters until the Mueller report was released in April 2019 and Democrats had retaken the House of Representatives, largely on the strength of thirty-one Democrats winning seats in Democratic districts won by Trump in 2016. Contrast the decision not to let voters know before the 2018 midterms that the claimed collusion between the Trump campaign and Russia was a hoax with Jim Comey's exoneration of Hillary Clinton's illegal use of a private email server while serving as Secretary of State.

Before the 2016 presidential election, Comey held a nationally broadcast news conference to announce that despite potential violations of several federal laws, as FBI Director he had determined Hillary Clinton had done nothing worthy of criminal prosecution. He went further; according to Comey, *no* reasonable prosecutor could conclude otherwise.[54] Obstruction of justice was not even mentioned as a possibility despite the fact Hillary allowed or authorized a mountain of evidence to be destroyed, including thousands of emails, computer servers, and cell phones.

Why not a similar national television announcement before the 2018 midterm elections debunking the Trump/Russian collusion fraud, which by then the FBI and Mueller team surely knew was nonsense? Progressives had savaged the President for nearly two years for supposedly colluding with the Russians. The Mueller team had to know those allegations were untrue but remained silent. Was there any reason to hide the truth from voters other than trying to swing the midterms in favor of Democrats? How many of those thirty-one seats would have gone Republican if the truth had been shared?

Bottom line: Inspector General Horowitz made and described a compelling case for political bias, improper motivation, and corruption at the highest levels of the FBI and DOJ, but then backed away from stating the obvious—the investigation of the Trump Campaign was a politically motivated witch hunt, as the President had long contended. What the inspector general appears to have done is similar to what Bob Muller did when he submitted his report—he tried to protect himself and his team from the wrath of the left. Mueller avoided becoming a target of the liberal crazies by giving them something to sustain their coup fantasies even though the evidence did not support it. Not much was needed—with the help of a sympathetic and complicit media, virtually anything, no matter how inconsequential, can be turned into the proverbial Sword of Damocles. In the case of the Mueller report, the "bone" thrown to the "mob" was outlining "evidence" the Mueller team found insufficient to support a recommendation to prosecute the President for obstruction of justice but hiding that fact by stating the team could not exonerate the President from obstruction charges. Mueller understood if he left the door even slightly ajar for Progressives to continue their insane investigations of the President, their fury would continue to be directed against Donald Trump rather than Mueller and his team. Horowitz essentially tried to do the same thing by avoiding a conclusion that political bias within the FBI and DOJ spawned the vendetta against the Trump campaign.

The final chapter may not yet have been written on the FBI's and DOJ's handling of the "Russian collusion" investigation. In May 2019 John H. Durham, a veteran federal prosecutor from Connecticut with a history of investigating wrongdoing by national security officials, was named by Attorney General Bill Barr to investigate the origins of the Russian collusion probe. The investigation eventually turned criminal. With Joe Biden's election, however, that investigation may be ended quickly, although before stepping down AG Barr named Durham "special counsel" in an effort to allow him to continue his probe regardless of who occupies the White House. We will see what happens.

Keep in mind how the Mueller investigation started. In May 2017, after President Trump fired James Comey as the director of the FBI, largely because of his public grandstanding and posturing over the continuing investigation of Russian interference in the 2016 presidential elections, Rod Rosenstein, deputy director of the FBI, appointed Robert Mueller as special counsel to continue the investigation. When Mueller stacked his investigative team with Clinton supporters, anti-Trumpers, and left-wing extremists, including Peter Strzok and Lisa Page, Progressives were ecstatic. They could smell blood in the water. Mueller's "dream team" would not let the cause down. Trump was finished.

For nearly two years, Progressives basked in the conviction the Mueller investigation and report would provide the definitive roadmap for a quick and easy impeachment. Trump might even resign. The Progressive talk shows and media were giddy with anticipation. Daily, radio and TV hosts speculated about the many illegal activities engaged in by the President. He was tabbed a Russian spy, a traitor to his country.

Then it all crashed and burned—no collusion, no obstruction. Not even an investigative team heavily stacked against Donald Trump could find either collusion with the Russians or obstruction of justice by the President. Progressives responded as Mueller knew they would. Infuriated and unapologetic, they doubled down. The House Intelligence Committee, chaired by Congressman Adam Schiff, arguably the most deceitful and lugubrious character in US political history—if he didn't exist, a cartoon strip would have to invent him—took up the "cause," the "resistance."

In truth, the Mueller report left the door only very slightly ajar for Progressives to continue investigating the President—there was not much left to go on. As one commentator put it, the twenty-two-month investigation, "[F]ailed to find Trump guilty of collusions with Russia in the 2016 election and failed to find actionable obstruction of justice pertaining to the non-crime of collusion."[55] The Mueller report, in other words, desiccated the essential premise fueling Progressives' convictions they would be able to bring down the Trump presidency—that the Trump campaign had colluded with Russia to influence the 2016 US presidential election. The one tidbit it offered, the only thin reed of hope, after 500 witnesses, 2800 subpoenas, the production of countless documents, 675 days of investigation, and the expenditure of over $45 million—no stone was left unturned—was the Mueller team's claimed inability to exonerate the President for obstruction of justice and, in an obvious overture to the "mob," an outline of the "evidence" the team considered in reaching that gratuitous conclusion.

As special counsel, it was not Mueller's or his team's responsibility to exonerate the President or determine whether or not obstruction of justice occurred, only to say whether sufficient evidence existed to prosecute obstruction of justice charges. It was a "thumbs up" or "thumbs down" decision. By stating he could not exonerate the President and then elaborately describing the "evidence" his team "considered" as "possible" obstructions, Mueller was trying to obscure the fact his investigation had not found the evidence legally sufficient to support a decision to prosecute. If it had, Mueller would have been obligated to say so, and the special counsel's team of angry Progressive crusaders certainly would have insisted that he do so. That is exactly what Attorney General Barr and Deputy Attorney Rod Rosenstein both subsequently found in their reviews—the "evidence" described by the Mueller team fell well short of criminal obstruction. Rosenstein, who appointed Mueller, clearly was not a Trump supporter.

By confusing the discussion of obstruction, however, Mueller accomplished what he needed—he gave Progressives enough "talking points" to keep them from turning their destructive anger against him and his team. The House Intelligence Committee took the bait. Determined to impeach the President for "something," it shifted into high gear, convening hearings, calling witnesses, floating new theories of misconduct daily, as Progressives attempted to salvage something from the Mueller Report's calculating treatment of the obstruction issue. Remarkably, despite Mueller's unequivocal rejection of "collusion," Progressives persisted in their efforts to delegitimize the President by maintaining Hillary Clinton lost the election only because of collusion between Russia and the Trump campaign. No reason to let facts interfere with the dysfunctional fantasies of the Progressives' base.

However, the Mueller report made it nearly impossible for the Progressives' collusion claims to gain traction; they quickly discovered that trying to manufacture a plausible obstruction case in the absence of a predicate crime was a daunting task. The investigation was floundering. But, as all of us should realize by now, when Progressives are involved, the show is never over until the "mystery guests" appear.

It truly is enigmatic how consistently provocateur witnesses surface—and then slide back into the alternative universe that produced them, never to be seen or heard from again—to prop up Progressive investigations or causes. It matters not what the occasion may be—a Supreme Court appointment, an impeachment—Progressives seemingly can dial up an unlimited supply of "witnesses" with "scandalous" information to share, often decades old.

In a courtroom, statutes of limitations prohibit the bringing of lawsuits more than a few years old precisely because the supporting evidence has become "stale" and unreliable. There are no such safeguards with the Progressive "shock troop" witnesses. They are programmed to either lead the assault or reinforce it, and they understand their role and the fact that they are expendable—"as always, if your treachery is discovered or exposed, we will deny any knowledge of your actions." Look how quickly Christine Blasey Ford was jettisoned by Progressives after her stumbling performance in the Brett Kavanaugh hearings. That said, the witnesses also know they will be provided with full legal support, their fifteen minutes of fame will be well-choreographed and stage-managed by the Democratic Party—book deals and talk show rounds could be on the horizon, perhaps even public office—and they will be idolized and protected by a mesmerized-media. Consequently, it was hardly surprising when, on cue, the latest iteration of a Progressives provocateur, this time a "whistleblower, materialized to try to resuscitate an investigation on life support and fading quickly. The whistleblower accused the President of "bribing" Ukrainian President Volodymyr Zelensky during a phone call by threatening to withhold military aid if Zelensky did not dig up "dirt" on Joe and Hunter Biden.

The basic premise, that it was necessary to "dig up dirt" on the Bidens, should have given pause to thinking people. For years, Joe Biden bragged about how as vice president he strong-armed Ukraine. The essential facts were well known, just never investigated seriously by the Obama administration. Hunter Biden, while his father was vice president of the United States and in charge of Ukraine policy, including gas and oil policy, accepted a position on the board of a Ukrainian gas and oil company, Burisma. Burisma paid him millions of dollars over a several-year period. Hunter Biden admitted he was offered the position only because his last name was Biden—he had no background or experience in gas or oil or with Ukraine. That is how bribery works—one of the better ways to make sure the vice president of the United States will advocate for you with his government is to take good care of his family.

As it turned out, the whistleblower, who never appeared or testified before Schiff's House Intelligence Committee, had no first-hand knowledge of the phone call between Presidents Trump and Zelensky, apparently was a Progressive activist—at least one report said he worked for Joe Biden—and essentially coordinated with Adam Schiff to stage the entire spectacle. Other reports indicated he was a member of the intelligence community, again raising concerns with "deep-state" interventions in domestic politics. A transcript of the call, which the whistleblower did not know existed, all but eviscerated the allegations.

Collusion? Abuse of power? Treason? What else can you call it when members of Congress make up "evidence" to impeach a president? Certainly, no civil or criminal litigant could fabricate evidence and avoid criminal penalties. Why is there seemingly no concern when members of Congress do the same?

As weak and unsupported as the whistleblower's allegations may have been, Progressives had been thrown a lifeline of sorts. It was a straw they eagerly seized, recognizing they were out of options. Last chances are, after all, last chances, and Progressives were not going to let this one slip away, the facts and the Constitution be damned. They determined to use the Zelensky call to impeach the President the moment they heard of it. They were committed to impeaching Donald Trump for something, it did not matter what, and feeble though it may have been, this allegation at least freed them from the withering constraints of the Mueller report.

Once again Progressives showed how fixated and partisan their focus is. Just as the actions of the Clinton campaign and the DNC in using foreign sources to compile a false dossier against President Trump, and the FBI's and DOJ's knowing misuse of that dossier, was ignored by the Mueller team, Adam Schiff's and the House Intelligence Committee's investigation of the phone call between Presidents Trump and Zelensky ignored the actions of Joe and Hunter Biden. Even though the Bidens' activities in Ukraine were at the heart of the controversy Progressives claimed gave rise to an impeachable offense by President Trump, the Schiff committee showed no interest in learning anything about those activities. It is something Progressives feel empowered to do—ignore actual misconduct by members of their party while they pursue made-up charges against others—because they know there never will be an outcry from the media.

Understandably, Progressives did not want voters to compare what Joe Biden had done in Ukraine with the innocuous conduct by President Trump they now were claiming constituted an impeachable offense. Hunter Biden profited handsomely from his father's position as vice president of the United States, and Joe Biden publicly acknowledged—bragged about—that as vice president he extorted Ukrainian officials into firing a prosecutor investigating corruption involving Burisma while his son was on the Burisma board. Hunter Biden remained on the Burisma board for several years until his father announced his candidacy for the Democratic presidential nomination.

Joe Biden, of course, insists there was nothing wrong with what he and his son did in Ukraine. The fact that Hunter Biden resigned from the Burisma board when his father decided to run for president, however, says everything anyone needs to know about whether or not Joe Biden believed what happened in Ukraine was legitimate. He understood his son receiving millions of dollars for serving on the Burisma board while he was vice president and in charge of the United States' Ukraine policy, and his manipulation of Ukrainian officials to make sure his son was not caught up in a corruption scandal engulfing Burisma, would be recognized during a presidential campaign for what they were—old-style political graft and corruption. Why else would Hunter Biden resign from the Burisma board when his father decided to run for president? If he could serve on the board while his father was vice president, he certainly could serve while his father ran for president, or even if his father was elected president. No, either Joe Biden or someone on his campaign staff recognized that while he may have been "under the radar" and immunized from criticism as vice president in an administration that could do no wrong in the eyes of the media, his self-dealing would become very visible during a presidential campaign. I am confident Joe Biden never envisioned running again for national office when the Burisma deal was struck, and if serving as vice president was to be his "last rodeo," there certainly was no reason to leave money on the table.

To show how evident it was to everyone except, perhaps, the Bidens, that the Burisma deal was "dirty," Christopher Heinz, stepson of Senator John Kerry and a business associate of Hunter Biden at the time he was appointed to the Burisma board, was so troubled by the arrangement he ended his business relationship with the younger Biden over it.[56]

I am confident the friends of Joe Biden were not surprised by the allegations of corruption against the former vice president. Many believe he made a cottage industry of using his office to enrich himself and his family. In another chapter, for example, I talk about how shortly after Joe's brother, James, was hired as an executive in a construction company, despite his lack of construction experience, the company was awarded a lucrative government contract. His other brother, Frank, profited handsomely as a developer in Costa Rico from Joe's position as the Obama administration's "point man" for Central and Latin America. Millions of dollars of taxpayer-funded loans went to a friend of Biden's to open a luxury car dealership in Ukraine. The list goes on. As one commentator summed it up, "Politicians have long used their families to route power and benefits for their self-enrichment," but "one particular politician—Joe Biden—emerges as king of the sweetheart deal, with no less than five family members benefitting from his largesse, favorable access and powerful position for commercial gain."[57]

Some consider Joe Biden the most corrupt politician in the history of American politics. I doubt he is that accomplished, but he was good enough to hook up his son with interests in Ukraine willing to pay him generously. One thing is certain: Burisma and Ukraine could not have been interested in Hunter Biden for his expertise, accomplishments, or personality. Hunter Biden has struggled with drug and alcohol problems for years. He was booted out of the Naval Reserve. He had no background or experience in either gas and oil or with Ukraine. But his last name was Biden, his father was vice president of the United States, and Ukraine was desperately in need of US aid. Are there any questions or uncertainties about how or why Hunter Biden's appointment to the Burisma board came about?

Think what the hue and cry would have been if Donald Trump, Jr., or Eric Trump, had traveled on official government business with their father, as Hunter Biden did with his, to countries seeking military aid and other assistance from the United States and came home with personal contracts worth millions of dollars. Is there any Progressive truly disingenuous enough to pretend they would not have cried "Foul" if the person who sat on the Burisma board had been named Trump rather than Biden? For that matter, is there any Progressive who can say with a straight face they would not have considered it an impeachable offense if a son of Trump had sat on the Burisma board in the same circumstances as Hunter Biden? In Joe Biden's world, what he did in Ukraine may qualify as little more than "family business as usual," but if he believed what he did was above reproach, you can bet Hunter Biden would still be a member of the Burisma board.

There was an appalling incident in September 2019 during the House Intelligence Committee's "investigation" of the phone call between Presidents Trump and Zelensky that illustrates with remarkable clarity the mendacious character of Progressives and how desperate they were to discredit the President. While Joseph Maguire, acting director of National Intelligence, was testifying during a Committee hearing, Adam Schiff purported to read a copy of the transcript of the call between Presidents Zelensky and Trump. The tape of the Intelligence Committee hearing needs to be heard to fully comprehend what happened. Essentially, however, Schiff completely misrepresented the nature of the call, at one point making the President sound like a syndicate crime boss making an offer the other side could not refuse: "I hear what you want. I have a favor I want from you, though. And I'm going to say this only seven times, so you better listen good. I want you to make up dirt on my political opponent. Understand? Lots of it, on this and on that."

The problem is, nothing of the kind was said by Trump. Schiff simply made it all up.

Schiff later would try to call it an "attempt at humor," a parody, but look at the video and see if you can detect anything but willful deceit and arrogance in this contemptible, two-bit caricature of a politician. Schiff knew casual followers of the investigation might never discover the fraud he was perpetrating and understood the media not only would not take him to task for it but almost certainly would find a way to defend his inexcusable dishonesty. Adam Schiff, more than anyone I know, exemplifies why you do not want your life controlled by politicians, although Jerry Nadler, Chuck Schumer, Richard Blumenthal, and Maxine Waters are some very competitive "seconds."

The actual transcript of the call between Presidents Trump and Zelensky confirms the comments referring to the Bidens were brief, completely nonthreatening and noncoercive, and certainly not a key part of the conversation. There was no follow-up then or later. In fact, after the call, the Trump White House had numerous contacts with Ukraine, and the Bidens never again were mentioned. It should have been clear to any fair-minded person that during the call, the President was simply doing his job, questioning the Ukrainian president to determine how serious he was about cleaning up corruption in his country—it has long been among the most corrupt nations in the world—before sending millions of taxpayer dollars to Ukraine.

If there is any doubt whether that was the President's intent, a story in the *New York Times* published in late December 2019, although certainly not intended to support the President, confirms it. The story quoted the President during an August 2019 meeting in the Oval Office questioning whether Ukraine's new president, Zelensky, was a "genuine" reformer, and cautioning that, "Ukraine is a corrupt country. We are pissing away our money." How much clearer could the President's intentions be? Corruption in Ukraine, not the Biden's, was his concern.

That said, I am not sure how any realistic discussion of corruption in Ukraine could exclude the Bidens. The President should be concerned when a supposed ally is willing to bribe an American vice president to curry favor with the United States. Could there be a better example of the type of conduct the President needed assurance would be stopped than what happened between the Bidens and Ukraine? Isn't understanding how a situation like that came about an indispensable component of determining whether adequate safeguards have been put in place to prevent it from reoccurring? Don't the interests of the United States in rectifying situations like this outweigh any possible collateral political benefits to a president? Suppose, for example, sometime in the future information becomes available that another presidential candidate may have committed a serious federal crime. Would it be an impeachable offense for a president running for re-election to ask the Justice Department to investigate? How about if the crime takes place overseas and a foreign government is asked to investigate? Progressives apparently believe so.

In carrying out the duties of the president, national interests frequently will overlap with a president's political fortunes. Politicians, presidents included, make decisions that are in their political best interests. As long as national interests are involved—and there certainly was a national interest involved in trying to fully understand what happened between the Bidens and Ukrainian officials—why is it even relevant that some political interest of the President also may be affected? Is it even possible to separate a president's political interests from the decisions they are asked to make daily? Isn't the essence of politics responding to voter preferences? Progressives understandably may have been sensitive to someone delving too deeply into the Bidens' activities in Ukraine, but millions of other voters wanted an explanation. Why should those voters have viewed attempts to impeach the President based on his call with the Ukrainian president as anything other than an elaborate cover-up by Progressives designed to enhance and protect the political interests and prospects of Joe Biden and the Democratic Party?

Keep in mind that Ukraine and the United States have an agreement to share and exchange information regarding criminal investigations. Corruption by the former vice president and his son, even if the House Intelligence and Judiciary Committees insisted on ignoring it, seems to fit comfortably within the intent of that agreement. Certainly, Democratic lawmakers thought so. In May 2019, for example, three Democratic senators wrote Ukrainian prosecutor general, Yuri Lutsenko, calling on him to reinstate an investigation against Paul Manafort, a former member of the Trump campaign, an investigation press reports alleged had been suspended to avoid angering American officials.

The hypocrisy is astonishing. It is fine, not an abuse of power or any other violation of law or the Constitution, for Democratic congressmen to ask Ukraine to investigate an American citizen when the target of the investigation is someone Democrats hope will cause problems for a Republican president and advance the political interests of Democrats. It is an impeachable abuse of power, however, for President Trump to mention the Bidens in a phone call with the Ukrainian president, even though it indisputably is in the interests of the United States to eliminate corruption between its public officials and allies receiving millions of American taxpayer dollars.

Progressives have tried to distinguish the letter from the congressmen and the phone call between Presidents Trump and Zelensky by arguing that the letter contained no threats or attempts to coerce. The easy response is, "neither did President Trump's phone call," as the transcript of the call very plainly shows. More to the point, Wasn't it coercive and threatening for Congress, which has absolute control over the aid received by Ukraine from the United States, merely to have sent a letter of this nature to Ukrainian officials? The letter, no matter how carefully crafted, could never eliminate the implicit threat of consequences if Congress was disappointed with the response of the prosecutor general, and the congressmen who wrote that letter knew it. That was its purpose.

Consider for a moment the hundreds of communications that take place every year between American presidents and their counterparts around the world. Does anyone believe these conversations are simple exchanges of pleasantries? Would you not expect American presidents to use every means at their disposal to advance American interests? Is there anyone who does not understand that threats to withhold aid are routine negotiating tactics for any president when dealing with foreign governments? The office of the president is called the "bully pulpit" for a reason. In lengthy discussions between world leaders, should we parse every word, every sentence, to see if we can find something to take out of context and characterize as an abuse of power or worse? Is everything a president says to a foreign official a potential "gotcha moment?" If so, how should we view former President Obama's exchange with then Russian President Dmitri Medvedev?

In 2012, Barack Obama was caught on camera sending a message to incoming Russian President Vladimir Putin by advising outgoing President Medvedev that if given adequate leeway by the Russians during his campaign, he would have more "flexibility" to deal with issues involving Russia after the US elections, including, presumably, the contentious issue of the European missile defense. Obama, in other words, was telling Russia that if it would do him a favor during the campaign, he later would be willing to make concessions he was unwilling to share with voters before the election, apparently because he believed the concessions he had in mind would not be viewed favorably. Obama had promised the American people that if elected president, he would "reset" the relationships with Russian and other protagonists of the United State. Seemingly, part of the "reset" included Russia helping the President get reelected. Obama unquestionably was striking a "deal" with Russia to protect and advance his political interests.

Obama enlisted Russia's help to influence the outcome of a US presidential election. There is no other way to describe his conversation with Russian President Medvedev. Was that an impeachable abuse of power? Could promising concessions the President must have believed would not be acceptable to voters in return for a political favor in any way be viewed as in the best interests of the United States? Was it consistent with our national security interests? How much of a *quid pro quo* did Obama provide the Russians for their forbearance? We do not know because there never was an investigation. Why didn't the media have even a mild interest in finding out? Does anyone doubt there would have been calls for impeachment if the American president having that conversation with Medvedev had been Donald Trump rather than Barack Obama?

How can anyone dismiss Obama's asking Russia for a favor to help him influence the outcome of an American presidential election, and Hillary Clinton's using foreign sources, including Russian sources, to compile a bogus dossier intended to discredit a political opponent, as inconsequential, but maintain President Trump's phone call with the Ukrainian president constituted an impeachable offense? This is not simply the law of the "caught and the uncaught." All of these incidents were known and publicized, but the media and Progressives, almost entirely silent when Obama and Clinton were the focus, went ballistic when President Trump was accused of far more innocuous conduct.

The Steele dossier, by the way, certainly was not the first time Hillary turned to foreign sources to promote her interests. As Secretary of State, more than a few people believed she was running an elaborate "pay-to-play" scheme in which the individuals most likely to be granted an audience with the secretary were those willing to be generous to the Clinton Foundation, including many foreign leaders and governments.[58] This was not eleemosynary altruism on the part of either the donors or the secretary. The Clinton's allegedly used the Foundation as a personal "piggy bank" to fund lavish travel and other expenses. Even when not a direct source of funding, however, foundations are "branding" and image-burnishing projects for the rich and famous and enhance their fame and economic opportunities. It was more than coincidence, I suspect, that as a prelude to breaking ties with the British Royal Family and striking out on their own financially, Prince Harry and Meghan Markle withdrew from the foundation they shared with Prince William and Kate Middleton to establish one of their own.[59]

I also doubt it was coincidental that as soon as Hillary Clinton went "out of power" donations to the Clinton Foundation plummeted. In her first year as Secretary of State, for example, the Clinton Foundation reportedly received $249 million in donations. In 2018, after she left office, it raised less than $31 million.[60] Was Hillary "selling her office?" The media certainly did not care, but you be the judge. By some reports, more than half, 85 of 154, of the people from private interests who met with her during her tenure as Secretary of State donated to the Clinton Foundation or international causes promoted by the foundation. These individuals accounted for a staggering $156 million in donations, with a significant number of seven-digit, individual donors.[61]

Can you imagine what the media would do if the data showed similar correlations between access to President Trump and donations to a foundation populated and controlled by Trump family members? Progressives never have to worry about their "heroes" being criticized for these types of relationships, however, because the media, spellbound as it is by the Progressive *weltanschauung,* protects them.

You should be starting to see how quickly an expansive view of what constitutes an impeachable offense can be used to attack anything a president does and how quickly it could destroy any semblance of stability in government.

Any rational, fair-minded person would have viewed the President's brief comments about Joe and Hunter Biden during the call with the Ukrainian president as innocuous and superfluous, just as Progressives argue President Obama's promises of future concessions to the Russian president were innocuous and superfluous. But Adam Schiff and his Progressive cronies on the House Intelligence Committee are not rational or fair-minded people. They immediately elevated President Trump's comments to what they maintained was an impeachable abuse of power. Once again, Americans should be alarmed. Actually, they should be outraged. Impeachment of a duly elected president based on ambiguous, casual comments, never acted upon, and, as President Zelensky confirmed, never viewed by him as a threat of any nature? No president had ever been threatened with impeachment over conduct so insignificant.

The impeachment clause of the Constitution, Article II, Section 4, like much of the Constitution, was a compromise. Initial drafts of the Constitution provided no means for removing a president or other federal official from office, largely because many of the founders believed elections were the best means for determining whether a president should continue in office. They also feared the legislative removal of executive branch officials would harm the separation of powers concept so crucial to the architecture of the Constitution. Others disagreed and Article II, section 4, reflects the compromise reached.[62]

The meaning of the impeachment clauses in the Constitution has long been subject to debate. In some respects, the language of Article II, Section 4, is crystal clear: "Treason and bribery" had and have well-understood meanings, "High-Crimes and Misdemeanors," less so. A fair reading of the constitutional debates, however, is that the founders were fearful of divisive, partisan removals of executive branch officials. Consequently, at a minimum, the impeachment power was to be used only in cases where the removal of an official had strong bipartisan political, as well as public, support. While the meaning of "High-Crimes and Misdemeanors," a phrase borrowed from British law, was better understood in the 18th century, I also think it is fair to say the founders believed an impeachable offense had to involve, if not a crime, at least a serious constitutional transgression, and one that not only caused significant harm to an important public interest but also was of such egregious nature that it effectively disqualified the official from further service. General claims of incompetence or unfitness for office were not sufficient, nor was dislike of a president or other federal official.

The founders, in other words, recognized impeachment as a powerful tool capable of changing election results. It was not to be used indiscriminately or lightly but was reserved for serious transgressions damaging to the public interest and only when there existed a bipartisan consensus that less-absolute redress was not available. Anything more stringent threatened to frustrate the will of voters and subjugate the executive branch to Congress. Impeachment was supposed to be the "nuclear" option.

Although abuse of power is nowhere mentioned in the Constitution as an impeachable offense, I have no quarrel with the proposition that some misuses of presidential power could be flagrant enough to justify removal from office. This just was not one of them, not nearly. How can impeachable abuses be identified? That is the role of bipartisan consensus and why it is so important to the impeachment process.

Interestingly, for a good portion of the last several years, Nancy Pelosi shared the view that impeachment was reserved for things "compelling and overwhelming" and required bipartisan support—until she didn't.[63] I honestly believe many Progressive leaders, Pelosi among them, ensconced as they are in the Washington "bubble," believed independent voters, maybe even some Never-Trumpers and RINO's within the Republican Party, could be persuaded to join the impeachment hoax Progressives were pursuing. However, when it became clear a significant majority of voters, particularly independents, were not buying what Progressives were selling and Progressives were running out of any plausible grounds for impeachment, Pelosi "adjusted" her standards. Impeachment no longer needed to be based on grounds either compelling or overwhelming, and purely partisan support was fine, at least as long as Progressives were in control of the House. Further dividing the country, setting precedents that would destabilize the government and damage the Constitution were acceptable costs as long as the goals of the "cause," remaking America in the image of the Democrats' "big tent" bacchanal, were advanced.

In the end, Pelosi engaged in her own flagrant abuse of power, opting in favor of her political interests—safeguarding her position as Speaker of the House—at the expense of the Constitution by allowing completely bogus and constitutionally infirm articles of impeachment to be voted on and adopted. Improvisation, after all, is a skill far more essential to political survival than principle.

The Trump impeachment met none of the constitutional requirements. It did not have bipartisan political or public support. It would be difficult for any fair-minded person to say a serious transgression occurred or that there was any harm, much less significant harm, to an important public interest. And, after reading the transcript of the telephone call between President Trump and President Zelensky, it would be impossible for anyone to seriously argue that anything which transpired was even remotely disqualifying of further public service by the President. Please, all of those who can say with a straight-face that Joe Biden did nothing wrong and should be allowed to serve as president without Ukraine, China, or Costa Rico even being mentioned, but President Trump should have been impeached because of his comments during a phone call with the president of Ukraine, stand and confirm how truly unprincipled you are.

So, what is the "new" standard for impeachment Progressives are endorsing? Is impeachment authorized anytime a president does something with which an opposing political party disagrees? Anytime a president does something his political opponents can characterize as an "abuse of power?"

What exactly is it presidents do that cannot be characterized as an abuse of power? Is there any president in the history of the Republic who could not have been accused of abusing power? Is there even sufficient agreement on the powers of American presidents to provide fair warning about what will and will not be considered an abuse? Isn't "fair warning" an essential element of due process and fundamental fairness? Is every abuse impeachable, regardless of its nature, impact, or intent? Is intent even a relevant consideration?

Arguably, isn't every executive order that *makes* rather than *interprets* law an abuse of power? There is no authority in the Constitution for the chief executive to bypass Congress and make laws by executive order. That being the case, did President Obama abuse his power by substantively amending Obamacare through an executive order? How about Abraham Lincoln who enacted the Emancipation Proclamation by executive order after running for office on a platform promising slavery would not be outlawed where permitted by state law? Or Harry Truman, who tried to nationalize the nation's steel mills by executive order?

In the early days of the Republic, George Washington, as president, led an army into Pennsylvania to put down protesters during the Whiskey Rebellion. Franklin Roosevelt attempted to pack the Supreme Court to neutralize justices who might be hostile to his New Deal plan. He also used an executive order to send 120,000 Japanese expatriates and American citizens of Japanese ancestry to prison camps during World War II. Presidents have sent the military into harm's way without a declaration of war by Congress. Harry Truman authorized the first use of nuclear bombs against civilian populations. President Obama knowingly lied to Americans—Jonathan Gruber, a chief architect of Obamacare, admitted it—when he told them, "If you like your health insurance plan or doctors, you can keep them." Gruber disdainfully blamed the deception as necessary because of the "stupidity" of Americans, too dumb to recognize their self-interests.

Is it okay for a president to engage in an abuse of power for a "good" purpose or is abuse, *abuse*? There likely would be a strong consensus, for example, that the Emancipation Proclamation served a good purpose, so does that merit a free pass despite clearly being outside the scope of a president's executive order authority?

How about the schemes to pack the Supreme Court or nationalize the nation's steel mills? Progressives might have endorsed both of these actions, while those more cognizant of constitutional limitations would recognize how unlawful they were. As a presidential candidate, Kamala Harris promised that if elected she would issue strict gun-control measures by executive order if Congress did not act. It would be a clear abuse of power for any president to bypass Congress and engage in this type of executive branch lawmaking, but Progressives likely would applaud any president taking such action, lawful or not, neither recognizing nor caring about the constitutional overreach. Would they be equally sanguine, however, if a president sent the National Guard into sanctuary cities to uphold federal immigration laws?

Who decides what is an "abuse of power" or a "good" or "bad" purpose? What standards guide the decisions or is "abuse of power," like pornography, something you recognize when you see it? Are we willing to leave a decision as consequential as the impeachment of a president solely to the judgement of the political party that controls the House at the time of an alleged transgression?

One thing is certain: if impeachments no longer require bipartisan support, a serious transgression, and harm to an important public interest, few presidents ever will complete a full term in office without being impeached unless their party controls the House of Representatives. If the opposing party holds significant enough majorities in both the House and Senate, no president is likely to escape removal from office. Abuse of power is such an imprecise and malleable "standard" that without bipartisan agreement a president has committed an impeachable offense, impeachment quickly becomes an agent of harassment and sedition. A president will act contrary to the wishes of a House controlled by the opposing party only at the risk of impeachment. Our system of checks and balances, carefully crafted to limit the power of each branch of government, no longer would have meaning. One chamber of Congress, the House, would be the "Uber Meister" of our government. Effectively, we would be a unicameral government and direct democracy. Progressives no longer would need to obsess over eliminating the Electoral College.

One of the most troubling aspects of President Trump's impeachment was that no Democrat ever seemed to ask the most basic questions: "Under the Constitution, what is an impeachable offense, and what are the thresholds and standards required for impeachment?" They simply assumed the President could be impeached for any reason or no reason. An impeachable offense was what they said it was, and all that was needed to impeach was a majority in the House. The President was not charged with treason, bribery, or any other crime. He was impeached, as I heard one commenter say, simply for "being president." In one particularly revealing statement, then first-term Representative Abigail Spanberger described her decision to vote affirmatively for the article of impeachment against President Trump as follows:

This vote is about more than one man's abuse of power; It is about the power of the presidency and whether we, as citizens, can expect that our elected officials, and most powerfully, our president, will fulfill their obligation to uphold the Constitution.[64]

Is she kidding? If this was coming from a fifth-grader running for class president, it might be excusable. Coming from a sitting congresswoman, it is frightening. Is the representative suggesting she was voting to impeach a president, not for what he had done, but what she "feared" he might do in some unspecified way at some unspecified time in the future? Her "standard" for impeachment appears to be nothing more than if she does not "trust" the president, the president may be impeached. Does that mean any president she trusts is free to do whatever they want? How about the congresswoman's obligation to abide by the constraints imposed on impeachment by the Constitution, assuming Rep. Spanberger has ever read the Constitution? If you want to see what an abuse of power looks like, look no further—this was it—one of the greatest corruptions of the impeachment powers conceivable. Many have called what happened an attempt at a "soft coup." I see nothing "soft" about it.

An outburst by Texas Representative Al Green illustrated with even more clarity the degree to which Progressives have weaponized and trivialized the impeachment power and process. On the floor of the House, he reminded his colleagues, "There is no limit to the number of times we can impeach the President." Green himself already had introduced articles of impeachment against the President on three separate occasions.[65] To Progressives like Rep. Green, impeachment is a political weapon to be deployed with or without cause because the goal is not to vindicate the Constitution but to impede an opposing political party's ability to govern. If serial impeachments will accomplish that, then Rep. Green, "patriot" and constitutional genius *nonpareil*, is all for it.

Impeachment

Progressives were frustrated. For nearly three years, they had been frenetic in their search for something they could use to impeach the President. For two of those years, they were nearly orgasmic in the certainty the Mueller team would hand them President Trump's head on a platter. Then came the Mueller report, and the oxygen was sucked out of their world.

House Progressives struggled for months after the Mueller report to put the Russian collusion Humpty Dumpty back together again, relying on the report's equivocal discussions of "obstruction." In the process, Adam Schiff and the House Intelligence Committee trotted out a constantly changing array of impeachment theories—abuse of power, collusion, obstruction of justice, bribery, and extortion among them. Progressive operatives conducted endless focus groups, searching for a theory of wrongdoing that would resonate with independent voters. None of it persuaded anyone. The investigation was floundering, going nowhere. When the whistleblower threw Progressives a lifeline, they grabbed it frantically, recognizing there was nothing else and would be nothing more. The "standard" that guided their impeachment effort was straightforward enough: "It's the last chance, stupid."

Ultimately, the House of Representatives, controlled as it is by Progressives, voted two inane articles of impeachment against the President: abuse of power and obstruction of Congress. Obstruction of justice, the charge Progressives claimed the Mueller team sent to them for final determination, was never mentioned.

The first article of impeachment, "abuse of power," as already noted, is not expressly mentioned in the Constitution as grounds for impeachment. It also was terminally vague. And, the second article of impeachment, "obstruction of Congress." was not something that could be adjudicated by either chamber of Congress.

Congress and the Executive Branch are separate but co-equal branches of government. Under our Constitution, if one branch has a dispute with the other, that dispute is resolved by the third branch of government, the Judiciary. If the House believed it had legitimate grounds for overriding the White House's assertions of executive privilege against the subpoenas and other demands for information and witnesses served by the House—and that was the essence of the obstruction of Congress claim—it was obligated to go to the courts to resolve the stalemate. The House did not have the right to determine the legitimacy of its subpoenas to a co-equal branch of government, and by choosing not to test its position in the courts, it forfeited any right to contend its processes had been obstructed. Congress is not above the law either.

All other claims of wrongdoing shopped by Democrats during their "investigation," including bribery, extortion, and collusion, were dropped from the articles of impeachment without comment or explanation. While there was not a shred of evidence against the President supporting any of those charges, it is unlikely that was the reason they were eliminated—lack of evidence is not something that generally bothers Progressives. It's easier to imagine that what they believe to be true is true without doing the hard work of trying to substantiate it. Their media allies are perfectly fine with that approach.

No, bribery and extortion likely disappeared because those charges would have drawn attention squarely to the "Ukrainian unpleasantries" involving Joe and Hunter Biden. Progressives understandably were not keen on highlighting behavior they could neither explain nor justify by the party's leading presidential candidate at the time. "Collusion" likely was dropped because even Progressives, shameless as they may be, could not conjure up a plausible collusion theory after the Mueller report. For months following publication of the report, they managed to deceive the public by continuing to insist the Trump campaign, despite what Mueller found, colluded with Russia to "fix" the 2016 election. Extending the collusion hoax, and public anxiety and agitation, for those extra months was "value" enough. And if collusion continued to be brought up, there also was the matter of the Clinton campaign's very real collusion with foreign sources, the FBI, and the DOJ in an attempt to frame candidate Trump; no benefit in reminding voters of that con and the millions of taxpayer dollars spent to debunk it.

Interestingly, and distressingly, many in the country believed adoption of the articles of impeachment meant Trump had been removed from office. The days before the impeachment vote, social media went crazy as our undereducated, uninformed lunatic lefties reveled in the fantasy that the President soon would be dragged from the White House kicking and screaming. Some probably thought that when they woke up the morning after the impeachment articles were adopted, Hillary would be president. Clueless doesn't even begin to describe how benighted and intellectually challenged some of these people are. Then again, without a critical mass of clueless supporters willing to follow manipulative leaders over the precipice, the Progressive ideology could not exist.

Lest there be any confusion, adopting articles of impeachment does not oust a president from office. Articles of impeachment by the House of Representatives are only charges, much like an indictment in a criminal proceeding, nothing more. Those charges go to trial in the US Senate. Bill Clinton, for example, was impeached by the House for lying under oath in connection with the Monica Lewinski affair, an actual crime, but was not convicted in the Senate trial, so he served out his term as president. Likewise, Andrew Jackson was impeached in the House but acquitted in a Senate trial. Now President Trump has been acquitted as well.

Let's be clear: impeachment is supposed to be a solemn, seldom-invoked, and carefully constrained power that Progressives, in utter disregard of the Constitution, attempted to turn into a cheap political ploy. No duly-elected president from either party will ever again escape the tyranny of constant investigations or have the opportunity to govern if this is allowed to become the new normal. What Progressives did to President Trump was the real abuse of power, and while it is unclear whether congressmen and senators can be impeached—in the early days of our Republic, Congress self-servingly decided they could not, but no court has considered that issue—American voters should exercise their right to "impeach" the Progressive fanatics who tried to tear apart our Constitution and form of government by voting them out of office. The Adam Schiffs of the world hate America, want to change it fundamentally, have utter disdain for the Constitution, and are a disgrace to the offices they hold.

To show how truly "unserious" Progressives were in their impeachment efforts, immediately after the House approved the articles of impeachment, Nancy Pelosi announced she would delay sending them to the Senate. The purported reason: she wanted to "make sure" the procedures governing the impeachment trial would be "fair." She held the articles for over a month.

For weeks, Progressives had fended off criticism that they rushed to judgment on impeachment by claiming they needed to move quickly to prevent President Trump from continuing his interference with the 2020 election. Never mind there was not a shred of evidence the President was engaging in any type of interference with the 2020 election, that was the justification for supposedly rushing through the impeachment process.

Then urgency evaporated. Suddenly, Nancy Pelosi did not want the articles of impeachment delivered to the Senate, and her concerns with "fairness" quickly morphed into demands that the House impeachment managers be allowed to call additional witnesses during the Senate trial.

The irony is breathtaking, the hypocrisy beyond the pale. The House conducted the most one-sided, partisan, and unfair investigation of President Trump possible. Adam Schiff held secret hearings from which Republicans were excluded. When Republicans finally were allowed into hearing sessions, they were limited in their cross-examination of witnesses and were not permitted to call witnesses. Purely partisan articles of impeachment were adopted—there was not a single bipartisan vote. Progressives violated basic due process and fairness in too many ways to count. Then, with articles of impeachment going to the Senate for trial, a chamber of Congress Progressives did not control, they demanded "fairness," which included the right to call new witnesses. Why does the adage, "What's sauce for the goose is sauce for the gander," come to mind?

Think how disingenuous it is to maintain, as Progressives did, that the House proceedings produced "overwhelming" proof the President abused the powers of his office and obstructed Congress, but then insist additional witnesses were needed at trial to establish his guilt. Does anyone believe for a moment that if House Progressives thought the additional witnesses they were seeking to call in the Senate would have strengthened their case for impeachment in the House, they would have hesitated to call them? Their claim that the witnesses were not called during the House investigation because it would have taken too long to resolve anticipated claims of "executive privilege" by the White House always was nonsense. In a case involving a showdown between the president of the United States and the House of Representatives, the courts would have expedited the proceedings, and resolution of the issues would have been swift, even with appeals.

That is exactly what happened when Charles Kupperman, a former National Security Council official, was subpoenaed during the House investigation. A subpoena was issued for Kupperman's appearance before the House Intelligence Committee. The White House invoked executive privilege and directed him not to testify. Kupperman's attorneys filed what in essence was an interpleader action, asking the courts to determine whether his obligation was to respond to the House subpoena or obey the directives of the White House. The matter was promptly scheduled for a hearing. The House just as promptly withdrew the subpoena. It should tell you all you need to know about how genuine the Progressives' "need" for additional witnesses was.

More to the point, however long it may have taken to resolve executive privilege claims during the House investigation, it would have taken just as long during the Senate trial. That was not the reason the additional witnesses were not called in the House. Progressives were eager to add names to the list of witnesses for a trial in the Senate so they could keep the Senate, *which cannot conduct any other business during an impeachment trial*, tied up, shut down, and "out of business" for as long as possible. From their viewpoint, it would have been ideal if the trial lasted through the summer or even into the November elections.

The witness issue was a trap from the beginning. If the Senate had fallen into it, the trial would have gone on for months with the Senate effectively out of business for its duration. Without a functioning Senate, the President could not have done most of what he was elected to do, which is exactly what Progressives hoped to achieve.

When we had statesmen and patriots who cared for the country and believed in the Constitution, the worst of political instincts were tempered by adherence to commonsense standards, whether stated or not. The impeachment power was recognized for what it was: a powerful remedy of last resort. It was not treated as a political strategy for preventing opposition parties from governing. Now that Progressives have brought their "big tent" of crazies, malcontents, socialists, communists, anarchists, disciples of political correctness and identity politics, environmental and diversity terrorists, and other extremists into the political mainstream, there no longer are any rules, standards, or thresholds, much less due process or fundamental fairness. It's mob rule and mob law— "Hang-em high."

So flawed were the articles of impeachment, they should have been summarily dismissed by the Senate. Conducting a trial was a travesty, the equivalent of a court prosecuting an individual based on a legally insufficient and constitutionally infirm indictment. I suspect the Senate decided to address the articles of impeachment on the merits in an effort to prevent Progressives from recycling the same charges in the next

Congress if the President won re-election. I do not know if concepts of "double jeopardy" exist in the impeachment context, but if allowing an impeachment trial to proceed, flawed as it may have been, offered a possibility that the Progressives' reckless assault on the Constitution and wasteful expenditures of taxpayer dollars could be slowed, it was worth it. This, unfortunately, is what happens when the "rule of law" is replaced by the "rule of the mob."

Only the most credulous possibly could have bought into the charade Progressives were promoting. Progressives made a strategic decision not to call certain witnesses during the House investigation to strengthen their case for calling them during the Senate trial. Nancy Pelosi knew she could not withhold the articles of impeachment for long; she had a constitutional obligation to deliver them to the Senate, and it was an abuse of power not to do so. But she also understood the Senate would not impeach the President on legally insufficient charges. The trial would be over quickly if Progressives could not find a way to extend it.

She held the articles for as long as she could to give House impeachment managers time to try to coerce vulnerable "blue state" Republican Senators into voting with Progressives on the witness issue. Mitt Romney, Lisa Murkowski, Susan Collins, Rob Portman, and Lamar Alexander all were targeted. If they had been leveraged into joining Progressives, the House managers then would have selected and called the witnesses most likely to provoke legal skirmishes with the White House, extending the trial for months.

The ploy worked only with Romney—his animosity toward the President overrode any remaining vestiges of judgment—but Progressives happily accepted the consolation prize: help for their efforts to retake the Senate in 2020. The Republican margin in the Senate was razor-thin and depended significantly on the blue state senators targeted by Progressives. By forcing them to take positions on issues ranging from calling additional witnesses to the guilt or innocence of the President, Progressives believed they either could coerce them to vote with Progressives or, if they did not, inflict enough political damage on those running for reelection to provide a real opportunity to "flip" the Senate in November.

None of the new and additional witnesses Progressives were demanding in the Senate would have resuscitated impeachment charges that were incurably flawed from the outset. That never was the point. Pelosi, Schumer, and the gaggle of other Progressives leading the impeachment debacle simply were searching for ways to stop the President from governing. If they could shut down the Senate, they would shut down most of what the President was doing, in particular, sending more federal judges to the Senate for confirmation. It was not a big stretch for Progressives to believe enough blue-state Republicans could be pressured into joining them to make it happen.

The witness subterfuge also produced another important collateral benefit. Even though the gambit failed to shut down the Senate beyond the relatively brief period of the impeachment trial, it created new talking points for Progressives leading into the 2020 election. It allowed them, for example, to tell voters that during the impeachment proceedings, the Republican-controlled Senate and the President were trying to hide damaging evidence from them. To be sure, that strategy would have been followed even if additional witnesses had been allowed. No matter how many witnesses Progressives were permitted, they would have insisted on at least one more. There never would have been enough.

The President had been wildly successful in delivering on most of his campaign promises, but nowhere more effective than in appointing and having new judges confirmed at all levels of the federal judiciary. In the process, he managed to offset some of the massive majorities Progressives built under Obama in many judicial circuits. But new federal judges must be confirmed by the Senate, and the confirmation process would have ground to a halt if Progressives had managed to extend the Senate trial through the summer, perhaps even into November. Chief Justice John Roberts of the United States Supreme Court, a nominal conservative, also would have been committed to presiding over the impeachment trial and unable to participate in the usual manner in the deliberations of the Court.

Progressives understand that imposing their radical agenda on the country depends in significant measure on controlling the courts—think Franklin Roosevelt and his court-packing scheme to protect the New Deal policies that gave birth to the American welfare state—and were frantic to interrupt the President's appointment of judges committed to the Constitution and the rule of law. Preventing the Senate from conducting business was the easiest way to do that.

Progressives were particularly desperate to block any further Trump appointments to the Supreme Court. They may not have been confident about defeating the President in 2020, but they knew for a certainty they had a better chance of winning the election than they did of defeating his Supreme Court nominees, the Biden rules notwithstanding.[66]

Progressives' biggest fear was realized when "RBG," Ruth Bader Ginsburg, associate justice of the Supreme Court and a pop-culture icon for liberals, died in mid-September 2020. The eighty-seven-year-old justice's health had been deteriorating for several years.

Justice Ginsburg's death opened the way for President Trump to appoint Amy Coney Barrett, a conservative jurist sitting on the Seventh Circuit Court of Appeals, to the Court. While her confirmation by the Senate in late October 2020 created a solid majority of conservative justices on the high court, Progressives already have made clear they intend to expand the number of seats on the Court and fill them with Progressive loyalists, finally accomplishing what Roosevelt failed to get done during the Great Depression. Names like Clinton, Warren, Booker, and Buttigieg come to mind as potential "justices." It is unlikely that judicial experience will be part of the job description; only a willingness to "re-imagine" the Constitution.

I also believe impeachment was a key piece in a larger Progressive game plan—fomenting enough turmoil and chaos to mentally exhaust the American people. The theory seemed to be, "when not in the White House, create enough agitation to disrupt the sitting president's ability to govern and make people yearn for quieter, less discordant times." That was a prominent part of Joe Biden's messaging during the presidential campaigns—he would return the country to a "calmer" state and be "president to everyone," even those who did not support him—as his Progressive puppeteers plotted to deliver the country to socialism. Joe, whether he retains the cognitive abilities to understand it or not, was the Judas goat, nothing more. After nearly 50 prosaic years in Washington as an apex swamp creature, Joe Biden's chief legacy is destined to be that of a false prophet.

Progressives effectively declared war on the President and his supporters and deemed them guilty of the crimes of being pro-American and conservative. It was the equivalent of a bill of attainder.[67] Because they had been unable to defeat the President at the polls, all of their time and energy was focused on trying to prevent him from governing. This was done without regard to the damage inflicted on the Constitution or the country. The fact that attacking the President also gave aid and comfort to America's rivals and enemies across the globe was of no moment—resistance at any cost was the goal, and lies, deceit, false accusations, and bogus impeachment proceedings were the means.

The Progressives' obsession with impeachment was consequential to the nation for another reason. While Progressives were fixated on the impeachment hoax, they were oblivious to the coronavirus threat, which was just coming to the world's attention. Fortunately, the President, despite being forced to respond to apocryphal impeachment charges, maintained his focus on the affairs of state. He quickly imposed travel bans to and from China and established a coronavirus task force. Predictably, he was immediately labeled "xenophobic" by Progressives, including Joe Biden, for doing so, never mind that the President's preemptive actions unquestionably slowed the spread of the virus to our shores and saved countless American lives.

Amazingly, despite the President's quick response to the virus, it took several more weeks before the threat began to dawn on Progressive leaders. Bill De Blasio, mayor of New York, for example, urged New Yorkers to "get out and take in a movie," in a tweet on March 2. Three weeks later, New York City became ground zero for COVID-19 in the United States. There were 80,000 COVID-19 cases worldwide at the time of the tweet, and President Trump had extended his travel bans to South Korea and Italy, but the good mayor had a "Pelosi moment."[68]

A "Pelosi moment" in what sense, you ask? In this sense: in late February 2020, as COVID-19 began to spread, Nancy Pelosi visited Chinatown in San Francisco and urged people to "come join her."[69] When the speaker finally began to grasp the significance of the outbreak, she scurried underground, disappearing from public view, barricaded in her walled estate in San Francisco. Much like Joe Biden, she remained "missing in action" for most of the next months as the pandemic ran its course. In usual Progressive guerilla war fashion, on the occasions when she momentarily "surfaced," it was only to criticize something the President or his coronavirus task force had done, not to offer anything constructive, with one exception. To show just how in touch she was with the millions of Americans filing unemployment claims, she did a televised interview during which she proudly showed off the trove of designer ice cream safely stored in her twin, $24,000 each, refrigerators. Apparently confident she had stockpiled enough ice cream to sustain her government in exile, she continued to use the coronavirus as an excuse to keep the House out of session, even after the Senate returned to Washington, as part of the continuing Progressive strategy to prevent the President from carrying out the business of the nation.

These are not good people. These are not brave people. These are not even smart people. They are political opportunists whose agenda is power. And anyone who has seen Nancy Pelosi interviewed recently has to question seriously whether she or Joe Biden is the most cognitively impaired.

What is happened adds new meaning to the idiomatic phrase, "fiddling while Rome burns." The Roman Emperor Nero allegedly let Rome burn so that he could bypass the Roman Senate and rebuild Rome to his liking. Progressives have been just as intent on destroying our Constitution and an elected president of the United States so they can remake America to their liking.[70] Their overheated rhetoric is figuratively burning the nation, and legions of their foot soldiers are in the streets calling for resistance and insurrection. The riots following the death of George Floyd show graphically their ability to spark widespread insurgency and violence in our cities, supported by a network of Progressive "deep state" operatives, governors, mayors, and members of Congress. These people do not like America. They plan to destroy it. And they will not hesitate to take advantage of the opportunities the election so unexpectedly gave them.

Barack Obama's election as president in 2008 invited socialists and communists to inundate the Democratic Party. Bernie Sanders's good showing in the 2016 Democratic presidential primaries emboldened them to stop pretending to be mainstream Democrats. Donald Trump's election in 2016 caught most of them off-guard—the polls had Hillary a double-digit winner until suddenly she was not. That combination, however—Bernie's surprising showing in the 2016 primaries and Hillary's loss—had the effect of kicking any remaining mainstream Democrats to the back of the bus. The upheaval propelled the Progressive lunatics into control of the party because the election results mistakenly were interpreted as meaning moderate and traditional Democrats no longer were electable in America.

Progressives were so close to the ultimate prize. If Hillary Clinton had been elected president, socialism would have been enduringly embedded into the fabric of this country. Having come so close, their efforts to get Trump out of the White House and a Progressive loyalist into the office turned frenzied.

Hillary and Barack Obama were not moderates, but both disguised their more extreme views well. Even though Obama had taken the Democrats from the party of Bill Clinton to a party controlled by Progressives, he was enough of a politician to hide the transformation from public view. The campaigns of most of this cycle's Progressive candidates, however, unknowns and underachievers that they were, could have exposed just how radical the Democratic Party had become. It was another reason the impeachment proceedings were so helpful to Progressives; during the primaries the impeachment hoax diverted voters' attention from the fanatical views of the Progressives' candidates.

Once Joe Biden became their nominee, Progressives immediately started to moderate their message. Joe's "name recognition" was a significant advantage; he had been around so long, he seemed harmless. Unfortunately, he is the biggest "apparatchik" of all, and someone other than Joe will be making the presidential decisions. It will not be Kamala Harris. Obama had his Rasputin,[71] and there is no reason to believe that either Biden or Harris will be any less controlled by the political commissars who will be dispatched to "manage" them.

The message from Democrats may have moderated during the general election, but the ideology remained the same. It was a strategy Barack Obama had urged Progressive to employ for some time—if you plan to transform America, hide your true agendas from voters until after elections. It was an approach Obama followed when he told Russian President Medvedev he would have more "flexibility" to accommodate Russian interests after the 2012 election.

At the end of the day, the COVID-19 outbreak stifled more of what the President had hoped to get done than anything the Progressives managed to do with their pointless impeachment efforts. It also provided an excuse for Progressives to keep Joe Biden out of public view, where his growing cognitive difficulties would have become increasingly visible. A separate chapter in this book addresses the nation's response to the coronavirus outbreak, and I will not discuss it in detail here except to say that Progressives did more than coincidentally benefit from the pandemic; they manipulated it to increase the damage to the economy and the suffering of millions of Americans.

As Rahm Emanuel, former chief of staff for Obama, congressman, and mayor of Chicago has said, "never let a serious crisis go to waste," and Progressives did not. COVID-19 was used to accomplish what three years of unrelenting attacks against the President had not been able to do. The country was kept locked down and afraid by Progressive governors, mayors, and city councils, crushing the economy and wiping out wealth on a scale not seen in America since at least the Great Depression. Millions of people became newly dependent on government. But most critically, voting schemes that reduced ballot security and made voter fraud more likely were authorized across the country. Under the auspices of "emergency powers" ostensibly needed to quell a pandemic, *1984*,[72] Progressive style, was ushered in.

In a sense, Donald Trump was a gift to Progressives. The President has a manner, personality, style, and approach that is anthemic to many otherwise reasonable Americans. They view him as crude and overly strident. They cringe at his tweets and wish he would act more "presidential." Others begrudge his wealth and success. Many conservatives do not consider Donald Trump "conservative enough," or a conservative at all. To put it bluntly, some voters did not like Donald Trump personally and would not support him regardless of how much good he had done for the country. Their Trump Derangement Syndrome (TDS) was so great they could not vote for him even if it meant a socialist would be elected president and set in motion forces intended to tear apart the country they knew and loved. They were willing to risk their prosperity and well-being, and the prosperity and well-being of their families, simply because they disliked Donald Trump— or thought they did.

Some of the people suffering from TDS recognized the incongruity of not voting for the President because of his style and personality even if it risked electing someone likely to destroy everything they valued. The threat posed by Progressives was so antithetical to the American experience, however, they were not convinced it could happen. Having no history with socialism and communism, they did not believe Progressive candidates were as extreme as they sounded or meant what they said. They persuaded themselves that these candidates, no matter what they might claim to represent, ulti- mately would do "what was best for America." I also heard people rationalize that, "four years of these guys and voters will become Republicans forever."

How catastrophically mistaken. The proud people of Venezuela, the most prosperous country in South America until socialists took over, undoubtedly thought the same thing. Venezuela now is the proverbial train wreck. Also lost in these self-indulgent fantasies was the fact that while many "Progressives" are approval-seeking "useful idiots" and social justice warriors as close to brain-dead as humans can get while still breathing independently, Progressive leaders and the money men behind them are committed revolutionaries. Self- styled though they may be, their goal is to re-make America in the socialist image they prefer with them in control, and they are deadly serious.

Like Rome in the final days, too many of us have forgotten the sacrifices that were necessary to establish and preserve the freest, fairest, and most prosperous nation on Earth. We have become overly tolerant of those trying to bring it down. We have forgotten the immutable law for sustained success: as difficult as it may be to reach the top, it is infinitely more difficult to stay on top. No nation, neither the Greeks, nor the Romans, nor anyone else, has been able to fend off the debilitating complacency that so persistently accompanies success, sapping nations of the spirit, resolve, and discipline that nurtures achievement and progress. We may have climbed the mountain, but our perch is precipitous, and unless we are willing to defend what has been attained, it will be taken from us. The barbarians never truly leave the gates or stop attacking, and unless we have the fortitude to resist their ceaseless efforts to snare the inattentive, the uninformed, and the most vulnerable segments of our society with the seductive illusions of progressivism's ruinous ideology, we will succumb to it. Progressivism, in true parasitoid fashion, inevitably kills the host that harbors it.

Buckle up, America. This is another fence that does not have to be taken down to understand why it was put up. Progressives never imagined that one day they might be able to take control of America without a shot being fired, but they now sense more than a "puncher's chance" to do just that. Going into the election, they needed your vote to make it happen. They no longer do, and that is troubling; in the words of George Orwell, "We know that no one ever seizes power with the intention of relinquishing it."

CHAPTER 4

ROBERT MUELLER

Was Robert Mueller the most duplicitous man in America or just the most intimidated? The Mueller Report, more than four hundred pages divided between alleged "Russian collusion," which was the only thing Mueller was appointed to investigate, and alleged "obstruction of justice" by the Trump administration, which was not within Mueller's original mandate, provides some insight. You be the judge.

As special counsel, Mueller had only one basic responsibility—to decide whether or not sufficient evidence existed to prosecute a crime. He had no obligation to write a meandering, over four-hundred-page report summarizing the portions of the evidence the investigative team wanted America to see. The report could have been one paragraph: "After investigation, we find insufficient evidence to justify prosecution." Everything else was simply an effort to assail a presidency and feed a media frenzy that handcuffed the Trump administration from the day the President first took the oath of office.

The handwriting was on the wall from the moment Mueller took charge of an investigative team stacked with "Never-Trumpers." There was not even a pretense of neutrality in the selection and make-up of the team, which was intended to be a lynch mob, nothing less. Progressives maintained the President was a traitor, a Russian spy doing the bidding of

Vladimir Putin. Why did they believe that? Because of a false dossier compiled on candidate Trump by Christopher Steele and Fusion GPS and paid for by the Clinton campaign and the DNC. Turned over to law enforcement and intelligence agencies populated by Obama appointees, the unverified dossier then was used to scam a FISA court into authorizing surveillance of the Trump campaign. The "deep state" may not have been able to prevent Donald Trump from becoming president, but it had every intention of making his tenure in office as short as possible.

The Democracy Integrity Project, a Progressive media-influencing operation allegedly funded by Progressive billionaires and supporters like George Soros and Tom Steyer, but also reportedly including the heads of social media giants Facebook, Twitter, and Google,[73] poured millions of dollars into Fusion GPS to maintain a massive misinformation campaign against the President.[74] I have described the malignant nature of the Democracy Integrity Project earlier in the book, but clearly, this organization was a major factor in keeping the Russian collusion hoax alive over the nearly two years of the Mueller investigation. It shows the type of money Progressives will spend and the machinations in which they will indulge in their fanatical efforts to change the nature and form of the American government. It also shows how badly the press and other media have failed America, accepting and republishing stories planted by what effectively is a deeply partisan, counter-intelligence operation committed to taking down a duly elected president and imposing a new "order" in America.

I think it is difficult for many Americans to believe any of their countrymen could take progressivism seriously. For those who have experienced the horrors of socialism and communism first-hand, it is difficult to understand the naivete of those unable to recognize and dismiss the false promises of Progressives. But make no mistake about it, these people are deadly serious. They want to change your way of life and your government and are relentless in their efforts to do so. The election of Barack Obama provided the best opportunity yet to undermine democracy in America, and they are taking full advantage. Most Americans celebrated the milestone of our first Black president in 2008 when Obama defeated John McCain and became the 44th president of the United States, even those who did not politically agree with him. Few, however, realized how deeply radicalized Barack Obama's politics were.

Progressives, by contrast, understood they now had a comrade in arms in the White House and moved quickly to capitalize by infiltrating and co-opting the Democratic Party. So quickly, that as early as 2012, Congressman Allen West of Florida estimated seventy-eight to eighty-one members of the Democratic Party in Congress were communists "hiding in plain view" in the party's progressive caucus.[75]

The extent to which Progressives successfully infiltrated the top echelons of government in the United States during the Obama administration's eight years in office is nowhere better illustrated than in the surveillance effort undertaken against the Trump campaign by our most venerated law enforcement and intelligence agencies, both during and after the 2016 elections. Mark Steyn, the celebrated Canadian political commentator and author, was wrong when he said in a radio broadcast, "Interference in political campaigns by members of a country's intelligence apparatus only happens in banana republics." It happened here.

Perhaps it was easier for the Progressives in our spy agencies to justify launching a counter-intelligence operation against a domestic political campaign because they believed

Donald Trump never was serious about winning the White House. His goal, they convinced themselves, was simply to bolster the Trump brand, build hotels in Moscow and elsewhere, and get richer through the publicity a run for the presidency would bring. His candidacy was a fluke and came about only because a basket of deplorables too dumb to understand what was in their best interests mistakenly believed he was a serious candidate and supported him. Regardless, Trump's election represented a threat to the ascendency of progressivism in America, and it needed to be ended.

How disappointing it must have been to Mueller's band of partisans to find there was no evidence to support the case they thought would be a "lay-down"—no collusion, no conspiracy. The finding of no collusion should have ended the investigation since that was what it was supposed to be about. The media had been in full song for months, salivating at the possibilities and sure of the outcome. Stories circulated about conspiratorial meetings between Trump or his emissaries and Russians. Collusion was a foregone conclusion. Trump, his son, son-in-law, and other family members all were going to jail.

It should have been a tip-off to Progressives when Mueller indicted twenty-five Russian nationals and three Russian entities for interfering with the 2016 election, but no one connected to the Trump campaign. The individuals associated with the Trump campaign charged by Mueller all were indicted for "process" crimes—things like "false statements" in connection with the investigation—or for crimes completely unrelated to the campaign. Progressives were so convinced Mueller and his team would not let them down, and so buoyed by daily media reports of pending indictments of the President and family members, however, they were impervious to any possibility other than collusion.

It is important to understand what process crimes are. Think Martha Stewart. She was charged with insider-trading violations but never was convicted of those charges. Instead, she spent time in federal prison for conspiracy, obstructing an agency's proceedings, and making false statements to prosecutors; those are process crimes. It is a tactic used routinely by federal law enforcement. It works like this.

Investigators call a potential witness or their lawyer and ask for an interview. If the request is granted, the investigators show up with a plan for tripping up the witness, trapping them into false statements or at least something the prosecutors can claim was false. Investigators usually possess documents they use for questioning without showing them to the witness. Questions are intentionally framed to be narrow, technical, and focused on small points in what may be lengthy documents written a long time ago. If the witness tells investigators anything that appears to contradict something said in the documents, they pounce, accusing the witness of false statements, perjury, obstruction, and anything else that seems to fit. The idea is to string together as many charges as possible with potentially significant criminal penalties either to create grounds for sending high profile individuals to prison or to coerce witnesses into implicating others in exchange for a "deal" carrying less or no jail time.

It is a variant of what happens in law enforcement every day. Let's take the example of an investigation of a corporation for suspected violations of federal, white-collar criminal laws. Investigators start with lower-echelon employees, offering immunity from prosecution if they will testify against individuals higher up in the organization. The investigators are trying to implicate the highest level of management possible, and they "squeeze" lower-level managers and others for "evidence" against their bosses. The coercion is not subtle. The clear message is, "cooperate or we will put you in jail," and "cooperation" has a very special meaning. To be sure they are getting the evidence they want, investigators typically require a hypothetical "proffer" of the information a witness would provide if granted immunity. If the initial proffer is not strong enough to suit prosecutors, the witness is offered an opportunity to "improve" their testimony. The process is rife for abuse—the incentive for witnesses obviously is to embellish testimony, even to the point of making it up, to avoid prosecution—and the process frequently is abused. If you are a law-abiding citizen, are married with children, have a good job, go to church on Sundays, and belong to the local country club, the prospect of a stay in a federal "hotel" is terrifying. People will do and say almost anything to avoid it.

If a defense lawyer did the same thing, essentially "bribing" a witness for testimony favorable to his or her case, they would not pass "Go," would not collect $200, and would go straight to jail. Not so with the government; legal "bribery" is a staple of criminal law enforcement.

Shortly after I wrote the preceding few paragraphs, the Michael Flynn scandal became public and demonstrated how easily law enforcement powers can be abused by over-zealous prosecutors. The former three-star general and national security advisor to President Trump essentially was entrapped by the same cabal within the FBI responsible for the Russian collusion investigation. Flynn was forced to plead guilty to charges of willfully making "false, fictitious, and fraudulent statements" to the FBI, in part by using threats to indict his son for unspecified crimes if the general did not plead guilty.

Subsequently released FBI documents showed the FBI plotted to make it appear Flynn had lied. He was "set up" by FBI agents, including Peter Strzok, sent to question him during the very early days of the Trump presidency, before protocols for such interviews had been established by the new administration. Jim Comey, the former FBI director, later would brag about "slipping in" agents to interview Flynn without either Flynn or the administration realizing what was happening. Flynn was not represented by counsel during the interview and allegedly was told by the FBI that having a lawyer present would "just slow things up" and was "unnecessary."

It is exactly the prevalence of these types of abuses by law enforcement that made the Mueller team's inability to find "evidence" of collusion so unusual. They clearly "squeezed" several of Trump's former associates, including the President's lawyer, Michael Cohen, who had been fired and were hostile to the President, and still could find no one willing to support a collusion claim, not even to save their skins. Making it even more remarkable, allegations of "collusion" and "conspiracy" are among the easiest charges for a prosecutor to "prove." Put two people in the same place at the same time, sprinkle in a few phone calls, suggest a motive for "agreement," layer it all with a healthy dose of innuendo and conjecture, and *viola,* you have collusion and conspiracy. The fact Mueller could not do it provides great clarity about how corrupt the entire "Russian collusion" narrative was. So, it was on to "obstruction."

It is one of the great ironies of the Russian collusion hoax that the obstruction charges against the President were predicated entirely on his alleged obstruction of the completely specious allegations of collusion. The President was investigated for allegedly trying to obstruct an investigation of charges the Mueller team early on had to realize were false. These were not allegations that simply turned out to be unprovable or were found to be insufficient to justify prosecution; they were fabricated, made up, completely fictitious. The Mueller team also had to know early in the investigation that the collusion claims were premised on a fraudulent dossier paid for by the Clinton campaign and the DNC and that the dossier had been used by enemies of the President within the Department of Justice, the FBI, and the National Security Agency to justify surveillance of his campaign. As Attorney General Bill Barr testified before Congress, "spying on a political campaign is a 'big deal.'" Imagine just how big a deal it would have been had the Trump campaign commissioned and paid for a false dossier to discredit the Clinton campaign and encouraged the nation's top law enforcement and intelligence agencies to investigate the activities of Hillary Clinton? It is nearly incomprehensible that Mueller expanded the investigation into obstruction knowing what he knew.

Mueller was appointed to investigate alleged collusion between Russia and the Trump campaign to interfere with the 2016 presidential election, and the investigation should have ended as soon as Mueller and his team determined no collusion occurred. Instead, Mueller turned to a provision in the special counsel regulations that provided him with jurisdiction to investigate "crimes committed in the course of an investigation intended to interfere with the investigation." That includes obstruction of justice. Mueller's band of vigilantes did not hesitate.

It is hard to find any justification for expanding the investigation. What was obstructed? Progressives feared President Trump would have Mueller fired and were vocal in their warnings that they would consider it "obstruction" if he did so, but Mueller never was fired. The sheer volume of documents and testimony provided to the special counsel by the White House makes claims of obstruction delusive and pointless. Mueller also had to recognize very early that the claim he was appointed to investigate was a ridiculous fiction. What, then, was the purpose in trying to prove his investigation of a ridiculous fiction had been "obstructed?" Was the investigation kept open simply to try to induce behavior that might amount to "obstruction?" Entrapment, in other words.

It is difficult to rule out entrapment as one of the goals of the Mueller team, but there were several benefits to prolonging the investigation. If the determination of "no collusion" was reached before the 2018 midterm elections, for example, announcing the finding would have lifted a cloud that had hung over the Trump administration since the first day the President took office, giving Republican candidates a huge boost, perhaps even keeping Republicans in control of the House of Representatives. Progressives would have felt betrayed.

Ending the investigation early and with a finding of "no collusion" also would have made Mueller and his team piranhas among the Progressive faithful—no more celebrity status, power lunches, or cocktail parties with the politically connected—and might have quelled some of the fervor of the "useful idiots" progressivism depends on for its existence. Something was needed to keep alive the impeachment delusions that had become the Progressives' chief obsession, solidifying influence, rallying cry, and fund-raising magnet.

Mueller, however, had a responsibility not to artificially prolong what he had to realize was a "dead-end" investigation, and the decision to expand the investigation to "obstruction" and then conclude that he "would not prosecute but could not exonerate"" was an abdication of his responsibilities as special counsel. His obligation was to determine whether or not sufficient evidence existed to proceed with a prosecution, nothing more.

Analogize for a moment to a grand jury proceeding. A grand jury can vote to indict or not, based on the evidence, but it has no power or authority to "exonerate" the accused. Neither did the special counsel. Exoneration or conviction is up to a judge and jury, based on the evidence and the law. From Mueller's position, the decision was binary: there either was sufficient evidence to prosecute or there was not. It was not a decision he could delegate to Congress or anyone else. This much is certain: if Robert Mueller believed the evidence established a criminal obstruction of justice, he would have said so; his team of Trump-haters would have insisted on it. Even if he decided he could not prosecute a sitting president, he would have made his decision on obstruction clear to the attorney general, and the next steps would have been up to the AG. Mueller is the former director of the FBI, a seasoned veteran of the Washington establishment, and a savvy lawyer; it was not patriotic deference to Congress or uncertainty that caused his equivocations about charging the President with obstruction.

By not recommending prosecution of the President for obstruction, Mueller effectively admitted he lacked the evidence to do so, but by claiming he could not exonerate the President, he implied culpability where none existed. That artfully deceitful trope was important because it provided the staging for how the Mueller team wanted the "evidence" to be perceived and understood. It was a simple ploy intended to plant questions in the public's mind about the President's conduct, to provide Progressives with "cover" for starting impeachment proceedings if they chose to do so, and to keep the "pot stirred" heading toward 2020. I also suspect it was intended to make sure the fury of Progressives remained focused on the President and did not transpose to Mueller and his team.

After two years of investigation, review of millions of documents, interviews of hundreds of witnesses, and the expenditure of $45 million of taxpayer money, Mueller could not find sufficient evidence to pursue a claim of obstruction but could not summon the courage to say so. He chose instead to violate one of the most basic precepts of fundamental fairness by publishing a report intended to suggest there might be a prosecutable crime when he had not been able to find one.

I do not pretend to know with certainty what motivated the Mueller team to do what it did, but the conclusion is nearly inescapable that while investigating a president accused of colluding to influence the 2016 presidential election, the investigative team was trying to influence the 2020 presidential election. They did so not only by keeping questions about the President's conduct alive but also by attempting to inflate the significance of evidence. This much is clear: the moment Mueller's team concluded "no collusion," there was no predicate crime to obstruct.

And the actions of the Mueller team plainly did influence the 2018 midterm elections. How early they recognized collusion between Russian and the Trump campaign was a Progressive delusion has not yet been established, but the evidence supporting collusion was so anemic, they must have realized it very early. If they had this knowledge before the 2018 midterms, which they almost surely did, there would have been no reason to sit on that knowledge other than trying to influence election outcomes. Mueller and his team were fully aware of the way Progressives were sensationalizing the investigation, making up stories about the supposedly imminent indictments of Trump family members, recounting lurid details about meetings with Russians that never happened, and fantasizing about the impeachment of the President, but they did almost nothing to even dampen the speculation, much less stop it.

More than the mid-terms were affected by how the Mueller team handled the investigation. Mueller understood most of his report would be made public, although under the law there was no obligation for the President or the attorney general to release any of the details. Nevertheless, the report unquestionably was written for public consumption and to be as politically damaging as possible. While Mueller and his team claimed they could not determine whether the evidence they gathered amounted to obstruction, that did not deter them from wrapping it in a neat package, tied with a bow, and laden with all the sinister overtones they could muster for delivery on a platter to the President's political enemies. Mueller and his team realized doing so meant the battle over the President's conduct would rage on, perhaps to the 2020 elections, particularly if the report prompted House Progressives to open an impeachment investigation.

I do not necessarily believe Bob Mueller is a bad man; he may just have been an intimidated man. He understood a simple truth. After two years of investigation with the hopes of the left growing daily, if the Progressive attack dogs were not sated, they would tear him and his team apart. Character assassination is the weapon of choice in the cancel culture universe of Progressives, and they have become masters of the art. Mueller's reputation, built over many years of public service, would have been in tatters very quickly, shredded by the same people who for nearly two years viewed him confidently as the champion who would take down Trump. He knew it and took the measures he thought necessary to protect himself, his family, and his team against the flagrant abuses he understood were sure to follow if Progressives were not appeased.

That is one of the reasons the attacks Progressives mount against anyone who disagrees with them are so dangerous. You cannot challenge any element of the Progressives' narrative unless you are willing to subject yourself and your family and friends to all-out assaults. Progressives are indiscriminate saboteurs with allegiance only to the "cause;" they do not care how many lives they destroy. The goal is to eliminate debates they cannot win about ideas with which they cannot compete. Shouting down, discrediting, and intimidating the opposition are their only choices. It ensures that civil discourse on any subject will become impossible—it nearly is now—and compromise on any issue, out of the question.

Defenders of the special counsel will argue that he simply was not willing to decide the obstruction issue because of the effect it would have on the country and therefore deferred to Congress for a final determination of questions more political than legal. The fact Attorney General Barr and Assistant Attorney General Rod Rosenstein so easily were able to conclude that the "evidence" of obstruction provided by Mueller was insufficient to establish a prosecutable case, however, lays that contention to rest. So too does that fact that the special counsel sat on the investigation for months after he had to know it was pointless. Mueller was not a rookie. He understood Progressives would be enraged if he appeared to exonerate the President by finding no collusion, no obstruction, so he fudged the results and embellished his conclusions, claiming he was not exonerating the President. By suggesting the evidence of obstruction was "too close to call," Mueller took himself off the hook with Progressives and shifted their rage to AG Barr and Assistant AG Rosenstein, and in the process gave "aid and comfort" to those trying to overturn the results of a presidential election. He, in effect, reversed the burden of proof, forcing the President to prove his innocence by refusing to admit, unambiguously, what he knew to be true—there was not enough evidence of obstruction to make a case.

Realistically, how could the activities outlined by Mueller's team have amounted to obstruction? The Russian collusion investigation, bogus as it was, proceeded to its conclusion uninterrupted and without interference from anyone. Mueller was not fired or replaced. No predicate crime was found to be obstructed. The President provided full transparency, even making White House legal counsel available for interviews with the investigative team and producing over a million documents to the special counsel without claiming privilege for any of them. The President also agreed to make public everything in Mueller's report that lawfully could be made public, something he had no obligation to do.

The activities Mueller described as possibly "obstructive," are, at worst, expressions of frustrations on the part of a president who was cooperating fully with the special counsel's investigation, but whose agenda was being subverted by the baseless claims of political opponents so unmindful of the welfare of their country they spent every day fervently hoping the president of the United States would turn out to be a Russian spy.

What kind of Americans spend all of their time hoping the president of their country is a criminal? What type of politicians are willing to ignore the business and security of the country and devote the entirety of their time and effort to undermining everything a duly elected president is trying to do, and what most Americans want done, in an effort to nullify the results of an election they will not concede?

It is revealing to compare how Progressive candidates were treated by the Obama era law enforcement and intelligence agencies. Why wasn't Hillary Clinton and the Clinton Foundation, for example, investigated? Millions of dollars were poured into the Clinton Foundation by foreign interests seeking access to her while she was secretary of state. Her husband, the former president, was paid additional millions of dollars by foreign interests to give meaningless speeches about frivolous subjects during her time in office.

Why wasn't her participation in the giveaway of 20 percent of America's uranium to Russia, followed by a $145 million donation to the Clinton Foundation, ever seriously looked into? Why was she not criminally prosecuted for allowing thousands of emails to be destroyed and cell phones and computer servers to be crushed with a hammer during an ongoing criminal investigation? Jim Comey "exonerated" her on national television.

The list of equivocal activities surrounding the Clintons is nearly as long as the list of President Trump's accomplishments, but she is the "Teflon Lady," protected unwaveringly by the media, her election once considered key to the final empowerment of socialism in the United States.

Why weren't investigations launched against Joe Biden and his son Hunter? Burisma certainly was not the first or only time Hunter Biden benefitted from his father's office. For example, he also entered into billion-dollar investment arrangements with the Bank of China and other Chinese entities after accompanying his father on an official visit to China. At the time, the former vice president was in negotiations with the Chinese government over a host of issues, including nuclear security. Among the deals struck by the investment firm jointly owned by the Chinese government, Hunter Biden, and Christopher Heinz, the stepson of John Kerry, was one involving a major Chinese defense contractor accused of stealing US military secrets.[76] Substitute the name "Trump" for "Biden" and consider how Progressives would have responded.

Perhaps it just would have consumed too many investigative resources to look into Joe Biden's "family-friendly" deals. Joe spread the spoils widely. I earlier recounted how his younger brother, James, became an executive at a major construction company despite having no previous experience in construction. Six months later the construction company was granted a $1.5 billion contract to build 100,000 houses in Iraq with the president of the company reportedly telling investors, "it really helps to have the brother of the vice president as a partner."[77] I suppose it does. Joe's other brother Frank, sister Valerie, and son-in-law Howard Krein were not left out of the pillage.[78] The accounts of the reoccurring "good fortunes" experienced by Biden family members and friends have been reported extensively; you can read those stories elsewhere. My question is, why no investigations?

Prominent Progressives do not get investigated for activities like these because they are protected by a Washington establishment dominated by Progressives and a news media that has become a house organ for the Democratic Party. The allegiances are cult-like. Regardless of what candidates or elected officials favored by Progressives may do or say, they need not worry—an unfavorable story will not be pursued for very long.

Have you ever seen how a herd of black Angus cows with new calves reacts when threatened by a predator? They circle, heads facing out, calves in the center, and any animal foolish enough to challenge them is likely to pay the ultimate price. Progressives react to threats the same way. They instinctively circle to protect their own, and their responses to threats are every bit as savage as the Angus cows. They never can show weakness, admit to being wrong, or apologize for the lives they destroy when they are wrong. If some of them have violated the public trust by using their offices to enrich themselves or their families and friends, well, those are deserved rewards for the sacrifices they have made to "improve" the lots of "common" men and women. The media always considers their motives pure.

For Progressives, the Mueller investigation may not have produced the "perfect" scenario, but it proved very "useful" nonetheless. It provided, for example, a completely false narrative of "collusion" to distract and hinder the Trump administration during its first two years. A quick pivot to "obstruction" then handicapped the President for months after the Mueller report was released, eventually resulting in the President's impeachment. Because the media did not hold Progressives accountable for their egregiously wrong claims of collusion, they were free to move to "obstruction" as if the collusion hoax never occurred.

As I mentioned earlier, I believe a significant part of the Progressive strategies for defeating Trump in 2020 involved trying to keep the country in such upheaval that voters would tire of the turmoil and yearn for quieter times. The wide-spread rioting and violence just a few weeks before the 2020 election, with promises of more to come if the President was reelected, unquestionably was part of that strategy. Progressives understood that some voters, scared, weary from the constant strife, and not understanding what was at stake, were likely to capitulate and vote for a candidate they viewed as less "divisive," say, Joe Biden. It was far too steep a price to pay for "calm."

If we turn the country over to Progressives, it is unlikely we ever will get it back or that it will be recognizable if we eventually do. The only possible reason the election of Joe Biden or any other Progressive could make things appear less divisive and tumultuous is that conservatives are more respectful of election results and the office of the president. Even when they vehemently object to the person in the White House, conservatives do not conspire to foment "soft" coups or intentionally set out to frustrate the agenda of a duly elected president. There will be political disagreements to be sure, but nothing like the premeditated plan Progressives adopted to try to shut down the Trump administration. To most conservatives, Obama was an intolerably incompetent and divisive president, but they remained civil even as they watched him drive a wedge through the heart of the country and dither as our cities burned, policemen were killed, and American prestige and influence plummeted around the world.

Attorney General Barr sent shock waves through Progressives when he announced he was investigating how the spying against the Trump campaign originated and whether DOJ, the FBI, and the National Security Agency had a sufficient predicate for authorizing the surveillance. Predictably, he was attacked mercilessly by the Progressive cabal attempting to discredit and destroy yet another long-serving public servant with a stellar reputation and record. But stay tuned. There still may be justice. Before leaving office, AG Barr appointed John Durham, the prosecutor earlier assigned to investigate the federal officials involved in the surveillance of the Trump campaign, as a "Special Counsel," the same status enjoyed by Bob Mueller. The appointment provides a degree of independence from DOJ and the same protection against termination Mueller had and might suffice to allow Durham to complete his investigation without being terminated by the Biden administration. I suspect even now, post-election, Jim Comey, John Brennan, James Clapper, Andrew McCabe, Peter Strzok, Lisa Page, and others are sleeping less soundly as they wait to see if and when the hammer drops.

The real and dangerous legacy of the Mueller investigation is that senior members of the nation's top law enforcement and intelligence agencies first conspired to stop Trump from being elected and then to topple him if elected. The Mueller team aided and abetted those efforts by spending months investigating allegations it had to realize almost from the beginning were fabricated and then extending the investigation many more months looking into whether the President obstructed an investigation of events they knew never happened—nothing short of an effort to entrap the president.

"Banana republic?" I hope not, but that is the direction in which Progressives are trying to steer the country. Tampering with elections is a crime without an easy solution, and Progressives know it. It explains why their assaults on democracy can be so brazen. Progressives also have learned that the American people are easily intimidated by violence, so they turn to it quickly. They now openly threaten to burn and ransack cities if they do not get what they want, and their increasingly undisguised efforts to influence elections, whether through the surveillance of a rival political campaign or the wide-spread voter fraud many believe occurred in November 2020, is not something that is likely to be interrupted without intervention by the federal courts. Judges, unfortunately, tend to be ordinary people sometimes asked to do extraordinary things. Most cannot measure up and few have the inclination, desire, or fortitude even to consider traveling that road. Fewer still have the resolve to withstand the assaults that would be unleashed against them and their families, and the rioting, burning, and looting that would occur in the streets of our cities, if the courts even considered engaging. It is much easier, and safer, for judges to decline election cases for lack of standing or on grounds that a non-justiciable "political" question is involved. No one knows what those terms mean anyway. It leaves Progressives understandably confident there never will be consequences no matter how egregiously they corrupt the political process.

As the noted British economist Josiah Stamp once said, "It is easy to dodge our responsibilities, but we cannot dodge the consequences of dodging our responsibilities." The lines have been drawn. We either get this right now or our country and our freedoms will be taken away. If the integrity of elections cannot be protected, neither can democracy. Earlier in the year, President Trump declared that "America never will be socialist." Let's hope he was right.

CHAPTER 5

GUNS

When I first sat down to write this chapter, the guns had barely grown silent in the Parkland, Florida, high school shootings that left seventeen dead and seventeen wounded. It was the latest of 400 individuals shot in school shootings, with 138 deaths, since the tragedy at Sandy Hook Elementary School in Newton, Connecticut, in December 2012, at least according to a sportswriter for the *Richmond Times-Dispatch*.[79] Seems everyone has opinions on gun control and gun violence, even sportswriters. There have been additional school shootings since, including one at the University of North Carolina, Charlotte, where two students were killed, as well as the Easter bombings of churches and hotels in Sri Lanka, the Chabad of Poway and Tree of Life synagogue shootings in San Diego and Pittsburg, respectively, and bombing attacks on a Roman Catholic cathedral in the Philippines and a mosque in New Zealand. Shootings in El Paso, Texas, and Dayton, Ohio, just occurred.

I am not a gun-control advocate, but like all rational Americans, I deeply mourn the dead and wounded and condemn unconditionally those who kill the innocent randomly by whatever means. However, the contention that "guns don't kill, people do," while certainly an oversimplification, is not a frivolous perspective, as shown countless times by those who plant bombs in public places, drive trucks and automobiles into crowds, stab policeman and other first responders, and kill and maim people in many different ways not involving guns. That simple truth was captured in a cartoon on the editorial page of the *Richmond Times-Dispatch* that showed the ubiquitous mascot of the Democrats, a donkey, and the equally omnipresent symbol of the Republicans, an elephant, exchanging views on gun control. The donkey says to the elephant, "And why wouldn't more gun regulations reduce mass shootings?" The elephant replies, "Because there's no such thing as a law-abiding homicidal maniac."[80]

The same day that cartoon was published, the newspaper reported deaths and injuries from dynamite blasts in Bolivia, a crash of an Iranian commercial airliner, the death of a father and daughter in an avalanche on a French ski slope, the death of two Turkish soldiers swept away by a flood, and a follow-up report on the deaths and injuries of vacationers from a helicopter crash in the Grand Canyon. A day later, the same newspaper reported the death of seventeen at a Mozambique trash dump—literally buried alive in garbage—and the death of a seventy-three-year-old hit-and-run victim. Shortly thereafter a six-year-old died when a tree fell on the mobile home where he lived.

I place no equivalency on any of these tragedies, some of which resulted from unrepentant evil or mental illness, others from unfortunate circumstances, but they underscore the fact that the world is a dangerous place. People, including children, die daily from an assortment of violent acts, mistakes, misfortunes, and bad luck. The deaths are tragic beyond comprehension but largely unavoidable.

School shootings accelerated in 2018, but historically have taken, on average, ten lives a year.[81] Unquestionably, that is ten too many, but ten times that number lose their lives riding bicycles to school. Why are we less concerned about those deaths? We do not have to allow children to ride bicycles to school. Why do we do so? Among the tens of thousands of Americans who die each year in traffic accidents, almost 2,500 are teenagers.[82] Why are we not more concerned? Is it because teenage drivers are a convenience to families? They can transport themselves to athletic practices and other events, run errands, and ferry younger siblings. Do we tolerate the extra deaths, in other words, simply because it is useful to have the extra drivers available?

Like guns, cars and trucks are misused all the time. People speed. People drive recklessly. People drive poorly. People drive drunk. People drive distracted. People drive angry. People intentionally weaponize vehicles to kill, to destroy, and to terrorize. When a child is killed by a vehicle, however, we blame the driver who misused the vehicle, not the vehicle, even when it has been intentionally weaponized and used for mass murder, as occurred in Nice, France, on Bastille Day, 2016. Why is that? Why do we view guns differently? Why do we blame guns when they are misused, but not cars, trucks, and other potentially lethal instrumentalities?

Some will say, "Because guns are designed for only one thing—to kill—while cars, trucks, and other sometimes deadly objects are made for other purposes." But that too surely is an over-simplification. Cars and trucks may be built for other purposes, but we know for a certainty they will kill and maim thousands year after year and sometimes are used to do so intentionally. Why do we tolerate the carnage?

In Britain, knife attacks are a leading cause of violent crime. Over 32,000 "knife crimes" occurred in Britain in 2017, many of them fatal.[83] Knife attacks generally rank second in the United States' list of crime weapons, just ahead of personal weapons— fists and other body parts—and blunt instruments. Other "popular" ways of killing or maiming include strangulations, drowning, fires, narcotics, poisons, and explosives. Because they tend to be cheap and readily available, "acids and corrosive substances" are gaining in popularity.

Should we ban knives or at least certain types of knives? One look at the assortment of "sharp instruments" used for attacks in the UK—a vast array of knives, machetes, sabers, stilettos, meat cleavers, axes, lances, scythes, shiv's, razors, shanks, blades, swords, box cutters, bayonets, sickles, and daggers—many of them designed only to kill—will quickly illustrate the deadly mayhem a sharp-instrument-wielding intruder could inflict on a schoolyard of young children. What would you do about "blunt instruments," such as hammers, pipe wrenches, flashlights, bricks, rocks, baseball bats, and fireplace pokers? They may be intended for other purposes, but we know they sometimes are intentionally used to maim and kill. How about your fists and other "personal weapons?"

In 2014, more than 130 people were injured in a train station in Kunming, China, when a group of ten men and women began randomly stabbing travelers. Similar attacks have taken place in Chinese schools and shopping centers. As recently as late August 2019 one person was killed and nine more injured by a knife-wielding Afghan national near Lyon France.[84] "Knife crimes," including the killing and maiming of school children, have become such a problem in London the city now prohibits the carrying of most knives with mandatory prison sentences and significant fines for habitual offenders. The mayor of London, Sadiq Khan, has broadly warned, "There never is a reason to carry a knife," and if you do, you "will feel the full force of the law."[85] England already has some of the most restrictive gun-control laws in the world, but those laws have not interrupted the pace of violent crime in London, where the homicide rate now equals that of New York City.

In Canada, victims encountering an assailant armed with a knife suffer a serious injury at a rate almost double that of victims encountering an assailant with a firearm. Blunt instrument attacks produce injury rates nearly as significant as knife attacks, and the fatality rate increases only slightly when a firearm is involved.[86] Unfortunately, despite gun-control laws one publication calls "meaningfully more restrictive" than US laws, Canada is not immune from gun violence either.[87] As recently as April 2020, a gunman disguised as a police officer moved house to house in rural Nova Scotia, shooting people and burning houses. At least eighteen were killed, including a police officer. In Canada, all gun owners must be licensed and all handguns and most semi-automatic weapons registered. Gun safety and other training are required to be licensed to own a gun, and guns cannot be carried outside the home except with a special license that is only sparingly granted. Extensive background checks are required. Depending on the type of firearm owned, the controls become even more restrictive. Predictably, however, Canada had stricter gun-control laws on its legislative agenda even before the Nova Scotia shootings.[88]

But it is knife attacks, often involving multiple fatalities, not guns, that have continued to plague our neighbor to the north. Each one leads to a *moral panic* that immediately causes Canadians to reflexively call for emergency legislation to combat knife crime.[89] Sociologists like Marshall McLuhan and Stanley Cohen have long described the phenomena of moral panic, which they attribute to "moral entrepreneurs, groups that attempt to influence society to adopt certain norms, and the mass media."[90]

Put simply, moral panic is the widespread, but excessive and unreasonable fear over a perceived threat to society. All "panics" develop in much the same way. Real events occur; they are exaggerated to crisis proportions by moral entrepreneurs and the media; panic builds in the public until there are demands to "do something;" and government or other powerful institutions step in to control the "crisis."[91]

The opportunity for skewing public opinion and policy should be obvious, particularly among those lacking the information, knowledge, and inclination to think situationally and rationally. Guns have become a primary target of the moral entrepreneurs, but there are many ways to kill efficiently and on a large scale. Those determined to kill will not be dissuaded from doing so by laws attempting to limit access to specific weapons. They will simply move to the next, perhaps more deadly, option, whether that is using sharp or blunt instruments, driving cars or trucks through schoolyards of children, planting bombs in shopping malls, churches, or schools, releasing deadly poisons, or other equally lethal and readily available alternatives.

Why is so much of the moral panic that follows school shootings in the United States directed at guns rather than the things that motivate people to kill? As a rule, we do not ban things that can be misused simply because they sometimes are, but we blame guns. Another political cartoon made the point by depicting a gentleman advocating banning forks, blaming them for his weight issues. His cartoon-figure wife quickly pointed out it made no sense to blame forks when he was the one using them to overeat, but then she quickly called for a ban on guns as she read a newspaper account of a school shooting.

It is precisely this kind of confused and inconsistent thinking that leads people to advocate "remedies" for attacks on schools, churches, and other public places that have no possible chance of reducing attacks. It is the understandable, intuitive need to do something, anything, in the aftermath of an incident too horrifying to comprehend. People are in shock. They are angry. They feel helpless. They want to strike back. They desperately want to make sure something similar never happens to anyone again. The entrepreneurs go to work, and moral panic sets in.

The shooting in Virginia Beach, Virginia, on May 31, 2019, provides an example. Twelve people were killed, eleven co-workers of a municipal employee who submitted his resignation just hours before the attack, as well as a contractor in the building to apply for a license. The shooter did not meet the usual profile. He was, by all accounts, a long-term employee in good standing, a former national guardsman and civil engineer by training. The guns used in the attack were acquired legally. His letter of resignation to the City of Virginia Beach mentioned no grievances. Nevertheless, Ralph Northam, Governor of Virginia, almost immediately called a special session of the Virginia General Assembly (which meets only for a limited time each year) to take up a package of gun-control legislation without any suggestion the measures contemplated would have had the slightest effect on the Virginia Beach shootings.

Beto O'Rourke, once a Progressive candidate for president, and a staunch gun-control advocate, also hit the airwaves after the Virginia Beach shootings to promote his gun-control agenda. He too was unable to say how anything he was advocating would have prevented the tragedy.

As they say, "Hope is not a strategy and a wish not a plan." Simply doing *something* without trying to understand or deal with the root cause of a problem is, at best, a feel-good exercise for the intellectually lazy and politically opportunistic—the fork "blamers" and moral entrepreneurs. At worst, it is a dangerous and unnecessary tinkering with important constitutional protections.

We, as a free people with individual rights guaranteed by the Constitution, have chosen to protect those rights even when doing so may be inconvenient, even costly, because the alternatives are so terrible and dangerous. Our Constitution, and the individual rights it secures, were designed to protect against the repeated violations of human rights visited upon countess civilizations by centuries of autocratic rulers, whether called kings, queens, emperors, czars, fuhrers, duces, sultans, emirs, conducators, marshals, vozhds, capitanuls, or el jefes. When, through fear, ignorance, or complacency we cede basic civil rights to government, we erode those protections in ways we do not realize and cannot predict. Giving up our freedoms one right at a time is nevertheless giving up our freedoms. Despots can be patient—Hitler, Stalin, Castro, Idi Amin, Nicholas II, and Mao Zedong did not come to power overnight—and obtaining a surrender without having to fire a shot has its advantages.

Stated a bit differently, the "slippery slope" or, if you prefer, the "camel's nose under the edge of the tent," theories are not the imagined concerns gun-control advocates would have you believe. Government is relentless in its quest to expand its power, reach, and authority. Its greatest ally in doing so is an inattentive and poorly informed population, not recognizing what is being surrendered until it is too late.

So, is the Second Amendment a "fence" we want to take down to assuage feelings of panic, anger, and helplessness, particularly before we fully understand the consequences and whether "gun controls" will do anything to eliminate or reduce attacks on schools, churches, workplaces, and other "soft" targets?

I once read a letter to the editor of a local newspaper from a teenage student lamenting the Parkland High School shootings and declaring it time to do away with constitutional protections enacted 200 years ago and, in the mind of the writer, "without meaning in the context of the modern world." It was not an unexpected statement from a young student without the education or life experiences needed to appreciate the importance of the individual protections and rights he and his family enjoy under our Constitution. The letter sounded more like a student repeating something said by a teacher who may never have read the Constitution and was too uninformed to understand why it protects what it does, particularly minority rights with which a governing majority may not agree.

The writer may have been focused on gun rights, but most of the other protections of the Constitution also were enacted more than 200 years ago. There is nothing obsolete about the recognition of "life, liberty and the pursuit of happiness" as inherent human rights, or freedom of speech, religion, and assembly, the right to be free of unreasonable searches and seizures, protection against "cruel and unusual" punishment, the writ of habeas corpus, the guarantee of trial by jury, and a host of other protections and liberties conferred by the Bill of Rights. Gun rights are no less important and certainly anything but obsolete.

The young writer fell victim to a common temptation—trying to pick and choose among those rights protected by our Constitution with which he thinks he agrees and supports, and those with which he disagrees, or thinks he does, likely because he does not understand them. Most Progressives, I suspect, would be quite content to strip rights from the protection of the Constitution one at a time, as long as they eventually get rid of those rights. The Constitution is a significant impediment to their assumption of authoritarian powers. The list of dictators who have suspended their countries' constitutions as a first step to usurping or consolidating power is lengthy.[92]

People sometimes do not understand that the United States is a republic, not a direct democracy. We have a Constitution that protects minorities against abuses by majorities, and a representative government designed to dampen the animosities and negative impulses of governing majorities. A majority cannot wipe out the rights of minorities by a snap of its figurative fingers, as often is the case in direct democracies. More importantly, the form and essential nature of government cannot be changed at the whim of the majority.

The young writer's disagreement with gun rights proves the wisdom of the founders in establishing a republic rather than a direct democracy. He does not like gun rights. Others may not like freedom of speech, assembly, religion, or other liberties. If everyone gets to choose which rights to keep and which to discard, basic freedoms disappear quickly. That is essentially what happens in direct democracies: convince, bribe, or coerce a majority of voters—it only takes 51%—and the mob is free to do as it pleases. It makes direct democracies the favored means of dictators for consolidating power and disenfranchising populations. It also is a prime reason why Progressives so fervently want to do away with the Electoral College and choose American presidents by majority vote.

Republics and constitutions are designed to bring stability and consistency to governments and nations. It is not easy in a republic to make changes based on fleeting trends or passing fancies. The rigorous give and take required to bring about change tends to filter out bad ideas and make good ones better. Accommodations are reached on issues that divide, leading to greater consensus. It is one of the reasons bypassing the rough and tumble of the legislative process and allowing courts to resolve difficult social issues can be so destructive—there is no opportunity for consensus to occur or the ameliorative effects of compromise and reconciliation to take effect.

For over 200 years, our Republic and Constitution have preserved everyone's rights against debasement by those in charge. We have remained a free people precisely because majorities have not been allowed to pick and choose which liberties they will allow and which they will not. Changes certainly have occurred. In total, seventeen amendments to the Constitution have been ratified since the original Bill of Rights in 1789, but each of those changes reflected significant consensus among Americans. Keep in mind, it is estimated that 30 percent of Americans own guns, while an additional 11 percent live in households where guns are present, so gun ownership is, at the moment, one of those "minority" rights.[93]

The young writer also plainly did not understand the importance of the Second Amendment to our democracy. Guns serve as an obvious check against an overly intrusive and too-powerful government. That may be more symbolic today when the government alone possesses the advanced weaponry of modern warfare than it was 200 years ago, but it continues to lend an invaluable American "edge" to how we view and interact with our government. While that independent spirit may be waning as we become increasingly dependent on government, it persists in ways both large and small and continues to make the relationship between Americans and their government unique among nations. Guns also contribute to "life, liberty, and the pursuit of happiness" for millions by providing endless recreational opportunities, whether in the hunt field, on trap, skeet, and sporting clay courses, on rifle and pistol ranges, or as collector's items. "Men's jewelry," as my wife sometimes refers to them.

In large measure, we do not treat cars and trucks, knives, baseball bats, axes, hammers, and similar items as potential weapons because they have not yet become the focus of a political agenda. The media and the moral entrepreneurs have not yet stirred a moral panic among the population over these items, so the harm they do is less visible. We do not fear them despite their destructive potential precisely because we have not been conditioned to fear them. They are familiar to most and therefore assumed to be less dangerous than guns. Even though it is far more likely that a loved one will be killed or injured by an intoxicated or distracted driver than become the victim of gun violence, there is no moral panic over impaired or inattentive drivers. Driving may be dangerous, but they are dangers we think we understand and believe we can control, so the deaths and injuries that result are accepted as the unavoidable consequences of living life. The occasional use of cars or trucks as weapons, which happens periodically around the world, including Charlottesville, Virginia, during the 2017 confrontation between alt-right and left-wing thugs, are treated as aberrations. We love our cars and trucks, need them, and do not want to think of them as killers or lethal weapons.

As to knives, bats, and other "weapons," despite the experiences in the UK, Canada, China, and elsewhere, we mistakenly believe them not to be as deadly as guns, preferring instead to pretend gun controls will be enough to stop homicidal maniacs from killing children and other innocents.

Part of this is intellectual laziness and a desire for instant and easy answers. Part is attributable to political opportunism. Actual solutions to problems like mass murder are difficult, time-consuming, and expensive. They require identification of root causes and inquiry into areas we would rather not venture: mental illness; poverty; hatred, fanaticism and political extremism; racism; the breakup of the nuclear family; deterioration of educational systems; anti-Semitism; and a host of other seemingly intractable problems lie at the core.

A multitude of other questions also swirl around cultural issues. Does anyone doubt, for example, that violent video games desensitize and glorify death and mayhem in the minds of the young? Do we have an understanding of how graphically violent movies may motivate the mentally unstable? When schools succumb to demands by parents that their emotionally disturbed children remain in "normal" classroom environments rather than being placed in programs designed to educate those with special needs, or otherwise resist getting professional help, do we know what outcomes are being set in motion? Do we appreciate the costs of our assiduous protection of the health records of the mentally insane?

The list could go on endlessly, and against this bewildering backdrop of cause and effect, Progressives offer an alternative too seductively simple for many to resist: gun controls.

I would like to return for a moment to the proposition argued by some that guns are different from cars, knives, and other objects that can be lethal if misused because these other items are designed for purposes other than killing, while guns are not. That simply is not true—guns are used in this country for a wide variety of recreational and utilitarian purposes, several of which already have been mentioned. Some people depend on hunting as a significant source of food. But also consider for just a moment how many lives guns save every year. Estimates place the number of defensive uses of guns each year in the United States at approximately 1.2 million, and studies consistently show lower injury rates among gun-wielding victims of crime than among those using other self-defense strategies.[94]

That said, we tolerate many things in this country that have no utility other than someone's pleasure, are not constitutionally protected, but are capable of killing and maiming. Every day in the United States, for example, ten people die from drowning, many of them in bathtubs and hot tubs. Should we ban hot tubs because they have no utility other than the pleasure of the persons using them or require everyone to take a shower rather than a bath? Why is the pleasure of a hot tub user more important than the pleasure of a recreational shooter or hunter?

The fact that cars and trucks undeniably have utility, moreover, does not support an argument for allowing anyone who wants to own or drive a car or truck to do so. Unlike gun ownership, driving is a privilege, not a right, which is why the operation of a vehicle is subject to greater regulation by governments than gun ownership. Regulation of driving lies squarely within the police power of the states to protect the public health, safety, and welfare, and millions of vehicles could be removed from the road simply by limiting their use to professional drivers or at least to a much smaller and better-trained universe of licensed drivers. Public transportation could substitute for private transportation. Doing so would save thousands of lives and prevent even more injuries. Why isn't it done?

I can say with confidence there would be an immediate and sustained howl of outrage from most of us if the government proposed to confiscate our cars and trucks and take away our driving privileges in the interests of public safety. It would be viewed as an overt attack on our liberties, and it would be. Take note—it will happen eventually and likely sooner than you expect. The COVID-19 pandemic provided an unexpected look into how quickly governments can turn arbitrary and autocratic and how dramatically our lives can change when they do. With Progressives now in power, do not be surprised when environmental claims are quickly used to limit or eliminate disfavored items, cars among them. For the moment, however, the focus is on guns.

Tens of thousands may die in accidents on the highways each year, many from the misuse of cars and trucks, but we accept the casualties because people like their vehicles. They provide conveniences and freedoms most of us do not want to give up. Cars and trucks also do not interfere with any of the current narratives being promoted by Progressives. Even though many of the drivers on the highways are poorly trained, largely inept—few know even the most basic traffic rules—and despite recognizing it could save countless lives, we are not concerned enough with highway deaths and injuries even to propose better training for drivers or make it more difficult to qualify for a driver's license. Just the opposite. Because we have so many non-English speaking people in the United States, some states allow translators to help applicants with the written portions of driving tests. Others translate their tests into multiple languages. At least twelve states allow illegal immigrants to obtain a license. They may not be able to read or understand traffic safety signs, but they are allowed to drive. "Lethal," perhaps, concerning, no," seems to be the attitude regarding cars and trucks, and knives, blunt instruments, poisons, bombs, and corrosive substances, as well.

Not so with guns. It is a Progressive dream to disarm America, and they have convinced many Americans there is a moral imperative to do so. A disarmed society is, after all, more submissive, easier to control.

Consider for a moment the difference in attitude toward gun usage, which is a constitutionally protected right, and drunk or distracted driving, which are not. Even though those driving intoxicated or under the influence kill thousands of people every year,[95] far more people than "active shooters," no one, MADD included, is advocating measures confiscating cars and trucks from people who have not misused them as a means of controlling unsafe driving by those who do.

Every day, thousands of people also misuse cars and kill people, many of them children, by driving distracted while texting, eating, smoking, combing hair, putting on makeup, reading newspapers, or engaging in a host of other diversions. We sometimes punish the drivers involved, but we do not attempt to take cars from people who use them safely, even though there is a possibility they may misuse them in the future.

I ask again if we place the blame for misuse of cars and trucks squarely on their drivers, not the vehicles, why are we unwilling to do the same with guns?

Mobile devices, phones, and tablets, by the way, are now showing up with regularity as the newest "dangerous instruments;" drivers distracted by calls and messages on cell phones are rapidly replacing the drunk driver as the main causes of injuries and deaths on highways.[96] Who should we blame, the mobile devices or the distracted drivers when people are killed or badly injured by a driver's inattention?

The attitude toward guns, to be sure, is influenced by the fact several high-profile attacks have involved schools and children. Understandably, nothing quite stirs the emotions of most Americans more than the murder of children, at least those children who have survived abortion, with the possible exception of pets, particularly dogs and cats. I sometimes wonder if parents were forced to choose between their children and their dogs or cats, how children would fare. Threatened harm to either, however, tends to unhinge even seemingly rational people.

The natural concern for the well-being of children does not explain why we blame guns rather than shooters for gun tragedies when with almost every other weaponized object we blame the person using it if deaths or injuries occur. If natural concern for children was the explanatory factor, we would not put our children at risk every day, as we do, largely without thinking about it. For instance, parents routinely put their children in cars with nannies, friends, neighbors, older siblings, classmates, mothers and fathers of classmates, and other drivers of mixed abilities and competencies. Usually, this is done with no idea whether the driver is capable or not. In most states we allow, even encourage, sixteen-year-old children to drive despite statistics showing the fatal crash rate for drivers under twenty is three times higher than drivers twenty and over.[97]

We also allow our children to participate in any number of high-risk sports and activities. Mountain climbing, sky-diving, hang gliding, bungee jumping, base jumping, big wave surfing, skiing, heli-skiing, proximity wing-suit flying, ATV and mountain bike riding, scuba diving, boxing, and almost any of the X-Games activities come immediately to mind. When deaths or injuries occur, we seldom blame the activity or talk about banning it. Why not? Isn't the logical answer, "because no moral panic has been created over deaths or injuries of children from these causes? Or is it because we compartmentalize those injuries and deaths as essentially "self-inflicted?"

If someone drives a truck through a crowd walking along a beachside promenade, killing dozens and injuring hundreds, as happened in Nice, France, on Bastille Day 2016, I think most people would agree the driver, not the truck, is responsible for the deaths and injuries. Suppose, however, after running over several dozen people, the driver leaves the truck and begins shooting into the crowd, killing several more. Is the driver, rather than the truck, now responsible for the initial dead and wounded, but the gun for the additional victims? What if the driver uses a machete rather than a gun—is the machete or the driver responsible for the subsequent deaths and injuries? Should we ban machetes? If the next maniac who drives a car or truck into a crowd, leaves the vehicle and uses a knife to kill additional innocents, should we also ban knives? How about tire irons? Or baseball bats? Among the dead and wounded are some killed or injured by vehicles, others by guns, machetes, knives, tire irons, or baseball bats, and the only common denominators are the identities of the persons driving the trucks, pulling the triggers, or swinging the machetes, knives, tire irons, and baseball bats. Why should we view guns differently than the other "weapons?" All are simply objects misused to kill and maim.

We have been conditioned to think about guns differently. In most instances, we can place the deaths or serious injuries that occur from the use or misuse of products into some rational perspective. There is grief, but no "moral panic," even when children are victims. No perspective is brought to bear when guns are involved, however, because the Progressive agenda will not allow it. With guns, we do not even pause to consider whether a proposed solution for ending gun violence can be effective, much less whether the "cure" will be worse than the "disease." The moral panic stirred to fever pitch by Progressives is such that we demand immediate answers, instant solutions. Enacting new laws allows us to feel like we have done something. Gun-control legislation, a step along the way to the Progressives' ultimate goal of banning guns entirely, always is proposed first. It is intended to sound reasonable and has the added benefit of drawing attention away from the more difficult problems surrounding gun violence—things like mental illness, political extremism, suicide, and domestic violence. It gets the "camel's nose under the edge of the tent," and that's all it is intended to do.

I happen to believe mental illness is the root cause of most school, church, and workplace shootings, but that is a difficult, messy problem to address, much less solve. Incredulously, some in the mental health community continue to resist the notion that mental illness plays any role in gun violence. As stated by Dr. Louis Krause, chief of forensic psychiatry at Rush University Medical College in Chicago following the Parkland, Florida, shootings, "The vast majority of gun violence is not attributable to mental illness."[98] He apparently discounts the fact that over 60 percent of gun deaths in the US are suicides or at least disputes that those committing suicide suffer from any type of mental illness or disability.

More likely, the statement reflects the doctor's desire to protect the mentally ill from criticism or his unwillingness to deviate from the narrative Progressives so passionately embrace: there is a crisis in America involving the mass shootings of school children, religious congregations, and other innocents; guns are the problem, not mental illness, criminal activity, or anything else; guns are inherently evil and need to be eliminated; if guns are eliminated, mass killings will stop, and the lions will lie down with the lambs.

Let me propose two thoughts that will seem preposterous to Progressives. As a rule, "normal" people do not use guns to shoot other human beings unless it is in self-defense. And owning a gun does not turn an otherwise rational human being into a homicidal maniac, as the concealed-carry statistics demonstrate. Across the nation, people with concealed-carry permits are far less likely to be involved in violent crimes than the population as a whole, and violent crimes decrease in concealed-carry states. Gun-control advocates dispute those statistics, arguing that many different factors contribute to the decline in gun violence in states that permit their citizens to carry a concealed firearm. Identifying or producing empirical support for those other factors, however, has proven elusive.

Let's face it: gun-control advocates just do not like guns. They want them gone, and the only narrative they are willing to consider is one that begins from the premise that guns, not people, even mentally ill people, are the root cause of gun violence. So committed are they to this view, they cannot even allow the families of shooting victims a respectable time to mourn and bury their loved ones before showing up and trying to use the tragedies to promote their gun-control agendas. Some, however, may be beginning to understand how gun-control advocates are using them. On May 19, 2019, for example, during a vigil in Colorado to honor Kendrick Castillo, who was killed when he lunged for a fellow student who entered a classroom with a gun and ordered students "not to move," the students in attendance walked out in protest when speakers at the vigil turned out to be mainly gun-control advocates and politicians with gun-control messages and agendas.[99]

I sometimes wonder if Progressives welcome shooting tragedies. Each incident renews the moral panic and provides an opportunity to push their gun-control agenda on newly traumatized audiences. They prey on the uninformed and misinformed, people who never have owned or used a gun and have not taken even a moment to review the underlying facts or data. In the horrific aftermath of a school shooting, these people are ripe to be drawn to the narrative of the inherent evils of guns and are easy to convince that the only way to keep school children and others safe is to ban guns. Quite frankly, given the ties between Progressives and violent leftist groups like Antifa, and the powerful, galvanizing effects a shooting event provides gun-control advocates, I cannot shake the concern that some shootings may be more than random attacks by disturbed individuals.

Part of the gun-control narrative, of course, is based on the implicit premise that gun violence is preventable, and stricter gun-control laws will end attacks on schools and other targets. In a world where the number of critical thinkers is shrinking quickly, it is becoming an easier fiction to sell. No one even pauses to question the basic premise. The interest of Progressives, however, is not in gun controls or even reducing gun violence. They want guns gone—hunting guns, home defense guns, recreational shooting guns—all of them. They do not just want to take guns out of the hands of the mentally ill, criminals, and domestic terrorists; they want to take guns out of the hands of everyone. "Reasonable" gun-control proposals are simply the first step in the progression to outright bans and confiscations of guns and ammunition. Kamala Harris, now the vice-president, for example, announced during her abbreviated presidential campaign that if elected, she would take immediate action, by executive order if Congress was unwilling to cooperate, to impose strict gun controls.

If she was elected president, in other words, Congress would either go along with whatever gun controls she demanded, or she would bypass Congress and legislate by executive order. Elsewhere in this book, I commented on the abuse of executive orders by other administrations, usually Democratic administrations. The danger to our form of government by this type of rogue action on the part of the executive branch cannot be overstated. It is a fundamental rejection of the separation of powers and principles of federalism that underlie our Republic. Legislating from the executive branch is unlawful and represents nothing more than an effort to consolidate power and authority, the early steps to the authoritarian rule socialism invariably produces. Expanding the power of the executive branch, ending the Electoral College—it is all aimed at the same thing: paving the way to totalitarianism.

Kamala Harris did not say she would ban guns outright, but if "President" Harris was reluctant to do so, it would work like this. Gun controls of some nature would be implemented. Public shootings nevertheless would continue because the laws would hamper only law-abiding citizens, not the criminals, mentally ill individuals, or terrorists carrying out shootings. Consequently, even more onerous controls would be enacted. Shootings would continue for the same reasons. Finally, declaring controls alone inadequate to end the "gun crisis," the government would make gun ownership unlawful. By that time, the Supreme Court would have been "packed" with Progressive zealots who would find ways to make the ban lawful. Gun confiscation programs would begin shortly thereafter, perhaps starting with a voluntary "buy back" program, which is an interesting euphemism since the government never owned the guns in the first place. When that effort "recovered" only a fraction of the estimated 393 million guns in the country, true confiscation efforts would begin with heavy fines and jail terms for those who refused to comply. Guns bought in recent years would be traced through law enforcement and registration records. Rewards would be offered for information leading to the identification and collection of older or unregistered firearms, potentially turning friends and neighbors into "snitches." Neighbors spying on neighbors has been an effective surveillance tool of socialist and communist governments for a very long time and only recently was used in some localities during the coronavirus outbreak. The mayors of New York and Los Angeles, for example, promised rewards if people would use their cell phones to photograph and turn in anyone violating "shelter in place" or other coronavirus orders. Some locations used drones purchased from China to do the same thing. Is this America? Make no mistake— they want your guns, and they intend to get them, using whatever means it takes.

This is how totalitarianism works. You do not have rights. The government tells you what to do and how to do it, and you refuse on pain of a fine, imprisonment, or worse. Need examples? Look at North Korea, Cuba, Nicaragua, and Venezuela. History is a marvelous teacher for anyone willing to pay attention.

Confiscating guns will not stop mass killings, either in schools or anywhere else. Criminals will still have plenty of guns. They will remain readily available from multiple, black-market sources, just as drugs are now. If for some reason those bent on mass homicides of children and other innocents are unable to access a gun, they will turn to other, likely more lethal, alternatives. If those alternatives are knives, blunt instruments, and similar objects, they too may be banned, as knives currently are in London, with equally ineffective results. Cars as weapons will become less a concern only because cars, as already noted, almost immediately will become casualties of radical environmental policies. If you own a gasoline-powered vehicle, expect to be taxed or shamed into giving it up.

The same moral panic strategy was used to enact Obamacare. The hysteria was created by grossly misrepresenting the number of people supposedly without access to health care. It is similar to the approach used by activists to advance any number of issues, including abortion, LGBTQ rights, and illegal immigration. The uninformed, misinformed, and gullible are first misled and co-opted. Those who know better are cowed by charges of racism, homophobia, or being on the "wrong side of history" or unremittingly stupid. The media goes to work, creating the desired narrative, and building a sense of urgency and anger. To get the camel's nose under the edge of the tent, reasonable-sounding steps are proposed to "solve" the manufactured "crisis." Those early steps are soon declared failures and more "solutions" are legislated until the camel is in the tent. If more is needed, or if things are perceived as proceeding too slowly, Congress and state legislatures are bypassed, and lawsuits are filed in friendly courts with predictable results.

It doesn't hurt that the strategy is making Progressive moral entrepreneurs rich. The admonition that if you want to find the truth, "follow the money," popularized in the 1970s movie, *All the President's Men,* is seldom off the mark. The formula always is the same. Money is raised, events are organized, and television, radio, and print media events pump up interest and concern. Donations flow in to support organizers and provide generous travel and other allowances—the hard work of revolution is better done, after all, in a Ritz Carlton than a Motel 6. Entourages grow, and cars, limousines, first-class air travel or private jets, and a host of other amenities soon are folded into the package. There are no incentives to approach problems reasonably and certainly not to resolve them on a consensual basis. There is no money in resolving problems. Panic is the prescription and outcomes consistent with the Progressive agenda are the goal.

This does not mean there are not many dedicated people with earnestly held beliefs involved in causes, including gun control. There are millions of volunteers all over the world, trying to do what they feel is right and benefitting not at all except by experiencing the satisfaction of engaging in a cause in which they believe deeply. We can all be grateful for these kind souls. But people of good-will, no matter how strongly they may feel about a subject, at some level should be willing to listen to facts, to try to understand opposing points of view and, when warranted, change their minds. Moral entrepreneurs never will. They may be socialists, communists, or some fringe group bent on revolution and the overthrow of the US government, or they simply may be opportunistic mercenaries, but their goals are to panic the public into the outcomes they desire, not effective or reasonable solutions to real issues.

Make no mistake about it; the leaders of the Progressive movement are committed revolutionaries. It is not the good of the country they have in mind. Their ultimate prize is power. Like all central planners, they have no idea what is in the best interests of the country, nor do they care; no "collective" government ever does. Instead, they intend to impose their "vision" on the country. They do not trust you and want to control how much education you receive; what you do for a living; where you live; what and how much you eat; where and how you travel; what you do, say, see, read, and watch; what medical care you receive; how much money you make and keep; and how you vote. They intend to control everything. How do I know? Easy. That is the way socialism always works. It also is essentially what the Green New Deal says.

If you need further evidence, the Covid-19 pandemic should have provided a peek into how monocratic Progressives consider their authority over you. Anyone who watched Lori Lightfoot snarl threats into the camera about what she intended to do to Chicagoans who had the audacity to disobey her stay-at-home orders, for example, should be very concerned. She is going to "lock you up, period!" This is the same imperious scold who posted viral memes featuring a frowning Lightfoot standing guard over the city and warning people to stay home. She also flippantly admitted to getting her hair done in defiance of the prohibitions she imposed on the rest of the city. Her excuse: she is "in the public eye," and "takes her personal hygiene seriously," which explains exactly how she feels about the rest of you filthy, unhygienic, uncaring cretins.

Gretchen Whitmer, governor of Michigan, arguably went even further. Her lock-down orders, for example, went through retail stores virtually item by item, specifying what people could and could not buy while in the stores. The governor's order quite literally dictated which store aisles could be opened and which had to remain closed *for people already in the store;* they could buy only what was in the aisles they were permitted to shop. Her classifications of "essential" and "nonessential" businesses, those permitted to remain open and those that had to close, likewise were mostly arbitrary. So draconian were her actions, the Michigan legislature sued to strip the governor of her "emergency" powers.

I wonder if it even has occurred to those who have been panicked into accepting the Progressive gun-control narrative that banning guns or making them harder to get might shift the paradigm toward even more destructive possibilities? It is easy enough, for example, for a deranged student bent on revenge against his school and classmates to find instructions for building a bomb on the internet, using materials available at the local hardware store. How difficult would it be to drive a car or truck through a schoolyard? Molotov cocktails are easy enough to make—some gasoline, a bottle, and a rag are all that is needed—and have only recently been popularized by the anarchists roaming the streets of American to burn and loot, theoretically to protest police "brutality" and racial injustice. Locking doors and setting fire to school or church buildings is almost as simple, particularly as police are removed from schools. Bludgeoning victims to death or using an ax, machete, or any one of the dozens of other, easily available "sharp instruments" to maim and kill may be the most accessible alternative of all, particularly for the maniacs who have watched too many *Rambo* movies. A gun very well could be the least lethal of the possible alternatives. Think about the unintended consequences that resulted from the banning of narcotics—the creation of an enormous, worldwide criminal enterprise that quickly expanded the drug trade and human suffering beyond anything previously known.

Just as importantly, where is the evidence suggesting that depriving everyone of guns to keep them away from the few who might misuse them would result in fewer or less-lethal attacks on schools or any other venue? To many who have joined the Progressive's anti-gun movement, the justification for gun control seems to be nothing more than the speculative proposition that, "I am tired of hearing we cannot do anything, so let's take away guns and see what happens." It is, in other words, the equivalent of a Nancy Pelosi moment: "We need to pass the bill (Obamacare) to find out what is in it."

Some will point to Europe or other areas where the cultural and social norms are very different from the United States, as evidence that gun controls work. However, consider this: while citizens in the United States own an estimated 393 million guns, there are nearly 857 million guns in the hands of civilians in the rest of the world, and that number is likely significantly underestimated because of the illegal gun trade and other factors.[100] That is not a figure you ever hear from the mainstream media because it means something other than access to guns is influencing the misuse of guns. There are plenty of guns available even in countries that largely prohibit gun ownership, just not the same levels of gun violence.

Or is there? Let's pause for just a moment to take a closer look because "gun violence" is another one of those labels Progressives so skillfully manipulate. It disguises a multitude of circumstances, very few of them related to "mass shootings" or "active shooter" incidents. A seldom-stated fact, for example, is that in the United States, the majority of firearm-related deaths, approximately 60 percent, are self-inflicted—suicides. Fatalities in mass shootings account for a very small fraction of gun deaths in the US each year. Using the FBI's terminology, 85 people died in the US in 2018 from "active shooter" incidents. While gun death rates in the United States, if suicide is included, are higher than in most countries of Europe and places like Canada and Australia, it is lower than any number of nations in Latin America.[101] And let's not forget: in Europe several countries have liberal doctor-assisted suicide laws, making improvisation unnecessary and undoubtedly reducing the number of deaths attributed to "gun violence." More to the point, can anyone reasonably say that someone bent on suicide will be dissuaded by the inability to access a gun? No more so, I would suggest, than someone intent on mass murder.

That said, commentators long have talked about a "culture of violence" in the United States different from the cultures and norms in most other parts of the world. It harkens back to our founding, the "cowboy" attitudes that developed as the country expanded to the west, the romanticizing of the "gangster" culture of the early 1900s, and a glorification of war, sex crimes, and violence originating in Hollywood. Progressives have tried to downplay the role of culture in gun violence, just as they have tried to downplay the influences of mental illness, poverty, terrorism, domestic violence, class, race, and gender envy, and a host of other determinants. They want the focus to be guns. But there are cultural influences and differences between the United States and other countries of the world that do not permit easy transfer of experiences when it comes to gun violence and certainly not gun controls. And as the experiences in England and Canada show, even when a "gun culture" does not exist, it is easy enough for criminals and the mentally ill to find ways to kill and maim on a mass scale.

I recently read an editorial by a writer I generally have found reasonable and level-headed: Marsha Mercer.[102] The gist of the story involved the weakening stand of many in America against gun-control laws, even among some leading Republicans, the waning "clout" of the National Rifle Association, and the lingering despair of parents of students killed at Virginia Tech in 2007 over the failures to enact stricter gun-control laws. Marsha Mercer ends her column with these words: "No one wants more mass shootings. The 2020 campaigns and election offer us the chance to show we care enough to try to stop them."

Once more, a singular focus on guns derails the logic of the analysis. What no one wants are more *mass killings,* and if every gun in America disappeared from the face of the Earth tomorrow, mass killings at schools, workplaces, synagogues, churches, mosques, nightclubs, concerts, and other public places would not stop or be reduced until the root causes of mass killings are addressed and resolved. The notion you can stop mass killings by stopping mass shootings is a complete *non sequitur* unless you are willing to assume that taking guns from people turns homicidal maniacs into model citizens.

How can we seriously believe gun-control laws would be effective in stopping attacks on schools, churches, and other public places anyway? Did Prohibition prevent the illegal sale and consumption of alcohol? If there is any evidence the drinking age laws have prevented a single teenager inclined to do so from drinking, I am unaware of it. Has the "War on Drugs" done anything to solve the sale of illegal drugs in the US? We currently have an opioid epidemic raging in the country that is killing 130 people a day, and the government cannot even slow it down. We spend billions of dollars every year on bans that try to prevent the unpreventable. In most cases, the cost is only a loss of money. When guns are the target, however, the loss will be much greater: our civil liberties and freedoms.

Put slightly differently, how realistic is it to believe laws will prevent criminals—those who intentionally and willingly break laws—from obtaining and using guns? When you make breaking the law profitable, the law will be broken; it is as simple as that. Isn't ensuring that the "bad guys" continue to have free access to whatever is banned, while the "good guys" do not, the enduring legacy of government prohibitions? And even if gun-control laws occasionally are effective in preventing a homicidal maniac or domestic terrorist from obtaining a gun, are we happier with the outcome when he or she bombs a school or church, or drives a rented truck through a school-yard, or wades through a playground swinging a machete? It simply is not rational to advocate experimenting with consti-tutional rights, hoping it might do some good without doing too much harm.

Moving shooters to more lethal options is not the only unintended consequence of disarming law-abiding gun owners while not affecting criminals at all. The statistics from across the country demonstrating that the incident of violent crime goes down in states that have enacted concealed-carry laws, for example, may be an inconvenient truth for gun-con-trol advocates, and one they would prefer to ignore, but the evidence is far too compelling to be dismissed casually. So, what does happen when the good guys are disarmed?

Unfortunately, we already have too many examples of what happens when criminals or the mentally ill have access to guns, but those who obey the law do not. In most states, we make schools and churches "soft targets" by banning guns on school or church property. Law-abiding citizens obey. Shooters take advantage. It is no coincidence that so many of the mass shootings in the US occur in schools and churches or other places of worship. Why not "harden" these targets? Isn't putting armed individuals on-premises a more rational response to school and church shootings than hoping that taking guns away from people who have not shown any propensity to misuse them will reduce mass shootings? We have the recent example of Jack Wilson, an armed security agent for West Freeway Church of Christ in Hood County, Texas, who unquestionably saved many lives when he shot and killed a gunman who already had murdered two parishioners.

The claim by some, that putting armed personnel in schools or other locations might result in accidental shootings or make students feel "unsafe," is nonsense and exactly the type of muddled thinking gun-control advocates encourage. School-aged children routinely encounter armed individuals: airport security guards; guards in banks and jewelry stores; guards at the US Capitol, national monuments, and parks; guards at courthouses and military bases; and guards at dozens of other locations, including some movie theaters. They also play video games, watch television, and go to movies that are graphically violent and portray mass murder by guns, explosives, and other means as common themes. We celebrate eighteen-year-old "children" who take up arms in the military with the express intent of using them to kill.

How many mothers do you know who have been dissuaded from taking their children into a jewelry store or a bank because an armed guard was inside? Have you ever seen parents avoid armed park rangers when they visit national monuments or parks or armed guards at airports? And how many take video games away from their children because they fear the graphic displays of homicidal mayhem will make them feel unsafe or desensitize them to violence? No, we may be raising children who need "safe spaces" from speech, thoughts, and ideas they would rather not hear, or debates in which they would prefer not to engage, but most of them seem to handle quite well the violent, the murderous, and the cruel in the games they play and the media they watch.

The reasons we refuse to take logical steps to protect vulnerable targets, like posting guards or allowing concealed-carry on school or church premises, has very little to do with a reluctance to expose children to accidental injury or things that might make them feel unsafe. It has much more to do with the Progressives' agenda—they want the focus, the rage, the moral panic, to remain squarely on guns so they can continue to press to ban them. It would expose the basic falsity of the narrative that banning guns is the only feasible way of stopping attacks on schools, places of worship, and other targets if simpler, more constitutionally acceptable measures, proved effective.

The other, seldom-talked-about reason many people do not want to see guards or other security measures in place at schools, churches, and similar locations is cost. School districts and many other venues simply do not want to pay for increased security. It is much easier and cheaper for school boards, school administrators, and others in the educational bureaucracy to blame guns for school shootings, propose various schemes for regulating and eventually eliminating guns, and periodically give indignant speeches to local Rotary or Kiwanis clubs about the need to end gun violence in America. It makes for good theater and provides abundant opportunities for virtue signaling.

When I was growing up, it was common for teenagers to carry hunting rifles and shotguns in the cars and pick-up trucks they drove to school. If you had ventured into the parking lot of my high school, for example, most trucks would have had a gun rack in the back window with two long guns, usually a rifle and a shotgun. There were dozens of guns on school property, and I believe that was true for most high schools of the time. When I went to college, we kept our hunting guns under our beds in dorm rooms or in our cars. Again, I believe this was common practice at many colleges. Never was there an incident involving a gun, either in high school or college. There certainly were no mass school shootings; the schools were the very epitome of "hardened targets."

Gun-control advocates nevertheless will continue to insist that "doing nothing is not an option; we have to try something." The argument is easy, has "curb" appeal, and helps keep anxieties high and the desire to do something out front and prominent. It also is the same type of sound-bite sloganeering people have grown accustomed to in the political arena, so it is familiar.

I get it. After a shooting, people naturally want to do something. They are distraught and vulnerable. An innocent group of kids has just been attacked, some of them killed, others injured, and all traumatized. No one questions the need to do something, but doing something always ends up meaning the same thing—gun controls. The discussion is never about addressing the actual causes of gun violence, increasing security or otherwise "hardening" targets, identifying and dealing realistically with the dangerously mentally ill, or the host of other common-sense responses that need to be made if violent attacks are to be reduced. It would be too difficult. It would be too costly. It would require thought and planning. And if people started to focus on the fact that "guns don't kill, people do," it would be too destructive of the gun narrative Progressives want everyone to embrace.

Believe me when I say that I understand the moral panic that results from a school shooting—I am a parent and grandparent. But where is the evidence that disarming people who do not misuse guns will have a positive influence on those who do, or that banning the sale or possession of guns will keep guns out of the hands of people who should not have them? What if we reacted to every tragedy as we react to gun events—*ad hoc* and without any effort to determine and address root causes? You would quickly strip away any number of individual rights and liberties in the hope that what you are doing *might* have some beneficial effect without too many unintended consequences.

If advocates of banning guns were serious about taking a hard, open-minded look at possible ways to reduce gun violence, many things short of putting guards in schools and churches could be done to help keep guns out of the hands of those likely to misuse them. One option would be revamping the privacy law protections afforded to the dangerously mentally ill. I also am not opposed to reasonable laws requiring background checks for commercial gun sales. We could consider allowing concealed carry on the premises of schools, places of worship, and most public places. Statistics from concealed carry states consistently and uniformly show violent crime goes down when criminals understand their intended victims might be armed. The people attacking schools and places of worship may be mentally ill or fanatics, but most of them also are cowards who usually quickly surrender or kill themselves when confronted with anything more menacing than unsuspecting children.

It doesn't take long for the camel to end up in the tent, however, if each time an attack occurs, we look for "easy solutions" in laws that progressively impinge on basic rights and liberties. We have to understand that as long as we have mentally ill people, "revolutionaries" willing to kill for a cause, the angry, the evil, the malcontent, and those desperate for fifteen minutes of fame, there will be attacks on schools, churches, and other public places. The "softer" the target, the more likely it is that it will be attacked. If guns are not available, something else will be used.

Don't be misled. Gun-control advocates are not after "reasonable" controls on the sale and ownership of guns. Those are just "first steps," which they expect to fail, and when they do, Progressives will move, one law at a time, to more onerous controls until guns can be banned without much opposition. Think about it; if you are unwilling even to entertain the thought that mental illness might play some causative role in school shootings, how can there be any real discussions about how best to address gun violence?

I end this chapter with these observations. It is amazing to me how little gun-control advocates seem to know about guns. They appear unable to grasp, for example, the difference between fully automatic weapons, which essentially already are banned in the US, and a semi-automatic gun, which describes a broad range of rifles, shotguns, and handguns. At least they pretend not to know the difference. They also do not seem to understand that the basic inaccuracy of a hand-held weapon on fully automatic fire, and the rate at which it uses ammunition, in most instances makes it less of a threat than a semi-automatic weapon. Even in warfare, soldiers typically do not use their rifles on automatic for those reasons. Too many war movies showing stationary, belt-fed machine guns firing hundreds of rounds a minute at enemy bunkers have convinced too many people that firearms of all kinds are killing machines with virtually unlimited firepower. It is the image Progressives want you to have.

Gun-control advocates also continually make the claims that AR-15 rifles are not "sporting guns" and "are intended only to kill people," when, in fact, the AR-style rifle is one of the most popular hunting guns on the market. They may look" military," but the "look" of a gun does not turn an otherwise lawful user into a terrorist or murder, and it should not have any influence on whether or not it can be sold to private citizens. If you believe otherwise, you also must believe that violent video games and movies are dangerous for children and adults alike and should be banned as well. No? What is the difference?

Unlike military rifles, an AR-15 does not have an automatic fire option. Except for magazine capacity, they operate like any other semi-automatic rifle, shotgun, or handgun used for hunting, recreation, or home defense. While the larger-capacity magazines available for AR rifles are common targets of gun-control advocates, large-capacity magazines do not turn people into killers either. A madman or terrorist committed to mass murder can use smaller-capacity magazines, changed more quickly and frequently, to create all the firepower needed.

Guns are no different than the many things that can be weaponized and used to kill on a mass scale, and like them, efforts to curb abuse should focus on the people misusing them and the reasons for their misuse, not on guns themselves. This is particularly true since the Second Amendment plays such an important role in the relationship between Americans and their government. There is no evidence suggesting banning guns would reduce violent crime, reduce school attacks, or otherwise improve public safety, or any real reason to think it would. We have to understand that the "moral panic" that ensues every time a shooting occurs is the result of a politically driven agenda. It is intended to arouse fear and anger and interfere with rational thought. The fact Canadians experience the same thing each time there is a knife attack demonstrates the manufactured nature of these crises.

Doing something just to be doing something, and without having fact-based reasons for believing the outcomes will be positive and the unintended consequences modest, cannot be the response. The government has demonstrated conclusively, time and again, that it is incapable of effectively banning anything, but in the process of trying, it is likely to trample rights and liberties and provide a new source of revenue for those willing to violate the law.

That may be the greatest danger of the gun debate. As the hysteria—moral panic—increases, people may become more willing to forfeit rights and liberties simply because they do not know what else to do. They may, in other words, be panicked into ceding more to the government than they understand. Progressives want America disarmed for a reason, and it has nothing to do with gun violence or school shootings. If Americans want to believe otherwise, Progressives are more than happy to indulge them.

At the very least, a ban on firearms would lead to the development of an enormous black market in guns, the disarming of lawful citizens, and a rise in violent crime as all targets go "soft." More ominously, while bans never will prevent criminals and terrorists from obtaining guns, if a firearm's ban makes it more difficult for the disturbed, mentally-ill "amateur" bent on terror to obtain a gun, it will simply steer them to other, more lethal alternatives. Progressives hope that is something you never will understand.

CHAPTER 6

RACISM AND BIGOTRY

*R*acism and *bigotry*, two words that have been milita-rized by Progressives and used casually to intimidate and silence those with whom they disagree. President Trump regularly is labeled a racist and bigot, even though people who have known him for years, including many prominent African American leaders and personalities, sharply reject those claims.

The problem, once again, is labels. Racism once meant prejudice, discrimination, and hostility directed to persons of a different race or ethnic group solely because of the belief that your race or ethnic group was superior. Bigotry likewise was reserved for those who treated other races or ethnic groups with hatred, intolerance, and contempt. The terms were not used lightly but were confined to proven instances of prejudice, discrimination, and intolerance.

No longer. Today, the terms are used "promiscuous-ly,"[103] their meanings almost purely subjective.[104] They have become "protean" and have "accreted" to such an extent "psychological, anthropological and sociohistorical sophistica-tions" are needed even to understand them.[105] If something "feels" unpleasant to someone of a different race, it's racist,[106] whether intended to be or not, because the terms "racist" and "bigot" now encompass an "animus" beyond the conscious and deliberate.[107] Without any requirement of intent, the labels can be applied broadly and indiscriminately.

Stripping "conscious intent" from the racial narrative is particularly important to Progressives. It provides the rationale for achieving their goal of re-structuring the country and changing its form of government. Because the country, its laws, and its institutions were established by White Western Europeans to benefit White Western Europeans, other races and cultures were disadvantaged, remain so today, and even centuries later, and after the election of a two-term Black president of the United States, nothing can happen in this country that is not "racialized."[108] If the structure of the country invariably results in racialized outcomes—systemic racism, if you will—it must be changed.

It takes only a moment's reflection to understand that the terms "racism" and "bigotry" have been redefined to support a Progressive agenda that depends heavily on racial and ethnic distrust, hatred, and envy. The meaning and understanding of the terms have "accreted" to such a degree that *everything* is racist and bigoted, the intended and unintended, the real and the imagined. Even those acting without the slightest racist animus produce racialized outcomes.[109] No other outcomes are even possible because the country was founded and built on racist principles that persist to this day. And in the Progressives' cancel culture world, even a single allegation of racism is sufficient to forever brand the alleged perpetrator as a racist and bigot, at least conservative perpetrators.

These are surpassingly unfair interpretations, uses, and understandings of the terms "racism" and "bigotry." It assumes a system frozen in time, place, and circumstance, unchanged from its origins. It completely ignores both historical context and the occurrence of almost too many metamorphic events to count and tarnishes a nation of over 330 million people with the sins of a few. As a basis for legitimate debate, reform, and agreement, it is chimerical. As an instrument of insurrectionary anarchism, however, it is masterful.

There are no limits to what today is considered racist and bigoted. You are a racist and bigot any time your actions or words can be recast as hindering, opposing, or disagreeing with a minority person or group in some respect, regardless of intentions.[110] Expressing opposition to an entitlement program, for example, is "racist" because entitlement programs benefit disadvantaged groups. No matter how ill-advised or illogical a program or proposal may be, no one is permitted to criticize or oppose anything that might be deemed advantageous to minorities. Debate and discussion are not possibilities, and certainly not disagreement; that would be racist.

The concepts are infinitely elastic, adaptable to any circumstances. If you oppose a decision to release prisoners during the coronavirus pandemic, you are a racist because many of the prisoners are Black. It does not matter that your opposition is based on the legitimate fear that released criminals, Black, White, or Brown, will commit new crimes, some of them violent, as happened in several states which adopted such programs, including New York. The fact you opposed the program for reasons unrelated to the color of a person's skin, or their culture or ethnicity, is beside the point. Racist motivation or intent no longer are necessary precursors to racism and bigotry.

You also are a racist and bigot if you oppose "open borders" for the United States. Again, it does not matter that your opposition is premised on protecting the country from being infiltrated by terrorists, exposed to contagions, or any of the other reasons the immigration laws long ago were adopted to address.

President Trump has been accused of "racism" and "bigotry" from incidents ranging from referring to Haiti and some African nations as "s—hole countries," to demanding construction of a border wall to prevent caravans of immigrants from South America, Central America, and Mexico entering the United States. In an earlier chapter of this book, I discuss the President's "s—hole" comments, which were not race-based but were directed to countries so mired in corruption they were not housing, clothing, or feeding their people despite receiving massive amounts of Western aid. The criticisms of his calls for secure borders were even more off-base.

Isn't it the job of the president to uphold our laws and secure the country's borders? Why should any president speak kindly of people who demonstrate contempt for our laws? Most are not refugees seeking political asylum—that much was made clear by the busloads who turned down Mexico's offers of asylum and continued to the US border.[111]

Why do we allow Progressives to control this narrative? Labels like "racism" and "bigotry" should be reserved for unambiguous instances of prejudice and intolerance of a different race or ethnic group, not used as a means for silencing critics and shutting down debate on important political and social issues. When no one can criticize, talk about, or disagree with any policy impacting a person of a different skin color or cultural or ethnic background, the "speech code" merchants unquestionably have managed to expand their reach well beyond our college campuses. Think what a powerful tool it is to be able to end any debate or controversy simply by charging your opposition with being racists and bigots. Nothing ever has to be defended on the merits because the stigma of being labeled a racist or a bigot is the scarlet letter of the day, worse than being called a pedophile. Powerful figures from business, entertainment, sports, the media, and many other segments of our society are routinely driven from office or position by unproven charges of racism and bigotry, not to mention sexual harassment, domestic violence, and more. But on what possible rationale should the color of a person's skin, or their culture or ethnicity, exempt them from criticism or defending their positions if we truly aspire to a color-blind world?

Progressives do not want a color-blind world. Why would they? Their venomous ideology is built on class, race, ethnicity, and gender envies. They have weaponized "racism" and "bigotry" precisely to insulate their extreme positions and causes from question and challenge. Because the opinions of racists and bigots merit no responses, Progressives never have to justify anything they do or say. If President Trump and a huge number of Americans want a border wall, then obviously they are racists and bigots, part of Hillary Clinton's "basket of deplorables," afraid of the demographic handwriting on the wall. End of discussion.

The opprobrium of being labeled a racist or bigot is not even necessarily limited to other races, cultures, or ethnic groups, as evidenced by the controversy that erupted over Will Smith being cast to play the role of Richard Williams, father of professional tennis stars Venus and Serena Williams, in a Hollywood production. One of the industry's biggest attractions, Will Smith is a light-skinned African American. When it was announced he had been tapped to play the role of Richard Williams, a darker-skinned individual, in a film about how Williams, without a tennis background, coached his daughters to international tennis stardom, there was an immediate protest from the African American community. The complaint? Will Smith was not "black enough" to portray the darker-skinned Williams, and it would be discriminatory and "racist" to select him for the role.

"Colorism," the prejudicial or preferential treatment of same-race people based solely on their color, is a major point of contention in the African American community, where many believe lighter-skinned African Americans with European features are favored and receive privileges, preferences, and treatments not accorded darker-skinned African Americans with more African features."[112] It is discrimination by complexion, and by choosing the lighter-skinned Will Smith to play the darker-skinned Richard Williams, darker-complected African American actors were "discriminated" against.

This is more than hypersensitivity. It is evidence of a worldview immutably committed to the proposition that everything happens because of race, and not just the color of a person's skin, but the shade of a person's skin, rather than skill, talent, experience, hard work, or any other metric normally associated with success. It is an assumption of racism in all things, at all times. Will Smith got the role, not because he arguably is Hollywood's top actor and box office draw, but because his skin is a lighter shade than darker-skinned African American actors, who only coincidentally happen to lack his acting skills and box office appeal.

"Colorism" has been an issue of contention in the African American community for many years.[113] The fact African Americans admit they discriminate against each other based on darker or lighter skin tones and facial features may help explain their susceptibility to the Progressive's narrative that White America, certainly conservative White America, is racist and bigoted, interested only in exploiting African Americans. Projection—attributing things you do not like about yourself to others—is a widely recognized psychological defensive mechanism.

How very little it takes to be branded a racist and bigot is illustrated by the case of Pam Northam, wife of the governor of Virginia, Ralph Northam. The governor was the toast of the Democratic Party until a news story broke about a 1980's photo in his medical school yearbook depicting him either wearing "blackface" or a KKK hood and robe. The governor first admitted he was one of the individuals in the photograph and then denied it the next day. He did, however, admit to other uses of blackface. At the very least, the change in story suggests the governor initially must have believed he was the figure in the KKK hood and robe—why would he not be able to identify himself in blackface?

The incident provided Democrats with an unusually opportunistic moment. The Lt. Governor, Justin Fairfax, a young Black activist attorney, would become governor if Northam stepped down. It was the ultimate "twofer"—an opportunity to "virtue signal" by forcing Northam, an old White man Democrat, to resign over a pet Progressive issue, racism, while at the same time elevating perhaps the next Barack Obama to the governor's mansion in Virginia, a key battleground state in the 2020 elections.

The party moved in quickly for the kill, as prominent Democrats everywhere called for Northam's resignation, including the state's two long-time United States senators, Mark Warner and Tim Kaine. When Terry McAuliffe, Northam's Democratic predecessor as Virginia governor—many believe he still runs the state—confidently predicted the governor would "do what was right" for the Commonwealth and step down, the stage was set for a coronation of a new crown prince. Progressives were giddy with anticipation. Then it all fell apart. Two women from Justin Fairfax's past came out of the shadows to accuse him of sexual abuse and violence, and Mark Herring, the Virginia attorney general and next in line to become governor if Fairfax could not serve, confessed to his own use of blackface.

There were tepid calls for all three men to step down—nothing like the fervor over the Brett Kavanaugh appointment to the United States Supreme Court, of course. Strangely missing was #MeToo demonstrators chanting "believe survivors" in support of Fairfax's accusers or any of the other machinations or dramas surrounding the Kavanaugh hearings.

The calls for Northam, Herring, and Fairfax to resign faded quickly. Faced with the prospect of the speaker of the Virginia House of Delegates, a Republican, becoming governor if the three Democrats were forced out of office, the outrage over Northam's offensive medical school escapades receded quickly. The governor announced a "reconciliation" tour to "heal" the Commonwealth, and Democratic Party elders suddenly became staunch believers in "due process" for Justin Fairfax. Herring faded into the background. The mainstream media quickly stopped covering the accusations against Fairfax. The stories shifted to Northam's rapprochement meetings with Black leaders.

I am not sure there is a much better way to expose the hypocrisy of Progressives than to compare their reaction to Justice Kavanaugh's nomination to the Supreme Court and their reaction to the morass involving Virginia's top three elected officials. When it appeared politically advantageous to do so, they were perfectly willing to sacrifice one of their own, but the wagons were circled and "principle" quickly abandoned when political expediency intervened.

Back to Pam Northam.

Throughout her husband's ordeal, she seemed to be a steadying influence and a model of grace and dignity in very undignified circumstances. Nevertheless, just a few weeks after the calls for her husband's resignation subsided, she was conducting a tour of the governor's mansion for a group of students, something she did periodically. Pam Northam was a former teacher and advocate for hands-on education. She also served as a trustee on the board of the very interactive Virginia Museum of Science.

A cottage adjacent to the governor's mansion that once served as a kitchen staffed by slaves recently had been added to the tours curated by Pam Northam. Because of her interest in interactive education, Mrs. Northam routinely invited those on the tours to touch and handle agricultural products and other artifacts in the cottage. On this occasion, in February 2019 those artifacts included balls of cotton, which Mrs. Northam reportedly handed to some African American students and asked them to "imagine being an enslaved person."[114]

Indignation exploded. Immediately after the tour, state lawmakers received a letter from one of the students, an eighth-grader, describing the incident as "beyond inappropriate."[115] The student elaborated:

> It was very testing to know I had to go somewhere, and I had no choice as to if I went, I had to be respectful, and be on my best behavior, even when the people in positions of power I was around were not doing the same.[116]

The student's mother also wrote a letter saying the actions of Pam Northam did not lead her to believe the governor's office had "taken seriously the harm and hurt they had caused African Americans in Virginia" (by the blackface/KKK incident) or that they (the governor and his wife) were "deserving of our forgiveness."[117]

On one level, I cannot view this any other way other than being emblematic of the hypersensitive nation we have become. Even taking into account the baggage her husband created with his blackface/KKK antics, Pam Northam had done nothing to suggest she was a racist, bigot, or anything other than a committed teacher who believed in interactive, experiential learning.

It is also indicative of something else—how unforgiving we have become as a nation. Perhaps cotton has become such a symbol of slavery that merely seeing, touching, or talking about it is hurtful to African Americans. I do not know. Assuming that to be the case, however, was there anything suggesting Pam Northam intended to offend or that she was aware of the hurt for African Americans associated with cotton? Or perhaps it was the mention of slavery that the student found upsetting? Regardless, wasn't this exactly the type of teaching moment where a private letter to or discussion with Mrs. Northam pointing out the sensitivity of this type of behavior for African Americans would have been a more appropriate and constructive response?

Not in a world where any perceived affront to a disadvantaged person or group, intended or not, real or not, is immediately viewed as "racist" and "bigoted." A White teacher asking a Black student to consider what being enslaved would have been like and providing a visual and tactile teaching aid to enhance the presentation is "racist" and the entire discussion therefore impermissible and "off-limits." How is it even possible to teach subjects like the Civil War in our schools if the mention of slavery is considered a racial affront to Black Americans? Which teachers would dare broach the subject?

Could only Black teachers even attempt it? Could it be taught only from the "Black perspective?" How narrow would that perspective have to be? Isn't it likely that most teachers would simply characterize the war as a monstrous atrocity and move on? Why would any teacher take the chance of doing more?

In the chapter of this book entitled, *"Taking Down Statues,"* I address some of the dangers of what has been called historical negationism—the deliberate censoring or distortion of historical records. Typically, southern states are accused of being revisionists, of trying to rewrite Civil War history and recast themselves as defenders of things like state rights and limited government. While no one can or should deny the central role of slavery in the outbreak of the war, however, it is just as damaging to the historical record to deny the legitimate roles played by issues like state's rights, the shifting balance of power between North and South as the nation expanded westward, the differing perspectives of urban versus rural economies, and a host of other underlying political, social, cultural, and economic issues. That is the essence of education. Not everyone in the South was a plantation or slave owner, and these issues played a role in the lead-up to war in a country still in its early stages of development. Many Southern political and military leaders were important actors in our history, both before and after the war, and it is impossible to ignore their contributions, both good and bad, without also eliminating important elements of history.

None of that is a defense of slavery, which cannot be defended on any ground. However, when events are removed from history, history itself is erased. A report in 2016 from a committee appointed by Yale University to determine the principles to be applied in determining whether to remove controversial historical names from buildings and other structures cautioned against the dangers of rewriting history, a favored propaganda tool of totalitarian regimes:

> Ill-fated renaming has often reflected excessive confidence in moral orthodoxies. One need only consider twentieth-century regimes that sought to erase their own past in the service of totalitarian propaganda. The Soviet Union conducted aggressive renaming campaigns of a kind captured by George Orwell's dystopian novel 1984, in which a so-called "Ministry of Truth" wrote and rewrote history.

* * * *

> Nearly twenty-five years ago, the late Robin Winks identified a critical distinction between liberal and illiberal alterations of historical monuments. Winks, the former master of Berkeley College, who served on the Yale faculty from 1957 to 1999, wrote that there are "two different concepts of history." In one conception, history is a record of things from the past that should not be forgotten. In this view, removing an item from the historical record is like lying; as Winks put it, such removals are akin to the work of the infamous "Great Soviet Encyclopedia," in which history became whatever the Party leaders wanted it to be at any given moment in time.[118]

In the 1920s, the "Ministry of Truth" of the newly formed Soviet Union created the "Great Soviet Encyclopedia" to write and rewrite history in ways pleasing to party leaders.[119]

People will argue that her husband's conduct put Pam Northam in different circumstances, and perhaps it did. But are we no longer capable of giving anyone the benefit of the doubt? Why is it so important to pounce, regardless of how innocent, unintended, or minor a comment or action may be? Is it simply the lure of the proverbial fifteen minutes of fame: "Look at me—I am a victim"? Victimhood unquestionably has become a sought-after status.

I believe more is involved. No opportunity to label someone a racist or bigot can be passed up because to do so would weaken the disciplinary impact of the tactic. The power of playing the racist and bigot cards comes from their relentless deployment. The more expansively they are used, the greater the intimidation factor, and the more broadly and effectively discussion and debate are muffled.

This is not necessarily even a conscious tactic on the part of most. They have been conditioned to interpret everything as a racial or ethnic affront by those who understand that when even the innocent is met immediately and aggressively with charges of racism and bigotry, people will hesitate to criticize or question anything advocated by people of different races or ethnic or cultural backgrounds. Cautious silence becomes the prudent course. We saw what happened during the riots following George Floyd's death. Even though the chaos expanded far beyond issues relating to Civil War statues, police brutality, or racial justice—it quickly became open warfare on democracy itself—people largely remained silent, knowing they would be labeled racists and bigots if they spoke out, and might be targeted by violent protestors.

Earlier in this chapter, I mentioned the connection between speech codes on college campuses and the indiscriminate accusations of racism and bigotry that have become staples of the Progressives' attack on American democracy. Both are part and parcel of a political strategy designed to shut down opposition to Progressive policies and quell dissident voices.

Once upon a time, it was accepted pedagogy in American colleges and universities that discussions of controversial or unpopular issues and subjects, even those that made students feel uncomfortable or unsafe, were indispensable elements of teaching and learning. That was the essence of academic freedom and the reason for tenured faculty members—tenure protected and promoted academic freedom because tenured members of the faculty could not be terminated simply for engaging students on controversial issues. The free exchange of competing ideas, even distasteful, hateful ideas, was considered the lifeblood of education and the bedrock of democracy. How can you study subjects like slavery, the rise of Nazism, the Holocaust, sexual violence, and a host of other topics without raising issues that may be uncomfortable for many and painful for some?

No longer. Today students are told they are entitled to be protected from any thought and speech that upsets them. They are offered "safe zones" on many campuses where they do not have to come into contact with speech, ideas, or individuals with which or with whom they disagree, and where they can be shielded from information they prefer not to hear. What makes them uncomfortable or unsafe, however, is selective and limited, which is the problem with all forms of censorship. What is considered harmful, noxious, or unacceptable is defined by the predilections, sensibilities, preferences, and favored issues *du jour* of those in charge, while the very purpose of free speech is to give voice to minority positions and ideas that may not be popular, at least at the moment. Where might we be in America today, for example, if speech critical of *Plessy v. Ferguson*,[120] and the "separate but equal" doctrine, had been suppressed?

There are many issues dear to the hearts of Progressives—abortion, LBGTQ rights, open borders, affirmative action,

separation of church and state, to name just some of them—
that are objectionable and upsetting to others. During the
long time-period of this country's history when a majority of
Americans found some of these subjects to be deeply troubling and unacceptable, should supporters have been banned
from advocating for change, as Progressives today try to ban
conservative commentaries and viewpoints on many of the
same subjects? What is fair game for debate and discussion
cannot be determined by "whose ox is being gored"—that is
the essence of censorship. Once established, policies quickly
can become engrained and untouchable if sheltered from criticism and opposing viewpoints. The position of Progressives
that *Plessy v. Ferguson* was correctly overturned, but *Roe v.
Wade*[121] cannot be questioned, illustrates the point.

It is a natural human inclination to want to ban that with
which you disagree. But protection of free speech, particularly
political speech, is a key part of the genius of our Constitution
and one of the great differentiators between our form of government and the governments of countries that are less free.
It is the reason that upon assuming power autocratic governments everywhere immediately begin to censor speech. The
fact that "the pen is mightier than the sword," is not something
lost on those focused on destroying democracy.

I once was on a college campus to attend a lecture by a
noted First Amendment scholar. At the time of the program,
the campus had been roiled by allegations of a racially inappropriate, but private email supposedly sent to a friend by a
member of the student government. It later would turn out
the email was a hoax, sent by agitators on campus. Regardless,
during a question-and-answer period following the lecture,
several students were visibly upset and questioned why
"hate" speech ever should be allowed. Despite the scholar's
best efforts to explain the dangers of censorship, particularly

when the governing majority does not share the views of political opponents or others in the country, the students were unable to come to grips with what many of us would consider among the most basic of constitutional principles, one we were taught from a young age was of crucial importance in preventing government abuse and overreach. We understood intuitively that whatever the "costs" of free speech, the alternatives were so inimical to our freedoms and liberties, they had to be rejected. The fact that so many of the students attending this lecture could not grasp why even "hate speech" needs to be protected spoke volumes about how completely we have jettisoned serious study of our history, Constitution, and form of government.

Protecting liberty is difficult and costly. Aristotle first postulated the idea that "nature abhors a vacuum," and will move quickly to fill it. Tyrants and despots will move just as quickly to fill any economic, leadership, or military vacuum in the free world. Virtually by default, the United States has long assumed leadership of the world's democracies and has shouldered a disproportionate share of the costs, burdens, and sacrifices of defending the free world. Millions of Americans have sacrificed their lives, many more their futures, to protect democratic freedoms, including the right of freedom of speech. College students with even a modicum of appreciation for the sacrifices made to guarantee the liberties they now enjoy at least should have the courage to confront, on the merits, ideas with which they disagree. They have not earned the right to shelter in "safe" places when faced with speech or ideas that upset them. "When I was a child, I talked like a child, I thought like a child, I reasoned like a child. When I became a man, I gave up childish ways" (1 Cor. 13:11). It is time for everyone to grow up.

Students are not entirely to blame for their confused and timid state. They have been programmed to be overly sensitive by an educational system that has been increasingly radicalized for decades. Students now cry, grieve, and express outrage virtually on command. Conditioned to respond to stimuli determined by those manipulating them, they respond predictably and unconsciously. As Rush Limbaugh once said, the one indispensable element for progressivism, socialism, and communism to take root is *abject ignorance,* and too many college and university students today are simply too unaware, unknowing, and undereducated to understand what is being taken away from them or how they are being misled by the Progressives' narrative.

It is important to recognize that the battle over speech codes on American college and university campuses is not a fight, as some have argued, "over ideas which lack value."[122] That is exactly the type of verbal gerrymandering on which the entire false narrative of progressivism is built. If you can censor information simply by claiming it "lacks value," you can censor anything. The importance of the First Amendment to our Constitution lies in its recognition that no person or group has the acumen, neutrality, or foresight to assign values to competing ideas, "kicking to the curb" those they consider unacceptable or "lacking value." Assigning values to ideas— allowing some, prohibiting others—is precisely what censorship does.

Rather than being an important and integral part of the "marketplace of ideas," too many of our colleges and universities today are limiting the scope of the education they offer and are closing, not broadening, young minds by enacting speech codes that restrict any speech deemed unwelcome, "wrong." disagreeable, or offensive.[123] Free discussion and debate have been strangled to such a degree, the University of Chicago formed a committee chaired by Geoffrey Stone, one of the nation's leading First Amendment authorities, to draft a statement setting forth the university's commitment to "free, robust and uninhibited debate and deliberation."

That the University of Chicago felt compelled to issue a statement endorsing free speech on campus speaks volumes about how deeply Progressives and other advocates of "assigning value to ideas" have taken over many of our institutions of higher education. Equally enlightening is the fact that the Chicago statement, which does no more than confirm a commitment to the First Amendment of the United States Constitution, has met resistance on many campuses and still has been adopted by only a distinct minority of colleges and universities in the country. To be fair, some campuses already had adopted free speech policies of their own, but everyone should be asking hard questions of schools that have enacted speech codes and adopted "safe" zone policies that run counter to First Amendment principles.

Despite the importance of race and ethnicity weapons in their ideological war against democracy, it is clear that some types of discrimination are not as "upsetting" to Progressives as others. Why don't anti-Semitic slurs, for example, engender the same degree of backlash as racially inappropriate statements about African Americans or Hispanic migrants? Where is the outrage over what appears to be continuing discrimination against Asian students in the college admission process?[124] It has been shown time and again that to matriculate at many of our colleges and universities, including some of the most elite, Asians are required to have considerably higher test scores and credentials than other races.[125] I recall an official in the California state university system some years back, perhaps before the passage of Proposition 209 amended the California constitution to make it unlawful for public institutions to discriminate based on race, sex, or ethnicity, attempting to explain why it was necessary to take fewer Asian students: they "studied too much" and did not "add enough" to campus life, or words to that effect. Bill Clinton made similar comments while he was president. Isn't this the type of thinking that was used to limit the number of Jews admitted to Ivy League schools in the first part of the twentieth century? By what measure is it acceptable?

It is acceptable in many of our colleges and universities because the Progressives' diversity blueprint for our campuses, as well as our workplaces, does not include everyone. The focus is on a small number of favored races and ethnic groups. Asians and Jews are not welcome. Nor is anyone included within Hillary Clinton's "basket of deplorables." Certainly, there is no desire to promote diversity of religious belief or political thought, or any knowledge that competes with the Progressives' orthodoxy. It is an allegorical form of diversity— concentrated, non-diffuse, and intended to exclude at least as many as it includes.

Have we strayed this far from our constitutional roots? Is the current generation of college students simply too frail to shoulder the responsibilities of democracy? Are they turning to socialism because they believe it will be a "safe" space where they can be taken care of, sheltered from a competitive world, and protected from ideas they find upsetting? The world can be a frightening place, and students too uninformed to engage issues meaningfully do not seem ideally suited for the rigors of democracy.

The current trajectory of America suits the Progressives' agenda well. They do not welcome dialogue and debate. They do not want anyone, particularly students, to understand the vast differences between socialism and the constitutional form of market-based government they are privileged to live under. They do not want them to understand or appreciate American exceptionalism or how the unprecedented prosperity the United States introduced to the world has relieved poverty and raised living standards everywhere. They want them to hate their country and everything for which it stands. What they seek are undereducated, indoctrinated "loyalists" who will buy into the race-baiting divisiveness, class, race, and gender envies, and "social" and "racial" justice absurdities on which progressivism depends for survival. The bastardization of terms like "racist" and "bigot" is an easy-to-execute part of the strategy for trying to ensure that happens.

It is one of the reasons control over the education system is so important to Progressives. It provides the most fertile ground for proselytizing young minds and the most direct way to diminish the quality of education sufficiently to prevent students from gaining the knowledge needed to think critically and logically, engage in meaningful public discourse, participate constructively in the civic, cultural, and economic activities of their country and communities, and develop the intellectual competencies that promote independent thinking and allow for the assimilation of complex facts, ideas, and conceptual frameworks.[126]

Take the example of the school children confronting Sen. Diane Feinstein (D, CA) in the Senate Office building.[127] The children were in near hysteria over the Green New Deal's forecast that the planet would effectively end in twelve years unless the dramatic steps outlined in this ridiculous parody of a political agenda, at a projected cost of $100 trillion—more than four times the current national debt—were implemented immediately. Even the most ardent climate change advocates talk about the effects of global warming taking place over many decades, not twelve years, but that's not the point. These young school children were in Washington with their teacher who, had she been doing her job, should have been able to bring balance and perspective to climate change issues and the Green New Deal. Her panicked students obviously had not been taught to think about or question a flawed, illogical, and unsound political manifesto proposed by self-identified social-ists. Neither had the teacher. The causes may have been very different, but were these children any less indoctrinated than the youth corps of Nazi Germany, the "Deutsches Jungvolk in der Hitler Jugend" and the "Edelweiss Pirates?" This is what happens when people become dependent on government for direction, guidance, and purpose—they are told what to believe, how to react, and what to do.

Once upon a time when a person encountered hardship or failure, we were taught resolve, perseverance, and resilience. The value of picking yourself up and never giving up was a life lesson in toughness and determination that led to the devel-opment of a hardy, confident nation, leader of the free world. Today we teach "victimhood" and "exploitation" and silence critics with charges of racism and bigotry. For the "hardened" combatants of progressivism, these are powerful weapons in their "no holds barred" assault on American democracy, but it is rapidly turning generations of Americans into frail, pro-grammed pawns, unaware and unappreciative of the gifts of their heritage or the threat progressivism poses to their freedom and prosperity.

This is where militarization of the terms "racism" and" big-otry" has left us. Nothing said or done in America is too innoc-uous not to have racial dimensions. Indiscriminate charges of racism and bigotry are used to intimidate and silence critics and have become a dominant line of attack in the Progressive's reckless assault on democracy. We, unfortunately, have been complicit in the spread of this contagion by tolerating the casual and promiscuous use of these terms and by allowing too many of our schools, including our colleges and universities, to be turned into the equivalent of modern-day "book burners."

While President Trump routinely is blamed for the deterioration in race relations in American, it is the great "Agitator in Chief," Barack Obama, who should be held responsible. Obama had the greatest opportunity in the history of American politics to bring the races together. How did he do? At the time he took office, most Americans believed race relations to be "generally good"; by the time he left office, 69 percent of the country believed race relations to be "mostly bad." As some have noted, the Black Lives Matter movement is part of the Obama racial legacy.[128]

During his presidency, every time Barack Obama had an opportunity to heal America, he did exactly the opposite, promoting racial anger, distrust, and divisiveness. Think Trayvon Martin; Harvard professor Henry Gates; Michael Brown; Dallas, Texas; and the constant charges from the Obama administration of racial bias and discrimination in the judicial and law enforcement agencies of the United States. Obama's message never was one for calm and reconciliation, but of a racially divided America with brutish police forces slaughtering young Black males in the streets while a complicit, supportive judiciary and White population looked on. The anger he engendered among African Americans resulted in the killing of five police officers and the wounding of nine others in Dallas, Texas, in July 2016 by a military vet allegedly angry over police shootings of Black men.[129] It now has culminated with calls for defunding police departments as anarchists and Marxist revolutionaries march in the streets of many of our cities.

What lay behind the former president's "divide and conquer" approach to race relations?

Perhaps it was his friendship with Bill Ayers, leader and co-founder of the violent Weather Underground, and a committed terrorist and communist, or his wife, Bernadine Dohrn, another member of the Weather Underground. They were neighbors of the Obamas in Chicago, their children attended the same schools as the Obama children, and one of the first meetings of Obama's political career took place in the Ayres's home.[130] In case you have forgotten, throughout the 1960s and 1970s, the Weather Underground conducted a domestic terror campaign of bombing public buildings in the United States, including the US Capitol.

Or maybe it was the influence of Frank Davis, another friend, confidant, and mentor of the former president, who was a self-identified communist and member of the Communist Party USA.[131]

It could have been the virulent, anti-American tirades of the Rev. Jeremiah Wright. For more than twenty years the Obamas attended Trinity United Church of Christ in Chicago where Rev. Wright, the head pastor, preached a gospel of hatred of America and everything for which it stands. Among the many anti-American rants attributed to Pastor Wright was the admonition to his congregations, "not to sing 'God Bless America,' but 'God Damn America.'" He married the Obamas, baptized their children, and is credited by Obama for the title of his book, *The Audacity of Hope*.[132] Michelle Obama's candid comment in an unguarded moment during the 2008 Wisconsin primaries that, "for the first time in my adult life, I am really proud of my country," suggests the good reverend's noxious screeds struck a receptive chord in the Obama household.

And how could it be otherwise? No one would sit through a pastor's anti-American harangues for twenty years if they found them offensive. Do you believe the Obamas would have attended a church where the minister was preaching a deeply biased and bigoted message from the pulpit? This background, affiliating with domestic terrorists and communists, attending a church where the pastor essentially urged "death to America," and a wife who admits to never having been proud of her country, should have alerted more people to the fact that the Obama version of "hope and change" was likely to be more revolution than change and anything but color blind. Maybe at another time in our history people would have paid more attention, but the country was deeply into a national act of atonement for slavery and segregation—the election of Barack Obama, a Black man, as president. No one was giving much thought to the fact they were electing someone who associated with militants and communists and had no governing experience, no business experience, no military experience, no experience of any kind that would suggest he was capable of leading America, much less the free world. No one questioned the role of Valerie Jarrett, an Iranian born, Chicago political operative, who essentially lived in the White House during much of the Obama presidency. Bill Clinton called her "Obama's Rasputin." I call her Obama's "political commissar and overseer." She was there to make sure the Obamas did not stray from their Progressive roots.

Not surprisingly given his background, lack of experience, and the "advisors" around him, Obama frequently governed like an inexperienced, left-wing oligarch. He routinely ignored constitutionally imposed constraints on the executive branch by using executive orders, recess appointments, and similar "workarounds" to negate or change laws with which he disagreed, including immigration laws. Other laws were enforced selectively. In one particularly egregious example, the Obama Justice Department refused to pursue to conclusion a Voting Rights Act case against members of the militant Black Panthers organization following the 2008 elections. Dressed in paramilitary uniforms and armed with billy clubs, members of the organization stood at the entrance of a Philadelphia voting station and shouted threats and racial slurs at White voters attempting to enter.[133] The failure to prosecute to finality what many believed was an open-and-shut case of voter intimidation was an early indication of the identity politics the Obama administration would pursue and the racial divides it would create.

Eight years of the Obama administration effectively erased many years of steady, positive progress in race relations in America. It is not something that can be easily corrected, particularly since the Progressives' playbook now has been finalized and put in place: incite anger and resentment among minority voters by convincing them they are being exploited by bigoted White supremacists; continue to weaken education; condition students and the general public to accept an ever-broadening palette of conduct as racist and bigoted; teach, preach, and never let people doubt that racism and bigotry are systemic in this country and account for every success or failure; never give anyone or anything the benefit of the doubt, but always assume every person of a different race or ethnic background is a racist and a bigot—even if they are not, their ancestors probably were; and stifle all opposition to the Progressives' ideology by instantly and angrily accusing anyone who disagrees of being a racist and bigot.

This certainly is not a fight that can be won by wishing or willing it away, by continuing to accept or tolerate bogus claims of racism and bigotry, or by retreating to "safe places." The election of Barack Obama in 2008 was the most significant signal yet that decades of effort to strengthen and grow socialism and communism in the United States finally was paying dividends. Eight additional years of a Hillary Clinton presidency would have sealed the deal and delivered the biggest prize of all:

a socialist United States. Having come so close, Progressives redoubled efforts to complete their "revolution," as evidenced by their ceaseless attacks on the Trump presidency and the riots that erupted after the death of George Floyd. The results of the 2018 midterms, when some of the most extreme left-wing candidates in the history of the Republic were elected to Congress, should have provided a hint of what was to come.

It once would have been unthinkable for a candidate running as a socialist or communist to be elected to high office in the United States. Today Bernie Sanders and others openly run for the office as socialists and attract crowds of supporters. Progressives showed remarkable patience and persistence as they plotted over the years to weaken the education systems in America, increase the number of people dependent on government, and create the race, class, and gender envies on which progressivism depends. They will continue to play the race, class, gender, White privilege, and racial and social justice cards for as long as they can; it works.

But they got impatient—the prize was too close, the disappointment too palpable, and the shock of Trump's election too much—and they exposed themselves for what they are. In the process, they also uncovered some of the secretive billionaires who fund and control so much of the Progressives' agenda and gave us a look at how completely progressivism has compromised the news media, Hollywood, social media, academia, and major businesses in the United States.

The New Green Deal is perhaps the greatest overreach in the history of US politics, and its hypocrisy is appalling. It shows clearly the fanciful character of the "promises" Progressives are willing to make in their efforts to buy elections and power—estimates place the cost of the Green Dream at over $600,000 per US household.[134] And like the ruling class of the old Soviet

Union, who lived in lavish apartments or homes, owned dachas in the country, were squired about in chauffeur-driven cars and enjoyed the finest in food, drink, entertainment, and other luxuries while the rest of the country endured shortages of everything, the aristocrats of the Progressive movement have no intent to live by the rules they intend to impose on everyone else. If you need proof, consider the antics of politicians like Al Gore and a bevy of Hollywood celebrities who push for "green energy," the elimination of fossil fuels, airplanes, flatulent cows, and large homes, and question the right of people to have children, but fly in private jets, own yachts and large-footprint homes, and ride in caravans of gasoline-powered SUVs.

The same things happen with the wealthy donors who assert so much influence over the Democratic Party and shape its agenda, and with the party's "intelligentsia," everyone, it seems, except the unsuspecting masses who are duped into voting for these Bolsheviks by visions of a "land flowing with milk and honey." In case you have not figured it out, folks, they may have needed your vote, but they do not want your advice, and they could care less about what happens to you, at least until the next election looms.

Donald Trump's election in 2016 seemed to have the effect of waking up the American people to the existential threat progressivism poses to their continued freedoms and prosperities. Ten million more people voted for him in 2020, but now that Progressives have regained control of the government, they will move quickly to undo most of what was accomplished in the last 4 years; 2016 likely will represent little more than a momentary pause in the Progressives' onslaught. So much of what America stands for—faith, democracy, opportunity, self-reliance, liberty, protection of individual rights and private property, and respect for the rule of law—is in danger of fading into the dustbin of history unless conservatives are able to regain control of Congress in the 2022 mid-terms.

In the meantime, let's be clear. It is not racist to uphold the laws of the United States, including immigration laws, because those attempting to violate them are of different races or ethnic groups. It is not racist to criticize countries too corrupt to function because their populations and governments are made up of people of color. It is not racist to raise legitimate issues concerning slavery with Black students simply because those issues may be uncomfortable. It is not racist to ask one of Hollywood's best actors to portray an individual whose skin tone is darker. It is not racist to disagree with the political positions of Black or Brown America on legitimate policy grounds. It is not racist to expose the Progressives' misuse of social and racial justice principles. It is not racist to denounce the actions of those who riot in the streets, destroy historical artifacts, and burn and deface buildings and properties. It is racist and bigoted when individuals and groups unable to address issues on the merits attempt to silence opposing views with contrived charges of racism and bigotry.

It also should be clear that the United States has not been frozen in time, place, or circumstance for nearly 250 years—things have changed meaningfully—and that "systemic racism" is a meaningless "label" that is being badly misused and exploited to excite the "useful idiots" on which progressivism depends. It can be applied to everything and avoids explaining anything. It sounds so *progressive,* so *enlightened,* so *consequential,* who could question it? If the United States is systemically racist, then obviously the current governance structure needs to be torn down and replaced with the socialist paradigm Progressives prefer. End of discussion. Let's go find some buildings to loot and burn. Sadly, for too many, that is as deep as the thought processes get.

Perhaps all of the puerile, pseudo-revolutionaries out there should have paid more attention to their mothers' readings of *Alice in Wonderland.* When Alice, immature child that she was, first chose to go down the rabbit hole, she did not understand the adult world either. It was the experience and maturity gained as she traversed Wonderland that finally allowed her to begin making better decisions. It is a lesson for all of you truculent social justice warriors.

In case you have not noticed, America is being manipulated. It needs to stop.

CHAPTER 7

GEORGE FLOYD

"We have two pandemics, COVID-19 and racism." That is the refrain of many—too many. It even can seem accurate if you give it no thought. Progressives do not want you to think about it because the notion that racism is pandemic in the United States is central to their efforts to foment civil unrest and change the nature and form of the US government.

Racism is not pandemic in America. America is not a racist country. Like every country, city, and community in the world, America has some racist citizens. They are a sharply dwindling minority, and their presence does not make the country racist. The country is not lawless because we have people who are.

America elected a Black president in 2008 and re-elected him four years later. That would not have happened in a racist country. The earnings of black college graduates in the US now equals the earnings of White college graduates. That would not have happened in a racist country. As the late, great Black economist and political commentator, Walt Williams, pointed out, if the earnings of African Americans in America were added and treated as a GDP, Black America would rank among the world's twenty wealthiest nations. That would not have happened in a racist country.[135] As Williams also noted, the world's mightiest military once was headed by a Black general, Colin Powell; Black Americans are among the world's most famous people; and some of them are among the world's wealthiest people. [136] None of that would or could have happened in a racist country.

The examples could go on endlessly. That is not the point. It is impossible to identify any country, race, or culture that does not include a least some individuals who are racist, including Black Americans. That certainly is not a defense of racism, which all thoughtful people reject unconditionally.[137] But the notion that it somehow is possible to eliminate all bias, intolerance, and prejudice from a world made up of imperfect beings, and not doing so makes an entire country racist, is an impossibly narrow and groundless perspective.

I understand some will disagree with everything I just said. For them, everything that happens in this country necessarily is racist because they have declared racism to be "systemic and structural." In the previous chapter, I addressed how the terms "racist" and "bigot" have been redefined and inflated to serve a Progressive agenda that depends heavily on racial and ethnic distrust, hatred, and envy. I know of nothing that carries a greater stigma than being branded a "racist" or "bigot," and the indiscriminate and promiscuous use of the words has become a powerful tool for silencing critics and stifling public discussion and debate. There is no need to respond to the racist views of bigots; they can be dismissed without rejoinder. "Racist" and "bigot" have acquired such malleable and boundless meanings, it no longer is even possible to question the propriety of their use. And if racism is structural, it cannot be eradicated unless the system itself is dismantled and reconstructed. *Workers of the World, Unite!*

Perhaps if recent generations had been better educated, it would be easier for them to understand how they are being misled. I do not think many have even paused to consider the distortions which have occurred to terms like "racist" or "bigot" or what that means for the viability of legitimate public discourse and racial assimilation. It is an appeal to ignorance directed to audiences cheated of perspective by years of listening to poisonous liturgies from radicalized teachers and professors who blame the United States for everything wrong in the world. Once stripped of pride in the country, the under-educated are easy marks for the race merchants, Marxists, and other worshippers of collectivism.

No one seriously questions that racism can take many different forms, personal, institutional, and cultural,[138] or that it can be latent. These are compelling societal issues that unquestionably must continue to be addressed. My point is different. Terms like racism are being distorted to create an irrebuttable presumption of racism in all things at all times and to attribute all adversities facing African Americans to a single cause: racism. It means when a Black person is shot by a police officer, for example, the reason must be police brutality directed against Black Americans, racism if you will. No other explanation is possible. There is no need to try to understand facts or circumstances. Since the reason for the shooting is indisputable, the rage is justifiably immediate.

George Floyd's death, and the widespread protests, looting, and riots in reaction to it, of course, are what make this discussion particularly pertinent. I am a powerful advocate for the presumption of innocence and will allow the legal process to run its course, but from the evidence publicly available, what happened to George Floyd is difficult to understand. We expect such brutality from gang violence or terrorism, but we do not expect it from our police, those charged with keeping us safe, all of us, regardless of race, gender, age or circumstances.

I will say this, however. The "knee to the neck" maneuver used on George Floyd is an authorized defensive tactic for police trying to subdue unruly suspects. It is considered "non-lethal." Evidence gathered since Mr. Floyd's death also suggests he likely was under the influence of drugs, resisted arrest, and may have died from causes unrelated to the method police used to control him. None of that means the police acted appropriately, but it does illustrate the importance of allowing the legal process time to provide an accurate and complete record of what happened.

Since George Floyd's death many prominent athletes, both professional and amateur, have joined the protests, calling for social and racial justice. As I mention elsewhere in this book, when dealing with celebrities, it always is difficult to separate the sincere from the hypocritical. Most did not attain their positions because of special insight, knowledge, or understanding, and strengthening or protecting their "brand" is just as likely to be the motivation for engaging controversial issues as anything else. Nevertheless, various sports writers have taken to praising athletes for using their "platforms" to advance racial and social justice, or for their "courage" in "taking a stand." Meanwhile, some of these "heroes" crank out shirts, caps, and other merchandise featuring logos playing off George Floyd's death and sell them to the public at a significant profit, as does The Black Lives Matter store. To be fair, some athletes made generous donations to various Black causes. I credit them far more than the rent-seekers looking to exploit what rapidly became a national crisis.

I fail to see, however, the "courage" in joining a movement already underway and popular among your peers and many others in the country. Where were these intrepid Paladins before George Floyd's death? Where were they when Colin Kaepernick claimed to be protesting the same issues? Where were they when China cracked down on the NBA after Daryl Morey, general manager of the Houston Rockets, sent a tweet supporting the Hong Kong protestors in October 2019?[139] You remember the story. Some of the most prominent NBA stars were openly critical of Morey despite the obvious "right and wrong" implications of China's suppression of demonstrators in Hong Kong, apparently more concerned with their endorsement and sponsorship deals in mainland China than the civil rights of Hong Kong's citizens. Since that time, China has increased its stranglehold over the rights of people living in Hong Kong, which by treaty between China and Britain was supposed to remain autonomous until 2047.[140] The NBA and its stars have remained mum.

Some will maintain that Floyd's death was simply the "last straw," that after the deaths of Tamir Rice, John Crawford III, Ahmaud Arbery, and others, enough was enough. Perhaps, but a majority of the athletes who spoke up following Floyd's death did so only well after protestors were in the streets and Americans of all races were recoiling in shock from the videos of George Floyd's final minutes. If it was the "last straw," it took time for many of them to realize it.

How much more confident would we be in the motivations of the athletes who reacted if they had shown the courage and judgment also to denounce the random destruction and violence taking place during the "protests?" How about at least a mild rebuke to Hawk Newsome, one of the founders of the Black Lives Matter movement, for his statement that if the country did not give them what they wanted, "then we will burn down this system and replace it."[141] Show us, in other words, that as athletes and citizens they are more concerned with protecting lives than jumping on the bandwagon to protect their "franchise." Show us their convictions run just as deep when it might cost them money and popularity. For truly courageous athletes, think Billie Jean King and Muhammed Ali, who did not pause to test public opinion before taking stances or supporting causes that were unpopular with most of America at the time.

I do not know what Black Lives Matter represents. Many consider it a terrorist organization, responsible for the deaths of police officers in Dallas, Texas, and elsewhere. Others accept the organization's claims that its intent is simply to encourage peaceful protests against police brutality toward Black Americans. If the movement's founders and spokespersons have communicated any peaceful messages, however, I missed them. And as I heard Glenn Beck say in a recent show, if you did not know what the KKK was, and it started to advertise a program to promote local food banks for the poor, surely you would look into who and what you were dealing with before signing up. No matter how laudable the program might be, it's still the Klan, still toxic, and still a group you would not want to support. I doubt many have tried to look behind the curtain of Black Lives Matter to see what is there, including the dozens of prominent corporations that have donated hundreds of millions of dollars to the organization.

Think about it. An organization whose leaders promise to "burn down" America and replace it with something more to their liking, receiving hundreds of millions of dollars from companies and individuals across the country. Even though it is anything but clear what BLM "wants" or what it stands for, corporate America is pouring enormous amounts of money into its coffers with no idea where the money is going or how it will be spent. Will it be used to kill cops? Destroy cultural artifacts and monuments? Burn our cities? Arm rebels to bring revolution and terror to our streets? Does anyone care? As with most "movements, only a few things are certain: the organizers and "leaders" will get rich; there will be no incentive to improve anything, just the opposite; and the public will feel better, at least for a time, because "something" has been done, no matter the eventual consequences.

If anyone spent a moment to look behind the curtain of Black Lives Matter, they might begin to understand just how far afield the movement has led them on the issue of police brutality. Like racism, police brutality is not pandemic in the United States.[142] Far from it. Missing from the furor over George Floyd's tragic death is the reflection that needs to take place when a tragedy like this occurs. There are thousands of interactions daily in this country between police and private citizens and at least 50 to 60 million encounters a year.[143] One researcher places the number of yearly civilian/police contacts many times higher than that.[144] Whites are more likely to have encounters with the police than either Blacks or Hispanics.[145] Almost all such contacts, Black, Brown, or White, are non-confrontational and civil. When violence occurs, the actions taken by the police almost always are justified and reasonable. In only the smallest fraction of incidents do things go wrong. Police departments, like every other organization in the world, are not perfect, but the number of Whites killed by police every year far outnumbers the number of Blacks, nearly double, and many from both groups are killed by Black police officers.

Despite those numbers, advocates argue that Black Americans are killed *disproportionately* by police. They rely on population figures to support their claims, but population figures alone cannot be used as the sole or even primary determinant when evaluating whether race-based disparities exist in police/civilian encounters. As one group of prominent researchers found, the violent crime rate and racial demographics of an area are far better predictors of the race of persons likely to be killed in an encounter with police:

Many people ask whether black or white citizens are more likely to be shot and why. If you live in a county that has a lot of white people committing crimes, white people are more likely to be shot. If you live in a county that has a lot of black people committing crimes, black people are more likely to be shot.[146]

A significant number of studies support these conclusions.[147] So does common sense. These researchers made another important finding completely at odds with the current Progressive and Black Lives Matter narrative: White officers are no more likely to shoot minority civilians than non-White officers.[148] Not surprisingly, in most cases of fatal shootings involving police the individuals killed were armed and had opened fire on officers *before* the police responded.[149]

When a White person is killed by police, no one blames racism even when the officer is Black. When a Black person is killed by police, racism is presumed even if the officer is Black. Why? Police officers are human, with all the frailties that implies. They sometimes are fearful, make mistakes, or get angry. Emotions, particularly fear, can have deadly consequences. When a police encounter results in the death of an unarmed civilian, rarely are the motivations unambiguous.

At this juncture, someone almost surely will say, "you have no idea what you are talking about. You are White, not Black, and you cannot possibly understand how people of color are treated by police."

I certainly do not pretend to fully understand the Black experience in America, but I can look to thoughtful Black commentators like Thomas Sowell, Walt Williams, and Robert Woodson for very different and more insightful views of that experience than those provided by Black Lives Matter. All three of these men are careful scholars who have spent their careers observing, studying, writing about, and trying to improve the Black condition in America and reversing the damage progressive policies have done to Black Americans. I trust their opinions and perspectives far more than the impassioned views of an organized protest movement dependent for its funding and existence on generating the widest possible civil unrest. Dr. Ben Carson is another Black conservative, a medical doctor turned politician and political analyst, who lends reason and context to Black issues. There are many others. For those looking for balance and perspective, you should read and listen to what they have to say.

The true intolerance of the Black Lives Matter movement is shown in its savage opposition to the simple reminder, endorsed by most Americans, including many Black Americans, that, in reality, all lives matter or should matter. Organizations interested in healing racial divides and creating racial justice should be concerned with the lives of all Americans, not just Black Americans. However, when Grant Napear, play-by-play announcer for the Sacramento Kings of the NBA for more than thirty years, responded to an inquiry about his thoughts on the Black Lives Matter movement, by tweeting, "All Lives Matter ... Every Single One," he was fired. One would think that if Napear was a racist someone would have figured it out over the last thirty years or so, particularly since he worked with mainly Black NBA stars. No matter. A single statement deemed contrary to the Black Lives Matter movement, and he was out. The "cancel culture" at work. Anyone who questions the movement's legitimacy and goals must be immediately and brutely disciplined so that the message is crystal clear: speech is anything but "free" if it is intended to challenge something Black Lives Matter says or represents.

Essentially the same thing happened to Mike Gundy, head football coach for Oklahoma State University. His sin? He wore a t-shirt displaying the logo of *One America News Network*. It is a cable channel that had been critical of the Black Lives Matter movement; it also had been mentioned by President Trump. Gundy was forced to apologize. It remains to be seen whether or not he will retain his job.

Whatever happened to the First Amendment? Why is it difficult for people to understand the role freedom of speech has played in securing the liberties they enjoy? What if our government attempted to ban all speech promoting Black Lives Matter? Obviously, it would violate the Constitution. Once that concept is mastered, it should be easy enough to grasp the fact that the same principles apply to someone speaking critically of Black Lives Matter. That, after all, is simply the other side of the coin. There cannot be discussion or debate if only one side is allowed to speak or express a point of view. No matter how vehemently two protagonists may disagree or how confident each may be in their position, it usually is helpful to recall the admonition of Judge Learned Hand: *"The spirit of liberty is the spirit which is not too sure that it is right."*[150]

Unfortunately, it is a "bridge too far" for many. The dots don't align. The synapses and neurotransmitters are too few. They fall into simple traps like, "there is no value in hate speech," without realizing that what constitutes hate speech, prohibited speech of any manner, for that matter, will be defined by those in charge. When those whose views you share are in power that may be palatable, less so when they are not and the harsh realities of living under a regime with the power and will to imprison you or worse for political differences become more evident.

Many do not even understand why the phrase "All Lives Matter" is considered racist. After all, what lives do not matter? Remember, however, *racism* is now an accreted term, subjective, unrelated to either conscious thought or intention. At a basic level, "All Lives Matter" implies criticism of the "Black Lives Matter" movement. That is considered racist. No one is permitted to criticize or question Black Lives Matter. Others object because they believe the phrase suggests racial "dismissal and denial." Some believe it implies all lives are equally at risk, and they disagree. For still others, it detracts from the notion that *systemic* racism permeates everything we do. Our society, in other words, is structured in such a way that it favors and puts White people in better positions to succeed than Black people, something that has persisted since the country's founding, never mind that we have had a two-term Black president, there have been thousands of elected, Black public officials in the country,[151] and hundreds of Black mayors run or have run most of our major cities, including New York, Los Angeles, Philadelphia, Atlanta, New Orleans, and Washington, DC.[152]

All of these interpretations of which lives matter are points that deserve discussion and debate. But that is what they are—positions to be defended on the merits if they can be, not imposed subjectively or by the fiat of a militant political movement and then protected by the harsh censorship of those who legitimately question them.

"Structural" or "systemic" racism" is key to understanding how race is being misused by extremists in their efforts to bring down the United States government. Few Americans even know what it means. Seldom is it explained. Yet to those more inclined toward revolution than democracy, it sounds plausible. For many years, however, thinkers like Thomas Sowell and the late Walt Williams, and more recently, Coleman

Hughes, have made compelling cases that "structural racism" is not a significant factor in denying life opportunities to Black Americans. William Julius Williams, the famed Harvard Black sociologist, reached the same conclusion in *1978*.[153]

It does not matter what is true. If you are a movement committed to completely changing American society, culture, and government, structural racism is a point far too valuable to give up, even if untrue. It, in fact, is your point. If the structure of America is racist, then the structure needs not just to be changed, but to be torn down, reorganized, and reconstructed as directed by Black Lives Matter and the mob in the street. To give you an idea of what that means in the minds of those trying to destroy America from within, the following came from the course materials for a workshop being presented by the Grassroots Policy Project and the People's Action Institute:

The key points we will emphasize in this workbook are:

1. Racism is dynamic and ever-changing. The critical aspect of racism that we must address today is the accumulation and incorporation of long-standing racialized practices into all of our social and economic structures.

2. Structural racialization is a system of social structures that produces and reproduces cumulative, durable, race-based inequalities.

3. Racialized outcomes do not require racist actors. Focusing on individual instances of racism can have the effect of diverting our attention from the structural changes that are required in order to achieve racial justice.

4. Organizers need to explicitly and implicitly challenge all manifestations of racism and racialization in our work and in our organizations.[154]

Racism is "dynamic,' 'ever-changing," essentially a moving target? "Racialized outcomes do not require racist actors?" It's all "structural?" We cannot escape racism because racism is inherent in the system? The only solution is to tear the country apart and start over?

In what image we are supposed to rebuild? Socialism, to be sure, but which manifestation? North Korea? Cuba? Russia? Venezuela? Amazingly stupid.

Or is it? Think about it for a moment. If racism is dynamic, constantly evolving, no "remedies" ever can be enough. No matter what is done, more needs to be done. The race merchants gain a perpetual "seat at the table."

As always, the "devil is in the details." Paragraph 3 of the Peoples Action Institute's workbook refers to "racial justice." What does that actually mean? Who defines it and on what basis? Who decides when it has been achieved?

The key for Progressives is controlling the dialogue by getting out front and defining the issues, in this case, "racial justice,"" in specific, rigid ways. Susceptible individuals are recruited and indoctrinated to think about the subject only in the thetic manner determined by proponents of the issue. Anyone who questions the validity of the perspective, or offers alternative viewpoints, is quickly silenced by charges of "racism" and "bigotry." The advocacy group grows by recruiting the "useful idiots" needed to spread the message, and the group becomes the sole arbiter of everything that will be considered necessary for "racial justice" to improve. The media joins the fray and adopts the group's "vision" without thought or introspection. No one questions the validity, truth, or fairness of how "racial justice" is being defined or how unchecked its parameters may be. The group's definition has become a cause to be protected with the same level of ignorance, intolerance, and fanaticism displayed by the Nazis in building and protecting the Third Reich. Whatever happens, there never will be a concession that racial justice has been achieved, or even that progress has been made, because doing so would diminish the power and standing of the group advocating for it.

The parameter of "racial justice," in other words, are unknown and unknowable, and unquestionably will evolve regardless of current "understandings." Consequently, it seems fair to ask: What countries or governments in history do Progressives view as race-neutral; and how is race neutrality even possible in a world where the parameters of "racial justice," as well as "racism and bigotry," continuously expand, bound only by the limits of the imaginations of their proponents?

The obvious follow-on question is, "Must we kill all the people we determine to be racists to have a society and culture free of racism?" How would it work otherwise? Is there a way to create a society free of racism if those considered racists are allowed to remain in the population? Perhaps internment in "re-education" camps for those suspected of racism would work. But if racism can occur without conscious intent and not only is "subjective," but also "structural," does everyone who may have *benefitted* from a racist system require re-education or possibly more? Generally speaking, second chances are not offered to those accused of racism in the Progressives' cancel culture world, at least not conservatives. It's "one and done, once a racist, always a racist." How can a re-education program possibly be reconciled with that understanding?

I urge you to read in its entirety this cultural platform of the Peoples Action Institute, which calls for actions that would put to shame Mao Zedong's cultural revolution in China. Mao wiped out any remnants of capitalism and traditional Chines culture to impose the groupthink that came to be known as "Maoism." The Peoples Action Institute is advocating the same thing for America—wipe out capitalism and destroy any vestige of existing American culture, which is irredeemably corrupted by racism and bigotry. Mao's cultural revolution was a political, societal, and economic disaster for China. The cultural revolution called for by the Peoples Action Institute would be the same for America. Here is an example of just one, and not nearly the most radical, of the exercises contained in the course materials for this troublesome workshop:

Activity: Community-Based Economics 45 minutes

Imagine that our communities collectively controlled serious amounts of capital. What could we do with it? How would we make sure that our collective resources are being used to target and address long-standing racial disparities in our society, around housing, access to loans, quality education, neighborhood development, etc.? Now, think of a big headline that we would like to see in the news 10 years from now, one that reflects the kinds of changes we are fighting for. **What will that headline say?**

All of this should be terrifying to thinking Americans, Black, White, Brown, or otherwise. Groups like this, and there are many of them, are organized, well-funded, and committed to turning America into a regimented, jackbooted, collective regime with "them" in charge. There will be no racial justice, no social justice, no justice of any kind, just arbitrary rule by a collection of radicals dedicated to a new order in America to be determined by them. For those of you who think your "cause" will be vindicated under a Progressive regime, but life otherwise will continue more or less as you know it, think again. Nothing of the sort is planned. If Progressives gain control, the country, and you, will be defenseless, bankrupt, and in complete social and cultural upheaval in very short order.

None of this has anything to do with racism, bigotry, or racial justice. Race is simply the stalking horse. It is the easiest way to lure young Americans into a fight they do not understand and convince them to make choices they do not realize they are making. The goal is revolution, to take down American democracy and turn the country to socialism. Once in power, very little would be heard about racism, bigotry, or racial justice from the Progressives in charge. Those are not the goals.

Derek Chauvin, the Minneapolis police officer who drove his knee into George Floyd's neck as he laid handcuffed, on the ground, while three fellow officers looked on, had at least eighteen prior complaints against him for various forms of misconduct during his nineteen years on the police force. While only two of those complaints resulted in disciplinary action of any kind, a complaint a year against an individual police officer seems unusually high. However, he also was recognized for valor on more than one occasion. I do not know how many of the complaints against him involved people of color.

Derek Chauvin may be deeply racist. I do not know. He may be a bully. Again, I do not know. In our lifetimes, most of us have encountered cops with bad attitudes, bullies, no different than those found in most organizations. Based on the actions that resulted in Chauvin receiving two medals for valor, both of which involved live shooters and considerable risk-taking on his part, he also may be a "Dirty Harry" wannabe, showing off for recruits newly assigned to him. He could be all of the above. Based on the number of complaints against him, however, it seems fair to question why he still was on the Minneapolis police force on May 25, 2020.

Police unions likely are the answer. Just as public education could be improved quickly if the powers of teachers' unions were limited, so too would the level of policing in the United States improve if the powers of police unions were reformed to allow police departments to discipline and eliminate bad cops. Unions have been protected by the Democratic Party for decades—the Party relies heavily on unions for both dollars and votes—and it will resist any effort to reform any union, teachers and police unions included. Until reform happens, however, it will remain nearly impossible to purge bad teachers and rogue cops from the systems.

Having said that, I also recognize how difficult those decisions can be. Effective policing requires men and women who have a deep desire to serve their communities, but also possess the level of mental agility and judgment, integrity, communication and negotiating skills, compassion, and empathy needed to execute a very sensitive position. It also requires individuals who are tough, aggressive, and emotionally stable. Training is designed to instill the discipline that makes it all work in the volatile, dynamic, and dangerous circumstances in which police officers frequently find themselves. Sometimes, unfortunately, it is not enough.

Two of the other officers charged in Floyd's death were new to the police force, with only a few days of service as police officers. One of them was Black, something the media did not report widely.[155] Chauvin was their "training" officer. The third officer in the group was an Asian minority with approximately eight-years-experience.

Police brutality at any level is unacceptable. But police work in a brutal and violent world. Few of us can understand, much less appreciate, what it would be like to work in a profession where even a routine traffic stop can cost you your life, and where "normal" often means interacting with the angry, the psychotic, the seriously mentally disturbed, as well as the naturally violent and those dangerously amped-up on drugs. Responding to crime scenes and other violent situations, terrorism, natural disasters, accidents, and a host of other circumstances all carry the potential for exposing officers to murderous attacks, contagious and infectious diseases, and chemical and biological hazards. Life-and-death decisions sometimes have to be made in an instant and in circumstances where a police officer fears for his or her safety. There is an epidemic of suicides among police officers for a reason.[156]

None of that, of course, justifies police brutality or racial bias on police forces. When either is uncovered, it should be dealt with quickly and forcefully. There is no place in policing for those who abuse the trust placed in them. But we depend on the police to maintain civil order, and it is completely nonsensical to call for the defunding of police forces or doing away with police entirely, as mayors across the country are mindlessly suggesting. The Progressive anarchists among us know the result would be vigilantes and roving gangs controlling the streets of America, as the young and dumb who have been duped into following the lead of these fanatics cower in their homes, wondering what happened to the country and the security, rights, and liberties they once took for granted. Simply because there are a few bad cops does not change the fact that every day hundreds of thousands of good cops, committed police officers and public servants, willingly put their lives on the line so the rest of us can live in safety and freedom, regardless of race, gender, age, or circumstances. I wonder how many of those protesting George Floyd's death even paused to reflect on how different their situations would be in China, North Korea, Russia, Cuba, or other socialist states?

So, what are the facts? Is there a "pandemic" of police violence sweeping America?

As it turns out, the number of civilians killed by police was many times higher forty years ago than today.[157] As reported by the Dolan Consulting Group, a respected law enforcement training and research organization, today "[t]he risk of death from a doctor or nurse is 254 times greater than the risk of death from police use of force."[158] While the compilation, analysis, and publication of this type of data usually lags its collection by two years or more, it is estimated that over 250,000 Americans die annually from errors made by doctors and nurses. [159] Every year in the United States more than 16,000 people are murdered.[160] Another 40,000 commit suicide.[161] Nearly 35,000 die in traffic accidents, [162] almost 40,000 from accidental poisonings,[163] and over 30,000 in falls.[164] The average number of deaths each year from the use of force by police for the ten-years, 2003 through 2012, was 429.[165] Of the 990 individuals the *Washington Post* estimated were killed by police in 2015, only 248 were African Americans.[166] *Six thousand, seven hundred and eight-nine* African American men were murdered in 2014, most of them by other African American males.[167] Why is Black Lives Matter so unconcerned with the far more lethal problem of Black on Black violence?

To put this in some perspective, in data collected by the FBI, 48,315 assaults against law enforcement officers occurred in 2014 alone. Twenty-eight percent of those assaulted, 13,654 officers, were injured badly enough to require medical treatment.[168] Nearly 2,000 of the assaults involved a firearm, while "cutting instruments" or other dangerous weapons were used in just under 8,000 additional attacks. All told, police officers were attacked with deadly weapons almost 10,000 times in 2014[169] but responded with lethal force in only a tiny fraction of the incidents. The FBI data also clearly understates the actual number of attacks on officers, as only 66 percent of the police forces in the country provided data. The Dolan Consulting Group projected the actual number of deadly assaults on officers in 2014, exclusive of instances when "personal weapons," fists and feet, were used to beat officers, as 14,703 or approximately forty a day.[170] It concluded:

> These (citizen) deaths occurred in only 0.0003% of all police-citizen contacts, only 0.009% of all arrest situations, and in only 2.1% of assault on officer situations. Deaths from police use of force are very unfortunate, often unavoidable, and extremely rare.[171]

Are police targeting people of color disproportionately? The Dolan report found no evidence to support that claim. Analyzing data on the race of individuals who murdered police officers from 2013–2015, for example, 33 percent were African American men, 19 percent were White with Spanish surnames, and 5.9 percent were identified as Asian, Pacific Islander, or Native American/Eskimo. [172] When juxtaposed against population figures and the number of African Americans killed by police, it was determined that African American men were five times more likely to kill a police officer than other races or genders, but only 3.7 times more likely to be killed by police.[173] African American men, in other words, were killed by police significantly less often than their violence toward police suggested they might have been.

We do not speak of "pandemics" when thousands of African Americans die as a result of criminal homicides at the hands of other African Americans or when tens of thousands of Americans die because of errors made by medical professionals. Why not? As pointed out by the Dolan Group, one difference arises from the fact that we expect the police to protect us, not kill us. We are shocked, understandably so, when those we trust fail us. But isn't the same also true of doctors, nurses, and other professionals? Why do we treat their mistakes differently than those made by a police officer? And why isn't Black Lives Matter concerned when Black men kill each other at rates nearly thirty times greater than those who die in encounters with police?

The answer is simple enough. Perceptions of police brutality and bias toward Black Americans have been *politicized and weaponized*. A *moral panic* has been created as those trying to take over the streets of America plot to weaken law enforcement in this country. The absence of police makes insurrection easier.

Much of the violence that broke out in American cities following Floyd's death was not spontaneous. Most of it was planned well before Floyd died, intended not to protest his death, but to usher in a "long hot summer of unrest," similar to the race riots of 1967, and aimed at destabilizing American cities, amplifying the economic harm caused by the COVID-19 pandemic, and putting police forces on the defensive. The head of New York City's Commission for Intelligence and Counter-Terrorism, John Miller, for example, described coordinated and preplanned networks of scouts; stand-by medics and lawyers; sources for bail money; inventories of rocks, bottles, and accelerants; stockpiles of communications equipment with encryption capabilities; and large numbers of out-of-state "protestors" imported to turn peaceful protests into violent encounters between police and civilians.[174] And whether part of the initial planning or not, extremist groups, domestic and international, moved quickly to capitalize on Floyd's death by initiating campaigns advocating for worldwide attacks on police.

Think about it for a moment. If anarchists so easily can spark violent national riots over a single incident involving four officers from a single police force in a single American city, as terrible as that incident may have been, how far can we be from a complete breakdown of social and civil order? Black Americans die disproportionately at the hands of other Black Americans every night in cities like Chicago without a murmur of protest against the Progressive mayors and city councils in charge, many of whom are Black. Police kill twice as many White suspects as Black without even a shrug of the nation's figurative shoulders. But narratives of systemic bias and brutality directed against African Americans, supposedly infecting every one of the nation's police forces, have enabled anarchists to conscript enough from the ranks of the ingenuous to provide cover for their plans to bring insurgency to the streets of America.

Debasing and weakening police forces around the nation is key to that strategy. If the police can be defunded, or even intimidated into inactivity, then the anarchists, Marxists, socialists, and other Progressives will control our streets and cities. Perhaps nothing has put the damage caused by the dumbing down of our education systems more plainly on display than the willingness of so many to seriously consider such profoundly idiotic "solutions" to "police brutality" as defunding or doing away with police forces entirely. Everyone who thinks that is a good idea, try to visualize just for a moment what you would do when the mob shows up outside your house to loot, burn, and deface, and there is no one to call or respond.

Is anyone truly naïve enough to believe that if the police simply disbanded tomorrow this somehow would be a safer, fairer nation where "the wolf shall dwell with the lamb and the leopard shall lie down with the young goat?"[175] If so, their thinking is at least as muddled as the confused economics of socialism described by Lawrence Reed in the quote included in Chapter 1, page 22, of this book. The more apt biblical reference would be, "lambs to the slaughter,"[176] as those looting, burning, and destroying neighborhoods and cities, supposedly to protest racial injustice and police brutality, turned their lawlessness against the innocents who have been misled into believing the rioting has something to do with racial injustice or police brutality. The organizers of these protests are not concerned with either. Their goal is to manipulate public opinion and foment civil unrest in support of a political movement whose goal is the overthrow of the government of the United States.

Getting rid of police forces, or hampering police forces by underfunding them, will make it infinitely easier to turn the streets of America into the violent battlegrounds the anarchists covet. It will happen quickly if the Progressive mayors in charge of many of our cities carry through with their threats to cripple police forces. When people like Minneapolis City Council President Lisa Bender respond to questions about what people should do if their homes are broken into and no police are available to respond to a 911 call by dismissively stating that, "Calling 911 comes from a place of privilege," it becomes difficult not to conclude that the inmates already are in control of the asylum.

Has anyone ever looked at the list of services a typical city police department provides to its constituents? It includes emergency response teams; security and crowd control patrols; child-abuse units; crisis intervention crews; crisis-response squads; air-support groups; SWAT troops; rapid response forces; and many other specialty responders. Few public events of any consequence could happen in any city or town without police assistance. Doing away with police also would exacerbate many of the economic disparities Progressives supposedly oppose. Those who could afford to hire private security guards would do so. Everyone else would be on their own. Americans would re-arm at unprecedented rates. There would be no choice.

Consider what it would look like. People will not stand by while their homes are burned and their property is stolen. Armed vigilante groups will form to patrol and protect neighborhoods and communities. Who will mayors and governors call to restore order—social workers and counselors? The national guard or military regulars would have to be called in. We effectively would be in a civil war, which is exactly what the anarchists want.

There are nearly 18,000 police agencies in the United States employing approximately 800,000 officers at an average annual salary of less than $54,000. Why pretend a cohort that large, for jobs that dangerous, and salaries that modest, will not contain at least some who may be racist, others who are incompetent, and a few who are just bad actors? What organizations of any size anywhere in the world are made up only of "perfect" human beings? The objective should be to weed out the bad cops as quickly as possible, not to punish the vast majority of officers serving honorably and on whom we depend to maintain order and safeguard our lives and property.

To carry the lunacy a step further, shortly after George Floyd died, the school district in Portland, Oregon, announced that it intends to withdraw police officers from public schools.[177] That seems like a sensible approach—let's make the schools "soft targets." Because four police officers who had nothing to do with the city of Portland, its schools, or the state of Oregon did something reprehensible somewhere else, let's punish the officers in Portland and make ours schools and city less safe.

The genius behind this decision, Superintendent Guadalupe Guerrero, apparently plans to compensate for the lack of police protection by increasing spending for social workers, counselors, and "culturally specific support" for students.[178] Brilliant. Good luck. Once again, underprivileged kids attending inner-city schools will be placed in harm's way and have their learning environment disrupted by disorderly students no longer constrained by a police presence. Teacher safety also will be jeopardized. Several other cities are clamoring for the same inane policy to be adopted in their school districts.

Do we have any thinking people left in the country? Have these pretentious worshipers of wokeness forgotten why police were in their schools in the first place? Safety concerns aside, do they not understand the benefits to police/community relations that arise when children and teenagers have positive relationships with the officers in their schools? Are they unable to recognize the importance of the role models police officers represent to many students? Are they incapable of acknowledging that information from uniformed police officers about drugs, alcohol, driving, and a host of similar social issues is likely to resonate with and be more practical, useful, and impactful to students than the hyperbolic jargon of social workers and counselors?

What message are these people are trying to send anyway? That all cops are "bad" and to be avoided by people of color? That it's okay to condemn an entire category of people for the sins of a few? That the rule of the mob is a better alternative than the rule of law?

This comes full circle to something I have written about often in this book. The race merchants, including the greatest race-agitator of them all, former President Obama, really do not want race issues in this country to be improved. For some, it is a matter of maintaining their power, position, and relevancy. For others, like the former President, it is about the revolution, the "cause." If Obama wanted to broker better race relations, he certainly retains the standing and influence to do so. As a first step, he could stop using the divisive rhetoric he commonly employs when addressing the nation about race. Recognizing the good work police forces around the country are doing and the fact that an overwhelming percentage of officers work diligently to keep every American safe would be a constructive next step. He would have to be honest about the fact that even the best of organizations, including police forces and the government he once headed, sometimes will have individuals who fail to live up to the high trust placed in them, but that alone does not taint the entire organization. He could help communities understand that among the millions of encounters that take place between uniformed police officers and the public every year, most are nonconfrontational, and instances of unjustified police shootings, while never acceptable, are rare. He could remind people of all the good deeds and acts of kindness police officers across the country engage in every day. He could teach the importance of due process and calm, and condemn violence as an appropriate public response on those occasions when police and others fail us. And he could help people realize that the hundreds of thousands of officers doing their job ethically, responsibly, and faithfully every day are not their enemies and are not responsible for the transgressions of a few.

Unfortunately, the former President has never shown any inclination to promote tolerance and understanding among the races or, quite frankly, any ability to provide this level of leadership. It also would require him to surrender the disdain he so obviously holds for significant segments of the American public. The Progressive mayors and governors, more interested in moral grandstanding and symbolic gesturing than serious dialogue, obviously lack the desire, and in some cases the intelligence, to be effective problem-solvers. If they were more competent and serious thinkers, planners, and administrators, the cities and states they run would not be failing in so many ways or such large numbers. It is not easy to get things done when power and public adulation become more important goals than accomplishment.[179]

It nevertheless remains a message that needs to be heard and understood, regardless of how delivered. The alternatives are too dire, the outcomes too calamitous, to think any other way.

CHAPTER 8

ILLUSIONS OF TRUTH

I read an interesting editorial not that long ago. It was before COVID-19. The essence was that the key issue in the 2020 elections would be health care because the vast majority of Americans are pessimistic about health care and have low expectations about the health care they receive relative to what they pay for it.[180] The editorial was based on an article by Sam Baker entitled, "Editorial: The American health care crisis," published on the informational website Axios in April 2019[181] The most revealing part of the report was the fact that while almost two-thirds of Americans say the health care system works well for their households, most believe it does not work well for most other Americans.

That is a startling disconnect between what Americans experience and their media-driven perceptions about the experiences of others. Most Americans like their health care and their doctors but have been deceived into believing other Americans are receiving inadequate health care at prices no one can afford. They have been misled, in other words, into accepting as true something inconsistent with their own experiences. In the process, they have become easy targets for those trying to socialize not just medicine, but the country as well.

Part of the problem, of course, lies with the twenty-four-hour cable news cycle. With many hours of "fill" programming needed each day, news stories get repeated, analyzed, dissected, and speculated upon endlessly. As with all things, repeated often enough, even the inconsequential can begin to feel meaningful. Said often enough by enough people, the "illusory truth effect" begins to take over.[182] Hitler recognized the value of the technique early on, writing in *Mein Kampf* that "slogans should be persistently repeated until the very last person has come to grasp the idea."[183] It is called brainwashing.

The underlying principles are easy enough to understand. As psychology has shown, the more *familiar* something sounds, the more likely it is to be believed, even by someone who has actual knowledge that it is untrue.[184] And while actual knowledge ultimately may outweigh familiarity in influencing whether or not a particular individual will believe something they know not to be true,[185] that is precisely why Progressives are so much more comfortable when college students are studying subjects like "gender equality in Hollywood films of the 1930s" or "cultural identity" rather than history, civics, and political science. The illusions are easier to create and perpetuate when the audience has no idea whether the information is true or not.

Social media, of course, is another significant part of the equation. Uninformed people propagating misinformation to burgeoning collections of credulous audiences make material almost instantly familiar. The "bandwagon effect"—doing something primarily because others are doing it regardless of your own beliefs and values—then takes over.[186] As Bertrand Russell wrote: "Collective fear stimulates herd instinct, and tends to produce ferocity toward those who are not regarded as members of the herd."

This powerful element of the bandwagon effect explains much of what is happening in this country. People forego their own beliefs in deference to a perceived collective "intelligence" regarding things with which they have no experience and know little about:

> A precondition of bandwagon effects is that persons accept an aggregate phenomenon beyond the realm of their personal experience, which therefore cannot be directly observed, as a point of reference for their own attitude and preference formation and thereby reify it as a social fact. Individuals' impressions of opinion or preference distributions in anonymous collectives can originate from several sources. The most basic background is simple rationalization or projection by attributing broad societal support to one's own position. This "looking-glass effect" may easily lead to distorted perceptions of mass opinion known as "false consensus" or "pluralistic ignorance."[187]

"Fake news" and unreliable data can play outsized roles in the formation of those perceptions:

> The main sources of information on opinion and preference distributions among the citizenry at large are the mass media (Mutz, 1998). Published findings from public opinion polls are the most important type of mediated mass feedback, although not the only one.[188]

*****

> As reporting on public opinion is a multifaceted phenomenon, the quality of the information on which citizens base their impressions is critically relevant. For systematic reasons it is often rather

questionable. The media's interest in quick publications of high news value tends to be at odds with the methodological requirements of careful survey research. In many countries there have been elections where the polls went utterly wrong. Moreover, media audiences usually lack the capability to distinguish between sources of valid information, such as well-conducted polls, and sources of dubious credibility. Parties' and candidates' campaign communications may contribute to further blurring citizens' picture of public opinion. These actors intuitively believe in the power of the bandwagon effect and try to capitalize on it during election campaigns by seeking to appear highly popular.[189]

People also clearly are predisposed to believe what they want to believe.[190] There are several physiological and psychological reasons for this, but at their core is the premise that *beliefs* often define *identities*, and if changing beliefs means changing identities and potentially alienating those with whom you share an identity, it may be impossible to do. When the need to validate identity makes facts "subjective, and malleable—a means to an ideological end—people end up living in a "self-created reality" from which there may be no escape.[191]

Elsewhere in this book, I write about how Progressive voters tend to band together around single issues, not to resolve those issues, but as a substitute for the community these socially isolated individuals do not otherwise have. They become affinity groups and because resolving the issues that bind them would threaten continuation of the group and the "passions" they share, they have no desire or incentive to make the accommodations necessary to improve anything they supposedly care about. Their "issue" substitutes for family, community, and country, and they have no goals, aspirations, or loyalties beyond it. They transfer all of their time, effort, and commitment to protecting and defending the "issue" and have little concern with anything else; certainly not the broader interests of the country as a whole. The country, in fact, often becomes the "enemy," particularly when their "issue" is not supported either by the law or a majority of voters. Their need for acceptance by the "sisterhood" or "brotherhood" that has formed around the "issue" and taken them in leaves no room for perspective, balance, accommodations, or trade-offs. Their loyalty is to the "issue" and other supporters of the "issue" on whom they depend for recognition and confirmation, not to country.

So, are we at a point where too many in the country are so uninformed about so much, they have no choice except to "follow the herd," are locked into believing only what supports their self-created realities, even when they know them to be untrue, and are unwilling to consider facts or circumstances that challenge the false narratives of their make-believe worlds? Is the country under the control, in other words, of those Robert Samuelson calls "economic entrepreneurs?"[192] Sadly, we appear to be.

Economic entrepreneurs prosper by selling new "political policies" to the public with economic or other benefits accruing to the entrepreneurs. They take much the same tack as moral entrepreneurs mentioned in the chapter entitled, "*Guns.*" A problem supposedly affecting a "national interest" is identified, publicized, and debated by the intellectual class, who then formulate their preferred "solutions." Both the problems and the solutions will reflect a particular mind-set or political bias. As in the case of the moral entrepreneurs, the goal is to manipulate and shape public perceptions and understandings in specific ways.

It is not difficult to influence the public perceptions of individuals too uninformed to do anything other than "follow the herd." More dangerously, when the uninformed and under-informed begin to outnumber everyone else, herd instincts become more compelling influences than either facts or truth. If you recall my analogy in the earlier chapter entitled *Robert Mueller* to the herd of Angus cattle threatened by predators, facts and truth are the predators the Progressive herd is intent on keeping away from those who have been propagandized into make-believe worlds.

What we are witnessing is more than normal political divisiveness. We have had political divisiveness in the past. My earlier comparison of the treatment accorded Presidents Lincoln and Trump, for example, certainly is not the first or only time we have had polarizing presidents. Thomas Jefferson absorbed his share of vilification, as did James Buchanan, Andrew Johnson, Warren G. Harding, and many others. But this is different. Third-world, revolutionary tactics have been introduced into the United States as Progressive have taken over the Democratic Party; infiltrated our top intelligence and law enforcement agencies; annexed the news media; brainwashed legions of gullible students through educational systems they have monopolized and weakened; rejected a peaceful transition of power and attempted to oust a lawfully elected president from office; encouraged violence against political enemies; and combined with the news media, social media, and others to suppress free speech and intimidate those who oppose them. Some of these forces have been underway for decades; others are more recent and opportunistic.

The success they have enjoyed should not be surprising. Never before have our educations systems been so radicalized and ineffective. Never before have the communication means existed that are available today for manipulating and dividing large populations. Never before has the level of wealth existed that today allows race merchants to foment large scale class envy. Never before has there been such a lack of understanding of our form of government and what makes it fairer, more just, and better able to protect the liberties and opportunities of Americans than any other. Never before has there been such a lack of appreciation for the economic miracles America's market-based economy has produced for so many, the millions around the world it has fed, or the suffering it has relieved. Never before has American exceptionalism been so undervalued and misunderstood. Never before have so many Americans been so willing to exchange their freedoms and liberties for government support. Religion, once a bedrock of American democracy, ideals, and values is under siege, the faithful accused of intolerance and worse for beliefs that have guided ethical and moral thought for centuries.

In the past, shared ideals, goals, and aspirations overcame differences in languages and cultures in a country of immigrants. There was a collective sense of the common good. No longer. Today, Americans are pitted against each other in what is claimed to be a zero-sum game in which some win, but many lose.

It seems only a short time ago that John F. Kennedy admonished the American people to "Ask not what your country can do for you; ask what you can do for your country." Today's Progressives are interested only in what they can do to change the country and President Kennedy's call to service on behalf of a country they barely acknowledge and no longer care about must seem like a quaint artifact from a very distant past if they even know who John Kennedy was. Their loyalties are to causes, and for most of them, causes they know little about other than what they have been told by those in line to benefit.

Where is all of this taking us? If Progressives retain control of our government, it means a weakened and devastated America. It means Americans will surrender freedoms and rights many barely understand and obviously do not appreciate. It means America's economy will contract and, with it, the economies of the world. It means America will become unrecognizable to the legitimate refugees and immigrants who flock to this country seeking freedoms and economic opportunities. It means the American military will be depleted and the defenseless democracies of Western Europe, which depend on our military to protect them, will face external threats they have no way to defend. It means the newly emerged, but equally defenseless democracies of Eastern Europe, which fought and sacrificed to break the bonds of socialism, will return to autocratic rule. It means the arts, the sciences, and all that lends substance and meaning to the world will fade over time into the gray backdrop of socialism, as always happens under "collective" governments. It means shortages of food, medicine, housing, clothing, and everything we today take for granted. It means the environment will languish because those who will be in control, assuming they even care, will not have the resources to address environmental issues. It means humankind once again will have proven its inability to sustain and nurture democracy, that it lacks the intellect, commitment, discipline, energy, and courage needed to defend liberty, and that for too many subjugation is preferable to the sacrifices and hard work required to live in freedom. It means the United States, the world's greatest force for good, no longer will lead the world, and all the world, including Americans, on a scale that cannot yet be imagined, will live in dramatically reduced circumstances; poverty, suffering, and misery are the only "fruits" that ever flower under socialism. It means no "white knights" will come to the rescue because there will be none capable of doing so. It means no second chances because history teaches that superpowers that fail never return to that status again. It means the bad guys will win, and the world will become a safer place for oligarchs, tyrants, and dictators because, as Edmund Burke observed, "The only thing necessary for the triumph of evil is for good men to do nothing."

If that sounds overly dramatic and aggrandized, consider how quickly and easily socialism destroyed Venezuela, once the richest country in South America. With the Green New Deal projecting the planet's demise within twelve years if dramatic steps are not taken immediately, there is no reason to believe that Progressives, having gained control of our government, will do anything but move quickly to take control of the economy and dramatically alter the course of American history. Aggressive attempts to implement the Green New Deal would have a nearly instantaneous impact, particularly if linked with confiscatory tax increases and other wealth transfers to try to fund its nearly $100 trillion projected cost. Some Progressives are suggesting income taxes of 70 percent or more in addition to a stiff value-added tax. Confiscating and redistributing assets through a "wealth tax" is also proposed.[193]

Do not confuse a "wealth tax" with an income tax. Progressives plan to tax your assets, all of them. It's an annual tax on your net wealth. If you have $1 million in net assets and the wealth tax is set at 15 percent, you would owe $150,000 annually in addition to the significant income taxes and other assessments you would be expected to pay. Most proponents are proposing the wealth tax only for the very rich at the moment, but like all taxes, that will change quickly as the government runs out of money to pay for universal health care, free higher education, student loan forgiveness, reparations, and the other reckless spending schemes Progressives propose.

George Will, among others, has described the "financial illiteracy" of Progressives and how quickly their spending proposals will bankrupt this country.[194] To make it even worse, many Progressives, Alexandria Ocasio-Cortez among them, are proponents of "Modern Monetary Theory," which postulates that governments can simply print as much money as they need to fund whatever they want to do.[195] How did that work for Venezuela?

One hundred trillion dollars is the estimated cost for the Green New Deal alone. We blanched at the initial $2.2 trillion relief package for COVID-19, and understandably so. The entire national debt is just over $23 trillion, and we struggle to find ways to deal with that. Progressives never seem to understand the crippling effects of tax increases, unless, of course, it suits their purposes. Listen to the promotion of "back to school" or other "tax holidays," which are widely promoted as reducing prices, incentivizing purchases, and, in general, providing a significant benefit to consumers, retailers, and the economy. The data supports those claims.[196] The same type of effect shows up when internet sales are tax-free.[197] When taxes are increased, however, there never is an acknowledgment that exactly the opposite effects occur.

There is only one certainty—now that they are in control, whatever scheme these economic simpletons settle on, will damage the country quickly.

Can this destructive path for the United States be reversed? Only if we come to our senses. Progressivism has to be recognized for what it is and stamped out. Education always has been and remains the key to democracy. Socialism and communism depend for their existence on the undereducated, the uninformed, and the resentful. Without creating class and race envy among the vulnerable, socialism and communism never take root.

It will take years to repair the damage done from decades of dumbing down our education systems; of pitting Americans against each other; of intentionally stirring class, gender, and race envies; and spreading divisive messages of "exploitation," "income inequality," "racial and social injustice," "White privilege," and the cacophony of other incendiary Progressive narratives.

It is far from certain that the damage can be reversed. Has a sense of complacency and entitlement permeated our society too deeply? Will those who have entrenched themselves in a make-believe world of resistance, revolution, rebellion, and commitment to "causes" ever understand enough to realize how far afield they have been led? Are too many people in our country so removed from the bitter sacrifices made by millions to establish and protect our way of life that we no longer understand what is required to maintain freedom and prosperity? Have we reached the point where the undereducated and uninformed, who have no understanding of the suffering and destruction socialism has caused throughout history, simply outnumber those who understand its ruinous nature? Are people too inattentive and unconcerned to realize why entire populations live in poverty and fear in places like Cuba, North Korea, Venezuela, Nicaragua, Russia, China, and significant parts of the African and Asian continents, while most Americans enjoy standards of living and levels of freedoms that are the envy of the world? Do we still have enough people with a basic understanding of how prosperity and wealth are generated to offset those susceptible to the deceptive promises of socialism?

I do not know the answers to these questions, but I have confidence in the exceptionalism of America and Americans. I believe the damage that has been done to our society and economy can be repaired if good men and women have the resolve and discipline to do it. It will require the rejection of identity politics, the herd mentality, the celebration of victimhood, and reliance on government. It will require rebuilding our educational systems. It will require that we reaffirm our commitment to market-based economics and meritocracy and make common-sense social and cultural accommodations. It will require secure borders, respect for the rule of law, and a return to times when Americans shared common goals, ideals, and values, and took pride in their country and what it stood for. It will require a willingness to engage forthrightly in civil debate genuinely intended to resolve the issues that divide us. It will require the reestablishment of an honest and unbiased news media. It will require a turn from single-issue politics to a recognition of the importance of country. It will require a lot of things.

Can it be done? Yes. Will it be done? What choice do we have?

CHAPTER 9
EDUCATION

From the early parts of this book, you have heard me refer to the importance of education to American democracy. The founders recognized very early that the complex federalist government they were forming, one built on three co-equal branches of government—yes, that's right Alexandria Ocasio-Cortez and Elizabeth Warren, it's *branches,* not chambers, and it's *three,* not two—each with distinct authorities designed to provide checks and balances on the powers of the others, could not sustain without an educated electorate. Education was necessary for a variety of reasons, including the creation of a meritocracy rather than an aristocracy of wealth, but more importantly to provide people with the knowledge necessary for sound decision-making concerning the government they would elect to represent them.[198]

Education was to be publicly funded, available to all, free from religion and ideology, and, at the college level, offer "classical knowledge:" modern languages; mathematics; natural philosophy, to include chemistry and agriculture; natural history; botany; civil history; and ethics.[199] The idea, as expressed by Thomas Jefferson, was:

> [t]o bring into action that mass of talents which lies buried in poverty in every country for want of the means of development, and thus give activity to a

mass of mind which in proportion to our population shall be the double or treble of what it is in most countries.

The founders struggled with leaving religion off the list of requirements for public higher-education, recognizing it as a "chasm" and "defect" in institutions professing to provide instruction in all "useful sciences," but ultimately were faithful to the separation of church and state principles of the Constitution. They instead suggested that the various religions establish their own "professorships" near universities so students could attend religious lectures while using the libraries and other facilities of the universities and colleges.[200]

In significant measure, this great vision for higher education has been turned on its head as Progressives have worked hard to steadily turn institutions of higher education from centers of learning where young minds are exposed to the wisdom of the ages and are challenged and developed through the free and robust exchange of competing ideas and opinions, into social clubs for adolescents. "Amenities"—dining venues, activities centers, health clubs, and swimming pools—have all become more important on campuses than libraries, classrooms, teaching, and learning.[201]

In earlier times, colleges and universities were true "crucibles of learning." Expectations of students were high and the experience rigorous—it could be unforgiving. Today, students show up on college campuses with "comfort animals" and medical folders, and the first visit for many is not with a classmate or roommate, but to a college counselor of some description. Helicopter parents hover protectively over them throughout their college days, making phone calls to school administrators and professors on their behalf and sometimes even to prospective employers. Rather than preserving and transmitting knowledge across generations, the goal of many institutions appears to be a "reset" of history, restarting it from the 1960s, as if nothing that came before possibly could be important or relevant. No longer a defender of meritocracy, too much of higher education today is devoted to studies of essentially contentless subjects designed to promote political agendas, not learning. As the American Council of Trustees and Alumni (ACTA) puts it:

> [C]olleges and universities continue to offer unstructured and chaotic curricula, causing students to sort through a plethora of course options in the name of "choice" and "self-discovery." General education requirements are saturated with academic jargon that focuses more on vague learning outcomes than on the specific courses and topics that students need. As a result, students are left even more confused as to what they are supposed to learn. We find that hundreds of colleges, large and small, prestigious and not, require far less of their students than they should. During this rapidly changing period of history, American higher education overall does not adequately hold itself responsible for the intellectual and professional development of American citizens and America's workforce.[202]

There still are, of course, many institutions trying hard to educate students the right way and doing a very good job of it, just not nearly enough of them. Take a look at the assessment of the core curriculums of hundreds of colleges and universities in the United States by ACTA.[203] Core curriculum or "general education" courses are the portion of college study, usually taken in the first two years, that coordinates and connects all other fields of study a student may encounter. These are the courses that cultivate logic, critical thinking, writing and communication skills, mathematics, and the other foundational learnings without which a college education becomes little more than a siloed mish-mash of disparate facts and information.

The core curriculum also provides the reservoir of information even the brightest students need to draw upon as reference points as they consider and analyze information. One of the many false premises of education in America today is the notion that students do not need to learn or memorize information because they can simply look it up on computers, tablets, or cell phones. That profoundly misguided belief completely overlooks the reality that without sufficient background information, a "cache" of knowledge, if you will, students are unlikely to know what questions to ask, much less what information to look up. It also becomes impossible for people to see or understand connections between seemingly independent data points. "Connecting the dots," even on a limited scale, requires a certain threshold of acquired and retained knowledge. The more extensive that knowledge, the more insightful and perceptive thought processes can be.

As a former Dean of Harvard College described the role of the core curriculum in higher education:

> At its best, general education is about the unity of knowledge, not about distributed knowledge. Not about spreading courses around, but about making connections between different ideas. Not about the freedom to combine random ingredients, but about joining an ancient lineage of the learned and wise. And it has a goal, too: producing an enlightened, self-reliant citizenry, pluralistic and diverse but united by democratic values.

Harry R. Lewis
Former Dean, Harvard College[204]

That is a role of education frequently not understood in today's world. Without a certain level of shared and connected information, it is difficult to share values, democratic or otherwise.

To illustrate, can anyone truly understand gun-control issues in the United States without knowing how central the right to bear arms was to the founding of America? Were you aware, for example, that British gun-control efforts in 1774 started the American Revolution, turning what was a situation of political tension into a shooting war?[205] The colonists believed strongly in the inherent right of an armed self-defense to protect the liberties they considered inalienable and to resist tyranny, whether manifested as an individual criminal or a criminal government.[206] The British knew they never could control America without disarming America. The colonists understood they never could allow themselves to be disarmed without ceding their rights and liberties to the British military.

It is one of the important lessons of history that has been lost in the current gun debate. The fact the Second Amendment derives from notions of the inherent right of an *armed* self-defense, whether against armies *or individuals,* lends a perspective to gun rights that often is ignored. It may not change the minds of gun-control zealots, but unquestionably it is knowledge those interested in an informed and responsible debate need to know. It connects a lot of dots. Unfortunately, many gun-control advocates are not interested in connecting the dots. At one level, they are afraid of guns and simply want them gone. At another, like the British, they understand that to control America, they need to disarm America.

The lack of stored knowledge explains, at least in part, the outsized influence social media has on so many. Without the information needed to put into context and analyze the diffuse claims flooding the internet, the uninformed are easy to confuse and convince. If you do not know the history of socialism and communism, it becomes easier to buy into the delusional "milk, honey, and fairness" claims of their proponents. If you have not studied American history and understand what a force for good America has represented in the world, you are far more susceptible to claims that America is the "Great Satan," the "Evil Empire," and responsible for virtually everything that afflicts humanity. To take the point a step further, one of the common criticisms of the currently popular STEM educational format—a focus on science, technology, engineering, and mathematics—is that it creates narrow technocrats, mechanically proficient but lacking the necessary "soft skills" needed to think logically or critically, communicate well, and lead ethically.

At least STEM education can provide technical proficiency. Many courses of study in American colleges and universities today offer almost no useful content. Puppet art; nannying; diving business and technology; bowling industry management and technology; auctioneering; cannabis cultivation; comedy; sexuality; popular culture; jazz studies; gender studies; costume technology; eco-gastronomy; packaging; comic art; bagpiping; and adventure education are among the degree programs offered at some of our institutions of higher learning. These programs typically are made up of courses not designed to tax the intellect or upset the relaxed atmosphere of the college experience. For many years, for example, it somehow slipped the attention of the administration at the University of North Carolina's Department of Afro-American Studies that most of its courses were "paper" or "independent study" classes, effectively without professors or any academic requirements and with grades oftentimes awarded out of sympathy to students viewed as less than the "best and the brightest."[207]

And therein lies the rub. Later in this chapter, I provide the appalling statistics Walt Williams cites about the "unreadiness" of most high school graduates for college, but we continue to insist that every high school graduate is college material. That may be the single most misguided premise ever articulated for higher education, and it has given rise to at least two calamitous setbacks.

First, it has caused a systematic "dumbing down"—a reduction in academic rigor—of the educational programs at too many colleges and universities. Once an institution accepts a student, it takes on a moral and ethical obligation to provide that student with a legitimate chance of graduating within a reasonable time. There are different ways this can be done, but the easiest and most obvious choice for many institutions is simply to reduce academic rigor.

Second, it has prevented the development of robust, post-secondary, technical and vocational schools similar to those that exist in much of Europe. If everyone is supposed to attend college, there is no need for alternative forms of advanced education.

It also has had another significant consequence—the rise of total college debt. I say "total" college debt because, despite the many misleading stories in the media, the average college debt per undergraduate student has risen more moderately since the 1970s than you may have been led to believe. What has risen steeply is "total student debt," largely because we insist everyone must go to college whether or not they have the desire or qualifications to do so.

The average debt for a four-year college graduate in 2018 was $28,650.[208] To provide some perspective, the average price of a new car in 2018 was $35,742,[209] and the average family income was $61,372 by year-end 2017.[210]

If we go back to 1970, the average borrowing by full-time students, both undergraduate and graduate, was $1,066.[211] The average price of a new car was $3,543,[212] and the median family income was $9,870.[213]

The increases between 1970 and 2018 were not insignificant, but over nearly fifty years perhaps not the kind of escalations you were expecting. Most of the very significant student debt burdens the media is fond of citing are incurred by students in professional schools in disciplines like law and medicine that also offer substantial earning potential.

The columnist Catherine Rampell provides some additional insights into student debt. Looking at students who first enrolled in college in 2003 and following them over the next six years, nearly half, 44 percent, had borrowed no money at all, while another 25 percent had borrowed less than $10,000. Only 2 percent of students had borrowed more than $50,000. Ms. Rampell also points out that approximately one-third of college debt is owed by people in the top income quartile, with only twelve percent of student debt borrowed by those in the bottom income quartile.[214] This may be one of the few times in history when a liberal has worried about the "rich" paying too much for something.

The media rarely distinguishes individual debt from total debt when discussing the "student debt crisis," but they are very different issues. In 1970, total student debt was $7.6 billion from approximately 7.2 million borrowers.[215] Today it is $1.5 *trillion* from 44 million borrowers.[216]

This enormous increase in total student debt is almost entirely attributable to forcing students onto an academic path by insisting everyone is college material, not providing robust, post-secondary, vocational or technical school alternatives, and offering abundant, cheap federal loans for education. For comparison purposes, total consumer debt in the United States, pre-coronavirus, was approximately $14 trillion. Credit card debt accounted for $1 trillion of the total, with auto loans ($1.2 trillion), home mortgages ($9.44 trillion), and student debt making up almost all of the remainder. Despite these kinds of statistics, while she was a candidate for president, Elizabeth Warren proposed making all four-year public colleges and universities free and forgiving up to $50,000 in college debt for everyone in households making up to $100,000 annually. Free education and forgiveness of student debt, not to mention free health care, remain popular proposals among Progressives.

Call it vote-buying, income redistribution, bribery, whatever, the incentive-crushing "free-stuff" just keeps flowing. Why not throw in a new car for every graduate and maybe forgive some credit card debt as well? Perhaps a government wage and paid summer vacation while in college should be considered.

Who can blame partially educated teenagers and uninformed parents for wanting their share of the swag? It is a basic law of economics that the cheaper the price of something, the more of it will be consumed. The costs of free education would be staggering. The impacts on higher education would be even greater. It would be very difficult to deny a "free" government benefit to anyone, regardless of their qualifications. Millions more would be enrolled in public universities. Many would not graduate, but academic rigor and standards would degrade even further as schools scrambled to maintain graduation rates and meet their "obligations" to students.

In the United States today only 34 percent of adults over twenty-five years old hold a degree from a four-year college or university.[217] Among current students, the six-year graduation rate from a four-year college or university varies from only 57.6 percent in public schools to 65.4 percent at private institutions.[218] The four-year graduation rates are considerably lower, only 33.3 percent for public universities and 52.8 percent for privates.[219] Since approximately 74 percent of students attend public colleges and universities, the lower graduation rates from these institutions swell the ranks of those who never graduate.[220]

In some states, the graduation rates are truly dismal, well below national averages. Arizona, for example, has a 26.3 percent, six-year graduation rate for its colleges and universities; Alaska, 26.4 percent; and Georgia, 42.6 percent.[221] The average for the fifteen states with the lowest weighted graduation rates is approximately 45 percent. The fact that the majority who graduate are taking longer than the traditional four years to do so also increases college debt significantly. Arguably, the quickest way to reduce college debt is simply to graduate on time.

Cheap federal dollars are another aspect of the "student debt crisis." The federal government has controlled the student loan program for years, first, as a "guarantor" of loans made by private lenders, later as a mix of direct loans from the government and government-guaranteed loans from private lenders, and finally, in 2010, a switchover to all "government direct" lending.[222] The bottom line: cheap federal loan dollars and claims that everyone is college material are sending a lot of students to institutions from which they will never graduate.

The fact private lenders have not been involved in the student loan program for nearly a decade was not something known to Maxine Waters, Chair of the House Financial Services Committee. During a hearing in April 2019, she tried to pin the blame for the student loan "crisis" on big banks and was visibly surprised to learn the federal government had been solely responsible for the student loan program since 2010.[223]

Like all public benefit programs, the government has little incentive to bring any discipline or standards to its lending practices. If the student loan program loses money, taxpayers bear the cost. If the government lends money to someone with no chance of graduating, taxpayers bear the cost. If it lends money to students taking frivolous course work or attending institutions of such low standing that a degree is essentially worthless, practically ensuring the students will not be able to repay their loans, taxpayers bear the loss.[224] Private lenders, who must show a profit if they want to stay in business, would exercise greater restraint and make more collectible loans.

However, Progressives love a good financial crisis. It gives them an excuse for government takeovers and government-based remedies. Taking control of education and eliminating private alternatives would allow Progressives to ensure our education systems produce only the technocrats needed to carry out the work needed by the state without producing graduates with the historical perspectives or critical thinking skills to challenge the Progressive's vision for a socialist America. Much of what is going on with higher education has less to do with education than social ordering, but get used to it. Unless and until Progressives stop using schools as sociological proving grounds, are willing to concede not everyone is college material or even interested in pursuing an academic path, and begin encouraging credible post-secondary vocational and technical schools to develop, billions of dollars will continue to be wasted amassing students in colleges and universities from which they are unlikely to graduate, taking contentless courses and majors which cannot provide them with either an education or a livelihood, and being proselyted with Progressive dogma.

Since it is unlikely that we will be able to interrupt the efforts by Progressives to diminish the credibility of our educational institutions or reduce the government's reckless waste of student loan dollars, the question arises: "Is there any way we can reduce the cost of a college education without making everything "free"?

You bet. In Germany, for example, higher education essentially consists of professors in classrooms teaching students who largely arrange and pay for their room, board, and sustenance. There are no frills—no co-curricular activities, no intercollegiate sports, few extracurricular activities of any sort. Just classrooms, professors, students—and learning. It is an inexpensive and effective way to deliver education, but it is not what the American public wants. People demand the full "college" experience for their sons and daughters with all that entails. They just would prefer not to pay for it or even acknowledge how much it cost to provide the bricks and mortar, services, opportunities, and entertainment options offered by modern American colleges and universities.

Online education is not the answer. There simply is no way to replicate the academic rigor of a serious college education part-time or online. Schools seeking "alternative revenue streams" promote online learning, and some of them have enjoyed tremendous financial success with it, but online programs cannot provide what is needed to create engaged, educated citizens able to communicate effectively and think critically and with the knowledge necessary for rational decision-making.

Stories are beginning to surface about college-qualified students increasingly turning their backs on colleges and universities because of the perceived high costs and what is seen as the reduced value of a college education. Several large companies also have announced they no longer will require a college degree as a prerequisite for employment, including Apple, Google, and IBM.[225]

I cannot say I am surprised. As too many of our colleges and universities continue to ratchet down academic rigor, the value of a college or university education diminishes as well. It is not something that can be hidden. Both students and employers soon begin to notice that a weaker higher education system produces undereducated, undertrained, and underqualified graduates. This is one of the reasons masters-level programs are becoming the new entry-level degree in many professions; master programs are likely to be the first time many students encounter legitimate college-level work. Adding an extra layer of education to get the training once offered by undergraduate programs may not be the smartest way to attack cost issues in education, but it at least provides Progressives with something else to eventually give away. However, if students truly are moving away from attending college because of the costs involved and a perceived loss of benefit, and if employers are becoming wary of hiring college graduates, both groups are misguided.

It would be a shame if students with the ability and inclination to attend college are discouraged from doing so. From a student's perspective, a college education remains a relative bargain—the debt a graduate incurs is likely to be less than the cost of the first car many of them will buy immediately upon graduation. Quality of education is a more serious concern for both students and employers. Students need to be selective in the institutions they choose and the programs they pursue—they should attend serious colleges and universities offering legitimate courses of study and sound core curricula. Never has the nation been more in need of a classically educated citizenry than today. Employers need to be just as selective and hire graduates who have completed demanding programs at institutions that remain committed to principled education.

Fortunately, there still are colleges and universities which take education seriously and not as an opportunity for social engineering or paternalistic "love-bombing." These institutions continue to provide educations that produce technically proficient graduates with the necessary knowledge and "soft skills"—critical thinking, writing, communications, ethics, leadership, self-awareness—to make them valuable, not just to employers, but also to their communities. Graduates of these schools will continue to be in demand as long as the schools remain committed to mission and maintain academic rigor and excellence. But the numbers are dwindling. The many schools that have made education secondary to other goals are the problem, but the solution is to fix the schools and demand accountability from college and university administrators and faculties, not to discount or dismiss the value of true education, a bulwark against tyranny over the ages.

I have made the point before but will make it again, just a bit differently. What Progressives would like to see are educational systems that produce a technically trained but under-educated "proletariat," lacking the knowledge to recognize the delusions of socialism but capable of doing the work demanded by the state. Progressives would be perfectly content to allow the abasement of higher education in America to continue, cramming increasing numbers of students into schools where they can be trained for state-approved work without fear they might be exposed to the disruptive lessons of history that would unmask the harsh legacies of collectivism generally and socialism specifically.

I also do not know what alternative training those disenchanted with higher education may be contemplating. We do not have developed vocational or technical post-secondary school systems in the United States. Most that profess to offer some type of vo-tech training are for-profit organizations of widely varying quality. The training received from companies providing internal training likewise varies in quality and transferability. And even "good" vo-tech and company training will not be focused on producing informed, engaged citizens; the goals, preparing people for specific jobs and developing defined, narrow skill sets, are considerably less ambitious. Students who have the interest and ability to succeed in a competent academic setting are far more likely to benefit in the workplace and develop as engaged citizens if they graduate from a college or university that offers a sound core curriculum and retains a good measure of academic rigor.

Bottom line: forfeiting the opportunity to attend college because of media-driven concerns about the costs or waning downstream value of a college education is unnecessarily self-limiting. For those who attend a college or university with a legitimate curriculum and respect for academic rigor, pursue a course of study that has substance, and graduate, their degrees will open life choices and opportunities other forms of education are unlikely to match.

The student total debt crisis is being fueled primarily by the many millions of new students who are told they need to go to college and are being incentivized to do so by cheap federal dollars. Large numbers of them borrow money but never obtain their degrees or pursue degrees that are not marketable, creating the worst of all possible circumstances. Graduates of college still earn considerably more over their working lives than noncollege graduates, but investing in their education generally pays only for those who graduate, assuming they study something of substance.[226] For those who leave school without a diploma or graduate with a degree that lacks integrity, student debt is just debt.

When unqualified students are admitted to a college or university, everyone loses. Most of the unqualified will drop out before attaining a degree, regardless of the accommodations made for them. That is one of the reasons the number of Americans with a degree from a four-year institution remains so low. The lessening of academic rigor that invariably accompanies the admission of unqualified students also reduces the value of the degrees of all students and alumni, regardless of race, color, gender, or creed, if not immediately, then over time. The biggest losers are the nation and democratic principles, which suits the Progressives' agenda perfectly. The young and dumb are easy to influence, and if Progressives can keep them undereducated and safely incubated among like-minded students until they are fully committed to the "cause" and dependent on the "herd," they will have created the marionettes needed to embrace and sustain socialism.

Understanding how our educational systems are being weakened also helps explain why imposing speech codes and eliminating conservative students, speakers, professors, and administrators from college campuses is so important to Progressives. It takes time to bring baby Progressives to full maturity. You would not want to expose them to any type of outside influences, particularly conservative viewpoints, while they are in "safe" surroundings, reciting their Progressive catechism. They may not be very well-educated, but some could retain a degree of common sense. Better to keep them sheltered from alternate worldviews until they are fully indoctrinated and safely in the fold.

The boycott of conservative voices on many college campuses is a national embarrassment. Can you imagine any circumstance where a conservative student could have attacked a Progressive student, like Hayden Williams, a conservative student activist, was assailed by a left-wing thug on the Berkeley campus, without the media calling for the stoning of the perpetrator, the expulsion of conservative "deplorables" from the country, and the impeachment of Donald Trump? The media would have exploded in frenzied rage if the roles had been reversed.

The same type of muted response from the media and Progressives occurred when Jussie Smollett faked a hate crime attack by MAGA supporters. There was some "muttering" among embarrassed Progressives to be sure, but where was the outrage? Progressives knew they had to "react," but when other Progressives are the targets of criticism, the backlash always is short-lived and restrained. Think Virginia Governor Ralph Northam's and Attorney General Mark Herring's blackface antics, or the sexual assault accusations against Lt. Governor Justin Fairfax. Whether on campus or elsewhere, the "hue and cry" dissipates quickly when Progressives are the ones on the wrong side of the issue.

Consider also the episode involving a Bernie Sanders campaign organizer. Asked what would happen if Donald Trump was reelected in 2020, he said: "f-ing cities burn... I mean, we don't have a lot of time left, we have to save f-ing human civilization."[227]

These people are hate-filled thugs, apparently with limited vocabularies, but they continue to get a free pass from the media. If a Trump staffer or campaign volunteer said anything remotely like these incendiary threats, no pun intended, it would have been national news for weeks. Congressional Progressives would have opened investigations and ordered the national guard to lock down Washington.

Why isn't faking a hate crime as objectionable as participating in a hate crime? Think about it. Is there anything more repulsive than a Black man faking what Black men have decried, and rightfully so, for years? What is the justification for unnecessarily occupying hundreds of hours of police time in a city where crime is rampant? What if Smollett's fake story had set off rioting in Chicago or retaliatory attacks on MAGA supporters, Black and White? Why is it acceptable to impugn half a nation that wants to "make America great again?" Why don't Progressives aggressively and genuinely condemn hatred and bigotry in their ranks when it is so plainly on display? The simple answer is, "They cannot and have no desire to do so anyway.

They cannot because when the "party" is nothing more than the "big tent" of single-issue advocates I have spoken about in other chapters, connected only by a shared commitment to "moral relativism," no person or group within the tent can be criticized. They have no desire to do so because when the big tent has been filled to a critical mass, as it has been, with revolutionaries, anarchists, Marxists, fanatics, radicals, extremists, malcontents, and other sociopaths and misfits, hate begins to supplant moral relativism as the unifying principle. The Democratic Party, controlled by Progressives, now is a party consumed by hatred, bitterness, and contempt for everyone and everything with which it disagrees. That hatred is so great Progressives, like the Bernie campaign worker quoted earlier, have begun to embrace the savagery of past heroes of collectivism, Hitler, Stalin, Mao Zedong, Castro, and the numerous others who slaughtered so many and represented such destructive forces in the world.

The rage has become so great Progressives no longer can hide it. It manifests in many different ways, from profanity-laced rants like those of the moronic campaign worker who believed the continuation of civilization depended on the election of Bernie Sanders, to incidents that reveal the true anti-American sentiment bubbling just below the surface among the Progressives' faithful, such as the claim that the slogan, "Make America Great Again," is a racist rallying cry for white nationalists fearful of becoming a minority in this country.

Why is that even a reasonable interpretation of "Make America Great Again," a phrase used by multiple American presidents, including Bill Clinton and Ronald Reagan? For eight years, the Obama administration weakened America, decimating its military, overseeing an exodus of industries and jobs, placating dangerous enemies, encouraging open borders and sanctuary cities, creating the most racially divided America since the Jim Crow era, and generally crippling America's reputation, prestige, and influence around the world. By 2016, "Make America Great Again" was an important national priority, given what had transpired under Obama. There was nothing racial about it, just a yearning to turn away from the failed policies of an incompetent president and administration.

That said, has there ever been a time in our history when the political party not in power did not believe mistakes by the party in power had damaged the "greatness" of the country in some respects? Isn't it nearly a reflexive reaction for presidential candidates to promise to "fix" things, to restore the greatness lost by the neglect of the president they hope to replace? Isn't it, in other words, typically *American* for presidential candidates trying to win the White House to promise voters a return to "greatness?"

The simple answer is, not to Progressives. They do not believe in America's greatness and define the country by only one event in its history—slavery. Even though the United States has freed millions from the slavery of Nazism, communism, socialism, and other malignant forms of progressivism, and has been the greatest force for good the world has ever known, Progressives are stuck on one chapter of a history crammed with unparalleled successes in every area of human endeavor. By whatever standards may be applied, however measured, never has any country accomplished more, or shared it more fairly and beneficently with humankind, than the United States. No one denies the significance of slavery or the need to continue to address its remaining repercussions. However, neither can anyone candidly deny the tremendous progress that has been made in doing just that, except Progressives. Their fixation on slavery appears to be born of necessity—given the massive good the United States has done around the world, it is not easy to come up with things legitimately to criticize. But it also reflects maleficence and an understanding that the easiest way to realize their voracious thirst for revolution is to foment divisiveness and discord among the races by insisting the effects of slavery continue in America, virtually unaddressed and unabated.

Responsible Black leaders, the late Walt Williams, Thomas Sowell, and Robert Woodson among them, know better and write about it often. Others, not yet ready to give up an issue which provides them with their source of power and authority, refuse to admit the obvious—that problems facing Black Americans today stem far more directly from policies, laws, and programs promoted by Progressives than any remaining after-effects of slavery, which ended nearly a century and a half ago.

I wonder how many Progressives understand the broader issues of slavery, know anything about its prevalence and history in other parts of the world, including Black-on-Black slavery, or understand that nearly 46 million people in 167 countries remain enslaved today, including China, India, Pakistan, Bangladesh, Cambodia, North Korea, and Uzbekistan?[228] Again, "connecting the dots" is important if you are trying to evaluate something rationally and in perspective, but Progressives, some of them uninformed and naïve, others intentionally and deceitfully oblivious to inconvenient facts, have no desire to engage in reasoned thought or fair debate.

Slavery aside, Progressives' obsession with keeping college students isolated from history and conservative viewpoints shows how acutely they understand the nonsense they are promoting cannot survive intellectual scrutiny. People confident in their position do not shy from defending it. But on what basis could you even begin to defend socialism? Every time I hear Bernie Sanders declare something Republicans are doing is "un-American," I am nauseated. What possibly could be more un-American than openly trying to make America a third-world s—hole nation by turning it to socialism? Bernie understands, unfortunately, an America too distracted, uncritical, and undereducated to realize socialism is the antithesis of American democracy will begin to feel it is "mainstream" if he and others say it often enough. The more familiar something sounds, the more likely it is to be believed, even by those who know it to be false. The chapter, "Illusions of Truth," provides the details.

I want to return to the second great harm done by the false message that everyone should go to college. This has nothing to do with intelligence, by the way. There are millions of highly intelligent, creative, and competent people who simply lack the motivation, inclination, or desire to go to college. Their passions lie elsewhere. Nevertheless, the notion everyone should go to college has stifled the development of a robust alternative track for post-secondary education in this country. In Europe, the opposite is true. In Germany, for example, students are divided into those college-bound and those technical-school-bound early in life. That determination may be made a bit too early, but at least there is the recognition that many very smart, capable people are not inclined or suited for study in a college or university setting even though they have gifts and skills that are just as important to develop as academic pursuits.

The technical schools in Germany are rigorous. It is not unusual for programs to be four years in duration, two and a half years of classroom work, and a year and a half of mixed classroom study and internships. They provide in-depth training in a wide variety of occupations, and in many instances provide courses in language, social studies, and other disciplines that provide some of the "soft" skills missing from the vo-tech programs that exist in this country. We have nothing like them in the United States. Much of our college debt "crisis" would go away if we did. More importantly, people would have options for how they train for their chosen professions.

I largely have focused on higher education in this discussion, but our educational crisis starts at much lower levels and with the teacher unions. We have many talented, dedicated men and women teaching in our primary and secondary schools. We also have many who are not, and the unions protect the incompetent. They cannot be replaced unless, perhaps, they say something politically incorrect or become Republicans.

Has there been any more disappointing group during the COVID-19 pandemic than teachers? In every state in the country, primary and secondary school teachers resisted returning to classrooms. However, they expected truck drivers, retail store clerks, workers in food processing plants, shelf-stockers—virtually every employee of any description needed to keep them "safe," entertained, and comfortable—to return to work. Teachers, in other words, counted on millions of others going to work to support them but were unwilling to do their part and teach the children of those who did. "Virtual" learning certainly was not an adequate substitute, starting with the fact that it was not available to everyone. Even when it was, many students, notably the very young, do not learn well "virtually," particularly in households where adult support and supervision is not available. In other situations, in inner-city schools, for example, if children did not go to school, many of them did not eat and others were isolated at home in abusive circumstances. With their children out of school, many parents, single mothers especially, were not able to work; child-care was too expensive or unavailable. The negative consequences for learning, social development, and potentially *life outcomes*, were enormous. Teachers did not care. It was shameful. Actually, it was more than shameful; it was elitist.

I am not being critical of teachers who found it necessary to stay at home because of circumstances that made in-person teaching particularly dangerous to themselves or others for whom they had direct care responsibilities. If you or someone you are caring for falls into a vulnerable group because of age, underlying health conditions, or other reasons, I get it. But that does not describe many of those who "protested" returning to the classroom. Some had political agendas; they wanted to hurt the President by adding to the chaos. Others may have been lazy, content to "game" the system and collect a check. I am sure a few genuinely believed they were helping contain the virus by staying home, although if they had "followed the science" even a little bit—something Progressives are fond of recommending, but seldom do—they would have realized primary and secondary schools had been open around the world for months without major incidents or problems. I do not pretend to know all the motivations, either good or bad, but all of us should be disappointed in what can only be described as an abdication of duty by so many of our teachers.

Then there were the teachers who did not even want to teach virtually; they were concerned that uninvited guests— parents, grandparents, older siblings, caretakers—might listen in on what was being taught. It speaks volumes about the quality of the "instruction" and the nature of the "messages" they are providing to students.

But I digress. Let me return to the discussion of the weakening of education in our primary and secondary school system over the last several decades.

School boards annually spend millions of dollars on bricks and mortar. States, regions, and localities perpetually lobby for tax increases to support education. State lotteries are approved on claims that what they extract from everyone who participates, but disproportionately from those who can least afford it, will be dedicated to education. Every candidate for political office promises to improve schools and education if elected. But no matter how many dollars we commit to education, the problems will not be cured until we replace the bad teachers with good ones and until a key cause of the educational crisis in America is addressed and resolved—the disintegration of the nuclear family.

How can anyone doubt that the breakdown of the nuclear family is among the significant root causes for so many in our nation being poorly educated? As someone who grew up in a household where education was valued and achievement in school encouraged and celebrated, I cannot even begin to imagine the problems facing a child in a household with one parent, or maybe none, and no one who respects education or has any interest in academic achievement, and often is not home or is too stoned, high, or drunk to provide support. Whatever else we try to do with education, or think we are doing, will have no effect until those problems are addressed and corrected.

As the late Walt Williams repeatedly pointed out, before the rise of the welfare state, started by FDR but brought to fruition by Lyndon Johnson, there were very few differences between the family structures of Blacks and Whites in America. Black Americans actually married and stayed together at higher rates than White Americans, and five of six Black children under the age of six lived with both parents. Today, more than 70 percent of Black households are headed by a woman.[229]

As Williams also pointed out, however, Black Americans have made the "greatest gains ...of any racial group in mankind's history."[230] Williams illustrated that proposition by noting something I mentioned earlier in this book: if the earnings of Black Americans were totaled and treated as the GDP of a separate nation, Black America would rank among the world's twenty richest nations. It is not a statistic you are likely to hear from the "fake news" media. Williams attributed that remarkable progress to the greatness of the nation in which it occurred and said flatly, "Nowhere else on the face of the Earth would such progress be possible except in the United States of America."[231]

Once again, this is not something the media wants you to hear; it interferes with the narrative of an "oppressive" and "unfair" America, where the rich stay rich and the poor forever remain poor, exploited by a system that is "racialized" and where racism and bigotry abound. Something else Progressives would prefer you not hear: the median earnings of Black college graduates now equal the earnings of their White counterparts.[232]

In his writings, Williams also addressed the 30 percent poverty rate among Black Americans but pointed out that poverty rates among Black, intact husband-and-wife families have been in the single digits for two decades, another statistic you never hear. A significant reason for the persistence of the 30 percent poverty rate among Blacks, according to Williams, is simple—government programs that reward inferiority and irresponsibility. As he put it, "When some people know that they can have children out of wedlock, drop out of school and refuse employment and suffer little consequence, one should not be surprised to see the growth of such behavior."[233]

There is an additional factor—political correctness that results in White America applying lower standards to Black students than other students.[234]—Progressive politics at its virulent best.

In other articles Williams sharply criticized the education of Black students in America today, calling it "grossly fraudulent." As proof, he pointed to the fact that most Black students graduate from high school with the equivalent of a sixth- or seventh-grade education, at best.[235] The situation is not much better for White high school graduates, with a majority testing "not ready" for college-level work.

Progressives have been radicalizing and "dumbing down" our educational systems since the 1960s. It is another fence that is being torn down. Progressives will have it no other way. When "educators" are claiming education itself is inherently discriminatory, when courses in science, technology, engineering, and mathematics are intentionally watered down to make them more attractive to women and minorities, and when diversity has become a more important goal than learning,[236] it should be plain for all to see that Progressives have turned education into an ideological weapon, nothing more:

> Donna Riley, a professor at Purdue University's School of Engineering Education, published an article in the most recent issue of the peer-reviewed Journal of Engineering Education, positing that academic rigor is a "dirty deed" that upholds "white male heterosexual privilege." Riley added that "scientific knowledge itself is gendered, raced, and colonizing."

* * * * *

> Sympathizing with Riley's vision is Rochelle Gutierrez, a math education professor at the University of Illinois at Urbana-Champaign. In her recent book, she says the ability to solve algebra and geometry problems perpetuates "unearned privilege" among Whites. Educators must be aware of the "politics that mathematics brings" in society. She thinks that "on many levels, mathematics itself operates as Whiteness." After all, she adds, "who gets credit for doing and developing mathematics, who is capable in mathematics, and who is seen as part of the mathematical community is generally viewed as White."[237]

Claiming education is "inherently discriminatory" may sound outlandishly stupid and unserious to some, but the people making these statements are not trying to create cocktail hour chit chat or bolster their Progressive credentials. Many are deeply committed Bolsheviks attempting to bring America down by destroying it from within. The goal is to control America, not educate it. It is something everyone needs to understand.

CHAPTER 10

DOMESTIC VIOLENCE

This chapter arises from the controversy surrounding the signing of linebacker Reuben Foster by the Washington Redskins, now the "Washington Football Team." He was signed after being waived by the San Francisco Forty-Niners following his arrest for domestic violence involving a girlfriend. The incident occurred at the Forty-Niners team hotel in Tampa, Florida, during a game weekend. Some of it was caught on videotape. Foster, a former University of Alabama star, has had a turbulent beginning to his NFL career, with several off-field legal problems, including an earlier domestic violence charge involving the same girlfriend. That charge was dismissed when the woman recanted her story.

The howls of indignation were immediate when Washington claimed Foster off waivers. Fans, other NFL teams, television broadcasters, analysts, and others all self-righteously condemned Washington's actions, even though Foster had been placed on the "commissioners exempt list," meaning he could not practice or play with the team pending completion of an investigation by the NFL. Keep in mind, over forty NFL players have been accused of domestic violence, many of them still playing in the League, several on rosters of teams that thought it outrageous Washington would try to give Foster what amounted to a second chance.

In part, the reaction to Washington's decision to sign Foster is another example of the utter disregard for the presumption of innocence and the rush to judgment that has become the dangerous "new normal" in America. Some will say, "but there was a videotape of this incident." And so there was, just as there are confessions, eyewitness testimonies, smoking-gun documents, and mountains of other incriminating evidence in many criminal cases that result in acquittals of the defendants. We do not suspend due process and the presumption of innocence no matter how compelling the evidence appears to be. Things are not always as they seem, and reams of evidence attest to the unsettling unreliability of many "eyewitnesses" accounts.

I have no idea why people are willing to ignore protections so vital to the preservation of their liberties and freedoms as due process and the presumption of innocence. False accusations followed by imprisonment or worse are tools that have been used by despots throughout the ages to eliminate enemies. Who among us would want the government to be able to confiscate our property and send us to prison on made-up charges we could not disprove? Yet, supporters of #MeToo and similar organizations now routinely demand the most-dire consequences for people *accused* of acts of domestic and sexual misconduct, whether or not there is a shred of corroborating evidence and regardless of circumstances.

The Bret Kavanaugh confirmation hearings were prime examples, some of the charges so vague and unsupported only the truly naïve or politically blinded even would have paused to consider them. The accusations against President Trump during the 2016 presidential campaign provide other examples. Several women appeared, made accusations allegedly stemming from decades earlier, and then quickly disappeared before their stories could be seriously questioned. In another chapter, I described how routinely apparitions like these, "provocateurs," I called them, materialize in support of Progressives' causes.

The same rules, of course, do not apply when Progressives are accused of sexual misconduct, the allegations by Tara Reade against Joe Biden being the most recent example.

This is another instance in which it is important to keep in mind the danger of labels. Domestic and sexual violence are terms that have different meanings for different people. For some, they may suggest extreme physical behavior. For others, no actual physical contact or harm is needed—words more than suffice. If every accusation of domestic or sexual violence, regardless of its nature, however, immediately calls for the same reaction, proven or not—disparagement, loss of position and livelihood, public shaming, and possibly criminal prose-cution—without any effort to distinguish the serious and real from the trivial or imagined, not only does fairness become an immediate casualty, but it also arms the unscrupulous with the means for discrediting anyone they wish.

This is the juncture where someone is sure to say, "there are no trivial acts of domestic violence." But how can that be? When do we ever assign the same penalties to behaviors with different degrees of culpability? Even in the criminal arena circumstances matter, and all sentencing guidelines provide different recommendations for punishment depending on the presence of mitigating or aggravating factors and the nature of the crime committed. Why should claims of domestic or sexual violence be treated differently?

Let me ask this: should it make a difference if the domestic partners involved in a dispute identify as gay, transgender or bisexual? If the partners, for example, are both gay men and one strikes the other in the heat of an argument, should the incident be treated differently than a heterosexual male striking a heterosexual woman? What if everyone involved is drunk, high, or on drugs? Should we be willing to consider the possibility of a "set-up," particularly when celebrities are involved? Does it surprise anyone that a physically fit, twenty-something-year-old playing a violent, professional sport, fueled by alcohol or other stimulants, and constantly surrounded by women willing to have a fling with a star, may be subject to charges of domestic or sexual violence that need to be sorted out? Even understanding that people have been conditioned to react predictably to the labels "domestic and sexual violence," shouldn't we want to know what happened, whether the conduct, if proven, is serious enough to justify the punishment we are considering? Or is everything and anything we label "domestic violence" deserving of the "death penalty?"

Athletic skills erode quickly and careers in the NFL are short. For many players, the NFL not only is their best opportunity for success and financial security, it may be their only opportunity. A life ban from football, or even a significant suspension, is little less than a variant of the "death penalty." If accusations alone are enough to justify the "death penalty" for professional athletes, why is Justin Fairfax still Lieutenant Governor of Virginia and Joe Biden the president of the United States? In what sense was it fair to ban Foster from playing football simply because he was *accused* of domestic violence?

Please keep in mind. I do not know Reuben Foster. He may be a complete thug, and he may be guilty, but that is not my point. My point is not even that due process and the presumption of innocence were ignored, although they were, unquestionably. No, my point goes a step further. Many in the "mob" calling for the Washington Football Team's scalp for taking a chance on Foster almost surely are equally ardent supporters of restoring the voting and other civil rights of convicted felons once their sentences have been served, releasing nonviolent felons, not imprisoning people for various types of criminal activities and, in general, providing convicted criminals, even the most violent, "second chances."

Where is the same sense of fairness for Foster? The criminally convicted all were provided due process and the presumption of innocence and were found guilty. Foster has had no chance to address the charges against him. We know none of the details, and the videotape certainly is not enough to show how the problem started, who was responsible, or whether there were mitigating circumstances any fair jury should take into account before imposing sanctions. What if the woman had pulled a gun, knife, or other weapon just before the videotape started, and Foster was disarming her?

Is this "virtue-signaling" at its very worse—let us show you what commendable people we are by demonstrating our utter revulsion for anyone even suspected of domestic violence—or is it a mindless response to stimuli imprinted in our brains by clever and powerful advocacy groups? The treatment of Tara Reade's accusations against Joe Biden suggests politics and hypocrisy are in control.

Whether the behavior is approval seeking or a conditioned response, the result is the same. We are perfectly willing to strip the accused of his constitutional rights and livelihood before we even know what happened. We are unwilling to accord due process, the presumption of innocence, or any other right routinely provided to even the most violent criminals. We are prepared to presume the accuser always is correct and truthful, the accused always a liar and guilty, and the facts inconsequential and unnecessary. We, the mob, become prosecutor, judge, and jury and mete out our particular brand of justice swiftly and without regard for fairness, the facts, or the truth. We do so with a clear conscience because the "cause" we have adopted, domestic violence, is more important than any other consideration.

It was the same logic Democrats used to protect Ted Kennedy after Chappaquiddick. However reprehensible and cowardly his behavior may have been, Kennedy was a champion of the Progressive movement and therefore to be defended and supported regardless of what he may have done.

Why isn't this type of rush to judgment considered racist? It certainly has a hugely disparate impact on Black athletes. All of the NFL figures in recent memory who have suffered suspensions from football for domestic violence are Black. Think Kareem Hunt and Ray Rice. The vast majority of the more than forty NFL players who have been accused of domestic violence are Black. Ironically, most of the accused are either still playing or played without being suspended until they retired, which makes the "outrage" against Washington for claiming Foster, who cannot practice or play with the team unless and until the NFL's investigation exonerates him, seem particularly conspicuous and disingenuous.

There is a postscript to this story. The NFL lifted the suspension of Reuben Foster in May 2019. He then suffered a season-ending knee injury during a Washington practice and has not played since. It is unclear when Foster may again take the field, if ever.

CHAPTER 11

CLIMATE CHANGE

I have no doubt the Earth is in a period of climate change. It has undergone massive climate changes throughout its 4.5-billion-year existence. Every time there are changes in activity on the sun, the Earth wobbles slightly on its axis, changes occur in the oceans because of tectonic plate dynamics, or hundreds of other natural events, some well-known and understood, others not, the Earth's climate changes, often in significant ways. Many of the most consequential changes in climate occurred tens of thousands of years before man inhabited the Earth and certainly tens of thousands of years before large-scale industrial development occurred.

Oceans have expanded and receded; at times oceans have been more than 100 feet higher than they are today. Mountains have appeared and disappeared. Greenland was once green. Thirty-five million years ago, Antarctica was tropical. There have been multiple "ice ages" in the Earth's history—they happen approximately every 100,000 years—sometimes enveloping the Earth completely and making it a giant snowball. Between glacier cycles, there inevitably are warming cycles, and some have heated the Earth's surface to temperatures much higher than today with almost no ice to be found anywhere on the planet. During the entirety of its existence, the dominant climate conditions on Earth have fluctuated between "greenhouse Earth" and "icehouse Earth."

The question never has been whether the Earth's climate is changing. It always has and always will. The question is one of causality and impact. What are man's contributions to the Earth's constantly changing environment? Can those contributions be changed in any meaningful way? And would changes in man's contributions, assuming any impact at all, materially affect the climate changes that are destined to occur naturally?

The major controversy today centers on global warming and the role of "greenhouse" gases, particularly man-made greenhouse gases, in temperature increases. The main suspect in the global-warming controversy is carbon dioxide (CO_2), a byproduct of burning carbon-based fossil fuels. To simplify a very complex subject, the basic theory is that greenhouse gases like CO_2 "trap" heat from the sun in the Earth's atmosphere. This keeps the lower portions of the atmosphere warmer than they otherwise would be, heating the Earth's surface.

Although you would not know it from the current environmental debates, concentrations of CO_2 gas in the Earth's past have been considerably higher than current levels as major volcanic eruptions dumped millions of tons of CO_2 gas into the Earth's atmosphere. They continue to do so today. However, during the year concentrations of CO_2 gas change as the Earth periodically reduces and then regains carbon dioxide—the Earth literally "breathes," expelling or retaining carbon dioxide in response to seasonal needs.[238]

Today, we are in an interglacial period. There have been many in the past 800,000 years, eleven to be exact. The current one is known as the Holocene Period and has lasted nearly 12,000 years. Based on a hypothesis proposed by Siberian astronomer, Milutin Milankovitch, three orbital characteristics of the Earth, which occur every 19,000 to 23,000 years, determine the amount of sunlight that reaches the Earth's surface and control the planet's cycling into and out of glacial and interglacial periods: its tilt; the changing shape of its orbit around the sun; and its "wobble."[239] In terms of geologic time, we are a few milli-seconds late entering the next anticipated glacial period, which some scientists attribute to the effects of increased carbon dioxide in the atmosphere, even though two of the three Milankovitch cycles have yet to occur.

It is not my intention to engage the science of climate change. I am neither a climate change scientist nor a climate change denier, but I take issue with how the climate debate muddles the naturally occurring effects on climate, which largely are beyond the control of mankind, with effects that may be caused by human activities and potentially could be mitigated.

We do not know what we do not know, and science in this area is so laden with politics, it is difficult to know what information can be trusted. However, I believe this to be true: climate will continue to change significantly from natural causes, as it always has. Mankind cannot alter those natural events in any significant ways, although there are "scientists" who maintain human industrial activities have "forced" the Earth out of its natural cycles. Perhaps, but the Earth in its history has been much warmer than it is today, with far more carbon dioxide in the atmosphere, without interrupting those cycles. Keep that in mind every time someone speculates that human activity is interrupting the natural cycles of the Earth.

As all good scientists know, correlation does not imply causation. Consequently, whatever discussions ensue about climate change need to be honest about the naturally occurring impacts on climate versus the effects of human activities. If natural events will cause the seas to rise 100 feet over the next century regardless of human activities, as history predicts is likely to happen, will the additional carbon dioxide burden imposed by human activity increase those levels by 1 foot, 5 feet, 100 feet, or not at all? Former President Obama, despite the Green New Deal's projection of environmental catastrophes within twelve years, including steeply rising oceans if dramatic steps are not taken immediately, does not seem overly concerned—he recently bought a $12 million waterside mansion on Martha's Vineyard.

What we should be asking is whether human activities will increase in any meaningful way the climate changes we know are destined to occur because of natural events regardless of what humankind does or does not do. If so, will changing human behaviors and activities mitigate those added effects in ways that will make a difference? Put only slightly differently, we need to admit that consequential changes in climate will occur, with or without contributions from us, and then try to separate the changes that might be preventable from those that are not, excepting an act of God. If the seas are destined to rise 100 feet over the next century because of natural events, for example, does it matter that human activities, if left unabated, would cause the seas to rise an additional foot or even five feet? At the moment, the public climate debate tends to be little more than breathless hysteria, a moral panic, if you will, attributing climate change to a single source—human activities.

Systematic measurements of atmospheric concentrations of carbon dioxide gas started in 1958 when concentrations were determined to be approximately 316 parts per million or .0316 percent of the Earth's atmosphere. Today, sixty-one years later, it is just over 400 parts per million or approximately .04 percent. One letter to the editor I recently read concerning climate change used the analogy of a sports stadium to put these measurements in perspective—if the Earth's atmosphere was a 10,000-seat sports stadium, carbon dioxide would occupy four seats.

Since greenhouse gases are a natural part of the atmosphere and are necessary for life to exist, the question is not whether greenhouse gases can be eliminated, but whether man-made emissions of greenhouse gases are "upsetting" the natural concentrations of carbon dioxide gases in ways that are adding dangerously to the Earth's surface temperatures. The follow-up question, of course, is, assuming man's contributions to global warming are materially increasing the effects of natural changes, is there any realistic way to eliminate or mitigate man's impact? The question actually needs to be a bit more inclusive: can man's contribution to climate change, if it exists, be altered in ways that would bring about beneficial changes to temperatures on Earth without wrecking world economies, destroying our military's ability to defend the country, and creating mass starvation and shortages of essential goods and services, including medicines? Can it be changed, in other words, without sending humankind back to the caves? It is the rarely discussed "other side of the coin" of climate politics.

One estimate I have heard is that if the United States were to disappear completely tomorrow, the net temperature effect on Earth would be 0.1 degrees. While perhaps not insignificant, if true, it means anything the United States does to control CO_2 emissions is unlikely to have the necessary effect on Earth's surface temperatures unless there are significant reductions elsewhere in the world.

China leads the world in CO_2 emissions by a substantial margin, and many other developing nations contribute measurably to the world's total. The United States accounts for less than 15 percent of the world's greenhouse gas emissions and has made substantial reductions in its CO_2 levels in the last decade as it shifts away from coal and toward cleaner fuels like natural gas. As carbon dioxide removal technologies continue to evolve, and they are developing rapidly, reductions in US-generated CO_2 discharges will continue to improve. The United States unquestionably will bring its CO_2 emissions under control, but to keep the issue alive and motivate the frenzy that most benefits them politically, Progressives cannot let that be understood.

Solar, wind, and other "clean," renewable energy sources continue to be developed, but the technologies are not yet capable of supplying enough energy to replace carbon-based fuels and are unlikely to be able to do so for years to come, if ever. While the costs of these alternative energy sources are falling, they also remain more expensive than fossil fuels and require the use of much larger land resources than traditional energy plants. Building and deploying more nuclear generators would accelerate significantly the process of reducing greenhouse gas emissions, but, unfathomably, environmentalists object to this zero-emissions energy source that offers significant benefits over the alternative energy alternatives they prefer.

The giant Three Gorges Dam hydroelectric facility in China illustrates some of the potential shortfalls of "natural" sources of energy. The Three Gorges Dam across the Yangtze River, the third-largest river in the world, was an ambitious project intended to produce a significant portion of China's electricity needs, control the frequent flooding of the Yangtze, and promote navigation and agriculture, among other goals. Built at a cost of approximately $24 billion, the dam flooded millions of acres of land, destroyed hundreds of villages and cities, and buried thousands of years of cultural artifacts under hundreds of feet of water. It also displaced nearly a million and a half people and created an environmental catastrophe, as entire ecosystems along the Yangtze's banks were forever changed. Incredibly, the shift of water mass by the dam was so great the shape of the Earth itself was altered—rounder in the middle, flatter at the poles—and the Earth's speed of rotation was fractionally decreased. No one ever discusses what effects altering the Earth's shape and rotational speed may have had on climate, and the project never has come close to producing the 10 percent or more of China's electricity needs it originally was intended to satisfy. It also has slowed the seasonal flooding of the Yangtze only marginally.

If advocates of man-made climate change were rational in their concerns, the answer to "clean" energy unquestionably would be nuclear energy, which produces zero carbon emissions. Disposal of spent nuclear fuel, the major objection to nuclear power, is being addressed by the development of so-called Gen IV reactors, which will be the safest, most stable, and powerful nuclear reactors ever designed. Capable of producing energy from existing nuclear waste, they also will produce fifty times the energy from the same amount of uranium as older reactors.[240] As the World Nuclear Association, an international collective of countries using nuclear energy, has said, this generation of nuclear reactors is a "clean, safe, and cost-efficient way of meeting increased energy demands on a sustainable basis, while being resistant to diversion of materials for weapons proliferation and secure from terrorist attacks."[241] Not only is nuclear power considerably cheaper than either solar or wind power, but it also is far more dependable, and building a nuclear plant requires only a fraction of the land needed for a solar or wind "farm." No emissions, cheaper, more dependable, less use of natural assets—so what's the problem?[242]

There is none except in the minds of environmentalists who purport to be in love with "natural" sources of energy, regardless of how expensive, impracticable, damaging to the environment, or destructive of the economy, and resist even considering alternatives, whether it be clean natural gas or nuclear energy.[243] Consider for a moment what the landscape of the United States would look like cluttered with windmills and solar panels. Take a drive in Western Europe today, and you will get a sense—windmills on mountains and shorelines, solar panels on the roofs of ancient buildings. It's a mess, and it is not working. Because solar and wind energy is not easily adaptable or scalable to large industrial economies, crippling brownouts and blackouts are the norms when countries try to depend on these alternative forms of energy production.[244] If you need examples, think California, which virtually every summer endures energy shortages, as it struggles to make alternative energy sources work.

It is impossible to talk about nuclear energy without addressing the most common objection of environmentalists, which I alluded to earlier—how do you safely dispose of spent nuclear fuel? The traditional answer has been to store it in specially designed underground facilities like Yucca Mountain, Nevada, and the Morris Operation in Illinois, but the Gen IV reactors, which are capable of reusing spent fuel and producing clean energy, seem likely to do away with this problem. On a more macro scale, however, why are environmentalists not equally concerned about the disposal of the billions of lithium-ion and other batteries used every day, the highly toxic slag produced by municipal "energy from waste" plants, or the hazardous residue from the disposal of spent solar panels and the hundreds of other components and materials needed for non-nuclear energy production? Why aren't they also more candid about the massive amounts of electricity it takes to manufacture and recharge batteries and produce the equipment needed for "natural" energy sources?

Is it possible Progressives are not being entirely candid about their actual concerns with nuclear energy? Stephen Moore of the Heritage Foundation[245] thinks so. He suggests the true agenda of the "Greens" may be far more ambitious and sinister than environmental or safety concerns—the real agenda may be to permanently reduce human populations and slow human growth and advancement to protect the "carrying" capacity of the Earth. And it makes sense when you consider that rejecting nuclear power—a cheap, clean, and more dependable energy source in favor of the two forms of energy, wind and solar, most likely to stifle industrial and economic expansion—is mystifying unless the goal is to shutter factories and reduce industrial capacity until we no longer are capable of sustaining even current populations.

If you are a true believer, regardless of how many people may starve, how many jobs may be lost, or what effects it may have on the nation's security, reducing humankind's footprint on the Earth by putting a brake on industrial development and capacity may sound like an ideal strategy. Similar to guns, the environment is almost a perfect subject for creating a "moral panic," and it provides the "duty, honor, country" passions missing for those who have been taught to hate their country and everything for which it stands. It is the inevitable outcome of the myopic vision of single-issue politics. Focus only on your "issue," refuse to consider or debate alternative approaches and solutions, attack all those outside your "herd" with ferocity, and continue to build the moral panic needed to prevent anyone from questioning the legitimacy of what you are doing.

As in all things, there is a "follow the money" element to energy and environmental policy. This is a zero-sum game, pitting traditional sources of carbon-based energy against developers of alternative energy forms with trillions of dollars at stake. And it is not just the energy producers who have a stake in the outcome of this showdown—everybody from academics applying for grants to researchers, suppliers of equipment, politicians, environmentalists, and hundreds of potential industry participants, regardless of which side they may be on, have "skin" in this very high-stakes venture. That means little can be taken at face value, although as with almost everything that occurs in this country today, people tend to accept and believe whatever fits the narrative they have accepted. Independent thought, reason, or rational analysis seldom is part of the equation.

Shortages of dependable, economical energy would have disastrous results for the economy, our national defense, and the health, safety, and welfare of every American. Abundant, inexpensive, and efficient energy is the lifeblood that has fueled the economic miracle that is the United States. Conversely, expensive energy has been a major economic obstacle in most other nations of the developed and developing world. Contrast the situations of the United States and Western Europe. Today, the United States is energy self-sufficient or nearly so. Western Europe is dependent on Russian gas and oil and must temper everything it does to avoid offending its chief energy supplier.

Without access to abundant, dependable, cheap energy, we have a very different, far less prosperous, economic outlook. It will become impossible to feed and support the current populations of the world. That may not be a concern for those determined to reduce humankind's' footprint on the Earth, but for most of us, mass starvation is not a serious part of our world vision.

From a national security standpoint, artificially raising energy costs by rejecting abundant, less expensive, more efficient, and practical energy sources in favor of less abundant, more expensive, less efficient, and far from ready for "prime time" alternatives would be a major strategic blunder. China understands the point and is feverishly increasing its energy capacity, including its nuclear energy capacity, with forty-five plants in existence now and many more either under construction or planned. China already has forged ahead of the United States as the country with the largest installed power capacity in the world. A "Five Year Plan," enacted in 2016, calls for China to approve eight new nuclear plants annually.[246]

I can hear already the reaction to that statement. "There is no such thing as an unacceptable cost when it comes to saving our planet and environment. How can you possibly not see that greenhouse gases are causing catastrophic damage to Mother Earth? No reasonable scientist disputes that global warming is a man-made event and if we do not immediately take drastic action, we all are doomed."

The Green Dream manifesto essentially takes that position, hysterically declaring that the planet will be lost within twelve years if dramatic measures are not taken immediately—and it is exactly the type of nonsense that will produce energy and economic calamities. The fact is, responsible scientists do not all agree on the cause and effect of climate change, and no one is predicting a "crisis" anytime remotely within the twelve-year "window" of the Green Dream. Evidence from the last inter-glacial period in Earth's history, when surface temperatures essentially were the same as today, suggests it will take a hundred years or more for seas to rise to the levels they reached in that earlier "warming" period.[247] More to the point, if the controlling causes of climate warming are primarily natural, man is not capable of reversing the process, slowing it down, or affecting it except, perhaps, in small increments, and to suggest otherwise is irresponsible. There simply is no reason to believe the seas will not again rise to levels reached during the last interglacial period regardless of what mankind does or does not do.

The environmental debate is a cacophony that has been ongoing for a very long time. In an article written in October 2019, the late Walt Williams revisited some of the more egregious environmental claims that have been made over the last several decades. The predictions from prominent scientists included: warnings in 1969 that humanity would "disappear in a cloud of blue steam in 20 years;" a prediction in 2000 that snow would become "rare" in a "few years;" a US Navy forecast that by 2016 the Arctic Ocean would experience an ice-free summer; warnings of virtually "world-wide famine" by the year 2000; and forecasts going back to the 1930s and 1940s that the world soon would run out of reserves of various essential metals, as well as oil and natural gas.[248]

As Williams noted, no one ever retracts or apologizes for these flagrantly mistaken predictions. They just double down, making even more extreme claims that never are questioned or challenged by the media. Certainly, the Green Dream has managed to scare young school children and gullible voters out of their wits with its predictions of the imminent arrival of the Four Horsemen of the Apocalypse. That is the goal. As with so many issues, moral panic clouds judgment and provides those with environmental agendas the opportunity to strike.

Please do not misunderstand. We should and must be good stewards of the planet—it is the only one we have. That includes taking all the steps we can, within reason, to control and limit emissions, if for no other reason, "just in case." However, I remain more than skeptical of claims that man alone holds the key to controlling climate change. There simply have been too many dramatic changes in climate across eons that cannot possibly be attributed to man, and too many naturally occurring events that affect climate, for me to unconditionally accept the premise that the global warming we appear to be experiencing during this brief interlude in cosmic time is largely, if not entirely, man-made.

Equally illogical is the claim that the climate changes which allegedly have occurred as a result of man's "reckless" conduct can be reversed, but only by measures so extreme they would reduce the industrial capacity of the United States and starve large human populations into oblivion. How exactly does man prevent or control changes in the Earth's rotation, tectonic plate movements, sun spots, volcanic activities, the Milankovitch orbital cycles, or, for that matter, influence any of the numerous natural influences on climate? None of this, unfortunately, changes the fact that the reckless scrambling to implement the Green New Deal by the Progressives now in charge of our government is likely to bring financial ruin and political chaos to the nation.

As most people understand, we have difficulty predicting the weather from hour to hour, much less the climate over decades or centuries. While the battle rages on over the reliability of computer climate models, at the very least it is difficult to validate models that are attempting to predict events many years in the future. Commonly the models are tested by a procedure called "hindcasting"—seeing if the model can predict events that already have occurred. Hindcasting, however, is too easily "fudged." With the benefit of hindsight, a tester, intentionally or not, too easily can conform the model to predict results already observed. We nevertheless rely on this type of "backward-looking" validation almost entirely because we have no better way to try to verify predictions of events that may not happen for centuries. We also do not know enough about the variables affecting long-time climate change, and the accuracy of climate models, like all models, is completely dependent on getting the variables correct. Junk in, junk out.

When I was growing up, scientists and the media were widely predicting the coming of a new ice age. It hasn't happened. Just a few years ago, I also was listening to a television program on climate change, which concluded with the admission by one of the scientists involved that their climate models predicted, with equal degrees of reliability, either a coming ice age or global warming. If true, then obviously something was very wrong with the specifications for the models they were using. We simply do not know what we do not know and never will, and when specifying computer models, we cannot control for variables we are unaware of or do not understand.

The "experience" during the coronavirus outbreak should have alerted most Americans to the basic unreliability of many mathematical models, particularly when the data is incomplete or unknown. Almost all of the coronavirus models wildly overestimated the expected number of cases and deaths, some initially predicting over 2 million deaths in the US alone. And no, it was not "containment" efforts that threw the forecasts off—containment already was included in the variables used in most of the models.

To complicate matters further, science is not always right, even when everyone agrees. Quite the contrary—science often changes its mind, giving rise to the truism that "what is accepted knowledge today is sometimes discarded tomorrow." Eggs are bad for you. Eggs are good for you. Tomatoes are the key to good health. Tomatoes should be avoided because they contain lectins. Everyone should take a daily low-dose aspirin to prevent heart attacks. Do not take a daily low-dose aspirin if you have not had a heart attack because it might cause a stroke. Science necessarily is premised on the available information, and smart people reach conclusions based on that evidence. When better information becomes available, the same smart people change their opinions—unless they are environmental scientists, in which case only ideology, not facts, seems to count.

Like Stephen Moore, it is difficult for me to take seriously anyone who maintains man-made carbon-dioxide emissions are the most important element in climate change but will not consider solutions, like nuclear energy, that would balance the needs of the economy and national defense with what are claimed to be the needs of the environment. Many of these people are simply naïve, gullible individuals in search of a "cause" and having joined, they never will question the narrative of the "herd" that has taken them in and given their lives a degree of substance and meaning.

Others, however, obviously have a different, darker agenda. They are the political and environmental extremists who surreptitiously lead and direct the herd. They have staked out positions they will not change or compromise, advocating energy policies that would bankrupt the country and reduce its industrial capacity without any proof those policies would have any greater effect on climate and the environment than more reasonable alternatives.

Even more concerning, if Stephen Moore is correct, are those who have adopted the darkest agenda of all. Convinced that unless arrested, growing human populations soon will overwhelm the "carrying" capacity of the Earth, their goal is to create an artificial "pandemic" by reducing energy capacities below those needed to sustain current populations. Even among their acolytes, however, mass starvation is not a popular subject, so they do not talk about it openly, nor is there a need to do so—the environmental "cause" alone is enough to stir the passions of the masses, the "useful idiots." Meanwhile, other countries, military powers which present a clear and present threat to the United States, continue their emissions activities unabated, as they scale up their industrial and energy capacities.

Trying to balance environmental policies with the other needs of the nation is not, as some argue, a failure of "moral leadership." It is a bluntly pragmatic understanding that human progress and well-being, as well as our national security, depend on the availability of abundant, dependable, cost-efficient energy. Solar, wind, and hydroelectric energy cannot meet those needs at the moment, and they are unlikely to be able to do so for the foreseeable future, if ever. They also carry their own, often significant, environmental consequences, something proponents never talk about, but which can be far more severe than anything caused by carbon-based fuels.

As Stephen Moore[249] points out, "nothing exposes the insincerity of the global climate change movement quite as much the left's hatred of nuclear power." It is a debate that needs to be taken over and led by pragmatic, thinking adults capable of balancing the needs of the environment with the needs of the nation. The contents of the New Green Deal prove beyond question that the authors of that manifesto, and all who endorse it, are dangerous ideologues, not thought leaders, and they are incapable of providing the independent judgement and decision-making needed to make the necessary accommodations.

CHAPTER 12

THE CELEBRITY POLITICIAN

The celebrity politician. Ronald Reagan arguably started it, Donald Trump may have perfected it, and Oprah Winfrey for a while toyed with institutionalizing it. The editorial pages of newspapers rail against the madness of it all: the dangers of "lack of experience in governing." But what exactly is "experience in governing," and is "experience in governing" necessary to be a competent president of the United States? After all, we have had military leaders, entertainers, governors, state and federal senators, and delegates with a diversity of backgrounds and experiences in the White House with no consistent pattern of results. Ulysses Grant may not have been considered a paradigm of excellence in the Oval Office, but most believe Ike did an acceptable job. Both were accomplished military officers, both unfamiliar with governing civilian populations. Were the disastrous presidencies of Jimmy Carter and Barack Obama the result of "inexperience" or their hard tack toward socialism and their utter disregard of constitutional limitations designed to protect individual freedoms? Was the success of Ronald Reagan a product of experience in governing or his commitment to conservative policies and deference to the Constitution?

No one comes to the presidency with much relevant experience. The closest would be a former vice president, assuming their role in the administration was something more than ceremonial and, unlike Joe Biden, they remain sentient. But even for governors, senators, congressmen, attorneys general, diplomats, business leaders, community organizers, doctors, lawyers, and Indian chiefs—you name it—the outsized scale and scope of the presidency make any level of governing experience parochial and more or less inconsequential. No one has sat with his or her hand on the nuclear trigger before becoming president, and even members of Congress make decisions as "one of many" and usually with the interests of their home states or districts being determinative of their views of the "national interest." To be sure, prior public service may provide some insight into temperament and style, and even into how an individual may deal with certain types of issues, but it is likely to produce as many false positives as useful indicators about what type of president they would make. Events also can strongly influence how a president will be perceived. Would John Kennedy, for example, be viewed less favorably if the Cuban missile crisis had never occurred? Would Lyndon Johnson be regarded more favorably if the American public had not turned so stridently against the Vietnam war?

Does it even matter? In today's world, a president may set the tone for the country, but their ability to govern is more questionable. The truth is, at all levels of government, the ability of our elected officials to govern is constrained by vast regulatory states that have been delegated powers theoretically reserved, in the case of the federal government, to the executive branch, the Congress, or the courts. Populated by millions of faceless, unelected bureaucrats virtually immune from termination or discipline, the rules, regulations, and standards churned out by these agencies dwarf the laws enacted by Congress and state legislatures and can have even more effect on everyday life. The most purposeful presidential intent can be circumvented by the powerful bureaucracies in Washington, all of them populated by substantial numbers of life-tenured individuals ideologically and philosophically opposed to the policies of any incumbent president, regardless of party. They can easily outlast even a two-term administration.

How did we transition from a young republic with a limited national government to a vast, centralized regulatory state where the president is just as likely to be a celebrity as a statesman? It has been an interesting journey with hundreds of events, ranging from wars to financial crises, influencing outcomes. Let's look at some of them.

In the chapter on *"Education,"* I talk about the effects the weakening of our educational systems over the last several decades has had on the ability and willingness of Americans to protect our form of government. Our founders understood the importance of education and that an educated electorate was necessary for this new form of government to succeed. As Thomas Jefferson put it:

> I know no safe depository of the ultimate powers of the society but the people themselves, (A)nd if we think them not enlightened enough to exercise their control with a wholesome discretion, the remedy is not to take it from them, but to inform their discretion by education. This is the true corrective of abuses of constitutional power.[250]

Noah Webster, considered by many to be the father of American scholarship and education, put it even more directly:

> Every child in America should be acquainted with his own country. He should read books that furnish him with ideas that will be useful to him in life and practice. As soon as he opens his lips, he should rehearse the history of his own country.[251]

The majority of voters today simply are too undereducated—even those with degrees from prestigious colleges and universities—to understand what makes our form of government different from others and why their prosperity and well-being, and the prosperity and well-being of their children, is so dependent on protecting the principles that have made America the most successful, powerful, and free nation on Earth. Since history, for all intents and purposes, no longer is taught in many American schools, and since large segments of voters never have experienced war or the "cleansings" and genocides that have taken place under socialism, communism, and other totalitarian regimes, they have no understanding that calls for "social justice," "economic equality," and similar shibboleths have been the siren songs of despots throughout the ages.

The American public's unfamiliarity with their form of government manifests in ways both large and small. For example, almost daily the news media reports the frustrations of the American people with the inability of Washington to "get anything done." However, the Constitution was set up to make it difficult for the federal government to do anything. It never was intended to be the all-powerful "Oz," handing out favors and benefits to the masses. The individual states were supposed to be the primary vehicles of government with the federal government limited to certain enumerated powers, such as national defense, the post office, and international trade. Because the powers of the federal government were limited and subordinate in most respects to the states, the Constitution was set up to make it difficult for changes to be made in federal law. It may seem like a quaint notion, but the Constitution never envisioned that federal lawmaking would be either quick, nimble, or easy.

The year 1913 was the beginning of the end for federalism as the founders designed it and the beginning of the rise in big government. Until 1913, United States senators were elected by their state legislatures, not by popular vote. The idea was to provide the states with a means of defending against encroachments by the federal government. The Congress was a "federal" government rather than a "national" government because the states were incorporated directly into the structure of the government through the Senate. That all ended with the ratification of the Seventeenth Amendment in 1913, which provided for the election of senators by popular vote.

The year 1913 was consequential for another reason— ratification of the Sixteenth Amendment, giving Congress the power to impose a federal income tax. Passage of the Sixteenth Amendment, and an expansive interpretation Article I, section 8 of the Constitution, the general Welfare Clause, by Franklin Roosevelt's New Deal era Supreme Court, led directly to today's welfare state and the enormous entitlement programs that fuel it. For the first time, Congress had cash it could give away, and the temptation to do so quickly became irresistible.

The Supreme Court certainly has been complicit in helping the federal government broaden its power and reach. Decisions like *United States v. Butler*[252] and *Wickard v. Filburn*[253] greatly expanded the spending and regulatory authorities of the federal government, and if Congress was reluctant or moving too slowly, starting with Franklin Roosevelt, presidents have not been shy about turning to *executive orders* as a means for bypassing constitutional restraints on executive branch powers and legislating from the White House.

Executive orders are nowhere referenced in the Constitution. They are "implied" from a president's power to enforce the laws and manage the government. Consequently, in theory, executive orders must be tethered to a specific law or delegation of power by Congress. They are not intended to be an independent means of lawmaking by the executive branch. While often used for declaring "national days of mourning" or special holidays, there had been few consequential executive orders before the administration of Franklin Roosevelt. One notable exception was the Emancipation Proclamation by Abraham Lincoln. Roosevelt, however, issued over 3,500 executive orders during his twelve years in office, many of questionable constitutional validity. For example, he created the Export-Import Bank of the United States by executive order, as well as establishing the National Labor Relations Board and enacting the National Industrial Recovery Act. It was not until Harry Truman tried to use an executive order to put US steel mills under federal control that the Supreme Court finally intervened and in *Youngstown Sheet and Tube Co. v. Sawyer,*[254] reestablished the principle that executive orders could not be used by a president to make new law.

If *Youngstown Steel and Tube Co.* managed to slow executive branch lawmaking for a time—and no president has issued nearly as many executive orders since Roosevelt—its palliative effects clearly have faded. Barack Obama, for example, changed key provisions of the Affordable Care Act by executive order, and Progressive candidates for the 2020 presidential elections, Kamala Harris among them, promised to regulate guns by executive order if Congress did not cooperate in their demands for more gun controls. As a measure of how widely the floodgates have opened, Joe Biden signed nearly as many executive orders during his first two-weeks in office as Franklin Roosevelt did in his first month in office, and they continue to come.

The willingness of presidents to "make law" outside the boundaries set by the Constitution erodes federalism, the core concept in our form of government. But so too do activist judges when they disregard their oaths of office and make decisions based on personal predilections and political ideologies. This is not something well understood by most of the American public. Our commitment to the rule of law, the protection of private property, and the protection of individual rights are among the most important distinctions between our form of government and others. We do not allow presidents to nationalize steel mills or any other type of private property. In collective governments there essentially is no private ownership of properly. The important production assets are "nationalized" and under the control of government central planners, who cannot possibly know enough to allow economies to function efficiently. Add a bit of corruption, and you have the classic output of socialism and communism—authoritarianism, shortages, loss of liberty, and social chaos. There simply is no need for any type of consensus rule, or any reason for any type of government other than dictatorship, when the government controls the means of production.

Think about what happens anytime there is a military coup or other takeover of a country somewhere in the world by a socialist or communist regime. The new government immediately limits free speech, rounds up and imprisons or executes its political opponents, and nationalizes the means of production. For a recent example, think Venezuela. The true socialist/communist regimes in the world—Cuba, North Korea, and Russia, to name a few of them—not only consistently have produced brutal dictators and governments, but also have impoverished their countries and turned them into armed prison camps. Everyone living under these regimes is completely dependent on the "generosity" of the government for their existence, and "social justice" manifests as everyone being equally poor and abused. The barons of industry in the US may generate criticism from many quarters, but the fact government depends on the economic activities generated by private enterprise serves as an important check on government power and over-reach.

The fact socialism and communism so reliably produce poverty, shortages, and suffering wherever and whenever they are tried is not a flaw in execution of an otherwise sound theory of governance, as many Progressives seem to believe. The simple truth is, no system of government based on principles that contradict human nature possibly can be successful, and socialism and communism contradict human nature. Arguably, in fact, the human motivation that has created more prosperity for more people, relieved more hunger and suffering across the globe, provided more jobs, and generated history's greatest advances in science, engineering, medicine, technology, mathematics, and the arts is simple "greed." Put in gentler terms, self-interest is the great motivator that drives almost all human endeavors and accomplishments. Without it, we tend to be a somewhat lazy and unimaginative species. "From each according to his ability, to each according to his needs" might be a noble-sounding sentiment, but there is no evidence supporting it as a workable economic system or governing philosophy and certainly not one that produces social justice, unless everyone sharing poverty is your idea of social justice.

The lack of understanding among voters, particularly young voters, of these essential differences between collectivism and market-based economies is startling. During the 2016 presidential campaigns, for example, a supporter of Bernie Sanders responded to questions about why he supported socialism with shouts of, "Free education, free health care!" When asked if he understood what socialism is, the individual, obviously an artifact of our crippled education systems, responded that it was when "you are social with each other." He was completely nonplussed when asked if he had ever heard socialism described as a system in which the government owns the means of production.

I have spoken about this elsewhere in this book, but one of the mistakes routinely made by supporters of socialism is the belief that most governments in Western Europe are socialist. From this mistaken premise, they derive the equally mistaken conclusion that socialism not only is working in Europe but also that there is greater "social justice" in Europe. The governments in Western Europe, however, are not socialist in the sense of Cuba, North Korea, Russia, China, Nicaragua, or Venezuela. The governments do not own the means of production. Most are parliamentary democracies with embedded social programs, much like we have in the United States. The Western European countries have nationalized larger segments of their economies than has the United States, but for the most part, they are market-based economies with the essential means of production remaining in private hands.

Because larger welfare states have been built in Western Europe than in the United States, however, productivity has suffered, economic output has been reduced, and many governments—Spain, Italy, Portugal, and Greece, for example— are teetering on the brink of financial collapse. This has happened even though the Europeans largely have escaped having to pay the full cost for their national defenses, relying instead on NATO and the US for protection against external threats. As can be seen from UN deployments to the Middle East, even European countries with significant military capacities, like France, generally lack the logistical capabilities needed to keep their armies fighting for more than a short time, the lone exception being the UK.

One reading of the "New Green Deal" will tell you that what Progressives have in mind for America is not the European welfare state. The Communist Party USA celebrated when Barack Obama was elected president and by the end of Obama's second term, the dream of socialists controlling the American government was coming closer to reality. Bernie Sanders was openly running for president as a "Democratic Socialist" and receiving significant support. The Democratic Party's Progressive caucus in Congress was growing. And increasingly, radical Progressives were winning seats in Congress.

But work remained to be done, and Hillary was the key. If she had been elected and been able to select Supreme Court justices to replace Justices Scalia and Kennedy, that alone would have forever changed the country. Obama already had appointed two Supreme Court justices and had filled the lower federal courts with more than 300 Progressive judges. Another eight years of Hillary would have amassed an overwhelming majority of radical Progressive judges at all levels of the federal judiciary. And almost certainly, before leaving office she would have taken it a step further and tried to fulfill a Progressive dream that started with Franklin Roosevelt: enlarging the Supreme Court and "packing" it with justices sympathetic to the Progressives' agenda.

That remains one of the most significant dangers of a Biden presidency. As quickly as they can do away with the filibuster, you can expect Progressives to expand the number of seats on the Supreme Court to 12 or 15 and fill them with Progressive extremists who will remain on the Court for decades. The appointment and confirmation of Amy Coney Barrett to the Court practically ensures it.

For some time now, Chief Justice John Roberts, nominally a conservative, has been drifting to the left, joining liberal justices on key votes. Essentially, he took over the role of Justice Anthony Kennedy, who retired in July 2018. Kennedy, also a nominal conservative, was considered the "swing" vote between the liberal and conservative factions on the Court, not infrequently voting with liberals on key social issues. The Roberts/liberals "alliance" may have been an uneasy one for Progressives, but the level of "comfort" it provided might have been enough to delay their efforts to pack the Court, which Progressives understand will not be popular with many Americans, particularly the more than 71 million who voted for President Trump in November 2020. They also understand it would be a visible indicator of the disdain Progressives hold for this country, its institutions, laws, and Constitution, and how radically they intend to change all of them. As Barack Obama, Abigail Spanberger, and others have counseled less patient members of the Progressives' cabal, if you plan to turn the United States into a third-world, socialist s—hole, it's better not to tell people what you intend until after you get in office.

Delay no longer is an option for Progressives. Justice Barrett's confirmation created a 6-3 conservative majority on the Court and eliminated Justice Roberts as a potential swing vote. The success of the Progressives' "revolution" now depends on establishing an unbeatable majority of true-believers on the Court, young enough to sit for decades, committed and unprincipled enough not to flinch when called upon to destroy the Constitution and the country.

Controlling the Court is key to replacing democracy with socialism; the quickest and easiest way to do away with constitutional safeguards is simply to "interpret" them out of existence. How long do you think it will take, for example, for a "collective government" to provide a "collective" interpretation of the Second Amendment, meaning that only state created militias, National Guard units, will retain the right to "bear arms?" It likely will be a National Guard unit that drops by your house to pick-up your guns that have been confiscated by executive order, as Kamala Harris, a candidate for the Democratic nomination for president at the time, promised to do. The Electoral College will be another early casualty; Progressives covet "direct democracies," where minority voices can be extinguished at the whim of the majority. Freedom of speech, religious freedom, constraints against unreasonable searches and seizures, and anything else seen as interfering with the inauguration of socialism as the transcendent political ideology for the country will be "re-imagined" almost as quickly. Whatever constitutional impediments might exist to whatever Progressives want to do—reparations for slavery and the displacement of Native Americans; wealth taxes; elimination of fossil fuels; free higher education; forgiveness of student debt; free universal health care—the "new" and re-structured Court will be there to deal with them. Welcome to Huxley's *Brave New World.*[255]

Few people realize that the number of justices on the Supreme Court is entirely a prerogative of Congress; the Constitution is silent on the subject. While the Court, by tradition, has been made up of 8 associate justices and a chief justice since the mid-nineteenth century, tradition will matter little to Progressives. Their interests are power and control. What Progressives have dreamed about doing since Franklin Roosevelt first thought of it in the 1930s, eliminating the Supreme Court as a barrier to autocratic rule, is now within reach.

Hillary Clinton's loss to Donald Trump in 2016 did not just interrupt Progressive's efforts to pack the Court. If she had been elected, Hillary also would have completed the changeover to the single-payer public health insurance started by Obamacare. She would have continued to underfund and weaken the military. She would have exploited the same race, gender, and class cards the Obama administration used so effectively to divide America. She, in other words, would have finished what Obama started. More importantly, it all would have occurred without having to reveal that Progressives were now in control of the Democratic Party. The fact an American version of the Bolshevik's "Red October" of 1917 was so close until Hillary managed to snatch defeat from the jaws of victory explains in large measure the "Trump derangement syndrome" Progressives display every day.

For several decades, Progressives have been increasingly effective in making millions of Americans dependent on government. We now are at a point where people have become accustomed to looking to government for solutions to almost everything. In the process, private industry has been vilified: "the prices of prescription drugs are too high;" "the petroleum industry is price gauging;" "doctors and hospitals are charging too much;" "there is no excuse for the high price of a college education." In a sense, the progression to dependence on government has been natural as the country increasingly has divided into urban and rural populations. People living on top of each other in urban centers need the protection of laws and regulations far more than individuals living in rural areas and insulated to a degree from the behaviors of their neighbors. But much of the dependence has been built by intentional government policies and actions, which have destroyed the nuclear family as the primary societal building block, dumbed-down education, and discouraged self-reliance by serially expanding government "safety nets" and welfare programs. People have been conditioned to expect their government to step in and make things right anytime there is a natural disaster, economic downturn, or other problem.

While watching the 2019 Kentucky Derby, I was struck by how expectations that everyone will be protected against any misfortune is affecting everything we do. You may know the story. For the first time in the 145-year history of the Derby, the winner, a horse named Maximum Security, was disqualified for interfering with other horses while leading during the stretch run. "Country House," the horse that finished second, was named the winner. It would not have been a particularly controversial call in any race other than the Derby—Maximum Security clearly "lugged out" and interfered with horses behind him. The rule, which calls for disqualification if "the leading horse ... swerves or is ridden to either side so as to interfere, intimidate, or impede any other horse or jockey," was clear. The only thing that made disqualification notable was the fact no Derby winner ever before had been disqualified. Despite the disqualification, Twinspires.com, Churchill Downs's online wagering service, announced it would refund up to $10 to everyone who placed a winning bet on Maximum Security. It was the equivalent of a participation trophy for bettors; no sense sending anyone away disappointed.

Expectations that the government will step in as a buffer against hardships changes behavior. Why not build houses on beachfronts if the government will provide cheap insurance against flooding and hurricanes? Why not put buildings on unstable canyon walls if the government will replace them if taken by fire or mudslide? Why not create developments in flood zones if the government will rebuild them if disaster strikes? We have become comfortable being taken care of by the government, and that is a dangerous change in attitude for a nation founded on principles designed to keep government out of our lives. It is a change that has been nurtured by Progressives for decades but now seems to be coming to full flower. The election of Barack Obama gave the Progressive movement the opportunity. The campaign of Bernie Sanders provided traction. But the unexpected defeat of Hillary Clinton and Donald Trump's successes as president forced the radical nature of the Progressives' agenda into the open more quickly than Democrats would have liked.

Single-payer, government-run health insurance has been the holy grail of Progressives for years. Health care represents nearly 18 percent of the US GDP, and if Progressives can gain control of it by taking over the health insurance system, they will have nationalized a huge portion of the economy. There does not have to be a military coup for socialism to take over; it can happen one segment of the economy at a time.

While I am not a conspiracy theorist, I cannot help but believe Obamacare was purposefully designed to fail. It was too poorly and haphazardly crafted to reach any other conclusion. Nancy Pelosi summed it up nicely when she infamously said, "We have to pass it so that we can see what is in it." Progressives did not care what was in it; the key was getting it passed as a first but significant step toward the introduction of a government-run and controlled health care system. The country certainly was not yet ready for national health insurance when Obamacare was passed. People liked their insurance and their doctors and wanted to keep them. They were told they could, one of many lies the Obama administration used to sell Obamacare to the nation. Jonathan Gruber, MIT economist and the primary architect of Obamacare, openly gloated about how the "stupidity" of American voters allowed the Obama Administration to lie about the true costs of Obamacare.[256] Imagine for a moment, if you will, the media reaction if someone in the Trump administration referred to American voters as "stupid" and admitted lying to them about the costs of a proposed government program.

Obamacare ostensibly was set up around "private" insurance plans, apparently to get people comfortable with the idea of universal health care coverage while the majority of the country still was covered by private insurance and unlikely to panic about losing either their insurance or their doctors. Once the idea of universal health care insurance was ingrained in the publics' conscience as a "right," it would be easy enough to make the switch to a government-run, government-controlled program. Simply wait for Obamacare to fail, declare that the failure demonstrated the inability of private insurers to meet the needs of the American people, and then nationalize health care through a rescue plan that would establish a single-payer system. Hillary Clinton was expected to follow Barack Obama into the White House, so there was no need to rush the process—everything was in place to make the transition comfortably within Hillary's expected two-term reign.

It was another version of the "camel's nose under the edge of the tent" strategy, and much of it has come to pass. Obamacare is failing, but the discussions no longer are about whether we should have universal health insurance, only the form it should take—President Obama was effective in selling universal health insurance as a "right" of every American. The one hiccup in the process was Hillary's upset loss to Donald Trump.

A strong indicator Obamacare always was intended to fail were the enormous deductibles and co-pays included in health insurance policies offered under the program. To make the policies "affordable," deductibles often ran into the thousands of dollars and co-pays were significant. Many insureds could not possibly afford them. The Obama administration knew that, but high deductibles and co-pays could be blamed on the insurance companies, providing yet another reason why government-controlled insurance was needed. Meanwhile, the government paid billions of dollars to subsidize the purchase of insurance policies by millions of Americans, many of whom continued to seek medical care in hospital emergency rooms, as they had been doing for years, because they could not afford the Obamacare deductibles and co-pays.

Let's be clear. It wasn't universal health insurance Progressives were after. We already largely had universal health insurance through a combination of private insurance, Medicare, Medicaid, the Children's Health Insurance Plan (CHIP), the Veterans Administration, and other government plans, as well as so-called "safety net providers," which include public hospitals, community health centers, clinics, and local health departments funded by state, local, and federal programs. What Progressives wanted was complete control over the 18% of the economy the health care system represents. They wanted Americans dependent on the government for their medical and hospital needs.

One of the great rope-a-dopes by proponents of Obamacare in their quest to nationalize the health care system was the claim that tens of millions of Americans did not have health insurance, implying that tens of millions did not have access to insured health care. Unquestionably, many in the country did not have *private* health insurance, including large numbers who could afford to buy it but chose not to do so, those between jobs who decided not to enroll in COBRA or take-out short-term coverage knowing their employers would provide coverage as soon as they returned to work, and illegal immigrants. But that did not mean tens of millions of Americans were without access to insured health care. The largest public health insurance program in the country, Medicaid, insured approximately seventy-four million people. Another forty-four million, mainly the retired, were enrolled in Medicare. Two hundred and forty-five million Americans carried private health insurance, the majority of it supplied by their employers. The Veterans Administration insured 15 million military personnel. By law, hospital emergency rooms were required to provide treatment to anyone who presented for emergency treatment, insured or not. If you were poor and uninsured and sought treatment at an emergency room of a hospital, you immediately were enrolled in Medicaid, CHIP, or another program for which you were eligible, and you received treatment even if you were not eligible for any program, emergency or not.

Only 330 million people live in the United States, approximately 327 million at the time Obamacare was being formulated. Do the math. Who was without access to insured health care? Included in the ranks of the "uninsured" by supporters of Obamacare were those who had access to private, employer-provided health insurance but declined it. Others who were eligible for federal or state health insurance programs but did not enroll. Some who were eligible for subsidized health care benefits but did not apply. A significant number were illegal immigrants. Still others had incomes above the generous eligibility thresholds for federal or state assistance and simply decided not to purchase insurance.[257]

Understandably, healthy young people may not see a need for health insurance. One of the major objections to Obamacare was the fact it required everyone to purchase health insurance whether they wanted it or not and regardless of their circumstances, a common feature of universal, national health insurance plans. In true socialist fashion, these plans need the healthy to enroll and pay premiums to fund the benefits paid to the unhealthy. It is a transfer of wealth from the young and healthy to the old and sick.[258] Citizens in Western Europe may be used to their governments telling them what they can and cannot do or what they must buy, but Americans are not.

Need proof that proponents of Obamacare understood almost all of those they claimed were "uninsured" had access to adequate health care paid for by private or public insurance? When amendments were proposed to Medicaid, Progressives immediately changed tune, arguing the modifications would "hurt a health care program on which 70 million Americans depend." There were no claims these people were "uninsured" or that they lacked access to free health care, as had been the case during their propaganda campaigns over Obamacare.

Generally speaking, Medicaid, which provides comprehensive medical insurance to the poorest Americans, is available to those making at or below 138 percent of the federal poverty level (FPL). The CHIP program supplements that coverage and extends it to uninsured children up to nineteen years of age in families with incomes too high to qualify for Medicaid. Many states will provide coverage for children in families earning up to 200 percent of the FPL, and some provide coverage for uninsured children in families earning 250 percent or even 300 percent of the FPL.

Health insurance can be expensive, and people who find themselves ineligible for Medicaid or other welfare programs may opt not to buy health insurance even when it is available from their employers at a modest cost. I get it. But why is that any different from the myriad of choices millions have to make every day? Few of us are fortunate enough to have unlimited funds; everyone has to make choices. Why should I pay for someone's decision to buy a smartphone, new car, or flat-screen television rather than health insurance—77 percent of Americans now own smartphones, nine out of ten use the internet, 85 percent of households own a car, and 96 percent own televisions.[259]

But, you say, 138 percent of the FPL is not a lot of money. Obviously, however, there have to be eligibility requirements for federal welfare programs. If the threshold for eligibility for Medicaid or any other free program is not generous enough, then change it, but dismantling what has been the best private health care system in the world and replacing it with an enormous, government-run bureaucracy because we do not trust people to make good decisions about what they will and will not buy makes no sense. Unless, of course, the goal is something bigger, like promoting dependence on government and changing our form of government.

If we as a nation want universal health care, let's put the costs on the table, determine how to pay for it, and make sure private insurance remains a key part of the equation. "Medicare for all" may be a catchy slogan, but it obscures the fact the government effectively would be nationalizing a health care system that makes up a huge segment of the economy. It also would not be Medicare in its current form. That is another Progressive lie. They like to promote universal health insurance as "Medicare for all" because most people find current Medicare acceptable health insurance, at least when augmented by a supplemental umbrella policy. But it is an expensive program, even as subsidized by the premiums paid by most of those enrolled, and is projected to be bankrupt by 2026.[260]

That is not the "Medicare" program Progressives are talking about making "universal." A much more limited plan would be developed, although it is difficult to tease that fact out of the policy statements Progressives publish about their health insurance proposals. It is equally unclear whether you would be able to opt-out of whatever public health insurance is put in place and buy private insurance, or even if you would be allowed to supplement the government insurance with a private plan, assuming private health insurance continues to exist. In Canada, for example, buying private insurance for things covered by public health insurance is not permitted—that helps combat "adverse selection" and is part of the wealth transfer from young to old.

Canada is a good example if you want to see the limitations of public health insurance. The perception is that the Canadian system works well. But it is a heavily regulated program in which the government decides everything from the number of hospital beds available and how many doctors and other providers will be allowed to practice, to the drugs, medicines, and procedures that will be included. Even with only approximately 37 million people living in Canada, the system is struggling to maintain fiscal integrity. Benefits are being reduced, and there are long waiting periods for even routine procedures. After all, it saves a lot of money if people die waiting for treatment. For a candid assessment of the Canadian system, ask some of the many Canadians who routinely come to the United States for medical treatment how their national health care plan is working. Conversely, see if you can find any prominent American Progressives who travel to Canada for their medical needs.

It is fashionable for Progressives to claim drug prices are lower in Canada, but they never tell the full story. Some drugs are cheaper in Canada because the Canadian government will not approve drugs it considers too expensive. That does not mean, however, that drugs in general are cheaper in Canada; it usually means many are unavailable in Canada. After thirty years of price controls on drugs, Canada ranks seventeenth out of nineteen OECD (Organisation for Economic Co-Operation) countries in terms of access to medications.[261] Just like having people die waiting for medical treatments saves money, denying drugs is a "twofer"—you save the costs of treating those who die, as well as the cost of the drugs that might have prolonged their lives but were not available.

There are many cautionary tales here. The world is awash with examples of national health care systems most Americans would view as utter failures if they knew the details, including over-regulation, long waits for treatment, unavailability of drugs and procedures, and decisions that people are "too old to treat" at ages most Americans would consider their retirement "golden" years. Pay attention the next time you are in Europe. The number of elderly individuals with walkers and canes, stooped over, in pain, barely ambulatory, is significant. Many of them owe their conditions to the fact they could not obtain a needed treatment or procedure either because they were deemed "too old" or because the treatments they needed were not covered under their national health insurance programs. Also keep in mind, in most of Europe, when it is allowed and they can afford it, people buy private health insurance either to supplement or replace the "national" insurance. Have a conversation with a European about their national health insurance plans. You might get a favorable response from a German, but for the majority of countries, the most you are likely to get is a lackluster, "It's okay," followed quickly by the comment, "We have private insurance as well."

We already know universal health insurance in a country the size of the United States will be enormously expensive. Estimates for the plan proposed by Bernie Sander ran from Bernie's estimate of $1.38 trillion a year to an estimated $2.8 trillion a year by the Committee for a Responsible Federal Budget.[262] Since the revenues collected by the federal government are less than $3.5 trillion annually, the higher end of that estimate would consume roughly 80 percent of all federal revenues. Add $600 billion for defense spending and another $1 trillion for social security payments, and the government is quickly out of money. The bean counters will be in full song. You can predict the outcome. With no competition for primary health care insurance and accumulating federal deficits, health care benefits will be slashed, procedures will be denied, drugs will be disapproved, and the number of people dying younger or living out their lives in pain will rise.

Of this I am certain. If Progressives are successful in putting in place a government-run, national health care plan, your health insurance coverage will be degraded significantly. Perhaps not out of the box; to get it passed Progressives almost surely will present a relatively comprehensive program initially. Once in place, however, benefits and coverages quickly will be ratcheted back as costs mount. After all, there will be so many competing and more important initiatives, such as the Green New Deal, reparations for slavery and Native Americans, student loan forgiveness, and free higher education. There also is the inconvenient fact that private health insurance now pays a significant portion of the costs of Medicare, Medicaid, and other government health care programs because privately insured patients pay doctors and hospitals more, usually substantially more, than patients enrolled in government plans. The private health insurance subsidies provide doctors and hospitals with the revenues they need to stay in business.

Private insurance will disappear or be greatly reduced if our health care system is nationalized. So too will the subsidies privately insured patients pay to doctors and hospitals, many of which will go out of business. The entire health care provider system will contract and change. Less qualified "professionals" will take the place of doctors, who will be in short supply. It's hard to attract people to a profession that requires eleven to eighteen years of higher education and training but pays government wages. You instead will be in the care of physicians' assistants, nurse practitioners, midwives, and other non-physician providers, many of them trained overseas and with questionable credentials.

While I seemingly have deviated a long way from the "Celebrity Politician" theme with which this chapter started, the meanderings were intended to take us through a discussion of some of the threats of progressivism that were brought into focus only because Donald Trump, a celebrity candidate, defeated Hillary Clinton. His election forced Progressives into revealing the truly radical nature of their agenda earlier than planned. Suddenly, it was not just crazy Bernie ranting counterculture slogans from the 1960s, but a host of Democratic candidates, not all of whom had been considered as radical as their messages suddenly turned, embracing Marxist and socialist dogma as a new and better way for America.

Donald Trump may have been the ultimate "celebrity president," but the country needed him badly. His "outsider" status and inexperience in politics were instrumental in bringing to light a Progressive insurgency in Washington the American people needed to understand. In the process, he exposed Progressives for what they are: intolerant hypocrites and dangerous revolutionaries on a scale the American people could not have imagined.

We may not always have agreed with the President's tone or methods, but he got things done. After the lethargy of eight years of Barack Obama when almost nothing happened except turning the Democratic Party into the American Socialist Party, widening the nation's racial divides, and tarnishing the standing and prestige of the United States all over the world, it was past time to return to the principles that fueled America's successes. As the President reminded us, it was time to make America great again.

The fact that 10 million more Americans voted for Donald Trump in 2020 than in 2016 indicates people were alert to the Progressive threats. It did not matter, and Progressive now control our government. Many blame voter-fraud. You know the allegations. I have no idea if any of them have merit or, even if they do, whether it was enough to have changed the results of the election. My concern is, neither do election officials.

As a nation, it is in everyone's best interests for all Americans to have confidence that our voting systems are secure and accurate. That confidence was shaken for many in 2020. Some question the election outcomes because too many voting procedures were changed unilaterally by Progressive governors in ways that seemingly weakened ballot security, such as the prolific use of mail-in ballots. For others, the proposition that Donald Trump attracted almost 10 million more votes than 4 years ago, but a halting, visibly impaired, Joe Biden still beat him by campaigning from his basement and turning out more voters in key battleground states than Barack Obama, is an impossibly difficult tale to swallow.

We need to know what happened.

CHAPTER 13

ROBERT REICH

Periodically, something so shameless, so flagrantly wrong, occurs to remind us of the extremes to which Progressives are willing to go to mislead the American people and accelerate their dream of making everyone in the country entirely dependent on government. And so it was when an editorial by Robert Reich, the former Democratic Secretary of Labor, was published not very long ago in a local newspaper.

Reich was purporting to explain why welfare isn't welfare, and why, in any event, "red" states benefit more from government aid than "blue" states. To do so he had to stand logic and economics on their respective heads, and his arguments illustrate the dangerous zealotry that drives so much of the Progressive stratagem to steer this nation sharply left.

Essentially, Reich was railing against the Trump administration's plans to consolidate welfare programs under a federal agency that has "welfare" in its name—shame on us if we describe something accurately. He then went on to decry lumping Medicaid, food assistance, and housing aid into the category of "noncash welfare." According to Reich, if you define welfare this broadly, "a large chunk of America relies on welfare—including a lot of people who wouldn't like to think of themselves as being on the dole."[263]

Really? What exactly are Medicaid, food assistance, and housing aid if not welfare? And while those receiving it might not *like* to think of themselves as being on the dole, how else can you think about it? More to the point, isn't that the concern—there already are too many people in the US "on the dole?" The generous people of this country do not object to helping the needy, but they object to being taken advantage of; they balk at being scammed. Although many legitimately question the federal government's authority to provide federal assistance to anyone, something I will speak to in more detail in a moment, in the minds of most, the question no longer is whether federal assistance should be available to the needy, but who are the needy, who decides, how much should the needy receive, and under what circumstances?

These are perfectly sensible questions, and answering them is essential to any type of honest debate and consensus about federal assistance to the poor. Progressives, however, are not interested in debating federal assistance; they are committed to expanding it as broadly as possible. In their worldview, dependence on government is a necessity, even a virtue, not a last resort. It is how they plan to control populations and how they most easily can change the character and government of the United States. In typical Progressive fashion, however, Reich accuses the President of trying to make the United States look like a "vast welfare state" by calling welfare, *welfare.* If it looks like a duck, swims like a duck, and quacks like a duck, well, perhaps it's time to start thinking about it as a duck.

The diversionary political strategy of "bread and circuses for the masses" dates to antiquity, and Reich and other Progressives understand the tactic well. Consequently, rather than acknowledging the true nature of the debate over federal assistance and offering concrete suggestions for resolving the issues, Reich creates his own version of "bread and circuses."

According to Reich, red states actually benefit more from government assistance than blue states because—hold tight here—federal money being paid to defense contractors for goods and services, price supports for certain agriculture products, and subsidies to the states for land and forestry management means the economies of red states are heavily dependent on federal dollars.

Only someone committed to defending the unsupportable, and one who must firmly believe the American people are brain dead or nearly so, would even attempt to equate Medicaid and food and housing assistance with *purchases* from defense contractors and payments to states to ensure the availability of strategic resources. Nonetheless, according to Reich, the dollars spent by the government to do just that are the equivalent of welfare payments. Presumably, that also makes the salaries of federal workers, a majority of whom are Democrats, welfare payments. Essentially Reich is arguing that since many are benefitted in some way by federal *spending,* it is unfair to describe federal *benefits and assistance* in the form of Medicaid, food stamps, and housing support as "welfare." And ignoring the adage "when you are in a hole, stop digging," he goes further, claiming that when you take into account the advantages red states derive from federal spending, blue state residents send more tax money to Washington than they get back in federal help, while residents of red states receive more in federal assistance than the tax money they send to Washington.

I have no doubt many government contractors set up shop in states where taxes are lower, regulations fewer and fairer, and the right to work guaranteed. We can only hope most federal spending flows to more efficient suppliers operating in more capable, better run, lower-cost states. But arguing that federal dollars going to contractors and states for goods, services, and resources is the equivalent of welfare is utter nonsense. Reich also laments the fact that under the tax reforms enacted by Republicans in 2018, blue states now will give even more "welfare" to red states because, get this, blue state residents pay more state and local taxes than residents of red states, and the new federal tax laws limit the amount of state and local taxes that can be deducted from federal taxes.

The irony of using the excessive taxes paid by residents of high-spending blue states as "evidence" blue states are giving welfare to red states is so transparently idiotic that it requires little response beyond this. Blue states have subsidized their undisciplined, free-spending "habits" for years on the backs of more prudent, responsible red states. The big government, higher taxes, free-spending states learned early on that they could shift some of the burdens of their gluttony to other federal taxpayers simply because the more local and state taxes increased, the less federal tax they were required to pay. Incentivizing gluttony on the part of states too feckless to put their own houses in order should have no place in federal tax policy, and it is past time for California, New York, New Jersey, and the other overly extravagant states to shoulder the full brunt of their out-of-control spending. Why should I, a resident of Virginia, help California pay for sanctuary cities, uncontrolled immigration, the destruction of the central valley by unwise environmental decisions, and a host of other Progressive calamities?

Reich ends his head-scratching screed with the usual effort to shame— "We are all in this together, so we ought to help out those in need"—but then engages in a remarkable sleight of hand. He first observes that "We," whoever "we" may be, "don't regard the help (Medicaid, housing payments, and food stamps) as welfare handouts. We call it social insurance," but then tries to support his argument by referencing Medicare and Social Security which, unlike Medicaid, housing payments and food stamps, are true social insurance programs paid for by almost all working Americans through payroll taxes and, in the case of those receiving Medicare benefits, monthly premiums.

It's a lot to unpack. Where to begin?

Reich is an economist. He surely knows the difference between welfare handouts and federal spending, and he certainly understands that for most of us Social Security and Medicare are anything but free. I am retired and paying considerably more for my health insurance coverage under Medicare and a Medicare supplement plan than I paid for unsubsidized (my employer paid nothing) private health insurance while I was working. Over my working life, I also paid significant amounts of money into the Social Security program, as most working Americans do, more than I may ever take out of it. I fully appreciate the fact that my Social Security payments were to support workers already retired, just as what I now receive from Social Security will be paid for by current workers. My point is not that everything I paid into Social Security should be repaid, but simply that most who receive benefits from Medicare and Social Security made significant contributions to those programs. For some, Social Security and Medicare may be a windfall, but for the majority of people, these are programs paid for over a working career and, in the case of Medicare, will continue to be paid for as long as benefits are available.

As a matter of constitutional power, I have reservations about the federal government's authority to give away money to anyone, even the poor and unemployed. Article 1, section 8 of the Constitution sets out the federal government's spending power and is limited mainly to matters of national defense. As early as 1794, James Madison said of a proposal to allocate a $15,000 expenditure for French refugees, "I cannot undertake to lay my finger on that article of the Constitution which grants a right to Congress of expending, on objects of benevolence, the money of their constituencies." Years later, Colonel Davey Crockett made this impassioned plea in opposition to a proposed grant of $10,000 to the widow of a naval officer:

> We must not allow our respect for the dead or our sympathy for the living to lead us into an act of injustice to the balance of the living. I will make no attempt to prove that Congress has no power to appropriate this money as an act of charity. Every member upon this floor knows it. We have the right as individuals to give away as much of our own money as we please in charity; but as members of Congress we have no right to appropriate a dollar of the public money.[264]

Hundreds of appropriation bills, many for beneficent purposes, were vetoed by Grover Cleveland as recently as the late 1880s because they were outside the authority of the Constitution.

Ratification of the Sixteenth Amendment allowing a federal income tax in 1913 was the beginning of the end for this type of fiscal constraint. "Flush with cash" for the first time, the US government had money it could give away, particularly after World War I ended. Better still, the progressive nature of the income tax allowed politicians to play "Robin Hood," taking from the "rich" and giving to the "poor." The temptation was far too much for even constitutional limitations to contain, and it did not take long for Franklin Roosevelt and his New Deal Supreme Court to remove any constraints on congressional spending by interpreting the general welfare clause of the Constitution, Article 1, section 8, in ways that gave Congress the right to spend money virtually any way it pleased.

At this point, the train has left the station on that issue. The argument against unfettered government spending powers long ago was buried by zealous proponents for remaking the American government, a Congress willing to disregard constitutional restraints for political gain, and judges derelict in their duties, so I will stifle my objections to programs like Social Security and Medicare. There at least seems to be a consensus in this country supporting those programs, they have funding mechanisms, albeit flawed, and most of the people benefitting from them have at least some "skin in the game."

What is clear is that Medicare and Social Security are not "welfare," but food stamps, housing assistance, and Medicaid are. What else could they be? No one "earns" them. They are largely paid for out of the general revenues of the federal government and the states. There are no repayment obligations or mechanisms. There is nothing like a consensus supporting the breadth and scope of these programs. And they are precisely the types of programs that bring out the worst instincts in politicians. The temptation to "buy votes" by constantly expanding benefits, both in terms of what is provided and who is eligible, is overwhelming. As dependence on government grows and the number of people benefitting from these programs begins to outnumber everyone else, the incentives for expanding them build.

I believe most Americans are willing to extend a helping hand to the needy. But like all things, the "devil is in the details." While Americans may be perfectly willing to help those truly in need, I do not sense any appetite for extending government assistance to people making multiples of the poverty level, for allowing the welfare ranks to be swollen with the "unneedy," or for creating public assistance programs that disincentivize work and family. While the welfare system needs revamping, that can never happen as long as Progressives oppose every change, reject every suggestion that welfare should have work requirements for those able to work, and attempt to thwart debate about the proper role and scope of "welfare" by insisting, like Reich, that welfare isn't welfare, but some form of "social insurance." We never will get a handle on welfare in this country if we are not honest enough even to define it properly. "Welfare" cannot be treated as an infinitely expansive term justifying what essentially is a massive redistribution of wealth.

There once was a stigma attached to accepting welfare. It served to ensure people would work hard to get "off the dole" as quickly as possible. This is just another "fence" Progressives are taking down in their ceaseless quest to make and keep as many Americans as possible dependent on government. If redefining welfare as "social insurance" makes it easier to grow welfare programs, Progressives are for it. It is similar to the change in name from food stamps to "Supplemental Nutrition Assistance Program (SNAP)" and the change from actual paper coupons under the Food Stamp program to Electronic Benefit Transfer (EBT) debit cards. Don't change the program; just change the name of the program to disguise what it is. Tell people they "deserve" what the government gives them and more. Remove any guilt from receiving welfare by calling it "social insurance," and convince people their social insurance payments are no different from the payments the government makes to contractors for goods and services. Insist that people living in "blue" states are even more deserving of "social insurance" payments because "blue" states pay more federal taxes than "red" states and receive less.

As the proverb goes, "Beware of false prophets, who come to you in sheep's clothing, and inwardly are ravening wolves" (Matt. 7:15).

CHAPTER 14

THE CANDIDATES

The 2020 elections spawned a far more dangerous form of presidential candidate than celebrities like Ronald Reagan, Donald Trump, and Oprah Winfrey. Many were young; all were radical. They were unwilling to credit the United States for the great good it has done around the world at unprecedented costs in blood and treasure. They came with no promises to defend and protect the Constitution or the laws of the United States. Just the opposite. They sought to end constitutional government in America and replace it with socialism. They made no pretense of wanting to be president for all Americans; they did not. They were zealots with extreme worldviews and intolerant of anyone critical of their ideologies. They demanded loyalty to strict Progressive orthodoxies, and those Americans unwilling to commit were not welcome. They considered speech to be free only to the extent they agreed with it. Social justice was what they said it was. "Fairness" was whatever resulted from what they decided.

Make no mistake about it, these candidates, if elected, intended to eliminate the Constitution; place the means of production under government control; distribute society's opportunities and advantages not by merit, but by preferences based on the color of a person's skin or their gender or their ethnicity; strangle the economy through the rigid application of an extreme environmental agenda and expansion of the regulatory state; confiscate and redistribute wealth; pay reparations to Native Americans and those they considered victims of slavery; collect America's guns; open its borders; take down its monuments; eliminate religion, and weaken its military. They intended, in other words, to implement an entirely new social order and economic system designed by them, in which personal and economic liberties and freedoms would be nonexistent. They may have called themselves "socialists" or "Progressives," but their raptorial attitude was more reminiscent of the oppressive attitude of fascism at its goose-stepping best: "All within the state, nothing outside the state, nothing against the state," and as pointed out by one commentator, "Everything for the state."[265]

Progressives now control the Democratic Party, and the candidates running as Progressives were not shy about saying exactly what they planned to do. For most of them, their web pages only thinly disguised their intent. Andrew Yang's website provided a particularly good tutorial on what intrusive government looks like and what Progressives view as the appropriate role of government. Yang listed over 100 "policies" he would implement if elected, some so "in the weeds," you would have thought he was running for mayor of a small town in rural America, not president of the United States. I will have more to say about Yang later in this chapter.

In addition to Yang, Corey Booker, Beto O'Rourke, Kirsten Gillibrand, Kamala Harris, Elizabeth Warren, Wayne Messam, Marianne Williamson, and Pete Buttigieg were among the early contenders seeking the Democratic nomination. Several washed out early, casualties of their ineptitudes and lack of money. Others, like Tom Steyer and Michael Bloomberg, billionaires who sensed an opportunity to buy the presidency, later joined the field. Joe Biden also eventually threw his hat in the ring, presumably convinced to do so by more "traditional"

Democrats panicked by the prospect of a Democratic ticket so underwhelming and radical a safety net was needed. I am confident Joe, at age seventy-seven, thought his run as Barack Obama's vice president had been his last "rodeo."

Many of the "first to declare" were the types of candidates Bernie Sanders unleashed with his successes against Hillary during the 2016 Democratic primaries. Suddenly, the unknowns, the unaccomplished, the losers, were scrambling to prove they were presidential material by positioning themselves as far left as possible and promising to tear the country apart and turn it into a third world "s—hole" if elected. The thinking presumably was, if a tired, old, unaccomplished, treasonous wacko like Bernie can generate that much support, why can't younger, more energetic, and equally unaccomplished, treasonous wackos like us do even better? Even Joe Biden seemed to feel the "heat." Once he entered the race, he tried to carve out a place at the table by claiming he was the most "progressive" Democrat of all.[266] It shows how much control Progressives have over the Democratic Party when old-timers like Biden feel the need to burnish their Progressive credentials.

In an early effort to prove just how "progressive" he was, Joe floated the idea of naming Stacy Abrams as his running mate if he became the Democratic nominee. That should have been a scary proposition for everyone. Stacy Abrams is a committed pro-choice, anti-gun, anti-voter identification, flag-burning Progressive who was endorsed by Bernie Sanders in the 2018 Georgia gubernatorial race, which she lost. Despite that loss, she was chosen by Democrats to give the response to President Trump's 2019 State of the Union address. Kamala Harris, who ultimately turned out to be Joe's choice as a running-mate, was not a significant "upgrade".

Joe's name recognition unquestionably helped him during the campaign. He has been around so long he felt and sounded "familiar" and "unthreatening" to voters as long as they were not paying attention. And even if Joe was more a "swamp creature" than the progressive crusader he claimed to be, he had little choice other than to become the frothing-at-the-mouth extremist needed to maintain the support of the lunatics who make up the Progressives' base. Joe now needs Bernie supporters to suspend their rioting and building burning long enough to make it appear he has brought a degree of calm and reconciliation to the country. That was the implicit promise his campaign used to target the timid and dupe them into voting for him. It won't last for long, but even a brief interlude will allow the media time to gush about the "civility" Joe has re-introduced to the White House.

Biden is an old man, older when he took office than Ronald Reagan was when he left office. What is the likelihood of Biden even making it through a first term, much less eight years, in the White House? Joe went out of his way during the primaries to assure voters that if nominated he would "choose his vice president carefully because he was old," which sounded like an offer of a Faustian bargain—"Give me a stint in the White House, and I will make the radical of your choice my vice president; she will be president very soon."

The choice of Kamala Harris, young, inexperienced, and unaccomplished, as his vice-president means Joe's death or disability would hand the presidency to someone who enjoys the support of the Democratic Party's most extreme elements; that's why she was chosen. She clearly is the most radical candidate ever to run on the presidential ticket of a major political party in the United States. And brace yourselves; it could end up being a ten-year term as president of the United States.

How could that happen? Under the Twenty-second Amendment to the Constitution, someone who serves two years or less as a "stand-in" for an elected president remains eligible to run for two additional four-year terms as president. In other words, if Joe Biden dies, steps down, or is removed from office under the Twenty-fifth Amendment for health or other reasons after two years in office, his vice president would serve out the remainder of his term and still be eligible to seek two terms as president.

At the end of the day that may explain why Progressives were willing to stick with the visibly impaired Biden as their nominee, particularly since the COVID-19 outbreak allowed Joe's "handlers" to shelter him from public view where his growing cognitive difficulties were less visible.

Grand choice isn't it? A president who, as President Trump said, "is not playing with a full deck," and a vice-president who co-sponsored the socialist manifesto known as the "Green New Deal" and threatened to disarm America using executive orders, if necessary.

It would be comical if it weren't so dangerous. But it is dangerous, and it confirms two basic truths about the Democratic Party.

First, the Party unquestionably has been commandeered by socialists and communists calling themselves Progressives, as Rep. Allen West of Florida warned as early as 2012.[267]

And second, it lacks any semblance of a legitimate agenda and now has been reduced to pandering to its most extreme elements.

In truth, even if the Democratic Party had not been hijacked by Progressives, Democrats had no options other than looking for support from the radical left. President Trump already had occupied the center and right of the political spectrum by doing something rare in politics. He did what he told voters he would do if elected: appoint judges to the Supreme Court and other federal courts who would adhere to the Constitution and their oaths of office; shrink the "regulatory state;" enact tax reforms to help millions of Americans, but particularly the middle-class; renegotiate NAFTA and other bad trade deals; withdraw from the disastrous Iranian nuclear deal and the equally bad Paris environmental accord; reduce nuclear tensions with North Korea; punish China's repeated trade and intellectual property violations; rein in Russia's adventurism in Ukraine, Syria, Venezuela, and elsewhere; expand the economy; grow the stock market; bring manufacturing jobs back to the US; reduce unemployment, particularly among minorities; and build a wall along our southern border. The list could go on nearly indefinitely, but it makes the point: President Trump, more than any other politician in recent memory, was true to his campaign promises.

Most of that now will be undone. Progressives will do what they can to disguise how radically left they intend to take the nation, and Barack Obama, who remains personally popular among many voters, will continue to make cameo appearances to "reassure" Americans that their country is not being dismantled one plank at a time. But they will not be able to appear "too mainstream." The base will not tolerate too mild a message or delays in implementing the "new order" they envision. They will demand immediate action on issues such as the adoption of the Green New Deal; reparations; universal, government-run health insurance; the right to abortions up to and even beyond birth; "racial and social justice;" free tuition and student loan forgiveness; and expansion of the Supreme Court to create the super-majority of Progressive Justices that will ensure the ascendency of socialism in the US. Kamala Harris's presence may placate them for a while— most know Joe is too old and sick to be in office long—but they will be impatient to get as much in place as possible before the 2022 mid-terms. However, one thing is certain; for whatever time Joe manages to stay in office, neither he nor his vice president will be the ones in charge.

Sadly, Joe no longer is capable of being the one in charge. It was painful to watch his press conferences and other public appearances during the Democratic primaries, including the empty stares into the television cameras until his wife came on stage to "fetch" him; his losses of thought in mid-sentence; confusing his wife with his sister, and the angry outbursts he directed at supporters. He was struggling and continues to do so. He is easily confused.

But that is not the primary reason Joe and Kamala will not be in charge at the White House. I never believed Barack Obama was in charge of the executive branch while he was president—he had far too much time to play golf and visit Hawaii and Martha's Vineyard to have been engaged in much decision-making. No, Progressive handlers were in charge of the Obama White House, just as they will be in charge of a Biden/ Harris White House.

Before that starts to sound a bit too far-fetched and "conspiratorial," let me introduce Valerie Jarrett, Obama's "Rasputin."[268] The Iranian-born Jarrett—her parents were American expatriates—had been a close friend of the Obamas for years. A power broker in the Chicago political scene where Barack Obama honed his political skills, Jarrett once was chief of staff for Mayor Richard Daley. Many credit her with being the power behind Barack Obama's rapid rise in Progressive politics.

When the Obamas moved into the White House, essentially so too did Valerie Jarrett. She was named a "senior advisor" to the President, often stayed in the family quarters, and regularly dined and vacationed with the First Family.[269] Jarrett reportedly had her own, six-person Secret Service detail, not usual for "senior presidential advisors."

Some of the same radical influences on the Obamas spoken about in other chapters of this book—Bill Ayers, Bernadine Dohrn, the Rev. Jeremiah Wright—also were part of Jarrett's world. Although she divorced in 1988, her father-in-law, Vernon Jarrett, a Chicago television personality, was a close associate of Frank Marshall Davis, a well-known communist, and Valerie Jarrett is credited with recruiting Van Jones, another self-declared communist, to Washington to take over as Obama's "green jobs czar."[270] To provide a sense of the extent of Jarret's power over the Obamas, the *Times* once ran a story about her entitled, "The Other Power in the White House."[271]

In the book, *The Amateur*, Edward Klein, formerly an editor for both *Newsweek* and the *New York Times magazine*, quoted former President Obama as answering, "absolutely," when asked if he ran all of his decisions by Jarrett. Klein also cited Bill Clinton as cautioning, to paraphrase, "an amateur is in the White House relying on the Rasputin-like influence of one Valerie Jarrett to call the shots, while we are told to pay no attention to the lady behind the curtain."[272] Another author, Richard Miniter, chronicles how President Obama three times called off Navy Seal operations to kill Osama bin Laden at the insistence of Jarrett before finally being permitted to complete the mission in May 2011.[273] Her influence reportedly extended even to overruling cabinet-level decisions with which she disagreed.[274]

Predictably, the media showed little curiosity in determining Jarrett's actual role in the White House or how much control she exercised over the President. Whether you call her "handler," "consigliere," or perhaps more accurately, "political commissar," however, her influence was considerable. The Obamas' politics had been nurtured and shaped in the shadow world of some of Chicago's most radical elements, which was Valerie Jarrett's playground. I suspect Michelle Obama's confession that the first time she was proud of her country was when her husband was elected president can be traced to the anarchical influences that surrounded the Obamas in Chicago. I also believe Jarrett's mission was to make sure the Obamas did not stray too far from the Progressive orthodoxy while distanced from the fountainhead of their ideological roots. Progressives knew Barack Obama was weak and indecisive and perhaps even considered him vulnerable to more moderate points of view. Someone might have convinced him, for example, that it was not appropriate to sing "God Damn America," or blame 9/11 on the United States, as his long time Chicago pastor, Jeremiah Wright, preached. But if it required a watchdog to keep Obama in the fold, with all that Joe Biden has going on, it likely will take a pack.

Initially, I do not think Biden's entry into the race was pleasing to the Progressives who now run the Democratic Party. I say that because one of their favorite tactics for bringing down those they oppose, accusations of "sexual misconduct," was unleashed against Joe early in the campaign. On that occasion, the accusations involved inappropriate "touching" and "hair sniffing" allegedly occurring in 2009 and 2014.[275] It may not have been considered serious enough at the time to disqualify Biden from serving as vice president in the Obama administration, but certainly something America needed to know if Joe insisted on being a nuisance and interfering with the Progressive's plans to install their extremist of choice in the White House.

At some point, Americans have to come to the realization that the constant parade of women who materialize to make accusations of sexually inappropriate conduct, almost always involving incidents allegedly occurring years or decades earlier, against everyone Progressive's oppose, now including, it seems, one of their own, is the cheapest of political ploys. It degrades the process, the accusers, and everyone touched by this madness. I am not defending Biden. I think he is a corrupt political hack, far more deserving of a term in federal prison than a term in the White House. He has hung around national politics for too long and now truly is operating without a "full deck." But dredging up women to smear every political opponent with "she said, he said" accusations is something that should have run its course long ago. If it is given credence by voters, however, Progressives will continue to use the tactic shamelessly. If the embarrassing spectacle of the Kavanaugh hearings was not enough to discourage them, I am not sure what could.

In this case, it's possible the accusations of "misconduct" were intended only as a warning that the Progressive *nomenklatura* already had a choice for the Democratic nominee, a warning Joe, simpleton that he is, did not recognize. It's also possible the accusations were a "test" of sorts—the accusations were mild as these things go, and given Biden's long-time and well-known "touchy-feely" antics around women, they may have been designed to see if anything more serious was flushed out. "Monkey see, monkey do" is a pretty typical scenario in situations like this. Or this could have been notice to Joe that he needed to toe the Progressive line if he wanted to avoid further attacks from within.

Somewhere along the way, however, it seems to have occurred to Progressives that pairing Biden with a young radical might be the best way, perhaps the only way, to defeat President Trump and get someone they could control into the White House. Use Biden's familiarity to voters to lend an appearance of moderation to the ticket, slip in the radical of choice as the vice-presidential candidate, and see what happened. America might be exhausted enough from the constant turmoil the media creates around the President to be looking for some "quiet time," or enough independents and moderates might opt for Joe simply to assuage their uneasiness over what they viewed as the President's sometimes "unpresidential" behavior. Voters who ignored the details of the food fight that was the Democratic primaries might well have believed Biden could provide the calm they were seeking, particularly if they had not been watching his painful struggles to stay sentient during campaign appearances. Since Joe was not likely to make it through a first term in office even if elected, much less two, the odds were good that it would be only a short wait until the Progressives' choice for vice president would be able to take over. If the process seemed to be taking too long, well, there always was the Twenty-fifth Amendment.

The strategy had the added benefit that if a "Biden paired with a radical" ticket did not win the election, not much would be lost. Progressives did not expect to beat the President in this election cycle, Joe no longer was prime-time material and certainly was not a factor in Progressive politics going forward, and the "radical of choice" for vice president was unlikely to be damaged by an unsuccessful run for vice president—the "fault" would be Biden's.

The COVID-19 outbreak changed everything. It gave Progressives a real chance in November, even with Joe. The country was shut down, the President's agenda slowed considerably, including the appointment of federal judges. The economy was in a shamble with a recession likely and a depression possible. Unemployment rose to the worst levels since the Great Depression. The virus handed Progressives everything they had been trying to achieve with the impeachment hoax, and then some.

Democratic governors did their part by using COVID-inspired "emergency powers" to extend the crisis and keep their states shuttered for as long as possible. The apparent goal was to ensure the public hysteria over the pandemic continued long enough to frighten people into using mail-in ballots in November 2020, while keeping emergency powers extant so state voting laws prohibiting or limiting the use of mail-in ballots could be over-ridden by executive decrees.

The rioting following the death of George Floyd gave Progressives a second unexpected boost. I go into this in much greater detail in the chapter entitled, *George Floyd*, but it appears that while Mr. Floyd's death may have served as an unexpected "trigger" for the chaos that ensued, Progressives already had plans to foment massive civil unrest across the country last summer. Whether or not that is true, Progressive governors and mayors across the country sat back and watched as anarchists looted, burned, and defaced cities, set up occupied "autonomous zones," and tore down national monuments. Police were told to "stand down," and offers of federal assistance to control the turmoil were rejected. As Rush Limbaugh said on one of his broadcasts, Democrats were perfectly willing to sacrifice small businesses and the middle-class because the upward mobility of the middle class represents a threat to the Progressive ideology.

The weeks of civil disorder unquestionably damaged the President's reelection chances. Many Americans were bewildered that the President did not act more decisively to stop the lawlessness, but it was a dilemma. If the President ignored state and local officials and deployed the National Guard, Homeland Security, or other federal law enforcement agencies to restore order, he would have been anathematized as a dangerous and reckless autocrat, sending federal troops and agents into states against the wishes and "advice" of their governors to maim and kill "peaceful" protestors. And make no mistake about it, people would have been injured and killed if federal forces intervened; there would have been almost no way to avoid it. By exercising restraint, however, the President appeared weak and ineffective, unable or unwilling to protect America. Some of his base, made up in the main of people who believe in the rule of law, lost confidence.

The fact Progressives realized a Biden/Harris ticket provided them with a realistic opportunity to build the Progressive equivalent of the "Deutsche Reich Forever" if Joe could be nursed through the first two years of his term became clear when Tara Reade, a former Biden staff member, filed criminal charges with the Washington, DC, police in early April 2020. She accused Biden of sexually assaulting her in 1993 and had considerable contemporaneous evidence to support her charges. The media remained almost completely silent. For weeks after the charges were filed, the media did not ask Joe Biden a single question about them—not one.

Think for a moment about the frenzy that engulfed Brett Kavanaugh's confirmation hearings following his appointment to the Supreme Court. None of the organizations which so viciously attacked Justice Kavanaugh, not "#MeToo," not any of them, uttered a word about the accusations against Biden. There were no claims that all women must be believed. Quite the contrary; each of the women allegedly on Joe's short-list of VP candidates at the time, including Kamala Harris, reconfirmed their allegiance to Joe. Less than two years earlier, the same women were unanimous in their support of Christine Blasey Ford's unproven accusations against Brett Kavanaugh. I have more to say about this incident in the chapter of this book entitled, "*News Media*," but the silence surrounding Tara Reade's accusations provided proof-positive that Progressives no longer wanted Biden out, if they ever did.

But Progressives were worried, and not just because their hypocrisy had done the full Monty. They understood Joe had to respond to Tara Reade's accusation, but they also knew he was barely capable of remembering who he was running against, much less providing a cogent rebuttal to serious allegations of sexual assault. Progressives had no shame running a cognitively impaired septuagenarian as their candidate for president of the United States, but they were terrified at the prospect of allowing him to try to explain away the accusations of Tara Reade. One thing is certain: Progressives would not have let those complaints fester for as long as they did, or allowed Joe to go through fifteen press conferences without addressing Tara Reade's claims, if they thought he could have offered a credible rebuttal to the charges. The lengthy silence only was possible because of an obsequious media uninterested in questioning the candidate about the accusations.

The Biden campaign eventually settled on a question-and-answer format in predictably "safe" surroundings for Joe's response; it was the only chance they had to try to keep him "on message." He appeared on MSNBC's *Morning Joe* and was questioned by co-host Mika Brzezinski, a noted Progressive. Joe made the required, perfunctory "denial" of the charges, but the interview was anything but convincing, particularly when Joe stumbled badly while trying to explain why he would not authorize a search of his Senate papers stored at the University of Delaware, his *alma mater.* The refusal destroyed completely the credibility of his denial.

Tara Reade maintained that she had filed a complaint of sexual harassment at the time of Biden's alleged attack, which she said occurred in the basement of a Capitol Hill office building in the 1990s, but the written complaint had not yet been located. Some believed a copy might have existed in Biden's legacy Senate papers. Reports that Biden campaign workers had gone through the records stored at the University of Delaware not long before Tara Reade's allegations became public fueled suspicions that the Biden campaign believed the university had materials relevant, if not to Reade's accusations, then to other "sensitive" issues that might arise during the campaign, particularly if Reade's allegations prompted an investigation.

Joe made the entire episode more curious by offering to allow documents he had stored elsewhere, in the Senate building, to be searched for references to Tara Reade. Perhaps he knew the Senate would not release those records regardless of his consent—the Senate secretary ultimately concluded she lacked legal authority to release the information and declined to do so—or maybe the campaign knew those materials contained nothing of consequence. Whatever the difference, Joe did not attempt to explain his refusal to allow the Delaware documents to be searched other than the plaintive claim that, "Nothing is there." It was the same response Hillary Clinton provided after she destroyed thousands of emails during the investigation of her use of a private, non-secure email server to conduct official business while secretary of state. The media didn't care in either case. Joe and Hillary both understood they would not.

Close your eyes for a moment and visualize the media reaction if Joe Biden and Donald Trump had changed places in this controversy. The outcries would have been unrelenting. More to the point, is there any circumstance in which a responsible, fair media would not have exhausted every effort to access the Delaware documents and flayed a political candidate unable to provide a legitimate explanation for why the documents were not being produced voluntarily?

I always believed the reason Hillary Clinton so frantically destroyed emails, cell phones, and servers was less about preventing discovery of classified government documents stored on her unsecured personal devices, and more about preventing the disclosure of documents relating to contributions to the Clinton Foundation. Elsewhere in this book, I have described the "pay to play" scheme many think the Clintons were using to generate donations to the foundation and how quickly and dramatically donations dried up after Hillary left office. I suspect the Biden campaign had the same types of concerns about providing access to his papers at the University of Delaware, at least until that stash could be "cleansed" of troublesome materials. Given Joe's long and well-deserved reputation for monetizing his name and office to the benefit of friends and family, I have little doubt there are many documents he would prefer remain unseen and unavailable. Think what those records might disclose about his dealings in Ukraine, in Costa Rico, China, and elsewhere around the world where Joe has been linked to political corruption and graft.

There is no logical way to explain why the allegations of sexual assault against Brett Kavanaugh and Joe Biden were treated so differently by the media and every other Progressive ally. If the same standards were applied to Reade's allegations as were applied to Blasey Ford's, Reade would have had to be believed and Joe would have had to step down as the

Democratic presidential nominee. Caught like a deer in the headlights by the absurdity of their own "rules," Progressives tried to do a quick pivot: women are to be believed initially and given a chance to tell their story, but then the "truth" must be investigated and determined. Application of the rule of law and due process, in other words, not something even remotely offered to Brett Kavanaugh.

It was an awkward position for Progressives and not very convincing. But with the media squarely in their corner, it was not an issue that was allowed to gain traction during the general election. Never before had the utter hypocrisy of Progressives concerning women's rights and sexual misconduct been so publicly on display, but the media buried it.

Most Americans, I am confident, did not understand how radical the Progressive agenda was when they cast their ballots for a Biden/Harris ticket. I am equally confident few knew much about Biden's background and record, much less Harris's, even though Joe had been the archetypal "swamp creature," wallowing parasitically in the muck of Washington, for nearly half a century.

As vice president, Joe was largely "eye candy," on the ticket to lend gray hair and name recognition to the inexperienced Obama without fear that he might bring any type of agenda or resist what Progressives had in mind for America. He was the ultimate "silly putty" vice-presidential candidate, moldable into any form the Obama camp desired. He spent most of his time as vice president feathering the nests of friends and family, as has been described elsewhere in this book.

It is difficult to say how his association with the Obama administration was viewed by voters during the 2020 election. President Obama remains personally popular with many

Americans, even though he accomplished little while in office other than widening the racial divides in the country and passing Obamacare, a program so deeply flawed I can only surmise it was designed to fail to pave the way for government-run health insurance. People may have felt less favorably toward the former president if they had understood what a godsend he was to the Communist and Socialist Parties in America; both quickly recognized an Obama White House, with its roots in Chicago radicalism, was the ally they needed to turn the country sharply left and took full advantage.

But Obama's handlers were clever. He never was allowed to openly declare as a socialist or socialist sympathizer and his more radical politics were carefully hidden from the public. As the saying goes, however, "the proof is in the pudding." His administration managed to expand an already bloated regulatory state regime, and the economy predictably languished. By the end of his second term, illegal immigration largely was out of control, an opioid crisis was raging, and the military was underfunded and struggling. On the world stage, Obama perfected the art of "leading from behind," and his efforts to appease the nation's enemies were making the United States look weak and vulnerable. North Korea, Iran, Russia, China, and others were fractious and looking for ways to leverage the leadership vacuum.

Joe largely was invisible for most of the eight years he served as vice president, much like he was as the COVID-19 crisis heated up and the rioting sparked by George Floyd's death spread. A decision obviously was made by his campaign to keep him out of public view. If we had a real media, Biden would have had a lot of questions to answer about the contrasts between America under Obama and America under Trump, what he would have done to contain COVID-19 and control the rioting, and his mental health, but we don't. Hunter

Biden's escapades in China and Ukraine also would have required explanation, not to mention Joe's use of his office to enrich other family members and friends. Nothing, however, could be more damning of Biden's astuteness and decision-making than the assessment of former Obama defense secretary, Robert Gates, who wrote in his memoir that, "Biden has been wrong on nearly every major foreign policy and national security issue over the last four decades."[276] Only a candidate coddled and protected by the media possibly could have survived such an obvious indicator of unfitness for office.

Think about it. The Obama administration's secretary of defense castigating Biden for being on the wrong side or every major foreign policy and national security issue for the last forty years. It is the same Joe Biden who was accused by fellow Democrats of completely mishandling Anita Hill's harassment claims during the hearings to confirm the appointment of Justice Clarence Thomas to the United States Supreme Court. Biden was chair of the Senate Judiciary Committee at the time. Throw in how frequently Joe's "behavior" around women has been called into question, and you have a candidate who is deeply flawed in both judgment and character. But that is not what the media reported. Donald Trump was portrayed as the poltergeist and Biden the exorcist. Sides were chosen, and the media refused to report the facts straightforwardly or fairly.

As flawed as Biden and Harris may have been, you would not have found any more substance in any of the other Progressive candidates.

Beto O'Rourke was a prime example of the type of candidate the "Bernie effect" created. Beto reminded me of an overly privileged, empty-headed frat boy who forgot to grow up. He never had a serious policy proposal about anything, and the fact he was even mentioned as a presidential contender shows how badly our political standards have eroded. This is a guy who once was arrested for burglary and another time for DWI, who as a teenager belonged to a computer hacker group called "Cult of the dead cow," where he went under the moniker, "Psychedelic Warrior," and played in a punk rock band.[277]

Elizabeth Warren, or "Pocahontas," as President Trump dubbed her, has spent most of her life lying about her ancestry, claiming Native American heritage, presumably to advance her career and acquire the "victim status" so treasured by Progressives.[278] However, the finger-wagging, scolding, grating style and delivery of "Harvard's first woman of color" always seemed more likely to drive even committed Progressives to conservatism rather than convince people to vote for her.

Andrew Yang was another product of a privileged background and ties to the Obama administration. His "Three Big Ideas?" Guaranteed universal basic income for life in the form of a $1,000/month "freedom dividend" for every citizen over the age of eighteen; Medicare for all; and "human-centered capitalism," which, in true quixotic fashion, he describes as "maximizing human well-being and fulfillment." The estimated annual cost of the "freedom dividend" alone? More than $3 trillion.[279] He also favored voting by cell phone, free marriage and financial counseling, gun buy-back initiatives, ranked-choice voting, an America exchange program, prosperity grants, and a host of other "giveaways" and extraordinarily intrusive government initiatives. Mr. Yang unquestionably believes government is the dispenser and source of all prosperity and happiness, and that everyone would be much better off if an entirely new government designed by him assumed power in America. Take a look at his web page, https://move-humanityforward.com/, if it is still up.

I have explained "rank choice voting" earlier in the book and will not repeat that explanation here except to emphasize once again why Wang and other Progressives are such devotees of this bastardized form of voting. It has nothing to do with "improving" elections or "ensuring officials are elected by a majority of the vote," as some contend. It is simply an effort to bypass the Electoral College and get closer to the "direct democracy" model Progressives covet. Wang showed his disdain for the Electoral College by also calling for "proportional selection of electors," meaning each state's delegation to the Electoral College would be chosen proportionately based on the popular vote results in the state. If one candidate received 51 percent of the vote and the other 49 percent, for example, the electors would be divided that way instead of the winner taking all. If enough states, or enough big states, adopted similar procedures, the Electoral College results would more or less mirror the national popular vote. That might not even be necessary—several states already are signing on to an interstate compact to allocate their electors based on the popular vote tally nationwide, a scheme which essentially would nullify the Electoral College. We will have to wait to find out if it is constitutional.

We are a republic, not a direct democracy, and it drives Progressives crazy—it is hard to take rights away or change the form of governments in a republic. In a direct democracy if you can bribe, coerce, or intimidate 51% of the voters, *viola*, all those messy protections against government abuse and overreach disappear.

Progressives certainly understand how to bribe voters—Progressive candidates, in one form or another, all were trying to win the Democratic nomination by buying votes and making unrealistic promises of "something for everyone." "Free" health care and education, annual stipends for all Americans, forgiveness of college debt, and many other promises of "free-bies" were used to seduce the uninformed, the gullible, and the increasing number of people who have grown depen-dent on government. The projected $3 trillion a year cost for Wang's "freedom dividend," one program out of dozens pro-posed, would have consumed nearly all of the annual tax rev-enues of the United States.[280]

If you want to understand what an intrusive government looks like, spend a few minutes studying some of Yang's other "policy" proposals. Over a hundred were listed, including my favorite, the "American Exchange Program." The description of that program eventually was modified to describe a pro-gram requiring high school seniors to travel to different parts of the country so they could make friends and be exposed to other aspects of American culture. As originally proposed, however, the program required rural and urban families from around the country to swap places. They do things like that in China, but Americans have grown accustomed to choosing where they want to live and work. China has over 700 million people still living in rural areas but plans to move 400 million of them into urban areas and is building millions of condominium units in cities across China to accommodate them. When the Chinese government decides the time is right, those selected for "resettlement" will be told to pick up and move to which-ever cities they are assigned. That serves several government goals, including aggregating small farms to make them larger and more productive and moving people into areas where labor is needed. Families in China are powerless to prevent these forced relocations, but it is not something even conceiv-able in a democracy where private property is protected and the rule of law and civil rights are respected. Obviously, Wang's "vision" for a new form of government in America was not even distantly related to democracy.

Wayne Messam was mayor of Miramar, Florida, and a former Florida State football player. He too threw his hat in the presidential ring, and although he mercifully dropped out early, the fact he even considered entering the race illustrates the fantasies the "Bernie effect" has set off among fringe candidates. Massam favored universal health care, forgiveness of student debt, infrastructure projects, addressing climate change, and banning military-style guns and weapons. He also would have eliminated the Trump administration's corporate tax cuts, which helped bring tens of thousands of manufacturing jobs back to the United States and fueled the robust economic expansion that was occurring in the United States until the emergence of COVID-19.[281] He was, in other words, an unknown, small-town mayor and run of the mill Progressive, who has done nothing of consequence in the political arena but was willing to promise lots of "free stuff" in exchange for votes.

Pete Buttigieg was the mayor of South Bend, Indiana, the fourth largest city in the nation's seventeenth-largest state in terms of population. He would have been our first openly gay president if elected, as well as the first millennial to hold the office. Americans have a fondness, some might say weakness, for achieving "firsts" that often overrides good judgment and common sense. I am convinced, for example, Barack Obama, an unknown and unaccomplished United States senator, an "amateur" in the view of Bill Clinton, was elected president only because America fell in love with the idea of electing its first Black president. Buttigieg took full advantage of those tendencies, and he received strong support in the early primaries before eventually bowing out.

Let me be absolutely clear. It does not matter to me in the least what Buttigieg's sexual preferences may be. I would have no problem voting for a gay president, man or woman, with the proper background, intelligence, experience, and competencies. My objections to Buttigieg, as they were to Obama, were much more granular. He had nothing to offer as president, no grand ideas, no vision for the United States other than turning it into another failed socialist state, no remotely qualifying experience, not even notable success trying to govern what is the 306th largest city in the country. As the 306th largest city in America, South Bend is just a tic larger than the metropoles of Vacaville, California, and Kenosha, Wisconsin, but considerably smaller than Miramar, Florida of Wayne Messam fame, which checks in at number 189 in the ranking of US cities by population. At thirty-eight years old, Buttigieg didn't even have sufficient life experiences, in my view, to govern. From what I have been told, many residents of South Bend would agree.

Mayor Pete is an engaging guy, earnest enough and seemingly intelligent, although it is an uninformed intelligence, but he owed his popularity to the fact he was gay, not accomplished. The most worrisome aspect of his early popularity was the apparent willingness of so many to "bet the country" to establish a milestone.

We will have women presidents. We will have LGBTQ presidents. We do not have to elect unqualified, unaccomplished, thirty-eight-year-old mayors of small towns and cities to bring that about. We certainly cannot allow ourselves to be bludgeoned into bad political choices by a Progressive narrative that decries a biased, homophobic America because it has not yet happened. It is a message with only one intent: to intimidate Americans into a wave of virtue-signaling voting.

This is not a game. The decisions of presidents of the United States affect billions around the world. Voting for unqualified candidates with extremist agendas may feel "enlightened," but it is a reckless misuse of the political franchise that can lead to unpredictable, dangerous, and potentially ruinous outcomes. Elections have consequences.

A quick review of Buttigieg's "positions" will show you what I mean. They reflected the typical Progressive pulp. He wanted: paid family and medical leave for up to twelve weeks; a $15/hour minimum wage; forgiveness of student debt; elimination of the Electoral College; limits on campaign spending; a ban on charter schools; the end of new leases for oil and gas drilling on federal land, as well as off-shore drilling; a buy-back of guns; "studies" to evaluate reparations for slavery; government subsidies for "affordable housing;" some form of "free" tuition for college; abortion-on-demand; open borders; elimination of the 2017 corporate tax cuts; legalization of marijuana; "wealth" taxes; citizenship for "dreamers;" and a host of other unaffordable, economy-strangling, culture-changing programs.[282]

While none of these agendas mention defunding the police, It is only because it had not occurred to any of these "Thurber men," a gender-neutral usage of the term in this instance, at the time—their campaigns started and ended before George Floyd's death. If they still had been running, however, you can bet defunding police would have been added to their dystopian visions. There are no more efficient or quicker ways to ensure that anarchists will control the streets than defunding the police.

I apologize for dwelling on programs of Progressive candidates who long ago left the stage. I do so only because it highlights the extreme positions Progressives are advocating and the type of agenda Joe Biden is promoting. He has no choice; the Twenty-Fifth Amendment will come into play sooner than expected, and President Harris will implement the Progressive vision, if Joe shows any hesitancy to act.

There is nothing democratic or even *American* about what Progressives are doing. They are advocating mass changes to the founding principles of this nation and the basic compact between the American people and their government. This is not "nuanced tinkering" to improve a system of government; it is a call to arms to change the form of government entirely. That needs to be understood by all Americans. Progressives are proposing that a country built on principles of individual initiative, self-reliance, and personal freedoms be surrendered to government central-planners, not to emulate the welfare states of Europe and Scandinavia, but to replicate the failures of Cuba, North Korea, Venezuela, and Russia.

How serious is the threat? As one magazine article put it:

> The cover story of the most recent issue of this very magazine is about contemporary socialism: what it means to be a socialist in 2019, and how the movement transformed from—as writer Simon van Zuylen-Wood put it—"irrelevant, [from] the dustbin-of-history" to something near-ubiquitous, at least among a certain type of under-35-year-old.[283]

"Near-ubiquitous ... among a certain type of under-35-year-old"? How distressingly alarming. The cover story itself paints a picture of dangerous social and political experimentation among younger generations who have not yet "paid their dues," but have taken full advantage of everything America offers. They understand little about the realities of socialism, communism, or any other collective form of government, and like all of those too ignorant to learn from history, they are destined to repeat it unless they abruptly change course. Not quite the original quote, but close enough.[284]

George Will has described what he styled the scientific and numeric "illiteracy" of Progressives and how unrealistic their proposals are. As just one example, he pointed out if "Medicare for all" was adopted, there no longer would be anyone outside the *public* health care system to subsidize the benefits for those dependent on the system. Without the higher payments received from the 245 million Americans who currently subscribe to *private* health insurance plans, approximately two-thirds of all insured individuals in the United States, many doctors and hospitals could not stay in business. Rationing of health care would become unavoidable. As he also noted, the "spending explosion" advocated by Progressives, and the tax increases proposed to fund it, would result in a 91.8 percent marginal tax rate without coming close to paying for what is planned. As to the Green New Deal, its attack on fossil fuel alone would threaten world food supplies and make it nearly impossible to feed the planet's 7.5 billion people.[285]

Progressives cannot stand economic prosperity. They simply do not understand how in a fair world, some can end up with more than others, but "know" it must have something to do with White privilege, racism, or luck, either good or bad. In their worldview, things like hard work, skill, creativity, ingenuity, risk-taking, sacrifice, perseverance, self-reliance, drive, passion, willpower, integrity, and patience have no place; they are largely inconsequential. People are forever "stuck" into one of two-tranches—the haves and the have-nots—and the have-nots find themselves in that condition only because of circumstances beyond their control. Without government intervention, the have-nots are powerless to succeed, never mind the success stories of millions of people in the United States who started with nothing but, on their own, took advantage of the opportunities offered by this country and prospered. The "American Dream" is not and never has been a fiction.

A few years ago, Mitch Daniels, the former Indiana governor and current president of Purdue University, in a graduation speech had this to say about luck:

> And yet, among many pernicious notions of our time, perhaps the most dangerous is the idea, sometimes implied and sometimes express, that life is more or less a lottery. That we are less masters of our fate than corks floating in a sea of luck. Or, even more absurd, that most of us are victims of some kind, and therefore in desperate need of others to protect us against a world of predators and against our own gullibility.
>
> I doubt you or your parents believe such nonsense. If you did, you wouldn't have come to Purdue. You wouldn't have invested the time, money, or hard work that brought you to this moment. And I hope you will tune out anyone who, from this day on, tries to tell you that your achievements are not your own.
>
> Oh, sure, we all get important help along the way. I hope you will never lose sight of those parents, teachers, coaches, and others who nurtured and assisted the growth of your intellect, skills, and character. But in the end, your successes, and your failures for that matter, are, like your diplomas today, really up to you.[286]

A statement generally attributed to Thomas Edison puts it more bluntly: "Opportunity is missed because it is dressed in overalls and looks like work."

These are the things Progressives never seem to grasp. They make no effort to try to explain how government programs that destroy the motivations to work, create, and innovate possibly can succeed. Socialism and communism always seem inspirational in theory because the things that prevent attainment of the promised "nirvana," human nature and human motivation, never are included in the discussions. Where are these supernatural beings who will work tirelessly to provide for those who choose not to work? Why have they never before materialized to rescue socialism from its self-destructive nature? Why should we expect them to show up this time? Progressives do not try to explain.

Progressives think they are smarter than you. They do not believe you understand what is in your own best interests. Their expectations for most disadvantaged groups are so low, in fact, they manage to turn them into self-fulfilling prophecies.[287] As social scientists well know, when expectations of a person or group are low, that person or group is more likely to act in ways that confirm the expectations.[288]

While Progressives are quick to slander almost anyone with reckless charges of "racism" and "bigotry," what possibly could be more racist, biased, bigoted, and discriminatory than the obvious disdain they have for the competencies and abilities of disadvantaged groups? Contrast that with the reality described by Walt Williams mentioned earlier: if the earnings of Black Americans were totaled and thought of as the GDP of a separate nation, Black Americans would rank among the twenty wealthiest nations on Earth.[289] As Williams pointed out, only in the United States would that be possible.

Much of this largely explains why we had such a variegated and freakish field of candidates seeking the Democratic nomination for president. Suddenly, any Progressive was a potential presidential candidate, whether or not they had accomplished anything of consequence, as long as they could contrive a platform just a bit more extreme than anyone else running. They were "pitching" to audiences easy to seduce with promises of "social and racial justice;" free health care and education; forgiveness of student debt; confiscation of guns; income redistribution; reparations for slavery and the displacement of Native Americans; dramatic and damaging environmental measures; and "solutions" to a host of other problems few of the candidates understood and even fewer had considered or analyzed in any meaningful way.

None of the platforms were coherent or workable. None were even remotely affordable. All trampled basic freedoms and liberties. It did not matter. Bernie Sanders invited Progressives to follow him down Alice's rabbit hole into a fantasy world, and they eagerly accepted. Even those inclined to be a bit more cautious, like Amy Klobuchar, the senator from Minnesota, were forced into the give-away bazaar now masquerading as the Democratic Party.[290] It was a race to the bottom and more closely resembled a sixth-grade class officers election—"Free ice cream for everyone, longer recesses, no homework ever, and hot dogs every Thursday"—than a national presidential election.

While much of what Progressives propose may sound hallucinogenic, the stuff of fairy tales, they are zealots and will try to implement every one of the radical policies they are proposing. They may be scientific and numeric illiterates, but they have been handed control of this country with all that implies. My advice? Support conservative candidates at all levels of government. Work with your state legislatures between now and the 2022 mid-terms to strengthen our electoral system, update voter registration records, curtail the indiscriminate use of mail-in ballots, and address the misuse of emergency powers by state governors. And turn out to vote. It will not be easy, but regaining control of the House and Senate in 2022 is essential iif the Progressives' assault on American democracy is to be slowed.

CHAPTER 15

NEWS MEDIA

I s there any doubt the mainstream media has lost all credibility as objective reporters of the news? The fact that objectivity in reporting, at the very least, requires a consistent pattern of analyzing and verifying evidence in an unbiased and fair manner seems to have escaped notice by almost all journalists, reporters, newscasters, and others engaged in public communications. I am not sure anything in recent memory illustrates the extreme political bias of the media better than the complete lack of coverage of Tara Reade's charges of sexual assault against Joe Biden.

When Supreme Court nominee Brett Kavanaugh, a Trump appointee, was charged with sexual misconduct allegedly dating to his high-school years, Progressives erupted with sustained fury. The accuser, Christine Blasey Ford, a California college professor, was unclear about almost every detail of the claimed assault, which allegedly took place during a high school party. She could not recollect time, place, or circumstances, and individuals she identified as corroborating witnesses denied any knowledge of the incident. Ford also admitted to political motivations for her accusations—she wanted to put an "asterisk" by Brett Kavanaugh's name before he "took a "scalpel" to *Roe. v. Wade.*[291]

Nevertheless, the accusations dominated the news cycle for weeks leading up to the confirmation hearing, and virtually every women's rights organization on the planet attacked and condemned Kavanaugh unrelentingly. There was not even a pretense of a presumption of innocence or due process. Kavanaugh was guilty because women who make accusations of sexual assault are to be believed, with or without proof and regardless of how incredulous their stories might be. The reputation of a brilliant jurist and, by all accounts, a wonderful husband, father, and public servant, was left in tatters.

Flash forward to Tara Reade's charges against Biden. Reade, a lifelong Democrat, once worked for Biden and was clear about the details of what happened to her, which were grotesque. She contemporaneously reported the incident to others, including a neighbor, another Biden supporter, who confirmed Reade's story. Reade's mother anonymously called the broadcast journalist, Larry King, within days of the attack to seek advice. During the call, which was videotaped, she told King her daughter was having difficulties with a "prominent senator." Co-workers also acknowledged that Reade complained in the mid-1990s—the attack allegedly occurred in 1993—of being sexually harassed by a former boss in Washington. Joe has long raised eyebrows with his "touchy, feely" behavior around women. Many would call it groping.

What was the reaction of the media, #MeToo, and the other organizations that had excoriated Brett Kavanaugh for weeks, just two years prior? Nothing. *Nada*. Dead silence. No calls for Biden to step down. No calls for him even to explain. No support for Tara Reade or demands that she be believed. It was stunning, inexplicable, unimaginable. Regardless of what you may think about #MeToo and the other women's movements that react immediately and mobilize instantly at the first hint of sexual misconduct by any conservative, it seems inconceivable they possibly could be this biased or unprincipled. Even if you question the validity of the charges, how can the standards be so different? Most disturbingly, by what possible measure can the news media's indifference to the story be explained or justified?

I do not know if Tara Reade is telling the truth, although she has a long-standing reputation for truth and veracity. The corroboration for her claims also was significantly greater than anything Blasey Ford was able to produce. But that is not the point. Dramatically different standards were applied to nearly identical charges, both directed at men seeking high office. Progressives quickly moved from insisting that women who raise sexual assault or harassment claims "must be believed," to maintaining that "women raising these claims should be *heard* and then an *investigation* must take place to determine the truth." If that sounds like a call for due process and the presumption of innocence, it is, but those were not the standards applied to Brett Kavanaugh, and they cannot be reconciled with any that were.

America needs to come to grips with what is quickly developing into a reality far more dangerous than simple hypocrisy. It is an alarming form of political warfare in which the media has chosen sides and elected to join the socialist movement in America. This has nothing to do with women's rights. If the concerns were women's rights, the political affiliation of the accuser and the accused would not matter. It is about political insurrection. Groups like #MeToo are being used to target and destroy the political opponents of Progressives. They are ideological hit squads, and the media has signed on, not only to provide support but also to lend aid and comfort.

How did this happen? In part, it's attributable to something I have talked about a great deal in this book, the deterioration of our educational systems. Without an adequate understanding of the history of their country or its form of government, and lacking any appreciation for the traditional and important role of the media in public affairs, those now working in the news media have no reference points to guide how they carry out their duties and responsibilities. Professional and ethical standards have all but disappeared. If, as the American Press Institute says, the purpose of journalism is to "provide citizens with the information they need to make the best possible decisions about their lives, their communities, their societies, and their governments,"[292] then the innuendo, rumor, and unverified information from "anonymous" sources that too often poses as "news" today cannot possibly serve any public purpose.

However, inadequate education alone is not responsible for what has happened to the news media. Essentially, what inadequate education started, conflicts of interest finished—the media is hopelessly conflicted. A twenty-four-hour news cycle has created an insatiable need for "content," meaning insignificant stories get repeated endlessly until they seem more important than they are, and "dead time" is filled with manufactured "entertainment" posing as news. Everyone knows the drill by now. Place a group of like-minded people around a table and allow them to aggrandize issues by giving them a biased tilt and rehashing them endlessly. Or, take proponents of opposite viewpoints, put them together in a studio, and encourage them to spar over issues that can range from meaningful to the manifestly non-serious. In either case, viewers gain a distorted understanding of both the importance of the issues and the value and accuracy of the views expressed.

The real conflict for the news media, however, is competition from the internet and social media, which allow anyone, regardless of qualifications, to opine about anything and everything and to do so in real-time. As society turns increasingly to these non-traditional sources for its "news" and information, the media comes under pressure to report stories quickly, whether or not they can be verified, and to sensationalize or spin stories in ways calculated to attract and hold audiences. The "real-time" nature of the internet and social media, in other words, has forced the media to abandon the profession's traditional safeguards and has driven it into tabloid journalism.

There is another biasing influence. Because younger audiences have the most long-term potential for the media, the issues covered and the slants given to the coverage tend to be directed at these audiences, most of whom are left-leaning. Providing the Progressive viewpoint comes naturally for most news organizations, which tend to be populated by young Progressives too poorly educated, mentored, and trained to see the problem with allowing their personal political beliefs to color how they report the news. Virtually everything they report is filtered through their views on various social issues—climate change, race and gender, social and racial justice, abortion, LBGTQ rights, gun controls, immigration—and everything is pitched in ways that reinforce Progressive viewpoints. Even the most complex, nuanced issues tend to be reported in a "good" versus "evil" format designed to appeal to audiences more comfortable with emojis than the English language and not inclined to read or listen to anything more detailed than a "tweet."

Just before the Mueller report was released, I was reading a story by the Associated Press entitled, "Redacted report set to be released; Barr, Rosenstein to speak," published on April 18, 2019. Here is how the AP speculated about what the public should expect to see when the report was made public:

The nearly 400-page report is expected to reveal what Mueller uncovered about the connections between the Trump campaign and Russia that fell short of criminal conduct. It will also lay out the special counsel's conclusions about formative episodes in Trump's presidency, including his firing of FBI Director James Comey and his efforts to undermine the Russia investigation publicly and privately.

Could the story have been written any more suggestively or pejoratively? Even though no one had yet seen the report, is there any doubt the AP believed there were connections between the Trump campaign and Russia, and that the President had taken steps to undermine the investigation? Wouldn't a news organization trying to be neutral and fair have reported the story more along these lines:

The nearly 400-page report is expected to reveal *whether or not* Mueller uncovered *any connections* between the Trump campaign and Russia. *Attorney General Barr's earlier summary of the report said Special Counsel Mueller had found no evidence of collusion between the campaign and Russia.* It will also lay out the special counsel's conclusions about formative episodes in the Trump presidency, including his firing of FBI Director James Comey *and whether there were any efforts to undermine the Russian investigation* publicly or privately.

When we turn to the "commentary" or "opinion" pages of newspapers or to talk shows, things get even worse. More than a few nationally syndicated columnists tend to be "one-trick ponies." They gain fame, wealth, and access—syndicated columns, book deals, speaking engagements, invitations to gatherings of the elite—by becoming advocates for particular points of view and specific issues. A few seem so blinded by hate and bitterness, however, the only thing they can write or talk about is hate and bitterness, particularly when it comes to President Trump or anything conservative.

If you are a one-trick pony, you are out of business if the issue on which you "made your bones" goes away, so few of these commentators have much interest in seeing issues improved or resolved. It is similar to those who become leaders of "causes"—no "cause," no fortune, fame, or influence. Consequently, the common theme of many columnists is directed to convincing readers that whatever progress may have been made toward resolving a particular issue or set of issues, it clearly is not enough; things, in fact, are worsening. Whatever advances may have been achieved, it is only the tip of the iceberg—the situation is as bad as it ever has been, maybe worse.

Leonard Pitt is an example. I once regularly read his syndicated column as a source of different views on certain issues, largely race-related. He is a good writer, sometimes tried to be fair, and seemed to have a degree of common sense. He always has been somewhat of a one-trick pony; his thing is "racial discrimination, which, if you read his columns, is worse today than during the Jim Crow era, maybe the worst ever. There is overt discrimination hiding behind every bush, denying Black people a fair shake and equal opportunity. It is discrimination and White privilege that have resulted in over 70 percent of Black babies being born out of wedlock, mostly to teenage mothers, and growing up in single-parent households. It is discrimination and White privilege that has caused Black students to graduate from high school with the equivalent of a sixth or seventh-grade education, even though many of the school systems are run by Black administrators and many of the teachers are Black. It is discrimination and White privilege that has caused Black-on-Black crime. And so it goes. From time to time, however, he would make a sensible point, and most of the time he wrote civilly.

Then came Trump, and Leonard came unhinged. Rationality at any level disappeared from his columns, at least when writing about the President. Pure hate, visceral, vindictive hate, replaced civility. In one remarkably revealing article entitled, *"No need to 'understand' Trump supporters,"*[293] he scolds a lady named "Rose," who he described as a "nice lady," for advocating "trying to understand supporters of Donald Trump." Using the common ploy of setting up a "straw man," he first characterized the "issue" this way: the problem with Trump supporters is they represent "a backlash among right-wingers deeply angry and profoundly terrified by the writing on the demographic wall"—which he interpreted as the "declining preeminence of White, Christian America." He then supplied his solution: Trump supporters do not need to be understood; they need to be "defeated." He truly went over the top, however, when he tried to explain his "they need to be defeated" rhetoric. As he churlishly put it: "We know what it means to live and let live. And we know that welcoming a stranger, caring for the stranger, is simply what you do as a human being." But not for Trump supporters. They were not welcome in America.

Leonard Pitt is not a stupid man, but he wrote a stupid article, and in the process revealed something too disturbing to ignore. What exactly is he advocating? He flatly says while we know what it means to live and let live, Trump supporters are not welcome in America—there can be no compromise; they must be defeated. Isn't this the type of rhetoric that resulted in the death of five Dallas police officers in July 2016? Isn't it the same mentality that caused Progressives to bus in protesters to rob and loot in Ferguson, Missouri; Baltimore,

Maryland; and Charlottesville, Virginia? Isn't it race-baiting in in its most unvarnished form? He always has been somewhat of a shill on race issues, but this somehow feels more sinister.

An equally disturbing piece was written by Jamelle Bouie, entitled, *There's No Such Thing as a Good Trump Voter,*[294] claiming that those who supported the President voted for "a racist promising racist outcomes." According to the article, the President ran a campaign of "racist demagoguery against Muslim Americans, Hispanic immigrants, and Black protestors." Worse, he "winked to the stream of White nationalists and anti-Semites who backed his bid for the White House." [295] Trump supporters did not deserve empathy.

Can you imagine the hue and cry if Donald Trump or any prominent Republican made statements like these about supporters of Hillary Clinton? Demonstrators would be in the streets calling for the President's impeachment, claiming he had advocated violence against Democrats. They would find no ambiguity in the meaning of a statement saying, "We know how to live and let live, but not in the case of Clinton supporters, who are not welcome in this country." It would be viewed as a call to arms, and as in Dallas, Ferguson, Baltimore, and Charlottesville, violence likely would follow.

Where is the media backlash over columns like these? Why can George Soros and other billionaire anarchists support Progressive causes without the media lifting a figurative eyebrow, but when the Koch brothers support conservative causes, there is an audible gasp? How can the media promote protests on college campuses against wealthy conservative donors supporting Republican political campaigns, but applaud when wealthy Progressive donors do the same thing for Progressive causes? Why does the media welcome liberal speakers to colleges and universities, but remain silent when the appearance of a conservative scholar on campus results in protests and violence?

Unfortunately, the type of incendiary diatribes made by Leonard Pitts and Jamelle Bouie against Trump supporters are not uncommon. Conservative America is under attack every day without a murmur of protest from the media. Could a Republican comedian, for example, have gotten away with calling for trees to fall on a top advisor to a Progressive president, as Michelle Wolf did with respect to Kellyanne Conway at the 2018 White House correspondents' dinner? Where was the media outrage? Is calling for the death or injury of political opponents now part of the Progressives' platform? This makes the Burr/Hamilton duel of 1804 look civilized, but why is it happening? Why is it tolerated? What makes it acceptable?

Leonard Pitts no longer seems to have any interest in being part of the solution, if he ever did. There are true atrocities taking place across the globe every day, sometimes at our southern borders. Women and children are trafficked or enslaved by the tens of thousands. Millions live in poverty, and babies starve because of autocratic regimes around the world. Anti-Semitism is again raising its ugly head, including in the Congress of the United States. Democrats, for example, could not muster enough support to pass a resolution condemning anti-Semitism and bigotry following grossly anti-Semitic remarks by Congresswoman Ilhan Omar. While the House of Representatives ultimately managed to pass a generic "anti-hate" resolution, the episode exposed the virulent anti-Semitic thinking of many of the young Progressives recently elected to Congress. Socialism and communism continue to wreak havoc from North Korea to Cuba to Venezuela to Nicaragua. Women's rights are trampled in too many countries to count.

There are, in other words, more than enough causes for legitimate champions of justice and fairness to advocate—but none nearly as lucrative as keeping alive the racial divides in this country. Fan the flames of anger, hatred, and division; write about the shame of it all; encourage massive resistance to a lawfully elected American president; and celebrate as you make your way to the bank to deposit royalty checks. Nice gig.

Leonard Pitt also apparently does not understand that many millions in this country felt the same about Barack Obama as he feels about Donald Trump. I believe Barack Obama will go down as the most ineffective and incompetent president in the history of the Republic. He came into office as one of the least-qualified individuals ever to be elected and lived up to his credentials. He was a puppet on a string—weak, indecisive, clueless on the world stage, and a committed socialist who wanted to change the form of government in the United States forever. Being the country's most incompetent president is quite an accomplishment in a nation that once elected Jimmy Carter, but while Carter was just naïve and incompetent, he loved America. Obama was equally incompetent but not naïve, and he had no discernible love of country. What he had was an agenda to change the United States from a constitutional republic with a market-based economy to a socialist "S—hole."

Part of that strategy was widening the racial divide that existed in the country. Barack Obama could have been the great healer of the racial divisions still existing in this country, but he chose to do exactly the opposite. At every opportunity, he drove a wedge into race relations, whether it was his remark that Trayvon Johnson could "have been my son," his comments that Boston police acted "stupidly" when arresting Black Harvard professor Henry Louis Gates, his refusals to condemn racially motivated riots in Ferguson, Missouri, and Baltimore, Maryland, or his refusals to criticize the targeting of police officers by Black activists. The media never once questioned his motives, criticized his lack of leadership, or even lamented the lost opportunities.

Michelle Obama commented before the Wisconsin primary in 2008 that, "for the first time in my adult life, I am proud of my country." This came from a woman who accepted without hesitation all the dollars and benefits the United States offered, including the opportunity to practice law at a major law firm and for her husband to be elected president of the United States. The media yawned. For years the Obamas attended a church where the pastor routinely blasphemed the United States. The media didn't care. In Chicago the Obamas associated with violent domestic terrorists Bill Ayers and his wife, Bernadine Dohrn. The media ignored the story.

Despite it all, conservatives did not attempt to derail the Obama presidency with bogus obstacles. There were no rants about there not being any place in the country for his supporters. "Resistance" groups were not organized to try to frustrate his agenda, and baseless investigations were not launched against him, his family, and everyone associated with him to keep him from attending to the affairs of state. No one suggested impeaching him, despite many instances when the power of his office arguably was "abused," not even when he enlisted the assistance of the Russians during his re-election campaign. There was the usual and expected political opposition, the Garland Merrick controversy notwithstanding, but nothing remotely like the systematic attacks that were directed against President Trump in an attempt to derail his administration and overturn the outcome of a presidential election.

Garland Merrick, of course, was the justice from the United States of Appeals for the Second Circuit nominated by President Obama during his last year in office to fill the vacancy on the Supreme Court created by the untimely death of Justice Antonin Scalia. The Republican-controlled Senate refused to hold a confirmation hearing on his nomination, maintaining that the next president should fill the vacancy, which, for the record, at the time looked like it would be Hillary Clinton. This was precisely the procedure Democrats, and Joe Biden in particular, had long insisted was necessary to protect the integrity of the Supreme Court. Senator Chuck Grassley dubbed it "the Biden Rules." Under the Biden Rules, if a president nominated candidates for the Supreme Court during an election year, the Senate, which was constitutionally obligated to provide or withhold its consent to a nominee as circumstances required, could decline to convene a confirmation hearing absent a compelling need to do so.[296] At the time Joe Biden first articulated his "rule," Democrats were worried that during George H. W. Bush's final year in office, a Supreme Court Justice might resign, creating a last-minute vacancy and providing President Bush the opportunity to fill it with a conservative nominee. But when President Obama nominated Garland Merrick to the Court during the 2016 election year, Democrats, and the media, suddenly lost all interest in the Biden Rules.

While Joe Biden suggested his "rules" for purely partisan reasons, the idea of adopting procedures intended to avoid manipulation of the Court by last-minute resignations and similar strategies is not entirely without merit; it just has no constitutional roots. It's possible, for example, that older justices could resign to allow a lame-duck president to replenish the Court with younger justices of his or her choice, particularly if the president's party also controls the Senate. A case in point: if the Senate had confirmed Merrick Garland, it's possible the late Justice Ruth Bader Ginsburg, who was eighty-three years old in 2016, would have stepped down to allow President Obama an opportunity to nominate a younger justice before leaving office. Justice Ginsburg, hardly nonpartisan, had been vocal in her opposition to Donald Trump, saying she could not "imagine what the country would be like" if he became president and vowing to move to New Zealand if he was elected.[297] The media was remarkably unconcerned that a sitting justice of the Supreme Court would inject herself into partisan politics to that degree.

The Biden Rules aside, these always will be matters determined by the balance of power in the Congress. The party that controls the Senate will decide whether a confirmation hearing is convened for someone nominated to the Supreme Court by the president. That is true whether Democrats or Republicans control the Senate. It is what the Constitution contemplates.

Justice Ginsburg passed away in September 2020. Before COVID-19, however, if she had an opportunity to reflect on the state of the country, she would have discovered an economy that was humming, benefiting in significant ways the groups she professed to care about deeply. Manufacturing jobs were coming back to the United States in record numbers. Unemployment rates were at all-time lows. People's retirement funds were building as stock markets reached unprecedented levels. The military was recovering from years of neglect at the hands of the Obama administration. Things were booming all over the country. Any fair observer, as well as a fair media, would have had to concede that things were going splendidly, infinitely better than during the Obama years, and said so.

Not that any of it was pleasing to the media. Supporters of socialism, a system more accustomed to dressing people in gunny cloth and feeding them gruel, understandably are apprehensive when prosperity threatens to expose the contrastingly dismal outcomes consistently produced by the bleak ideology they embrace. They do not want America to understand how dynamic a market-based economy freed from suffocating over-regulation can be or to compare America with Trump as president to America with Obama as president. They do not want people to understand the human disasters communism and socialism universally have caused. Under Obama, the country got an early peek at what the Progressives' agenda would look like, although the Obama administration was careful to disguise the more radical aspects of its plans. Even so, the country was alarmed with what it saw and the direction Obama was taking it. It was a matter of pride with most Americans that a Black president had been elected, and many Americans liked the President personally, but rational voters were unwilling to abandon more than 200 years of real progress and achievement. I honestly believe a majority of Americans had seen enough by the end of Obama's first term and re-elected him only because they did not want to make the first Black president a one-termer. But having glimpsed where extreme liberalism was taking the country, Americans had no appetite for going there and in 2016 opted for a return to more traditional American principles and economic values.

Yes, Hillary won the popular vote but only because of a huge majority in one state, California. The popular vote margin was 2,864,974 votes nationally, and Hillary won by over 4 million votes in California, meaning Trump won the popular vote everywhere else. The Electoral College thankfully did what it was supposed to do; it protected federalism.

I am not comfortable having one state, particularly California, or even a few, control national elections. Elsewhere in this book, I discussed the voting laws, demographics, and other problems that make fair elections impossible in California. It is only getting worse. And keep in mind: it is not unusual in this country for a president to be elected without winning the popular vote—it has happened on five occasions— and even more common for a president to be elected without winning a majority of the popular vote. Nineteen times, American presidents have been elected without winning a majority of the popular vote, including Bill Clinton (twice), John Kennedy, and Abraham Lincoln. As I said earlier in the book, the president who garnered the lowest percentage of the popular vote in the history of the nation was Abraham Lincoln. It is a function of our constitutional republic and the protections it offers to minority voices.

The media was nearly apoplectic after the 2016 elections. Its full-out assault had not been able to derail the Trump campaign. Calls for eliminating the Electoral College, adopting ranked-choice voting, making sixteen-year-olds eligible to vote, giving statehood to Puerto Rico and a vote to residents of the District of Columbia, all were floated as possible ways to prevent a reoccurrence of what unhappy Progressives viewed as an electoral catastrophe. Perhaps if the media had been more focused on what was happening in the country instead of smugly dismissing Trump supporters as knuckle-dragging, gun-toting, Bible-hugging, White supremacists who could be dealt with appropriately after the coronation of Hillary, they might have understood why Trump won, although I doubt it. After eight years of obsequious Obama worship and sycophantic obedience to progressive dogma, the brains of most reporters had turned to mush; little "free will" remained. The media had become the palace guard.

They still haven't figured it out. The media continues to believe President Trump was elected by 63 million KKK wannabe's who should not even be allowed to stay in the country. Essentially, they have been blinded by the logical fallacies in the arguments they set up to try to explain what they considered the country's unfathomable rejection of progressivism in 2016.

The fallacies took various forms, but "begging the question," "circular reasoning," and "straw man" arguments are in the forefront. A premise is stated as an established fact, whether it is or not. Positions, arguments, and conclusions are then built around that premise, which already includes the conclusion to be proved. Using Leonard Pitt's castigation of "Rose" for her suggestions of reconciliation with Trump supporters as an example, Pitts postulated that Trump supporters were terrified, white supremacists rebelling against the changing demographics in America and voted for Trump only because he too is a racist and white supremacist who would protect them. That premise was stated as an undeniable truth with no exceptions. No other explanation for President Trump's victory is possible under that premise. It is not possible, for example, that Trump voters were objecting to Progressive policies that: raised taxes; weakened the military; widened racial divides; advocated elimination of Second Amendment rights; attempted to nationalize the health care system; destroyed millions of jobs, sometimes whole industries, through excessive and intrusive government regulation; promoted unfettered access to America by anyone who wanted to come regardless of circumstances—"open borders," if you will; encouraged the establishment of sanctuary cities; continued the destruction of our educational systems; packed the federal courts with hundreds of Progressive judges willing to reinterpret the Constitution and "legislate" from the bench; generated ever-burgeoning budget deficits; failed to do anything to slow a raging drug epidemic sweeping the country; ignored gang violence; blundered in dealings with Syria, Iran, and international terrorism; and the other disasters that were visited upon the American people under Obama. No, in the mind of Pitts and his Progressive friends, none of the many calamities and disappointments under Obama could explain the support for President Trump, only the fact that his supporters were racist goons who were not welcome in this country.

Nor, in the view of Progressives, did the fact their standard-bearing in the 2016 elections happened to be one of the most flawed candidates in the history of American politics factor into President Trump's victory. Even a partial list of the controversies that have checkered Hillary Clinton's public and private life is daunting: benefitting financially from trading cattle futures while the first lady of Arkansas; "discovering" supposedly "lost" records relating to the Whitewater investigation under her bed in the White House months after they were first subpoenaed; fighting off allegations of involvement in the mysterious death of Vince Foster; granting preferred audiences as secretary of state to significant donors to the Clinton Foundation; authorizing false stories about the terrorist attacks on the US embassy in Benghazi and failing to take steps to defend the embassy or its ambassador; destroying thousands of emails during a criminal investigation looking into her use of unsecured servers and electronic devices as secretary of state to store classified government documents; and defending her husband's dalliances with a White House intern by trashing the intern. I know of no other politician who has collected as many question marks as Hillary Clinton over a career. Many voters simply did not trust her, they did not like her, and some understood that after eight years of Obama electing another Progressive could well have ended the great political experiment that is the United States.

The Monica Lewinsky affair, by the way, certainly was not the first time Hillary Clinton, a supposed advocate for women's rights, defended her husband's abuse and mistreatment of women. Remember Juanita Broaddrick, Leslie Millwee, Paula Jones, and Kathleen Willey? To charges ranging from rape and exposing himself, to sexual assault and "groping," Hillary staunchly "stood by her man" and condemned the accusers. There were no "I believe" epiphanies.

You will never convince Pitts and others of like convictions that any of these things played a role in the defeat of Hillary Clinton. She was defeated only because Donald Trump attracted a base of White supremacist cretins who viewed Trump as the equivalent of the "Imperial Wizard." I suppose anything else would be too much to expect from someone convinced Jim Crow is still with us.

Through it all, conservatives soldiered on. They did what Americans with regard for their country and Constitution always have done—they suppressed their disappointments, respected the office of the president, and gave the individual occupying it leeway to govern. Obama almost ruined the country in the process, but he was allowed to govern. The media adored him. The fawning coverage of the former president should have been humiliating to serious media organizations. It was reminiscent of, and just as dangerous as, the "fluff" coverage in the lead-up to World War II that transformed the image of Hitler from oddball loner to a caring, gentle statesman with refined tastes.[298]

As the adage goes, "all politics are local," meaning while people may be motivated by many different things, their priorities tend to be matters that affect them daily: jobs, taxes, schools, roads, the cost of a new home. To claim that a single factor was the reason any voter, much less 63 million of them, supported a particular candidate is simply a revisionist fairy tale. It does not take much insight to realize supporters of Donald Trump were motivated by concerns about the direction the country was going, the fact they did not have jobs, the reality of awful schools for their children, and a host of other issues far more important to each of them than Leonard Pitts' fantasies about "writings on the demographic wall."

As an opinion writer and commentator, of course, Leonard Pitts is under no obligation to be either "fair" or "unbiased." He is entitled to his opinions. Regardless of how hate-filled, wrong, or misguided those opinions may be, his right to voice them is protected by the First Amendment. News articles, however, are supposed to be unbiased, objective, and accurate, and that is where the real problems lie.

News, as reported today, and whether in the print or broadcast media, is largely indistinguishable from the editorial pages. It is not unbiased, it is not accurate, and it certainly is not objective. Ethics no longer seem to have a place in America's newsrooms, and reporters no longer recognize they are not supposed to be either advocates or entertainers. Their duties and obligations are to report the news factually and fairly, leaving it to the editorial writers to express the opinions of the newsroom. If competition from nontraditional news sources makes that impossible, then at least have the decency to admit advocating for specific political ideologies and viewpoints and stop pretending to be disinterested journalists presenting balanced, fact-checked accounts of events.

Perhaps after Watergate, it was too much to expect that reporters and journalists one day would return to impartially reporting the news. The success and fame of Woodward and Bernstein convinced too many that a sensational story of political intrigue and corruption lay just around the corner, waiting to make them rich and famous. As soon as news reporting turned from a search for the truth to a search for the "gotcha" moment, however, the truth became irrelevant. An increasingly radicalized education system and social media did the rest, leaving us with a news media largely consisting of a collection of apostates from the ethical moorings and traditions of the great calling they claim to serve but clearly do not respect or understand.

CHAPTER 16

ABORTION

C al Thomas summed up the abortion debate best. It is, "[t] he scientific, moral and theological battle between life as an 'endowed inalienable' right and the evolutionary view that we are just material and energy shaped by pure chance in a random universe with no author of life, no purpose for living, and no destination after we die."[299] Perhaps then the callous disregard pro-choice advocates appear to have for human life should not be surprising, a disregard that manifests in many ways. There is, for example, the story of Virginia Governor, Ralph Northam, pardoning a woman convicted of concealing a dead body when she disposed of her miscarried, thirty to thirty-two-week-old fetus in a trash can. Pro-choice supporters decried the conviction and five-month sentence and celebrated its reversal by gubernatorial fiat, according to news reports.

Flash forward several months to the same Governor Northam calmly explaining how a proposed Virginia law allowing virtually unfettered late-term abortions would affect the delivery of a baby born alive. According to the governor, a pediatric neurologist, the child would be "made comfortable" while the doctor and mother discussed whether or not to kill it. This is the same Ralph Northam who just a few weeks later confessed to wearing blackface or a KKK hood and robe in a picture in his medical school yearbook. While he retracted that admission the following day, he admitted using blackface in other circumstances.

Regardless of your views on abortion, shouldn't even a miscarried fetus be treated more respectfully than trash? Should a baby delivered alive be left to die at the whim of the mother and doctor? The abortion bill Governor Northam was discussing was patterned after a New York late-term abortion law enacted in early 2019. Although supporters of the New York statute argued that it added little to the abortion rights conferred by *Roe v. Wade*,[300]as usual, the "devil is in the details." The New York law, like the Virginia bill Governor Northam was discussing, allowed late-term abortions, or even killing babies born alive, if "necessary to protect the patient's life or health." That includes "mental health," and therein lies the rub. There are no limits on what might be considered a threat to the "mental health" of a woman in either the New York statute or the proposed Virginia law. When Ralph Northam was discussing how the doctor and mother would have to decide whether the delivered baby would live or die, he obviously felt the proposed Virginia law provided mothers with exactly those unfettered options.

What would the macabre discussions between mother and doctor look like? "Doctor, I am out of work and the financial burden of trying to raise this baby will be too much of a mental strain for me, so let it die." Or, "the mental strain of raising twins will be too much for me doctor, so let them expire." Or, "the disappointment of another girl is so depressing, let her go."

Supporters argue that late-term abortions are uncommon and not undertaken lightly. Maybe so, but close to a million abortions take place in the United States each year, and even if advocates are correct that only 1.4 percent of them take place after the twentieth week of pregnancy, that is 12,000 to

14,000 late-term abortions every year.[301] Where else would we so lightly dismiss the slaughter of thousands of children? We treat our dogs and cats with more compassion and respect.

More disturbing still are the reasons abortions occur. In one report by the Guttmacher Institute, a leading private source for abortion statistics, fully 25 percent of abortions reported occurred because the women "were not ready for a child," 23 percent because the mothers "could not afford a baby," 19 percent because the women were "done having children," 8 percent by individuals who "did not want to be a single mother," another 7 percent by women who did not consider themselves "mature enough" to raise a child, and 4 percent because it would have interfered with "education or career."[302] In Florida, there were over 71,000 abortions in 2015 with no reason given for the abortion in over 92 percent of the cases.[303] What is clear is that only a very small minority of abortions are performed because of fetal abnormalities, danger to the mothers' physical health, and rape or incest. Most are simply abortions of convenience. According to the Guttmacher web page, 24 percent of American women will have an abortion by age forty-five, and 59 percent of women obtaining abortions already are mothers.[304]

The problem pro-choice advocates have, of course, is that to acknowledge any degree of humanity in a developing fetus threatens their position that a woman's decision whether or not to abort a child must be entirely hers, even after delivery. Life, in other words, does not begin until birth and the mother's decision not to kill the baby. Until then, society has no interest in its life, and the child is not entitled to any protection, legally, morally, or ethically.

For many in this country, the rights of unborn animals are far more of a concern than the rights of human fetuses and babies. Look at the enormous efforts expended to protect unborn turtles, eagles, and countless other species. People, like Jeremy Bentham, considered the founder of the utilitarian school of moral philosophy, and organizations, like PETA, maintain that animal rights should not be premised on whether an animal can reason or talk, but whether it can suffer. Surely, a developing fetus, and unquestionably, a delivered baby, can suffer.

One of the paradoxical things about the abortion fight, however, is that outside of the abortion debate, children, for the most part, are worshipped in our society and protected fervently. Want to raise money quickly? Advocate a children's cause. Want to arouse righteous indignation and passion? Suggest that someone is threatening harm to a child. Want to avoid opposition to new or increased taxes? Claim they are needed to build or improve schools. Why are we less concerned with the welfare of a viable fetus or just delivered baby?

It was not that many years ago when Americans were shocked and horrified by China's "one-child" policy that resulted in the death of millions of Chinese baby girls. Under the policy, couples were allowed only one child, and girls frequently were aborted or killed by parents who preferred boys. Chinese authorities also engaged in forced abortions for women who conceived again after having a first child. The policy finally ended a few years ago when men began to so outnumber women, it became difficult for them to find wives. Today, the Chinese government still controls reproductive rights, but couples are allowed two children.

The only reason today's Progressives might balk at a similar policy in the United States is an objection to the intrusion on their right to do as they please; dead babies would not bother them at all. While they have no problem telling the rest of

Americans how to live their lives, they suffer no interference with their own or their right to do what they want, when they want, and where they want, particularly when it comes to the sensual and concupiscent. It is why the country is now seeing various groups advocating for rights to engage in polygamy, bestiality, pedophilia, and other forms of behavior that have been taboo for centuries, proving, once again, there is nothing so extreme that someone will not demand the right to engage in it.[305] It is moral relativism carried to its logical conclusion. *Que Será Será,* the doubters be damned.

The view of most hardcore, pro-choice advocates seems to be that because a woman's health is a private, personal concern, she must have complete discretion over whether a baby she has conceived lives or dies, even up to and after birth, whether or not the reasons for terminating the life have anything to do with "health concerns." Just as the lives of defeated Roman gladiators were within the discretion of the throngs who gathered to witness the bloodshed, the life or death of an infant depends on whether the woman bearing it gives a "thumbs up," or "thumbs down." No one else, not society, not the father, and certainly not the infant, have any rights or interests in the decision. Even though in most states a woman, or man, could not lawfully take their own lives, taking the life of an unborn or just-born child, as long as it can be tied to the mother's "physical or mental health," however tenuously, not only is acceptable but a constitutional right, the scope of which continues to grow.

I do not agree with *Row v. Wade.* It was an illogical expansion of the marital privacy rights "discovered" by the Supreme Court for the first time in *Griswold v. Connecticut.*[306] It is one thing, however, to conclude that privacy rights protect a couple's decision to use contraceptives to prevent life from beginning, quite another to say those same privacy rights justify taking a life already begun. But once the Supreme Court decided to stray into this area, I think it did the best it could with what it had to work with. The Court's trimester approach at least acknowledged some level of mortality in the fetus based on viability, similar to the "heartbeat laws" some states are enacting today. I certainly recognize and sympathize with the argument that most fetuses will become viable if simply left alone, and the window of viability necessarily will expand as science advances, but the Court was called upon to make a Solomonic decision, and it did so.

The logic of *Row v. Wade*, however, is entirely inconsistent with where abortion advocates are trying to take it today. Yes, *Row v. Wade*, provided an exemption from the ban on late-term abortions based on the mother's physical and mental health, but the tenor of the opinion was to protect the life of the unborn after viability, not to allow casual claims of "not ready to have another child," or it "interferes with "my education, work, and social calendar," justify the killing of a child. And there is not even a hint in *Row v. Wade* that the Court thought it was approving mother and doctor sitting in the delivery room discussing whether a delivered baby should live or die. Nor was there in *Planned Parenthood v. Danforth* [307] or *Planned Parenthood v. Casey.*[308]

Let me ask you this. If the mother's health is the justification for late-term abortion, why should a one-month-old, or a six-month-old, both completely dependent on their mothers for survival, not also be subject to the mother's decision whether they live or die? If the mother of a one-month-old decides that raising the baby is interfering too much with her social life and that, in turn, is negatively affecting the state of her mental health, why should she not be able to kill the baby? Why has the state acquired a greater interest in protecting the health and well-being of a healthy, but completely dependent one-month-old, than in protecting the health and well-being of a healthy, dependent five-minute-old baby on the delivery room table? How about a 3-year-old or a 6-year-old—neither can sustain life on their own? Why is the mother's "mental health" less a concern of the state three or six years later than when these children first were delivered? Or is this some type of timed contest—you have ten minutes after delivery to decide if you want the child or not, after which the child becomes "human" and a ward of the state?

Some believe the abortion fight is less about women's health than women's rights. They suggest abortion on demand actually is a rejection of patriarchy and the attitude that the most important obligation of women is motherhood. Abortion, in other words, is about establishing that something which comes through a woman's womb is less important and consequential than something that comes from her mind.[309]

So, does a desire to reestablish the "sacred feminine" lie at the heart of the effort to give women nearly unconditional control over whether the children they conceive live or die?

If that is the goal, there certainly are less radical and culturally crippling ways to achieve it than sacrificing thousands of babies every year. And in this day and age, when no pregnancy need be "accidental, why shouldn't the decision to conceive circumscribe, at least to some extent, a woman's power to terminate the life she intentionally created?

Although "women's health" may be the prime motivator for some, "women's rights" for others, social and emotional isolation plays a role and influences the thinking of many of those who advocate abortion on demand and the right to kill even a baby delivered alive. This is an era when smartphones, computers, tablets, and other devices often occupy peoples' full time and attention to the detriment of normal social interactions. How many times have you seen families go out to dinner—Mom, Dad, little Johnnie, and little Janie—and as soon as they are seated, everyone pulls out their phone and retreats into their private worlds? Essentially, no conversations take place among the family for the rest of the evening.

Socially and emotionally isolated, not educated enough to engage issues in any meaningful way, lacking self-esteem, and unable to appreciate the consequences of what they are advocating, people are increasingly desperate to be part of something—a "sisterhood," a" brotherhood," anything. Antisocial, histrionic, and narcissistic behavior patterns develop and control everything they do, say, and think. They become easy prey for "causes," including abortion. Being part of a group advocating a cause soothes feelings of isolation and inadequacy. It becomes an obsession. There is no desire to listen to, much less understand, opposing points of view, nor is there any capacity to admit the group or the cause may be misguided or wrong.

There are other influences, of course, including a public dialogue too often dictated and dominated by publicity-seeking celebrities. In his 1978 book, *The Culture of Narcissism*,[310] Christopher Lasch made the point that the narcissist typically identifies with an "individual of grandeur," believing he or she is like them. To a large extent, we have become a nation of narcissists whose dominant ethos, in the words of author Neal Gabler, is a "culture of celebrity."[311] In a world that largely is atomized, diverse, and mobile, celebrities offer a type of "shared culture," which even if shallow and artificial, injects some degree of excitement and passion into otherwise ordinary and mundane lives. If celebrities embrace abortion on demand as a cause, so too will those who identify with them.

It is an "ethos," unfortunately, that provides celebrities with excessive influence over public opinion with very little evidence to suggest they are the ones who should be controlling the discussions of important cultural and social issues. Many of Hollywood's most successful actors and actresses do not even have high school diplomas and live in insular worlds of privilege and fantasy. Too often, celebrities are commodities for sale, more interested in promoting themselves and their careers than the thoughtful debate of economic, political, social, or other issues. Most did not attain their celebrity status because of intelligence, specialized knowledge, leadership skills, or ethical values, but more commonly because of convention-defying behaviors, language, and lifestyles. For many, their images are entirely manufactured; it is impossible to separate their political and social views from their unceasing self-promotion. And unlike elected officials, if their views are entirely misplaced and wrong, even dangerous, perhaps intentionally so, they have responsibilities to no one.

Take a look at the chapter in this book entitled, "*Illusions of Truth*." If you live in a bubble where celebrity opinions substitute for facts and what is important is defined by "causes" and "groups," your perspectives begin to blur. This make-believe world may provide a sense of belonging missing in the real world, but it leads naturally to "causes" substituting for critical thinking and values. Allegiances once reserved for family, church, and country are redirected to groups and issues. Compromise becomes impossible because if the issue goes away, so too does the "shared culture" and "identity" it offers supporters. Any beliefs in one country, one people, or commitment to common goals or a common good, evaporate.

It was not that long ago that in times of dispute and disagreement over political or social issues, we considered which among competing positions would be better for the country as a whole. That might sound quaint in this day and age—notions of a "common good" are becoming virtually nonexistent in a nation that increasingly has turned from viewing itself as a "melting pot" of nations to embracing a multiculturism that intentionally seeks to divide Americans into competing camps—but once upon a time, it served as a useful tie-breaker, a way to reconcile competing proposals and bring closure to disputed and divisive issues. As Judge Learned Hand cautioned, "The spirit of liberty is the spirit that is not too sure it is right," and that understanding allowed us to reach compromises. Today, too often, the prevailing dynamic more aptly appears to be that summed up by former Secretary of the Treasury, William McAdoo: "It is impossible to defeat an ignorant man (or woman) in an argument."

The ascendancy of *moral relativism* as the structural philosophy of the Democratic Party has played a central role in promoting abortion as an elective procedure of convenience with almost no limitations. Think of it as the Progressives' version of the "mutually assured destruction" doctrine (MAD) that kept the peace during the cold war between the Soviet Union and the United States. Moral relativism is what keeps the peace among the competing factions of the Democratic Party, insulating "causes" like abortion from criticism or challenge.

How does it work? As I point out elsewhere in this book, the Democratic Party has become little more than a large tent where single-issue voters gather with no unifying principles or coherent policies guiding decision-making. Because everyone is different, diverse, and without shared languages, cultures, values, goals, or ideals, there can be no moral absolutes; everything must be relative. Right and wrong can be no more than viewpoints because no one can be judged on what they believe or how they act without completely fracturing the party. Every group, large or small, must be entitled to decide for itself what is acceptable and what is not. If the group decides cannibalism is appropriate, then it is. If the group decides killing infants a few moments before or after delivery is justifiable, who is to say otherwise? It does not matter whether others have a different viewpoint because everyone has the right to determine the code of conduct they will follow with no obligations or responsibilities to anyone else—unless, of course, the viewpoint is conservative, in which case the group can be as judgmental as it wishes.

That is moral relativism. It postulates that two actors engaged in different activities with very different ethical and moral implications nevertheless should be treated identically because the actions of one cannot be considered any better or worse than the other. Progressives have argued for years, for example, that 9/11 was justified because of US policy in the Middle East. They likewise have long maintained that neither side was morally superior in World War II because the Allies bombed Dresden and used nuclear weapons to subdue Japan. Some have attempted to justify the Holocaust by comparing it to the Israelis' treatment of the Palestinians.

But moral relativism depends for its existence on the absence of concepts of right and wrong, and that, in the end, might be the key to understanding the abortion-rights movement. You can only defend aborting a viable fetus on demand if you attach no moral or ethical concerns to the decision; otherwise, abortion represents one of the greatest genocides in the history of the world with over 40 million dead babies in this country alone.

Roe v. Wade started the process of taking down the fence around abortion, but advocates will continue dismantling that fence, one board at a time, until they either are stopped or gain unconditional control over the decision of life or death, even for babies delivered alive. That may be an untenable position for many, but it should not be surprising when no moral or ethical consequences attach to the killing of the unborn and the just born. Moral relativism is eroding the country's moral and ethical compass, its sense of right and wrong, at a rapid pace, and until that is corrected, if it can be, we are likely to continue as a nation divided, not just on abortion, but on most of the significant social issues of the day.

CHAPTER 17

OPEN BORDERS

Will someone please explain to me the justifications for advocating *open borders?* Isn't border security a basic element of sovereignty and a critical aspect of what the federal government is constitutionally obligated to ensure?

The spectacle of the initial caravans of migrants from Central America storming the US border in California, demanding immediate entry into this country, struck me as little more than a staged prelude to implementation of a larger plan essentially designed to overwhelm US border controls. I could not help but believe organizers were hoping for a catastrophe of some kind. What better outcome could there be for convincing Americans our border policies are cruel and unwelcoming than provoking an attack by panicked border guards that killed or injured women and children?

The migrants were well dressed and well-fed. They came complete with megaphones, signs, and other paraphernalia of "protest." Many refused asylums in Mexico, proof that asylum was not the goal. Even when reaching the US border, most did not surrender to US authorities, as would be customary for anyone truly seeking asylum. They instead immediately went to the border walls. Intent on provoking a confrontation, they tried to do so by hurling rocks, bottles, and chunks of concrete at guards, who displayed commendable restraint by using non-lethal pepper spray and tear gas to disperse the crowds.

Women and children, of course, were placed front and center of the melee. Terrorists and activists everywhere have learned that using women and children as human shields is the easiest way to maximize media coverage, generate public sympathy, and alarm those too naïve to understand that it is just a tactic. After all, only a mother more focused on "revolution" than safety would put her children in harm's way, particularly when there are easier, safer alternatives available, such as going to a border portal and peacefully requesting asylum.

Make no mistake, for the most part, the waves of illegal immigrants inundating our borders are not people seeking a safe haven from physical abuse or political prosecution. Most are fleeing economic conditions created by leaders in their home countries they voted into office, although a number are mercenaries being paid to participate in what effectively are border demonstrations. It is very similar to the protests that materialize when there is a police shooting or some other tragedy that sparks public outrage. Seldom are the protesters entirely or even mostly local. Many are bussed in from other locations, often college campuses, and are provided with signage, taught an appropriate selection of political chants, and are housed and fed. The riots that erupted following the death of George Floyd, although more "national" than most, provide an example: a well-coordinated, well-funded, nationwide, nascent insurgency on the part of Marxists and other anarchists trying to destabilize the country.

In the now-notorious confrontation between the alt-right and left-wing extremists in Charlottesville, Virginia, in August 2017, locals also essentially were bystanders, watching two armed groups of troublemakers get off buses and clash in the public square. Neither group was from Charlottesville. Both came armed and ready to create a media event. And that is exactly what they did—create a media event. The most serious injuries that occurred, sadly, were not among the thugs pushing and shoving each other, but two police officers who died when their helicopter crashed, and a young woman who was fatally injured when a deranged, out-of-state individual named James Alex Fields Jr. drove his car into a crowd. Several others were hurt in that incident.

Despite the fact these staged "protests" often incite violence and death—the shooting deaths of five police officers in Dallas in July 2016, being a particularly tragic example—no one ever seriously investigates, much less prosecutes, the organizers and sponsors. Stories continue to link billionaires like George Soros to Antifa, the ultra-violent leftist group, and other left-wing protest organizations, but no one appears to care.[312] Very much to the contrary, while Progressives repeatedly charge those who oppose them with being intolerant and discriminatory, they have adopted an agenda of confrontation with anyone who questions their increasingly manic worldviews. How else do you explain Maxine Water's shrill call to arms in the summer of 2018, encouraging liberals to harass and attack members of the Trump administration and their families whenever and wherever they encountered them?

Before you dismiss Maxine Waters as the nut case she is—although voters in California continue to return her to office—keep in mind that many other prominent liberals have advocated aggression when dealing with conservatives. Hillary Clinton, for example, in the same time frame remarked that "you cannot be civil with members of the Republican Party."[313] Really? And Eric Holder, Attorney General of the United States during much of the Obama administration, encouraged supporters not to take the "high road," but to "kick" Republicans whenever they went "low."[314] While that particular remark may have been intended to be more metaphysical than physical, statements made by conservatives rarely are accorded any benefit of the doubt, so why should Holder's? Earlier in this book, I commented on the dangerous diatribes Leonard Pitts, the well-known liberal political commentator, and others, have directed at Trump supporters.

The reckless statements of Maxime Waters and other Progressives, unfortunately, struck a chord among the Democratic faithful.[315] Several prominent Republicans and their families received credible threats of death or serious physical harm. Others were denied service in restaurants, gas stations, department stores, and similar public places and facilities. Dozens were confronted and publicly harangued or otherwise insulted and shamed. White House press secretary at the time, Sarah Sanders, was asked to leave a restaurant in Lexington, Virginia. It was a disgraceful, childish, and dangerous display of bitterness and vengefulness by Progressive hacks who lacked the courage and competencies to express their views civilly.[316]

Consider if Republican political leaders had called for the same kind of confrontations with officials in the Obama administration. The hue and cry would have been enormous, and rightfully so. This type of call to arms, unfortunately, is far more incendiary when issued by Democrats because of the large numbers of unstable individuals progressivism reliably seems to attract to its ranks.

In the same vein, what conservative judge or justice possibly could have gotten away with remarks like those made by the late liberal Supreme Court Justice Ruth Bader Ginsburg during the 2016 presidential campaigns? She publicly stated that she did not want to consider the possibility of a Trump presidency and might consider "moving to New Zealand" if it came about? Had she entered her dotage? It appears that way, but whether she had or not, one thing was certain—she was not going to step down voluntarily while Trump remained in office. Controlling the judiciary is key to the take-over Progressives have planned for this country, and now that they have regained the White House and control of Congress, I fully expect to see the Supreme Court expanded to twelve or fifteen justices and then "packed" with Progressive loyalists. FDR first tried to do it in 1937; Progressives have been trying to get it done ever since.

Civil debate and behavior are not of much interest to Progressives. Watch Chris Hahn sometime if you want to see an example of someone who has raised "shouting down" those who disagree with him to an art form. A Progressive activist and former aide to Chuck Schumer, Hahn hosts a podcast titled, "The Aggressive Progressive," and is a periodic guest on Fox News programs. While I understand he is on Fox as a foil of sorts, he never engages in discussions of issues—he just shouts. It's what you do when there is no substance to your positions. It also is likely the preferred style of his usual audiences, few of whom, I suspect, are advocates of civil anything. Just a guess, but I'm betting the Bernie Sanders campaign worker mentioned in another chapter, the imbecile threatening to "burn down" Milwaukee, site of the 2020 Democratic National Convention, if Bernie did not win the Democratic nomination, provides good insight into the profile of fans of "The Aggressive Progressive."

The barbarians are at the gates, and our independence and form of government are at risk. A significant part of the problem is that a biased and complicit media has forgotten its historic role of calling "balls and strikes" fairly, regardless of which party is in power and regardless of which way the facts shake out.

The Central American migrant story provides a good example. Other than on Fox News, you would have been hard-pressed to find any reporting of the fact that during the Obama administration, pepper gas and tear gas were used hundreds of times to suppress border incidents involving much smaller, less-threatening numbers of migrants. It would have been even more difficult to have found any criticism of those actions from Progressive congressmen, Hollywood celebrities, professional athletes, or any of the dozens of Progressive organizations or multitudes of "useful idiots" and social justice warriors running around with their hair on fire, over-dosed from drinking too much of the Progressive Kool-Aid, who regularly popped-up to protest the immigration policies of the Trump administration. Obama was one of their own and therefore beyond criticism. When President Trump adopted similar policies, the media quickly whipped the nation into an indignant frenzy.

What is any president supposed to do when thousands of migrants storm the borders, demanding immediate entry into the country? I was reading a letter to the editor in a local news-paper recently in which some poor soul confessed his "shame" that migrants had been tear-gassed by his country. He once had visited Guatemala and saw extreme poverty and squalor but was treated politely, and based on this "deep" experience and "expansive" world perspective, he was "sorrowful" that these good people had been treated so harshly. I am sure it never occurred to him that some in the caravans, maybe quite a few more than "some," were not "good people." Had he run into them, either here or in their country, they may have cut his throat. I repeat: what is any president supposed to do when thousands of unknowns show up at our borders demanding entry? And what, exactly, is this clueless individual suggesting—that we take in everyone from Guatemala? Why not everyone from Venezuela, Brazil, Nicaragua, and the rest of Central and South America as well? I am confident many American tourists have been treated just as politely in those countries as our "letter to the editor" friend was treated in Guatemala.

Obama used pepper and tear gas against migrants trying to breach our borders, the same approach taken by President Trump, but with significantly different reactions from the public because of how the incidents were reported, or not reported, by the media. Obama also routinely separated immigrant families, built holding pens to detain illegal immigrants, and generally took steps very similar to President Trump to stem the tide of unchecked migration, all without significant criticism from the media or anyone else. Keep in mind, during his campaign for the presidency, candidate Obama promised to shut down Guantanamo Bay. As president, he never did. Successful candidates frequently find after taking office that protecting America often requires keeping those who have not been invited out of the country. The COVID-19 pandemic has added another dimension to that understanding, one that few Progressives had even considered until now; keeping contagions out of the country.

Like it or not, the immigration policy of the United States cannot be premised on poverty. Over one-half of the world's population, more than 3 billion people, live on approximately $2.50 a day.[317] More than 1.3 billion live on less than $1.25 a day. Worldwide, more than a billion children live in poverty. We cannot possibly bring them all to the United States simply because they are poor, and if we did, the prosperity and opportunities they are seeking would not exist for long.

Put just slightly differently, the United States does not have unlimited capacity to absorb everyone who would like to be able to share in the prosperity that has been built here, where even the "poor" are rich by world standards. Eighty percent of "poor" households in the United States, for example, have air conditioning; nearly three-quarters have a car or truck and over thirty percent have more than one; two-thirds have cable or satellite television; half have at least one computer; and more than forty percent own their homes.[318]

That is something Progressives never acknowledge because they are far more focused on changing voting demographics and destroying the unity of America than "renewing" America or providing humanitarian assistance to immigrants. Few Americans understand, for example, that the number of illegal immigrants living in a state affects its allocation of seats in the United States House of Representatives. When allocating House seats, illegal immigrants are counted as part of the resident population, and states like California, with high numbers of illegals, gain House seats at the expense of states with fewer illegals.[319] It is another way for Progressives to influence the balance of power in Congress, not to mention outcomes in the Electoral College.

The immigrants coming to this country in the late 19th and early 20th centuries for the most part also came intending to become Americans, leaving behind the "old country" and its failed policies, and building a new and different life in America. They came legally, embracing democracy, and fully committed to accepting the laws, Constitution, and way of life of the new nation they were honored to call home. The resulting heterogeneous society blended culturally to develop a single identity as Americans, with a common language and broadly shared goals, ideals, values, and understandings of the "common good." This integrative process and cultural assimilation gave rise to the "melting pot of nations" metaphor often used to describe the United States. It always has been considered one of the nation's great strengths.

A heterogeneous but culturally unified America is not the type of "multiculturism" Progressives are seeking. Their version is what some have described as the "salad bowl" approach.[320] It is more accurately characterized as "cultural *pluralism*," with an emphasis on cultural *separatism* rather than assimilation. Every race, ethnic group, and culture within the population maintains its own unique identity, including its language. It is a model for building nation-states within nation-states, obviously heightening the probability of clashes between cultures.

The "melting pot" approach made the United States the most inclusive, tolerant, democratic, and free nation on Earth, sought out by millions for precisely those reasons.[321] The cultural pluralism of the "salad bowl" variant is intended to produce exactly the opposite result:

> Multiculturalism idealizes immigrant cultures and ignores their various dysfunctional practices and values. At the same time, it relentlessly attacks America as a predatory, soulless, exploitative, warmongering villain responsible for all the world's ills.

******

> Worse still, the identity politics at the heart of multiculturalism directly contradict the core assumption of our liberal democracy: the principle of individual and inalienable rights that each of us possess no matter what group or sect we belong to. Multiculturalism confines the individual in the box

of his race or culture—the latter often simplistically defined in clichés and stereotypes—and then demands rights and considerations for that group, a special treatment usually based on the assumption that the group has been victimized in the past and so deserves some form of reparations. The immigrant "other" (excluding, of course, immigrants from Europe) is now a privileged victim entitled to public acknowledgement of his victim status and the superiority of his native culture.[322]

Many of today's migrants are coming into this country illegally, and they are coming in such numbers assimilation is nearly impossible, even if we assume they want to assimilate. The cultural backgrounds, religious beliefs, and social values of large numbers of these migrants may never allow them to adopt American culture, values, laws, or the Constitution as their own. Some come from countries with authoritarian governments, and they arrive with no knowledge or traditions of democracy. They depended on government at home for their sustenance and welfare, and they come to this country, not looking for democracy or a different form of government, but with the hope and expectation that they will be taken care of more generously by a government wealthier than the one they are leaving. They seek out people who look like them, speak their languages, and share their religions, backgrounds, and experiences. They bring the same belief and value systems that contributed to the failures of their home countries, including dependency on government. Many are uneducated and unskilled. Some are criminals, terrorists, human traffickers, or drug smugglers. Others come with illnesses and infectious diseases. Significant numbers of women are pregnant and looking to establish birthright citizenship in the United States for their unborn child. It looks, in other words, more like a plundering of America than the "renewal" supporters insist will be the effects of an open-border policy. This much is certain: whatever else it may bring or do, balkanizing and overwhelming America will destroy the prosperity illegal migrants are hoping to share.

Mass migrations of illegals are not working anywhere. Since 2015 and the beginning of the influx of migrants from Syria and Africa to the EU at the invitation of German Chancellor Angela Merkel, for example, Europe has been virtually under siege. Migrants poured in and established "beachheads" for rebuilding the "old country" in their host countries. In Muslim enclaves, Sharia law replaced local law. "No go" zones sprung up where civilian authorities, including police, even today dare not venture.[323] It should not have been a surprise. Ten years ago, well before the recent mass immigrations into Europe, Angela Merkel declared multiculturism in Germany an "utter failure." The idea that people of different cultures with different values could work side by side and assimilate into German society simply proved not to be true.[324] The lesson for America:

> [W]e must be prudent in vetting people from other parts of the earth whose cultural values are so singularly different from ours to ensure that they can assimilate; that they are philosophically *capable* of "attach[ment] to the principles of the Constitution," which includes the notion that ours is a civil society, and that government at all levels is ruled by civil, not religious, law.

******

What happens when religious belief and cultural practice and mores are so ingrained in some individuals as to prevent them from meaningfully subscribing to the tenets of the American

Constitution, to American forms of government,
or to our social mores? They may wish to share
in our cornucopia of plenty, but at the same time
expect our society and government to adapt itself
to fit into their cultural and religious telescope. Is
this acceptable?[325]

And that, ultimately, is what is too often missed by those advocating open borders and unlimited immigration. Not everyone is coming to our shores to be an American, in part because they are unable to show allegiance to principles that run counter to their own deeply engrained cultures, beliefs, and values. They are not capable of becoming Americans, in other words, precisely because they cannot accept the shared foundational precepts that make America, *America.*

The principle that *compatible* cultures and values are indispensable to successful assimilation may nowhere be better illustrated than in the example of the Balkans. After decades of relative peace under a Soviet-supported communist government, as communism collapsed in Eastern Europe, old grievances quickly resurfaced. War broke out. The people of the Balkans, friends and neighbors generations removed from conflicts of the past, once again took up arms and began killing each other. Yugoslavia, the "Kingdom of the Serbs, Croats, and Slovenes," first formed in 1918, renamed in 1929, and reconstituted in 1946 after being liberated from Nazi rule, broke up officially in 1992.

Progressives understand the strategic importance of balkanization; it largely explains their infatuation with open borders. Progressives cannot show allegiance to the principles that make America great either. Those principles are, in fact, the antithesis of what Progressives believe. Consequently, weakening the foundational precepts of the country is not a concern; it is the objective. Their attacks on our shared bonds, our allegiances to flag and country, our sense of the common good for a single and united America, can all be hidden behind banalities like "multiculturism," which the "useful idiots" will embrace reflexively because it sounds avant-garde, cultivated, *progressive.* The goal is to separate us into rival factions where smoldering grievances, resentments, and jealousies can be more effectively churned and exploited until any remnants of unity disappear. The goal, in other words, is to create another Yugoslavia.

The strategy also explains why Progressives attack so vehemently those they perceive as Christian conservatives, but seemingly welcome people who embrace beliefs completely at odds with almost everything Progressives profess to support, including LBGTQs' and women's rights, moral relativism, and a host of similar social and cultural issues. In the short term, at least, dividing the country into adversarial camps is more important than ideological purity. As the experience of Europe has shown, when belief systems clash strongly enough, particularly when people feel religiously obligated to adhere to certain tenets, such as the ascendency of Sharia law, it can become nearly impossible to coexist under the same constitution and system of laws. These are exactly the types of differences Progressives are hoping to exploit.

Progressives fully understand the problems created by the mass influx of illegal immigrants. They do not want them in their communities and were nearly apoplectic when President Trump suggested sending migrants, who by law could not be deported from the United States pending a hearing on their immigration status, to sanctuary cities until their cases could be resolved. The President was attacked vehemently for making American cities "less safe" and for "punishing" political opponents. Progressives also claimed sending illegals to sanctuary cities would be "unlawful."[326]

Is that so? I thought the illegal migrants all were good people who would revitalize and reenergize America. How can it possibly make sanctuary cities less safe, or be punishment for political enemies, if they are asked to accommodate the illegals their Progressive mayors and city councils maintain are peaceful, hard-working individuals simply looking for a helping hand, posing no threat to anyone?

The notion that sanctuary cities, themselves in open defiance of US law, would claim it is unlawful to burden them with the care of the migrants they encouraged to come to this country illegally—effectively seeking sanctuary from the costs and obligations of attending to the incursion of illegals they invited—has to be one of the ultimate ironies. The hypocrisy truly is beyond astounding. However, the enormous homeless camps chocking the streets of Los Angeles, San Francisco, and other California cities, with the attendant risks of increased disease, crime, violence, and substance abuse, graphically demonstrates some of the hidden costs of the Progressives' agenda and explains why sanctuary cities reacted as they did to the President's suggestion that they host migrants waiting for their immigration status to be determined.

The panicked reactions of sanctuary cities should not have been surprising to anyone. It was reasonably certain that the billionaires, Hollywood-types, and other luminaries who set and control the Progressive agenda, many safely ensconced within walled mansions, others protected by bodyguards, would not welcome illegal immigrants into their neighborhoods and certainly would have no desire to deal with the social and economic issues created by their presence. Those are sacrifices for the rest of America to make, except, of course, for the occasional black-tie benefit dinners where the *intelligentsia* can be seen, drink champagne, nibble on canapes and blinis with caviar and dollops of crème fraiche, and shake their heads over the horrors of having to live in a country where such large numbers of "deplorables" voted for Donald Trump. Pass the shrimp toasts, please.

Wholly apart from the assimilation and social challenges unchecked immigration creates, the monetary costs are enormous. Multiple programs support illegal migrants in the United States at an estimated net cost of nearly $70 billion per million illegals.[327] Medicaid has become the de facto health care plan for most.[328] With nearly 11 million illegal migrants estimated to be living in the United States—many put the actual numbers at 20 million or more—you can do the math. As the costs approach and exceed a trillion dollars a year, you can keep things in perspective by remembering that a trillion dollars represent more than 25% of the total annual revenues of the United States. If you think borrowing money from China to pay for the support of those in this country illegally is a good idea and sound policy, then you should be thrilled by open borders and unchecked immigration. Perhaps Bernie Sanders, a millionaire a few times over with multiple homes—another person who has used to advantage the system he now criticizes—would be willing to chip in for the support of a few migrant families, maybe make a house or two available? Then again, probably not—Bernie, like many who prefer giving away other people's money, never has been particularly generous with his own.

I want to return for a moment to the criticism President Trump received for separating illegal immigrant families when they were taken into custody at the border. As I noted earlier, the Obama administration did much the same thing with hardly a murmur of protest from the media or the public, confirming the confounding hypocrisy of Progressives. This is particularly true since anyone with half a brain understands that a number of these children are not even with their biological families; the "bad guys" have learned that having children with you is one of the keys to gaining admission to the United States. Children are pawns being used by some pretty nasty actors not only to help them get in the country, but also to stay here.[329] Do you think it is difficult for them to "rent" or "borrow" a family back home?

But the most bizarre aspect of this controversy may be the fact that every day in the US, children are separated from their parents, and have been for decades, by welfare or child protection agencies for a host of reasons that would seem arbitrary to most thoughtful people. This happens without any protest from the liberal constituencies who so fiercely oppose every action by the President relating to migrant children. Many of the same Progressives condemning the Trump administration for separating families at the border, in fact, actively promote welfare agencies taking children away from their parents for almost any reason the government deems appropriate.[330] You also need to ask yourself a question: are parents who march children hundreds, sometimes thousands, of miles across harsh terrain under the most difficult conditions and then push them to the front of the line as "human shields" when they encounter border patrols, acting more responsibly than the American parents who every day are forced to surrender their children to government agencies, ostensibly to protect them from abuse and neglect?

Another fact you would not know unless you were listening to Fox News—the Obama administration oversaw the largest return of migrants to their native countries of any US administration in history. Between 2009 and 2015, more than 2.5 million migrants were deported under Obama, and that number does not include those who "self-deported." Immigration groups dubbed Obama the great "Deporter in Chief," but did you ever hear any criticism of what he was doing from the gaggle of "virtue-signaling" left-wingers in the media and Congress, more interested in demonstrating their refined sense of empathy than reforming immigration policy so that it works?

And that is one of the problems—no one is interested in reaching agreement on anything. Progressives were terrified of giving the Trump administration any kind of victory, even immigration reform, which the country badly needs. People can suffer, needless billions of dollars can be spent inefficiently and ineffectively on welfare and support programs, our national security can be weakened, and our unity as a nation undermined—all acceptable outcomes for Progressives if it denies Republicans what any rational person would perceive as a victory for all of us, including migrants.

While it is not supposed to be easy for the federal government to do anything—our founders clearly recognized the limitations of government and intentionally tried to restrain the powers of the federal government to an enumerated few—I doubt the founders ever anticipated the day would come when political zealots, waging an ideological war of attrition, would be willing to completely abandon any pretext of governing in an attempt to stifle American democracy and replace it with their socialist fantasies. Open borders are an important part of the strategy.

CHAPTER 18

TAKING DOWN STATUES

"When you change a name, you lose an identity." That principle from a recent editorial calling for the preservation of "Green Pastures," the only recreational area open to African Americans in Virginia during the Jim Crow era, is just as pertinent to the current frenzy to remove statues, the names of former slave owners, including George Washington and Thomas Jefferson, and all southern Civil War figures, from the public arena.[331]

There is a simple truth everyone should keep in mind—100 years from now, all of us will be considered vile, terrible people. I am not sure what the issues will be: we ate meat; hunted and fished; used carbon-based fuels; lived in houses that were too big; did not do enough to mitigate climate change; or any number of other possibilities. There is only one certainty—people of one era never will be able to measure up to the evolving social values and mores of future generations. Unless there are enough adults in the room to recognize that imposing today's standards on behavior taking place in different times under different circumstances and with different levels of understanding and information is unfair and countervailing, there never can be durable heroes, and history itself, mankind's greatest teacher and prophet, becomes little more than a convenient, self-edited fable. As the author of the editorial which started this chapter pointed out, "[m]emory is a slippery cog in the wheel of humanity, often ungeared by time and determined denial."[332]

No one can say, or even imagine, how they would have led their lives had they lived 100 years earlier. If you doubt it, try to explain, for example, why free Blacks often owned slaves, perhaps as many as 20,000 just before the Civil War? [333] Or why free Black men sometimes purchased wives but later sold them as slaves? Or why free Blacks sometimes sold their children as slaves?[334] Some free Blacks undoubtedly bought slaves to free them, but certainly not all.[335] They simply lived in different times, under different circumstances, and with different standards, understandings, and sensibilities.

People often forget, or simply never knew, that many different social, cultural, economic, and political factors led to the Civil War, although slavery unquestionably was at the core of most of them. The agrarian South was a cotton plantation–driven economy dependent on slave labor. That fact pitted the South against the industrial North, whose slave labor largely had been replaced over time by a steady influx of German and Irish immigrants, for political control of the nation. States' rights, meaning the division of power between the states and the federal government, was still a major issue in the United States in the 1800s. And as the country expanded westward, the alignment of new states between North and South became a major point of contention because of the effects it had on the North/South balance of power. When Abraham Lincoln, an anti-slavery candidate of the nascent Republican Party became president in 1860 without even being on the ballot in some southern states, the stage was set for conflict.

Because the United States was a republic, secession was considered by many to be a legitimate and natural right of the individual states. That had been a point of contention during the debates leading to the enactment of the Constitution, with some of the Founding Fathers arguing for including a specific prohibition in the Constitution against secession. It never was adopted. When Lincoln disagreed that the states retained the right to secede, shots were fired at Fort Sumter, South Carolina, on April 12, 1861, and the war was joined.[336]

I certainly am not defending slavery or the slave culture, both of which I condemn unconditionally. I am trying to demonstrate why it is important to consider circumstances and context when attempting to evaluate and understand history. Suppose, for example, today's environmental movement existed in 1860, and the industrial North had been told by a newly elected southern president who had not been on the ballot in several northern states that all industrial plants were to be shuttered immediately. Is there any doubt the North would have gone to war to protect its livelihood and way of life? Again, let me be clear. I am not trying to draw moral equivalencies between slavery and environmental concerns; I am only trying to make the point that context matters and even basically good people can act badly when threatened with the loss of everything they have known, economically, politically, socially, and culturally.

Take, for example, those who Tom Brokaw labeled the "Greatest Generation," our parents and grandparents who fought World War II and at great sacrifice, too often the ultimate sacrifice, preserved the free world. Is anyone willing to argue the United States was less racially biased during their era than now? Or less segregated? Or that women's rights were more respected? Or that the LBGTQ community was more tolerated? Or that the environment was better protected? It would be a silly exercise, wouldn't it? It certainly does not mean, however, that because the social beliefs and values of the "Greatest Generation" differed from what is acceptable today, we should not celebrate their heroism and sacrifice or what they achieved, not only in World War II but also in building the greatest and most prosperous democratic Republic the world has ever known.

Some of the people seeking to eliminate the names and images of slave owners and all Confederate monuments or statutes from our history are "virtue-signalers"—approval seekers grandstanding for attention. Others have been misled and manipulated by the entrepreneurial race merchants among us. Many of these same people likely worshipped Edward Kennedy of Chappaquiddick fame; would erect monuments to Bill and Hillary Clinton, two of the most character-challenged politicians in American history; and favor renaming schools after Barack Obama, the most racially divisive president since the Civil War. Others are adherents to principles of "moral relativism" regarding nearly everything except the Civil War. More than a few simply confuse themselves, never understanding that acknowledging the legacies of past generations does not require or imply approval of everything that happened or condone their failures. But a number are committed revolutionaries with no objective other than destabilizing the country.

Let me ask this question to those who believe Ted Kennedy was a paradigm of public service and an agent for good. Did leaving Mary Jo Kopechne to die in the water of Poucha Pond on the island of Chappaquiddick demonstrate better character than someone owning slaves 160 years ago when slave ownership was common and lawful in most states? Again, I am not trying to draw moral equivalencies or suggest scalable comparisons, but if there can be a surrogate for the horrors of slavery, at least on a singular basis, it might be the horror of someone leaving a young woman to drown slowly, over several hours, trapped and alone, in a cold, remote pond on Chappaquiddick Island.

Despite the atrocities of Hitler and the Nazis, today millions visit the death camps of Dachau, Treblinka, and Auschwitz. Hitler's retreat in the mountains outside Berchtesgaden, Germany, the "Eagle's Nest," also remains a popular tourist destination. Countless children first learned of the horrors of the Holocaust from a guide, a guidebook, or parents while visiting these sites. Should they nonetheless be torn down, obliterated from history, never mentioned or visited again? Does the fact these venues remain frequently visited places of interest mean visitors are celebrating the Nazis or the Holocaust? Does their existence represent an unspeakable affront to the Jewish community that needs to be ended immediately? Or are they more accurately described as painful elements of history, but powerful and important reminders of man's inhumanity to man and how quickly governments can turn abusive when people are inattentive?

Every year, countless American tourists also travel to countries around the world to visit and pose for photographs in front of monuments dedicated to emperors, kings, generals, and other historic figures responsible for savage wars, slavery, and countless deaths and atrocities. They do so without a moment's hesitation or the slightest criticism or objection. Millions visit the burial sites of figures like Napoleon, Mao Zedong, Joseph Stalin, Vladimir Lenin, Benito Mussolini, Josip Tito, Antonio de Oliveira Salazar, Francisco Franco, and Nicolae Ceausescu, all of them ruthless butchers. Palaces, castles, and other historic structures originally built and serviced by slave labor, where people were imprisoned, tortured, and executed, are toured by millions. Innumerable pictures are taken and shared on social media. Why are people seemingly able to place these "shrines" in historical perspective, but not slavery in America or the Civil War?

You know the answer. Socialism and communism depend on anger and envy at every level—class, race, age, and gender—to create interest in their lethal philosophies, so race has been made a "cause" in America that never will be allowed to abate or improve because it so usefully can be used to manipulate and divide America. It also is profitable. Race merchants and agitators write books and news columns, organize rallies, appear on radio and television, and benefit from millions of dollars in donations. There are no incentives to promote better race relations because were that to happen, the fame, fortune, and political power all would disappear. The goal is to whip America into a frenzy of class, race, ethnic, and gender rage and envy, rip the country apart, and divert attention away from the enormous failures of the governance principles Progressives are advocating and the more than 100 million people those principles have killed. It is to prevent the young from realizing that everything they have, and everything they are, they owe to the market-based economy of the United States and, more importantly, understanding that all of it will disappear quickly under the Progressives' plans for America. It is to conceal the fact that the only way socialism and communism ever prevail is "by way of a pistol to the back of the head and a death sentence in a forced labor camp."[337]

Slavery was a terrible and indefensible chapter in our nation's history, as it was in many other countries of the world. But it is part of that history, and hundreds of thousands of Americans died in a civil war which, from the perspective of 1861, both sides believed their causes to be "just." The fact that the harsh evils of slavery are better understood today than in the mid-nineteenth century does not mean history should be rewritten. Seldom is there unanimity about the justifications for war, Vietnam being an easy example. Should we condemn those who fought in Vietnam or refuse to acknowledge their sacrifices because many in the country opposed that war and believed it to be unjust? How about the American Indian Wars? Should the statutes of George Armstrong Custer be eradicated—all of them or only the ones depicting his role in the Indian Wars, leaving intact the monuments to his distinguished service for the Union Army during the Civil War?

You get the point. Historic figures, like all humans, come with blemishes, sometimes terrible blemishes. But before Robert E. Lee commanded the armies of the Confederacy, he was a highly regarded officer in the United States Army, who distinguished himself in the Mexican-American war and served as superintendent of the United States Military Academy. After the Civil War, he became president of what would become Washington & Lee University in Lexington, Virginia, one of the most respected schools in the country. Should we celebrate his service before and after the Civil War while expunging any evidence of his involvement with the Confederacy, shun him altogether, or, as we have done with even some of history's worst actors, treat history as history?

Part of that history is recognizing many Civil War figures were legitimate heroes to many in this country for reasons unrelated to slavery. Most of those living in the South, for example, were not slave owners. They were poor, rural farmers struggling to make a living. They did not own plantations, and they did not work on plantations. At most, they were on the fringes of the slave culture and had no power or ability to change it. For many of them, things like the right of self-determination, defense of their way of life, and similar factors were more consequential considerations in the war than slavery. Keep in mind, the Civil War started less than sixty-three years after the Constitution was ratified, and the nation still was finding its way.

In a very real way, I view the Civil War monuments and "names" controversy very much like I view speech codes on college campuses. Both are efforts to censor information and knowledge. Like it or not, history is made up of the good, the bad, and the ugly. You cannot sanitize it or preserve only those portions with which you agree without turning it into fiction. The destruction and pillaging of historic artifacts reflecting beliefs, cultures, or thoughts different from our own, including Civil War statues and monuments, might be something expected from ISIS, the Taliban, the Khmer Rouge, Nazi Germany, Mao Zedong, or other radicals, militant groups, and regimes afraid of history and committed to erasing it, but until now we always have been smarter, more tolerant, and willing to engage history in all of its dimensions.

To the virtue signalers and Progressive race agitators, however, Civil War statues and monuments and the schools, bridges, buildings, and other structures named after people who owned slaves or fought for the Confederacy during the Civil War provide easy opportunities for fomenting agitation and civil unrest. The game they are playing is simple enough: provide a one-dimensional view of history by characterizing every Civil War statue or monument, and every school, bridge, building, or structure named after a Civil War figure or former slave owner, as celebrating and perpetuating a monstrous evil; organize protests and rallies; and leave it to the extremists and media to take it from there.

The trick, of course, is to get out front and characterize whatever you plan to attack in the manner you want others to view it. Using Robert E. Lee as an example once again, he was a Confederate general for a short time, but a distinguished general in the United States military and respected educator for a very long time. Why does naming a school after Robert E. Lee imply the promotion of slavery rather than the promotion of leadership, service, or education? Only because activists say it is so.

Our capital city was named in honor of George Washington. Washington was a slave owner, as were many in the mid-eighteenth century, both North and South. He also was the general who won the Revolutionary War, our first president, and an American who did countless good. Should we assume the reason our capital was named Washington was to celebrate slavery or that continuing to call it Washington promotes and perpetuates a "monstrous evil?" Should we change its name? "Obama City" or "Clintonville" perhaps?

Why can't we accept the fact that historic figures are not the one-dimensional creatures the agitators and race merchants try to make them. Instead of focusing only on the flaws, why not attempt to tell a historically accurate story, including what they accomplished and how they may have failed? Why judge them solely on something that, regardless of how horrific we may find it today, tells only a piece of the story? How can we possibly be so fascinated by monuments to autocrats in other parts of the world who ruthlessly murdered and enslaved millions, but rage against Americans whose behavior we today understand as abhorrent, but which was prevalent and lawful during the times in which they lived? How will we measure up to the values of societies 100 or 200 years from now?

In truth, taking down Civil War statutes no longer has anything to do with slavery or racial justice. It has to do with revolution. That much should have been made clear when agitators supposedly protesting the death of George Floyd tore down, or threatened to tear down, statutes of Abraham Lincoln, Christopher Columbus, Queen Isabella, Ponce de Leon, Teddy Roosevelt, Hans Christian Heg, and a monument dedicated to the Texas Rangers, the law enforcement group, not the baseball team. There have been calls, however, for the baseball club to change its name, as well.[338] Some are now suggesting that Mount Rushmore should be obliterated. As one commentator put it:

> We've come to a remarkable moment when our culture supports the destruction of monuments designed to capture a sliver of our history. Often, both the mob and the liberal media that chronicle these destructive actions are illiterate in their understanding of history.
>
> When they first came for the statues of Confederate generals, it was considered justified. When they came for the statue of Union Gen. Ulysses S. Grant and the Emancipation Memorial erected in 1876, honoring Abraham Lincoln and paid for by freed slaves, it was something else they wanted to express: hatred of America.[339]

For those of you not convinced the violence has less to do with slavery, racial and social justice, police brutality, and discrimination than destabilizing our government and destroying our culture, consider this: The National Museum of African American History and Culture opened in Washington DC in the fall of 2016 without acknowledging one of the most consequential Black Americans in history, Justice Clarence Thomas of the United States Supreme Court. Why? Justice Thomas was a conservative legal scholar appointed by a Republican president.[340] While the museum eventually added an exhibit to Justice Thomas, the original snub was petty beyond reason but shows unequivocally that this is a fight about political ideology, not slavery or any other Black issue. The innocent protestors, those who think they are protesting things like social or racial justice and police brutality, are simply the "useful idiots" in the true Leninist meaning of the phrase for well-organized, well-funded, revolutionary groups committed to the downfall of the US government.

A few years ago, Yale University appointed a committee to recommend a formal framework for addressing renaming and removal issues involving historical figures who had become controversial.[341] It may have been an action born of necessity— Yale itself was named after Elihu Yale, a slave owner and trader—but I find it to be one of the better-reasoned policies regarding these types of issues.

The actual controversy triggering the appointment of the committee was an initiative to rename Calhoun College, one of the residential colleges within the larger Yale campus, and named after John C. Calhoun, once a presidential candidate and a former US vice president, secretary of state, senator, and congressman. He was considered a consummate statesman and brilliant political theorist, and in May 1957, at the behest of then-Senator John F. Kennedy, was named one of the "five greatest senators in US history."[342] He also was a staunch defender and advocate for slavery whose views were controversial even in the era in which he lived. Calhoun held similar beliefs toward Native Americans and played key roles in the displacement of some Native Tribes.

In its report, the Yale committee outlined the factors and principles it concluded should guide decisions on whether or not to change the name of buildings, structures, or significant spaces named after historical figures. It began with the proposition that renaming anything because of the perceived "values" of the namesake should be an "exceptional" event. Noting that "no generation stands alone at the end of history with perfect moral hindsight," and that historical names often

carry wisdom not immediately apparent to current generations, the report continued:

> A presumption of continuity in campus names
> helps ensure that the University does not elide
> the moral complexity often associated with the
> lives of those who make outsized impressions on
> the world. Controversy has attached to countless
> numbers of the most important figures in modern
> history. For example, Mahatma Gandhi, the Indian
> independence leader who inspired a worldwide
> movement of nonviolent protest, held starkly racist
> views about black Africans[343]

The committee next concluded that the presumption
against renaming should be strongest when a building or other
structure has been named after someone who made a major
contribution to the life and mission of the institution. Altering
a name in those circumstances was "distinctively problematic
because it threatens to efface an important contributing factor
in the making of the University."[344]

Proceeding from these foundational precepts, the committee then addressed the principles it believed should be
applied in specific cases to determine whether the strong
presumption against changing a name had been overcome.
The first of these principles involved placing the controversy in
historical context. Three different periods were relevant: the
era when a namesake lived and worked; the time of a naming
decision; and the present. The context was important because
evaluating a namesake's legacy by the standards of the era
in which they lived and worked, "usefully distinguishes those
who actively promoted some morally odious practice, or dedicated much of their lives to upholding that practice, on the one
hand, from those whose relationship to such a practice was

unexceptional, on the other." [345] It addressed, in other words, the reality that people can have "unexceptional relationships to moral horrors"[346] that do not preclude honoring the beneficial things they did or the positive contributions they made.

The committee found that considering time and place mattered for another reason; if a college or university named a structure or otherwise honored someone for reasons which, at the time of the decision, fundamentally were at odds with the institution's mission and value system, renaming becomes more likely. Again, a famous figure in history, American painter and inventor, Samuel Morse, was used to illustrate. If a building on the Yale campus had been named after Morse to honor his nativist and anti-Catholic views and support of slavery rather than his invention of the telegraph, renaming might be appropriate. Even then, however, if the structure bearing his name played a significant role in "forming community" at the school, or if other factors weighed more heavily in the analysis, a name change might not be indicated. As the committee pointed out, no single factor or principle is determinative:

> No single factor is sufficient, and no single factor is determinative. We expect that renaming will typically prove warranted only when more than one principle listed here points toward renaming; even when more than one principle supports renaming, renaming may not be required if other principles weigh heavily in the balance. We do not list the principles in order of significance because their importance may vary depending on the circumstances of the relevant name. [347]

The inquiry then turned to evaluating whether the namesake's *principal* legacy was fundamentally at odds with the mission of the school. Walt Whitman, who continually berated the

Lincoln administration for providing Black prisoners of war with treatment equivalent to White prisoners, but whose *principal* legacy was as a pioneering poet and writer, was the example used to show why that was important. Frederick Douglas, the celebrated Black American social reformer, abolitionist, writer, and statesman, but disparaging and biased toward Native Americans, was cited as another example of the "moral complexities" of human life that makes consideration of someone's principal legacy imperative. As the committee noted, all else held equal, appreciating the "complexities of those lives that have given shape to the world we live in" is a "virtue"[348] and an important part of history, learning, and scholarship.

Throughout its analysis the committee stressed the importance of avoiding the erasure of history:

> History is one of the forms of knowledge at the core of the enterprise. To erase a university's history is antithetical to the spirit of the institution. Erasing names is a matter of special concern, because those names are, in part, a catalog of the people whom the university has thought worthy of honor. Removing such names may obscure important information about our past.[349]

As the committee put it, "A university's ongoing obligation is to navigate change without effacing the past."[350] In part, that stemmed from the need to acknowledge "the moral fallibility of those who aim to evaluate the past,"[351] but also traced to the fact that students of today "are stewards of an intergenerational project,"[352] and the recognition that "[h]ubris in undoing past decisions encourages future generations to disrespect the choices of the current generation."[353] The committee then addressed some of the ways history can be preserved even when a structure is renamed or a statute removed:

When removing a name leaves other existing markers of the namesake on the campus, a name's removal from any one building, structure, or significant space poses a smaller risk of erasing history because the namesake has not been removed from the campus. Such markers may themselves require contextualization. But renaming one site does not require removal of a namesake from elsewhere on the campus. To the contrary, changing a name in one place may impose obligations of preservation in others. In many instances, renaming a building will make it incumbent on a university to take affirmative steps to avoid the problem of erasure. Such steps may include conspicuous museum like exhibits; architecturally thoughtful installations, plaques, and signs; public art; or other such steps. Selecting a new name that is thematically connected to the old one may be one further way to prevent renaming from becoming tantamount to erasing.[354]

Following the report, Yale University first determined to retain the name Calhoun College, but approximately a year later changed the name to honor one of the computer era's trail-blazers, Grace Murray Hopper.

The Yale report was focused on the somewhat unique setting of a university, but the principles it articulated apply to a far broader range of circumstances. I find it a compelling document on several levels, but most notably for its clear-headed understanding that history is an "intergenerational project" with no generation possessing perfect moral hindsight; that times and circumstances can place people into "unexceptional relationships" with "moral horrors;" and that "primary legacies" generally provide a better measure of someone's place in history than a focus on the human flaws we all share. These simple understandings, that all of us are flawed individuals, both the honored and those attempting retroactively to judge them; that the honored are entitled to be evaluated fairly within the context of the standards and conditions of their times and with a full appreciation of the legacies being memorialized; and that responsibilities to past, current, and future generations demand extreme circumspection and caution when intervening in historical events, are essential to any legitimate consideration of historical figures,

It is a call for *informed* decision-making and appropriate deference to historical determinations, recognition of the basic unfairness that can occur when people "not of the times" and applying standards that have evolved over decades attempt to make moral judgments about figures from other eras, and awareness that history cannot be a selective process defined by those intent on controlling it. One thing is certain: neither lawless mobs nor mayor nor governors operating preemptively under pandemic inspired "emergency powers" have the right to make unilateral decisions regarding the historical record or the artifacts appropriate to be included in it. If we entrust our history to those committed to erasing it, we will be doing nothing more than creating an American version of the *Great Soviet Encyclopedia*.[355]

Thinking people should recognize that the "naming' and "monument" controversies continue to exist largely because they are part of the larger strategy to keep race relations in turmoil. From my perspective, I am not sure why any school, public building, or other structure ever should be named after anyone other than the taxpayers who paid for it. This brings us to the issue of the schools, buildings, streets, and public spaces being named after Barack Obama. Does his legacy as the first Black president justify it, assuming we move past my objections to naming things to honor people who have not paid for them? Will that even be Obama's primary legacy, or is it more likely that his principal legacy will be more Marxist in nature—the individual most responsible for undermining American democracy by encouraging the takeover of the Democratic Party by communists and socialists, and the president who destroyed years of positive progress in race relations?

Tricky things, these legacies. What will people living 100 years from now decide? How will they decide? Should it depend on who is in charge? Are we happy turning history into a self-edited fable?

CHAPTER 19

CORONAVIRUS

Nine and a half million to 45 million illnesses, 140,000 to 810,000 hospitalizations, and 12,000 to 61,000 deaths annually. The Wuhan coronavirus, otherwise known as COVID-19? No, seasonal flu. These figures come directly from the CDC's webpage and help point out some of the incongruities between the extreme reactions of many to the coronavirus outbreak and the nonchalance most people accord the annual flu epidemics. As I write this chapter, the worldwide coronavirus count stands at 236,684 cases and 9,818 deaths. In the United States, the figures are 23,657 cases and 288 deaths. These figures undoubtedly will rise, perhaps steeply. However, seasonal flu, by CDC estimates, already has killed 22,000 to 55,000 Americans since the beginning of flu season in October 2019. Even though tens of thousands of Americans die every year from flu, fully half the country does not even bother to get a flu shot.

It is always problematic to write about something happening in real-time and evolving day by day. The situation can change quickly and unpredictably. Nevertheless, I am writing this chapter early in the COVID-19 outbreak, knowing this book will go to print before the COVID-19 pandemic has fully run its course, but having no intent to update the chapter as the virus progresses. I will not update the chapter because I am only trying to provide perspective on our response to the outbreak, not how serious it may turn out to be. I make no predictions in that regard, and I very clearly am not down-playing the risks posed by COVID-19 or any other epidemic or pandemic. All have the potential to wipe out civilizations. The Spanish flu alone may have killed as many as 100 million people. Pandemics may be more of a threat to the continua-tion of human existence than nuclear war, climate change, or any of the other existential threats to human life.

But I am questioning the unbalanced response being demanded by our media to this outbreak and because of the media, too large a portion of our population and too many of our state and local officials. As the World Health Organization points out, public health responses to pandemics and epi-demics that are disproportionate to the actual risks and ignore the social, political, and economic impacts of an outbreak are likely to be unnecessarily damaging:

> [t]he fear generated by the emergence of a previously-unknown infection may be greatly out of proportion to its real public health impact. Fear often generates inadequate decisions or inappropriate behaviours, including stigma of certain at-risk populations. The impact on travel and trade and on economies can be disproportionate, as it has been seen in the Republic of Korea during the MERS epidemic. To a certain extent, global health security also encompasses economic and human security. Thus, risk communication is critical to minimise the social, political and subsequently economic impact of an epidemic, and this is also a major focus of this publication.[356]

So, what accounts for the difference in how the public has reacted to the coronavirus and its indifference to the massive number of deaths caused each year by the seasonal flu? Or, for that matter, highway accidents? After all, dead is dead.

Certainly, the fact public health officials predict the mortality rate from coronavirus will be higher, perhaps substantially higher than seasonal flu, is part of the explanation. Projections of more hospitalizations, a larger number of people who can be infected by a single carrier, and a longer incubation time for the coronavirus all contribute to the narrative that the coronavirus is more "dangerous" than seasonal flu.

If people were being completely honest, however, they would admit the real figures for coronavirus essentially remain unavailable. Many people with the virus are asymptomatic. Others have such mild symptoms they never are tested or treated. Testing, in general, has been limited and sporadic. We just do not know how many people are infected with the virus. Projections about the possible effects of the virus are largely based on mathematical models and incomplete information. Models of this type are notoriously inaccurate, and the purpose for the model has to be considered; a model designed to predict "worse case scenarios" may not provide the most realistic assessments of actual risks.

To put it just a bit differently, there is a lot of speculation going on about COVID-19. The truth is, we let doctors completely take over a response to a problem that had significant nonmedical implications. As in all cases involving new pathogens, mathematical modeling based on inadequate data is likely to produce results that are exaggerated and hyperbolic, but those results have stifled debate over how we should respond to COVID-19 and limited input from important, nonmedical disciplines. Medicine unquestionably has a significant role to play in the response to COVID-19, but so does economics and some of the social sciences, all of which largely have been disregarded in the rush to contain the virus. We did this despite knowing the significant deleterious effects economic catastrophes can have on the health, welfare, and well-being of populations. We opted for short-term relief, knowing there could be a significant price to pay down the road.

In the United States, there clearly is a political element to the COVID-19 response. Democrats have spent most of the Trump administration's first term searching for ways to slow the economy and prevent the President from governing. With Joe Biden, their presumptive presidential nominee, showing obvious signs of age-related cognitive impairments, their fantasies of impeachment in tatters, and Bernie Sanders pushing the Democratic agenda so far left that most Americans now clearly recognize it as hardcore socialism, Progressives understandably were becoming increasingly desperate for something to interrupt the surging prosperity the President had brought to America before the 2020 elections. What James Carville, the lead strategist for Bill Clinton's 1992 presidential campaign, said then remains true today: It's the economy, stupid." Progressives well understand that principle.

Public health crisis or not, the coronavirus outbreak has been a political gift to Progressives in many ways other than slowing the economy. It essentially stopped the President from carrying out his agenda and continuing the changes that have been so important to a country finally regaining its footing after the disasters of the Obama years. For example, with the Trump administration preoccupied with the virus, the appointment and confirmation of new federal judges ground to a halt. The pandemic also provided Progressives with the much-needed means for shielding Joe Biden from debates with the President and other public appearances. Joe's cognitive difficulties would have become increasingly noticeable during a normal campaign. It is no accident he has practically disappeared during the early course of the coronavirus out-break and probably will remain out of sight for its duration—his one attempt at addressing the crisis, a televised "fireside chat," so plainly showed his confusion that he has been kept locked in his basement ever since.

Regardless of anything else, do not expect to see many live appearances by Joe during the fall campaign, whatever form it may take. He will be shielded, and his "appearances" are more likely to be prerecorded monologues so that his "forgetful" moments, gaffes, hesitations, and confusion can be edited out.

The media, as usual, has been more than willing to oblige Democrats, stirring the coronavirus pot breathlessly, intent on creating the same type of moral panic that drives so much of the Progressives' agenda. The worldwide media, for that matter, has been more than complicit in ratcheting up the fear factor, something the World Health Organization predicted:

> Given the effects of globalization, the intense mobility of human populations, and the relentless urbanization, it is likely that the next emerging virus will also spread fast and far. It is impossible to predict the nature of this virus or its source, or where it will start spreading.

> But we can say, with a high degree of certainty, that when it comes, there will be (a) an initial delay in recognising it; (b) a serious impact on travel and trade; (c) a public reaction that includes anxiety, or even panic and confusion, and (d) this will be aided and abetted by media coverage.[357]

I think it is fair to say that reporting on the coronavirus has been sensationalized to the greatest extent possible. If the number of confirmed cases in a locality increases overnight, for example, the reports always are: "Coronavirus cases in state X rose 50 percent overnight," rather than, "The number of coronavirus cases in state X increased from eight to twelve since yesterday." The same was done with the total case count in the United States when it was very low. In Virginia, authorities were counting as "Virginia cases" infected residents who were living in states other than Virginia at the time of their infections and had not yet returned to Virginia—anything to boost the totals. Media reports on the virus, print or broadcast, seldom describe it simply as "the coronavirus;" it always is the "rapidly spreading coronavirus," or the "surging coronavirus." Even when increases in new cases, hospitalizations, or deaths are modest—a small handful—the updates describe the caseload as "growing" or "spreading." All reports are for *total* cases, both recovered and non-recovered, never just *active* cases. Among active cases, no attempt is made to distinguish those that are serious from those that are mild, although the vast bulk of all COVID-19 infections, 95 percent based on the data available to date, have been classified as mild by health officials. News commentators recklessly speak of the need for a million ventilators at a time when the active cases in the world number 367,870, with only 18,538 falling into the serious category. Never are any benchmarks provided—figures from past pandemics and epidemics—to lend perspective. I have not heard anyone on broadcast media, other than Fox News, even mention the seasonal flu figures.

American politics do not explain the reaction of the rest of the world to the coronavirus, but it is easy enough to understand why most countries reacted as they did; it was driven by the need to lessen the impact on health care systems, many of them inferior or badly funded, which would have been overwhelmed if the number of cases requiring hospitalization grew too quickly. Italy, for example, has an aging population.

It is number two in the world, behind only Japan, in the percentage of its population over sixty-five. It has been evident from early in the outbreak that older people are more susceptible to the virus and more likely to suffer from underlying conditions that increase their risk of serious illness or death than younger, healthier individuals. That meant Italy, already financially stressed, had a problem.

The Wuhan Institute of Virology, the lab where some suspect the virus originated, also may have contributed to the "panic" around the world. The lab specializes in genetically altering viruses, and world leaders may have feared they were dealing with a weaponized "superbug."

"Flattening the curve of the coronavirus's progression" also clearly played a role in the US's response. Our health care system, superior as it may be to most in the world, had not stockpiled ventilators or test kits for a virus no one knew existed, and giving the system time to ramp up to levels where even "worst-case" scenarios could be handled certainly would not have been an irrational response if it had been balanced and focused. Unfortunately, it was anything but. In a sense, the extreme panic COVID-19 generated in America left even Republican lawmakers and state governors with limited options. If a governor did not show at least as much empathy and concern as those governors shutting down their states, they would have been pilloried in the media and already anxious state residents driven to mass panic. Governor after governor was forced into either adopting measures at least as crippling to the economy and our lifestyles as governors responding before them, or upping the ante. The states fell like dominos.

The initial recommendations for combating the coronavirus seemed reasonable enough. Wash your hands frequently, eliminate unnecessary travel, avoid overly large gatherings, and pay attention to "social distancing." But as the media fanned fears controlling the virus suddenly took on apocalyptic dimensions. Social distancing turned into social isolation. First, it was schools that were closed. Then came restaurants and bars. Major manufacturing companies followed. Virtually all professional and NCAA sporting events were canceled or postponed, including the NCAA basketball tournament, the Masters Golf tournament, and the season schedules for the NBA, NHL, NFL, and MLB. Travel, both domestic and international, ground to a halt, along with almost all other business and social activities.

I suspect fear of "social shaming," as much as fear of COVID-19, drove a number of the closures. Many events could have taken place safely with a few, reasonable precautions. However, we live in a society where people are reluctant to oppose what increasingly are becoming narrow and rigid norms imposed and transmitted through social media. Some have called it the *social media contagion effect*, and it may be a contagion more dangerous than COVID-19. By whatever name, however, the "herd mentality" is powerful, notoriously petty, and intolerant of those who are not disciples. Retribution can be swift and unforgiving, amplified by the power and reach of Facebook, Twitter, Instagram, and other technologies. No one wants to be on the wrong side of a negative social media attack. Consequently, as fears over the coronavirus spiraled out of control across the country, there was less and less appetite on anyone's part to try to tamp down the angst or place the risks in perspective. Reason already had left the building. Things shut down because that is what the herd demanded.

The state high school basketball championships taking place in Richmond, Virginia, relatively early in the outbreak were prime examples. The first game was played, and a champion crowned. Players, teams, spectators, officials, and others were in the building, ready to play the remaining four or five "finals." They were canceled. Good decision or faint-hearted response by overly cautious officials? As every athlete knows, the opportunity to compete for a championship, for most, is a once-in-a-lifetime opportunity.

Some of the suggestions for shutdowns I heard discussed were completely frivolous from the standpoint of containing the virus—closing ABC stores, preventing people from driving on the interstate highways—and can be understood only as products of an arm's race that had been touched off among states scrambling to demonstrate which were doing the most to combat the virus and protect their panicked citizens. The goals of much of it had less to do with public health than projecting a sense of urgency and engagement, and the ever-expanding restrictions were aimed directly at the weakest and most fearful among us. The clear message was: "We understand this may be the greatest existential threat mankind ever has encountered, and we intend to mobilize all the resources of government to defeat it. We are fighting for you. When all of this is over, you can look to us for the financial support that will be needed to repair the devastation this virus obviously will cause."

It was a message intended to instill a sense of foreboding, to panic the public into surrendering to their fears and committing their destinies to government, and it largely succeeded. Predictably, the stock market also panicked, wiping out trillions of dollars of wealth almost overnight. The effects are likely to reverberate in the economy for years.

For Progressives, it was a dream come true, a once-in-a-lifetime opportunity to expand government in America as never before. At no time in our peacetime history had there been such an opportunity to bail out Americas on such a massive scale or to make more of us dependent upon government. Politically, it was almost a perfect set-up for another reason—whatever the President did to respond to the virus, Progressives could criticize him for doing it.

In fact, the President was well ahead of other world leaders in responding to the COVID-19 outbreak. Democrats, ensconced as they were at the time in bogus impeachment proceedings, were oblivious to the threat. The Chinese covered up the outbreak for weeks; even though the Chinese government knew the virus existed at least as early as December 2019, it was not mentioned publicly until January 21, 2020. Wuhan and three other Chinese cities supposedly were put on "lockdowns" on January 23, but hundreds of millions of Chinese travelers, including 5 million from Wuhan, were allowed to circulate throughout the country between January 24–30, as they celebrated the Chinese New Year.[358]

President Trump responded quickly. He banned travel from China to the US for everyone except US citizens and dependents on January 30. Progressives, including Joe Biden, widely criticized him as being xenophobic for doing so. The next day, he created a coronavirus task force made up of top health experts and headed by the vice-president.[359] The task force would meet daily from that date forward.

Cutting off travel from China early in the pandemic was a decisive move that undoubtedly slowed COVID-19's arrival and spread in the United States. I have not heard Joe Biden or any Progressive acknowledge that, nor have I read anything from the mainstream media chastising Progressives for their criticism of the President's travel ban. Should we assume Joe Biden would not have stopped travel from China if he had been president? If so, he is even less qualified than I thought, and that is barely possible. Can you imagine what the criticism would have been if the President had not done what he did when he did it?

Despite the President's rapid and logical initial response—and remember, he was in the middle of an impeachment trial as the outbreak in China was first coming to the world's attention—when Progressives eventually shook off their impeachment lethargy and realized the potential gravity of the situation, the predictable chorus of criticism was quickly in full song. There was no sense of pulling together as a country. No sense of "we are all in this together." No sense of "common cause." Just the usual strains of hypocritical aspersions without any suggestions of what should or could have been done better or differently. In this country, we have a tradition of rallying around the president in times of national crisis, regardless of political affiliations. At the end of the day, we always have been Americans first, Democrats, Republicans, and Independents second. Not so anymore. It is similar to the rejection of the notion that "politics stop at the water's edge" I talk about in an earlier chapter of this book.

One thing is certain. No matter what the outcome of the COVID-19 outbreak in the United States, or how competently or incompetently the various state governments deal with it, the President and his administration will be vilified by Progressives for the federal government's handling of the pandemic. The attacks will be corrupt, unrelenting, and disingenuous. The President will be faulted for not controlling what he could not possibly control and for not doing what he had no authority to do. Americans will be angry, scared, disoriented, and confused by a world that very likely will look and feel different to them after the devastation being caused by the economic shut-downs becomes more evident. They will be looking for scapegoats, someone to blame, and they will be susceptible to the criticism and finger-pointing Progressives will direct at the President.

It is pretty evident that the Progressives' campaign to politicize the COVID-19 outbreak already has started. Virginia's Democratic governor, Ralph Northam, for example, recently announced that Virginia public schools will be closed for the remainder of the school year. A few days later, he issued an executive order suspending all "discretionary" surgeries in Virginia.

The decision to close Virginia's public schools was at the very least premature. Almost three months remain in the school year, and there is no need to decide this early whether schools should remain closed for the remainder of the academic year. It is not public-school-aged children who primarily are threatened by the virus. As of the date of the governor's announcement, Virginia had only 246 active COVID-19 cases and seven deaths, all among elderly or significantly compromised patients. Dialogue around the country also was beginning to turn in the direction I have advocated since the beginning of the COVID-19 outbreak—to avoid lasting damage to our economy and social and cultural institutions, we need to make sure the response to the coronavirus does not turn out to be worse than the disease. The response must balance public health concerns with economic and social interests to the extent feasible, and needs to be tailored to actual conditions and events on the ground. There would have been no downside to waiting a few weeks to see if Virginia students could return to school safely.

The same is true of the governor's decision to suspend discretionary surgeries. At the time of the order, not many Virginians were hospitalized for the coronavirus. The hospitals certainly were not overwhelmed, and there were numerous medical specialists not likely to be involved in treating COVID patients. Many elective surgeries also are performed on an out-patient basis in ambulatory surgical centers, facilities not likely to be used for the treatment of virus patients. Progressives, of course, were quick to point out that bans on discretionary surgeries should not be interpreted as banning abortions. Interesting perspective—measures purportedly designed to save lives should not be allowed to interfere with the operation of facilities dedicated to taking them.

Ralph Northam made the decisions he did when he did because they were not decisions driven primarily by public health concerns. They were intended to make things in Virginia appear more serious and chaotic than they were. Progressives want a train wreck, economically and socially, and I antici-pate Northam will continue to issue periodic executive orders, regardless of actual conditions on the ground, to ensure that people remain appropriately anxious about how the Trump administration is dealing with the outbreak. The orders will increasingly squeeze the economy. Some key state services, including the Department of Motor Vehicles, already have been suspended. Progressives want people to believe the federal response to COVID-19, which represents the most significant medical mobilization since World War II, has been inadequate, a failure, and more could have and should have been done. They want people to blame the President for the tragedies and dislocations that have occurred and will occur in their lives. Progressives want people afraid and vulnerable to their economic "salvation" message.

Need further proof of the political nature of the governor's actions? The governor just issued a "stay at home order" for all Virginians, effective through June 10, 2020. The length of the order has left everyone scratching their heads. Who knows what the world will look like by April 10, much less June 10, so why not issue the order for thirty-day increments, extending it as needed?

The scope of the order is puzzling only until you realize that June 10 is one day *after* the Republican primaries scheduled to nominate candidates to run against incumbent Mark Warner, a Democrat, for one of Virginia's US Senate seats. The lengthy time frame of the order, of course, also has the added benefit of conveying the sense of a constantly worsening situation, even though Virginia still has only approximately 1,200 COVID-19 cases.

On the same day as Northam's school-closing order, Progressives in the United States Senate were derailing a $2 trillion coronavirus relief bill by trying to add, at the last minute, funding provisions for various environmental initiatives borrowed from the Green New Deal and having nothing to do with relief for businesses and people hurt by COVID's economic dislocations. A version of the bill eventually passed the Senate, more or less stripped of the environmental add-on's, but newly laden with funding for NPR, the Kennedy Center, and other cultural favorites of Progressives.

Think about it. For more than a week, in the middle of a pandemic, Progressives held up a desperately needed aid package for people and businesses struggling to survive the government-mandated shutdowns, purportedly for "pork barrel" projects unrelated to the coronavirus or any possible health and safety concerns. At least that was the "cover." I tend to think the motivations for holding up the bill were more Machiavellian.

Progressives intend to ride this crisis straight to the White House if voters let them. They have very little interest in trying to mitigate the economic, social, and other damages caused by COVID-19 while a Republican is in the White House. If they can derail the President's agenda between now and November and go into the election with the country still reeling from the effects of the COVID-19 outbreak, that will be as close to their dream scenario as possible. The Americans and American businesses trampled in the process are simply "collateral damage," acceptable casualties of a "take no prisoners" war against the President and the Constitution.

Governor Cuomo of New York, another Democrat, also did his part. Cuomo initially seemed like a voice of reason among Democrats, handling early press conferences calmly and matter-of-factly, despite a rapidly escalating number of coronavirus cases in New York City and its environs. He even appeared to agree with the President over the need to restart sectors of the economy less impacted by the virus. There were mutterings of a "draft Cuomo for president" movement among some Democrats, likely those who recognized most clearly the frailties of Joe Biden and the political baggage he carries.

Then the Party got to the governor. He complained that New York had a shortage of ventilators needed to treat the most severely ill coronavirus patients, those who had developed severe acute respiratory syndrome (SARS). When the President pointed out Cuomo already had over 4,000 federally provided ventilators in storage, unused, he attempted to explain his ventilator complaint by admitting that while New York had not yet used any of the stored ventilators, if the number of COVID-19 patients requiring hospitalization continued to grow to the numbers projected, New York would need more than the 4,000 extra ventilators on hand. Cuomo subsequently exposed his autocratic propensities, which seem to reside in all good Progressives, by signing an order directing the New York National Guard to confiscate ventilators from other areas of the state for use in New York City. At the time of the order, he still had unused ventilators in storage.

And so it will go. Half-truths, gamesmanship, outright lies by politicians politicizing a pandemic in an effort to win an election. The lesson here: do not take at face value anything you hear about shortages of needed tests or medical supplies and equipment. There almost always is a backstory, and very often the problem lies with state officials not organized enough to get available supplies to the areas where they are needed.

Some experts doubt the COVID-19 can be contained regardless of what we do.[360] Because so many people who contract the virus will be asymptomatic or have mild, undifferentiated symptoms, COVID-19 is surreptitious and difficult to detect. Infected individuals may have no symptoms at all—they feel well—and spread the virus simply by continuing their everyday activities. By the time an outbreak is detected, it is too late—the virus already has spread. Victims of more deadly pathogens, who quickly become severely ill, are far easier to identify and isolate, and the pathogens therefore easier to contain. It is one of the reasons more lethal contagions like Ebola, SARS, and MERS kill so few people. These viruses, all zoonotic diseases—transmitted initially from animals to humans—are deadly killers, sicken victims rapidly, and many of the victims die quickly.[361] In a very short time infected individuals become too ill to be active and potentially shedding the virus. It also explains why seasonal flu spreads so widely—because infected individuals can remain asymptomatic and functional for longer periods, they can infect many others before becoming sick enough to withdraw from normal activities. Although the fatality rate for seasonal flu is relatively low, it infects so many the dead typically number in the tens of thousands in the United States alone.

If containment of the COVID-19 is not possible—Marc Lipsitch, a professor of epidemiology at Harvard, predicts that within the year 40 to 70 percent of people around the world will be infected—then everything we currently are doing to try to contain it essentially qualifies as "wasted effort" except to buy some additional time for health care facilities to marshal the resources needed to treat hospitalized patients.[362] Thus far, other than in New York, there have not been many COVID-19 patients in this country requiring hospitalization. For example, *Worldometer's* daily tabulation of coronavirus cases in the United States currently shows 23,657 active cases, with 288 deaths. Most of those cases, 23,593, are listed as "mild." Only 64 are identified as serious or critical. As of mid-February, by contrast, seasonal flu had *hospitalized* 280,000 Americans.[363] Interestingly, the most significant surge in COVID-19 cases in the United States appears to have occurred after the most stringent "shelter at home" orders by state governors went into effect.

Based on the same *Worldometer* posting, at the moment four states, California, Washington, New York, and New Jersey account for 67 percent of the total US active cases (15,770), and 62 percent of the deaths (179), with New York leading the way, by far, in the number of cases, 49 percent of the total, and Washington state in the number of deaths, 29 percent of the total. Many of the deaths in Washington state have been in nursing homes or assisted living facilities.

The main body of COVID-19 cases may be clustered in four states, but the entire nation has been shut down. The social and economic costs of this containment effort are staggering. Effectively, we have closed down our economy and most social activities, destroyed trillions of dollars of wealth, not just by crashing the stock market, but also through the loss of millions of jobs, many of which may never be recovered, and altering countless lives in too many ways to comprehend. Think, for example, of the athletes, young and old, professional and amateur, who have been denied the opportunity to compete for championships, the marriage ceremonies that were canceled, the once-in-a-lifetime trips and vacations that never occurred, the students who were not able to attend their high school or college commencement exercises, and the family members who could not visit hospitalized family members or properly eulogized their deceased loved-ones, examples that barely scratch the surface of the massive dislocations we have allowed COVID-19 to inflict on us.

Progressives do not care what you have to give up or how badly you may be affected financially. Nor do they give a wit about your health or welfare. In this pandemic, they see a path to power, and they want you scared, submissive, and dependent on government. Any decision by President Trump to try to balance our response to the coronavirus by easing restrictions on economic and social activities will be savaged by Progressives and the media. If the president determines not to ease restrictions, he will be lambasted for not doing more to protect the economy. When you have an unfriendly media with an agenda, there never can be a "correct" decision. Whatever was not done should have been done, and whatever was done should not have been done.

Unlike responses to previous pandemics and epidemics, nothing in the response to COVID-19 has been situational or tailored to meet circumstances. We are doing essentially the same things in states which have only a few cases as in states which currently have most of the cases. Proponents will claim that the nationwide containment efforts are the reason the virus has not spread more widely in the United States, and perhaps they are correct. Time will tell. But even if they are, the question left unanswered is whether containment measures less destructive of our economy and lifestyle would have been just as effective, particularly if the effort to contain the virus is one mainly intended to buy time for health care facilities to stock additional supplies and equipment. New York, Washington, New Jersey, and California have used essentially the same scorched-earth containment practices as the other states, but their COVID-19 cases continue to grow, supporting the view that the virus is not containable, at least not long-term.

Other countries have taken different routes, Sweden, for example, has not "locked down" its economy or people. The government encourages reasonable social distancing, frequent hand-washing, and other precautions, but when I last checked, its streets, cafes, restaurants, and other places of business were still bustling. Sweden has coronavirus cases, to be sure, but its coronavirus "profile" does not look much different from other Scandinavian countries and is considerably better than many Western European countries which imposed significantly more stringent, economy-crushing controls.

Another question that needs to be answered: are we creating a worse situation down the road by the extreme containment measures being taken today? Typically, viruses infect populations, peak, and then dissipate. Some infected individuals get seriously ill, others do not, but as a whole, the community builds a level of resistance, if not immunity, to the virus, which makes reoccurrences less severe. There are indications the COVID-19 is seasonal and may die down naturally in the US as warm weather arrives, much like the seasonal flu. However, if the combination of containment efforts and weather changes are successful in preventing COVID-19 from "peaking," does that mean the virus is likely to return with a vengeance later in the year? Does trying to contain the virus now, in other words, have any realistic chance of providing the time needed for the development of countermeasures, a vaccine, or other treatments, before there is a dangerous resurgence of the virus?

When containment of a virus is not possible, developing a vaccine to provide immunity against it becomes the most viable public health strategy. The race already is on to develop a vaccine for COVID-19, but it is unclear on what timeline an effective vaccine can or will become available and how many people will accept it once it does. We have had vaccines available for many years to combat seasonal flu, a serious killer, but only half the country gets an annual flu shot, even though the shots are free for almost all Americans. Approximately 20 percent of our population contracts flu every year. Tens of thousands die. No one pays any attention.

It's always informative to look back and see how previous pandemics were handled. In 2009, for example, near the beginning of the Obama administration's first term in office, the swine flu pandemic hit the shores of America. Eventually, there would be over 60 million cases in the United States, almost 275,000 hospitalizations, and nearly 12,500 deaths.[364] Worldwide estimates of the death toll resulting from the swine flu ranged from approximately 152,000 to as much as nearly 600,000. Of the many thousands of schools in the United States, approximately 700 closed, generally only those with clusters of students who were seriously ill with the flu.[365] There were no calls by the media for the large-scale shuttering of factories, restaurants, bars, or any other facilities. There was no interruption of professional, collegiate, and high school sports. Travel restrictions were not ordered, except for warnings about going to Mexico, where the swine flu originated. And the Dow rose over 40 percent during the pandemic.[366]

Has that much changed since 2009? Have we become such a fearful, risk-averse nation that we now are unable to bring any perspective, balance, or reason to this type of health threat? Does every new epidemic or pandemic demand the immediate and unconditional shut down of all aspects of our social and economic lives? We have lived through Ebola scares and outbreaks of avian flu, Zika, MERS, SARS, HIV, and AIDS in recent years. We also have endured epidemics of diphtheria (1921–25), polio (1916–55), measles (1981–91), and whooping cough (2010, 2014), not to mention the Spanish flu (1918), in this century. All of these pathogens were mass killers. None provoked a reaction like this, an almost total meltdown of society. Elsewhere in the book, I questioned whether millennials are strong enough to live in a democracy. The better question might be, "Are we?"

Progressives will attempt to justify the total shut down of the country on the premise that "you can fix the economy, but not your health." It is a seductive, but misleading *non sequitur.* It assumes the only possible, and mutually exclusive, alternatives are protecting health or protecting the economy. If that were true, and if health is the paramount consideration, the country should be shut down permanently and people confined to their houses year-round, not only because of the many contagious diseases that annually kill hundreds of thousands around the world but also because of the many other risks that threaten human health and well-being.

Never in my lifetime, and perhaps in no one's lifetime, have we as a nation responded to any other epidemic or pandemic as we have responded to this one. No one has been allowed to even consider alternative approaches, such as protecting the most vulnerable while allowing the less vulnerable to continue to work. The simple truth is that the vast majority of coronavirus patients, just like victims of flu and many other types of infectious diseases, show only mild symptoms and recover relatively quickly. With seasonal flu, we have decided that a couple of weeks of illness, sometimes severe, on the part of millions, and the deaths of tens of thousands annually, are not sufficient reasons to close down the nation every flu season. And how could it be otherwise? Flu arrives every winter, and we know, despite available medicines to fight it, it will sicken and kill many. But we also know that shutting down the nation to lessen the impact of flu would cause unacceptable economic and social harm and likely kill just as many, if not more.

So why do we think it makes sense to shut down for the coronavirus? Is it only because the virus is new and we are unfamiliar with it? If at least 25 percent of the people infected by COVID-19 are asymptomatic, as some medical experts suspect, if most of us will have "mild" symptoms, and if the coronavirus is now endemic, as it appears to be, how can we possibly continue this type of extreme containment strategy? Or, is this all about stalling for time while vaccines and other countermeasures are developed? Once those countermeasures are available, if they ever are, will Americans then be willing to accept at least as many deaths each year from COVID-19 as the 12,000 to 61,000 deaths that occur annually in the United States from seasonal flu?

The basic premise underlying the "public health versus the economy" argument also is bogus. You cannot always "fix" the economy, certainly not in the short term. No economy is resilient enough to withstand repeated shut-downs and interruptions of this magnitude. Each time a shut-down occurs, vast wealth and prosperity are wiped out. All of humanity suffers and not just economically. As health professionals know, disasters of many different kinds, natural, man-made, economic, and otherwise, result in widespread deaths and illnesses.

The collateral effects can be just as consequential. Nations suffering from contracted economies, for example, often lack the resources to invest in medical infrastructure, doctors and other health care professionals, health insurance, and social safety nets. Living conditions worsen. Supply chains break down. Food becomes scarce. It is not, in other words, the zero-sum game opportunistic politicians try to make it. The health of economies and individuals are linked in many different ways, both visible and opaque. Ignoring either to protect the other overlooks that obvious truth. Wrecked economies, lost jobs, lost opportunities, and a host of other fallouts from economic disasters cause illnesses, deaths, and suffering just as surely as biological pathogens. And whether we recognize it or not, by opting to focus only on the medical issues resulting from COVID-19, we have made a choice. The choice? We have favored those who may become sick from COVID-19 over those who will become ill, suffer, or die from the effects of the unbalanced responses we have made to the virus. The COCID-19 numbers may be more visible, but the collateral damages and deaths are just as real.

What we have at the moment is a completely media-inspired, fear-driven response to a new virus, a response that has not even attempted to mitigate the damages to our economy, social institutions, culture, and lifestyle. Essentially, the medical professionals seem to be betting that extreme containment measures and the arrival of warm weather will arrest the spread of the virus and allow effective countermeasures to be developed in the short time period before the next, perhaps more deadly, wave of the virus arrives. If that is the strategy, we have paid an enormous price trying to buy a few months. It may be comforting to some when state governments mandate practices with crushing and potentially lasting consequences for our prosperity and way of life, regardless of effectiveness and without even considering the availability of more reasonable or focused alternatives, but all of us will have to live with the aftermath.

Is everything we are doing to combat COVIS-19 even a public health imperative? How could it be? Too much of what is being done seems to be based less on facts, science, and public health principles than on the need for state governments to *look* proactive," quell panic, buy time, and play politics. For example, almost every state now is banning the gathering of groups of more than ten. Why ten? Why not five? Why not ban the gathering of groups altogether? What is the science that says ten is "safer" than eleven? Or twelve? If social distancing works, what does it matter how many are in a group? When we send college students home, do we expect they will stop gathering with friends, family, and acquaintances? How did that work out in Florida over spring break?

These are the types of events that bring out the worst instincts in governments and politicians. For example, Virginia has compiled a list of "essential" businesses, which can remain open, and a list of nonessential businesses, which have been ordered to close. The Virginia state government, in other words, has attempted to pick winners and losers, those who are being given a chance to survive the coronavirus shutdowns, and those who will be less likely to do so because they have been closed by government fiat. Two trillion-dollar relief packages or not, many of the closed businesses never will reopen.

Like most governments. Virginia does not understand that if a business truly is "nonessential," it would not exist. It is essential enough for enough people to remain in business. Why even try to close some establishments while inviting others to stay open? If people are circulating in pet stores, lawn and garden stores, home improvement stores, grocery stores, electronics stores, automotive parts stores, and the like, all on the "stay open list" in Virginia, will it make any difference if people also are allowed to frequent beauty salons, social clubs, indoor shooting ranges, farmers' markets, restaurants, and other businesses on the "must close" list? The businesses allowed to stay open all are instituting "social distancing" rules and other safety precautions, and there is no reason to believe any enterprise permitted to stay open would not do the same.

If state governments trusted you, what is "essential" and what is not would be sorted out quickly by the decisions of consumers who would visit only venues they considered "essential" and "safe." But state governments do not trust you, and like so much of what they do, the lists of "essential" and "non-essential" facilities are almost completely arbitrary

. I am confident there were members of a government committee convened somewhere in Virginia who exchanged congratulatory high-fives, perhaps only virtually, to celebrate their "brilliance" in determining the businesses that needed to be closed to make you "safe." Central planners always believe they have the answers. How fascinating would it have been to sit in while committee members struggled to differentiate pet stores, many of which offer pet grooming services and were considered "essential," from beauty parlors and barbershops, which were deemed "nonessential." It apparently was considered important for people to be able to get their poodles groomed but not important for the poodle owners to be able to get a haircut.

When does the cure become worse than the disease? I tend to think anytime reaction begins to masquerades as reason. Governments are playing the role of the Great Oz, and we have meekly assumed the part of Zeke, the cowardly lion, overly timid and anxious, trying to wring comfort from increasingly intrusive government limits on our liberties and freedoms. It will be difficult to wean many Americans from the dependency on government that will grow as the economy progressively weakens. I earlier said that government messaging was aimed at the weakest among us. That now seems to be most of us.

Brace yourselves. Other pandemics are on the horizon. You can count on it. Epidemics occur around the world frequently—on average 187 epidemics occurred somewhere in the world each year from 2011 through 2017, according to the World Health Organization—and pandemics occur periodically.[367] Since 1970, an astounding 1,500 new pathogens have been identified.[368] Globalization, urbanization, the extreme mobility of modern populations, mass immigration, and the ever-expanding interactions between humans and animals—the majority of all human infectious diseases originate through the cross-species transmission of microorganisms from animals to humans—all mean pandemics almost surely will occur with increasing frequency.[369] As a nation, we will have to come to grips with how to deal with outbreaks without creating an economic and social train wreck each time one occurs.

COVID-19 now has become our fifth endemic coronavirus. The other four we call "colds." It may be seasonal. If so, its prevalence is likely to ebb and flow, much like flu. It's also possible vaccines will be developed to combat it, although no one ever before has successfully produced a vaccine for a coronavirus, and vaccines seldom are perfect. Hopefully, antiviral drugs and other treatment options will be formulated as well, much like Tamiflu was created to treat the symptoms of flu.

Whatever the level of effectiveness of coronavirus vaccines or other treatments, we will need to learn how to deal more rationally with COVID-19 illnesses. It cannot be by shuttering the nation every time cases arise. We cannot let fear become the primary driver of our decision-making. Our economy is robust and resilient, but it cannot endure the "shocks" of repeated shutdowns. Every time that happens, tens of millions of those least able to afford it are badly hurt. Life savings, retirement plans, college funds, jobs, dreams, and aspirations all disappear. Most importantly, the threat to democracy is palpable—each one of these episodes cowers people into greater and greater dependency on government.

The message we are sending our enemies also is troubling to me. Terrorists around the world now have witnessed firsthand the widespread fear, panic, and chaos a biological agent can cause in a nation they viewed as strong and resolute. We have demonstrated just how "soft" we are. The usual safeguard against the terror or wartime uses of biological agents—the fact that those dispensing them cannot ensure that they will not become victims—may not be a sufficient deterrent to madmen willing to martyr themselves for a cause if our timidness in the face of COVID-19 provides a sense they might be able to win.

Bottom line: we have to be more resilient; we have to be smarter; we have to be braver; we have to be better prepared.

CHAPTER POSTSCRIPT

I began writing this postscript on May 2, 2020, and updated it in mid-May. I will not update it again; as you read it, keep in mind that it is written from the perspective of mid-May, 2020. I mention that simply to point out that the COVID-19 pandemic remains an ongoing health emergency and data is changing daily. By the time this is read, things may have changed significantly. I am encouraged, however, by the fact that nothing has happened to change the assessments contained in the original sections of this chapter, which was written in mid-March when the pandemic was in its early stages.

Coronavirus cases, both worldwide and in the United States, have risen sharply since I wrote the first part of this chapter, as I suggested they might. Nevertheless, world COVID-19 figures continue to lag significantly the World Health Organization's estimates of 3 to 5 million cases of severe illness from influenza epidemics in the world each year and 250,000 to 500,000 deaths.[370] In the United States, the figures are 39 million to 56 million flu illnesses, 410,000 to 740,000 hospitalizations, and as many as 62,000 deaths *this flu season.*[371]

Advocates claim that the social isolation created by "shelter in place" orders from state governors have been effective in containing the spread of COVID-19, but information increasingly becoming available calls that assessment into question. Specifically, we now have information about how countries, as well as some states in the US, that did not shut down have fared. Japan, for example, was not able to lock down its economy—it surprisingly lacked sufficient "at-home" technologies to allow people to work remotely. Consequently, subways, most businesses, and many other activities remained open. As of this writing, Japan has had excellent CVID-19 outcomes, with less than 500 deaths in a nation of over 126 million people. Keep in mind just how crowded the Japanese subways are; many of you have witnessed or seen pictures of the "pushers" on station platforms in Japan, shoving passengers into subway cars. It can nearly double the number of passengers per car.

The results have been just as good in South Korea, another country that did not shut down its subways, bars, restaurants, and malls. The same for Taiwan, which sits a stone's throw from mainland China. Sweden, one of the very first nations to reject the mathematical models projecting massive COVID-19 illnesses, hospitalizations, and deaths and remain open for business, continues to enjoy a COVID-19 profile no different from many countries that crushed their economies with lockdown orders.

In the United States, states like North and South Dakota, Nebraska, and Arkansas did not close but thus far have fared better than most areas of the country. Florida's and Texas's more targeted approaches, directed at safeguarding nursing homes and other enclaves of the elderly and sick, also have produced good outcomes. When Georgia and Colorado reopened their economies earlier than medical experts recommended, they continued to experience results at least as good as states which remained locked down.

Liberty University in Lynchburg, Virginia, welcomed students back to campus after spring break despite the pandemic. Twelve hundred students stayed on campus for weeks while virtually every other college and university in the nation closed. The media was apoplectic, widely predicting mass deaths and accusing the university's president, Jerry Falwell Jr., of a "staggering level of ignorance."[372] The "almost always wrong on just about everything," Paul Krugman, economist, professor, and columnist for the *New York Times,* accused Falwell of creating his own "viral hotspot."[373] As I write this, Liberty has experienced no outbreaks of the virus on campus, not one, and now is viewed as a model for reopening other schools.[374]

Perhaps most surprisingly, New York, the epicenter of the COVID-19 outbreak in this country, disclosed that 66 percent of its hospitalizations, not including nursing homes and long-term care facilities, involved individuals who followed the state's rigid lockdown rules and remained at home, isolated. That was a stunning revelation and one that should have sent everyone scurrying for an explanation. Instead, the media barely mentioned it, and Progressive governors continued to extend the length of their draconian "shelter in place" orders. Nevertheless, it is an outcome entirely consistent with the conclusions of those experts who early on predicted the virus was not the type that could be contained.

Is it possible the predicate on which the entire COVID-19 response seems to be premised, that social isolation is key to defeating the virus, may be wrong? Despite the indifference of the media and Progressive governors to the evidence that is accumulating around them, anyone with the slightest intellectual curiosity should be asking at least these two questions: are the experts and political class correct when they maintain that "shelter in place" executive orders are necessary to stop the spread of COVID-19; and is there any real science suggesting that less punitive measures, such as social distancing, handwashing, and covering your mouth when coughing would not have worked just as well? The data from New York, and the outcomes in countries and states that did not shut down, or reopened early, suggests that measure more respectful of the economy and our way of life would have been just as effective as the punitive actions taken by most states. If that turns out to be true, then the COVID-19 response will have been the most unnecessary and expensive overreaction to a pandemic in the history of the nation.

One thing is certain. A media truly doing its job would not immediately and universally condemn every deviation from the conventional wisdom, as our media is doing, but would investigate examples like the countries and states which never shut down or reopened early to see what could be learned about the optimum response to COVID-19. Our media, unfortunately, like all "captive" news organizations, is comfortable in its role as the voice of the Progressive Party, once known as the Democratic Party, and is not about to question the Progressives' narrative on COVID-19 or anything else.

COVID-19 unexpectedly presented Progressives with their greatest opportunity yet to establish socialism in the United States, and the media is nearly frantic in its resolve not to squander the moment. For that to happen, however, Progressives and their media allies need the country to remain locked down for a long as possible. The longer the economy is not functioning, the greater the number of people who will become or remain dependent on government. The more people dependent on government, the quicker the transition from capitalism to socialism can occur. To that end, Progressive governors across the country continue to mindlessly repeat the mantra, "we must be guided by the science," while ignoring not just the science, but also the mounting anecdotal evidence from areas that responded to COVID-19 differently and produced outcomes that suggest the supposedly "science-based" responses might have been mistaken.

The Department of Homeland Security, for example, announced testing at the National Biodefense Analysis and Countermeasures Center that shows sunlight, higher humidity, and warmer temperatures—being outdoors, in other words— can kill the virus quickly, within two minutes or less in some conditions. How did governors respond? They continued lockdown orders that closed beaches, parks, and other outdoor venues and discouraged people from going outdoors. Even when beaches started to reopen, impossibly arbitrary restrictions were imposed. One of my favorites— you can walk on the beach but not sit or sunbathe. Michigan authorized boating but not the use of a motor. In Illinois, no more than two people at a time were allowed on a boat, regardless of its size. A family of four or five locked at home together, in other words, could not get on the same boat, even a 90-foot yacht.

Decisions this capricious can only be viewed for what they are: power grabs. What else could they be? The decisions are too irrational to be unintentional. They are designed to intimidate, to send a message: "We are in control, and there is nothing you can do about it; no matter how arbitrary, capricious, wrong, and outrageous our decisions may be, you are obligated to obey and will be punished if you do not." Disciplining populations now sets the stage for what will be needed if Progressives regain control of the country and begin the serious business of implementing socialism. It is classic Leninism.

Governors also continue to tell people to wear masks even though many of the masks being used do almost nothing to prevent the spread of the virus. Few fit properly, particularly for wearers with facial hair. Most "filter" little, if anything, and certainly not the microscopically small virus cells;[375] it is like trying to contain mosquitoes with chicken wire. The same with gloves; unless people change gloves many times a day, at least as often as they would wash their hands, wearing them does very little to prevent spread of the virus. People are not contracting COVID-19 by absorbing the virus through the skin on their hands. More dangerously, to the extent masks and gloves provide a false sense of security that causes people to get closer or wash their hands less often, masks and gloves can have exactly the opposite effect on health and safety. And if the unfamiliarity and discomfort of masks cause people to touch their faces more frequently, they are not "safer."

Whether well-advised or not, the initial containment efforts were theoretically taken to "flatten the curve" and protect medical facilities and resources from being overwhelmed. Whether that was necessary or even prudent will be debated for many years, as the full effects of the damage to our economy and way of life become more evident. It also is a debate for another time and place. We are well past the point where we need to protect medical facilities and resources and have been for some time. Medical capacities have not been overwhelmed; doctors are being laid off and hospitals threatened with closures because of a lack of patients. Nevertheless, governors of many states, obviously intoxicated with the experience of exercising near-dictatorial powers for the last several weeks, have taken the COVID-19 response wildly beyond its original intent and purpose. The goal somehow has morphed into making sure no one, not a single person, gets ills or dies from coronavirus. In the minds of some of these newly minted, tin-pot totalitarians, unless and until a vaccine is developed that is 100 percent effective, or the virus is completely eradicated from the face of the Earth, we never will be able to reopen the economy completely or return to life as we once knew it. At least not until a Progressive regains control of the White House.

And why wouldn't they feel like that? Never before have they been allowed to exercise powers even remotely like this, without constitutions, state legislatures, or opposing political parties to interfere, and certainly not the media. It's rule by executive order, the closest they have ever come to the type of authority exercised by Napoleon, Mao Zedong, and Castro. The law is what they say it is. With a panicked and cowed public, no matter how irrational what they do or say may be, few object. Those who do are punished or shamed. It's good to be king. Fabulous actually.

It also is a complete overreach. By now it should have occurred to these petty tyrants that the type of containment efforts they are ordering are unnecessary and not particularly effective. Special efforts to protect unusually vulnerable populations from the coronavirus may be advisable, but when else have we ever completely locked down the country because of the possibility someone might contract a disease? Most people do not die from COVID-19; the majority never even know they have it. Fully 98 percent of all COVID-19 cases are classified as mild.

People die by the millions every year from flu and other communicable diseases, accidents, and other misfortunes, some of which are preventable or treatable, others not, but life moves on. We could take a variety of steps to reduce the annual slaughter on our highways, for example, some as simple as reducing speed limits, but resist doing so. Neary 40,000 people in the US die in car crashes every year as a result, with hundreds of thousands seriously injured. Worldwide, more than 1.3 million people die in highway accidents annually. Twice that number are injured. Why do we show such little interest in mitigating the carnage? Why do we not shut down our economy each flu season when tens of thousands die in America and hundreds of thousands more die around the world? The obvious answer is we recognize we cannot, that it would be far more damaging to shut down our economy than to soldier through seasonal flu and the other threats to our health, safety, and security that are part of living life.

Perhaps the most troubling aspect of the coronavirus response was how quickly Americans "came to heel." Almost without question, people quickly adopted the narrative of the "experts," virtually all of whom have been wrong about almost everything they predicted. We allowed our lives and livelihoods to be taken away from us without a whimper. Even now, every morning when I pick up a newspaper, there are stories about events still months away but being planned as if life as we currently know it will be a permanent condition. It truly is astonishing how docile and afraid of COVID-19 we have become and how readily we have forfeited basic rights and freedoms, not to mention destroying our economy and lifestyle, in a fearful effort to contain a virus that very likely is "uncontainable."

Realistically, I do not believe there is any way to view what many states are doing to keep their economies closed as anything other than political adventurism. We have a way to go before we will know how this pandemic plays out, but people waiting for a silver bullet, a vaccine, may be disappointed. The quickest development of any vaccine, for Ebola, took five years. Researchers have been trying unsuccessfully for thirty-five years to come up with a vaccine for HIV. No one has ever produced a successful vaccine for any coronavirus. Nevertheless, as I write this, there are reports of a potential "miracle" breakthrough in the development of a COVID-19 vaccine by Moderna that might be available by the end of summer or early fall. It obviously would be good news if true, particularly if it can be brought to market that quickly. I also suspect it would cause great agitation and disappointment among Progressives, who fervently hope the nation remains in the grip of the coronavirus panic at least through the November elections.

Every American should be disheartened by that last statement. One of our major political parties has so completely abandoned the principles on which this country was founded that it now is willing to make failure of the economy part of a strategy for returning to power. It is a cancer that has been allowed to grow because we have been careless with the freedoms and liberties we inherited. We have allowed the worst among us to shape our future. If there is an excuse for our negligence, it is no more than the fact the Progressive movement, for the most part, has remained out of sight, hiding in plain view, but hidden nonetheless. It is an excuse that endures no more. It is past time to rid our politics of this disease. To avoid being confused with Leonard Pitts and his vindictive against "Trump supporters," understand that I am speaking figuratively. But this menace to democracy needs to be convincingly rejected at the polls in November and sent back to where it belongs—the dust bins of history.[376]

Even without a vaccine, treatments will be developed for COVID-19, as they have been for HIV. Despite the media's refusal to acknowledge it, chloroquine, hydroxychloroquine, Remdesivir, and other existing drugs already are being used with good success to treat the virus, and as doctors learn more about the pathogen, they are improving the techniques for treating patients who contract it. A level of "herd" or "community" immunity may develop naturally, as well. Most experts believe at least 30 percent of all individuals infected with COVID-19 are asymptomatic, which means, if true, significant segments of the population already have contracted the virus but are unaware of it. At the moment, however, we do not know how adequately this type of immunity will protect people or how long it might last. A recent news story, for example, reported that seven Navy sailors appear to have developed the disease a second time.

The President also hinted at treatments that might "disinfect" the lungs. He, of course, was immediately ridiculed and accused of encouraging people to ingest Clorox, although he had done nothing of the kind. Shortly thereafter, researchers announced a promising inhalation technology that could stimulate the production of "super-oxides" in the lungs to combat coronaviruses and perhaps many other diseases. Isn't it startling how the media has yet to understand that each time the President says something they consider outlandish he almost certainly has information they do not? They are too absorbed with trying to find ways to criticize him even to consider the possibility

. The same thing happened when the President suggested UV light might be useful in fighting the virus. I have UV lights in my home's HVAC system, and UV light systems for eliminating bacteria and viruses in commercial buildings are becoming increasingly popular. The technology also is being used to disinfect hospital rooms and personal protective equipment, such as re-usable masks worn by medical personnel. The media nonetheless is uninterested and almost completely dismissive of the idea that UV light might have a place in the efforts to combat the virus. If the President suggests it, they reflexively oppose it.

Curiously, the media and many state governors continue to insist testing is the key to controlling spread of the virus. It has become a Progressive talking point, largely because it provides an easy way to criticize the President—no matter how much testing is done, it never could be enough.

Testing, as a containment strategy, is almost a complete fiction, at least until better testing technologies are developed. Estimates place the number of tests needed to control the spread of the virus in the United States at 35 million a day, assuming contact tracing also takes place, and as many as 100 million a day if it does not.[377] For those who do not know, "contact tracing" is the technique of identifying and tracing everyone who has contact with someone during a timeframe within which that person may have been infected with COVID-19. The idea is to identify and quarantine anyone and everyone exposed to the virus until doctors are sure they have not been infected.

Think how unrealistic it is to even consider testing on a scale this massive. An estimated 330 million people live in the United States. At 35 million tests a day, the entire population of the country would have to be tested every nine days, followed by a massive contact tracing effort. At 100 million, essentially the entire population of the country would be tested every three days. How is either option even logistically possible? The United States, which leads the world in total coronavirus testing, thus far has tested only 12 million individuals during the course of the pandemic. How could everyone in the United States even be required to submit to a test every three or nine days? And at what cost, not just in terms of money, but also in the interruptions in business schedules, schools, and daily life?

Is contact tracing even constitutional? South Korea has led the way in contact tracing during the COVID-19 pandemic, using digital devices such as cell phone apps and tracking bracelets to keep tabs on its citizens and visitors. Most discussions of contact tracing in the US currently focus somewhat more benignly on "assisting infected persons recall everyone with whom they had close contact," and then warning those people about the exposure and asking them to self-isolate.[378] The CDC publication just quoted, however, references another CDC paper entitled, *Digital Contact Tracing Tools for COVID-19* that broadly describes the various "proximity tracking technologies" available to support contact tracing. How long do you think it will take the data collection Nazis to conclude that "after the fact" interviews of potentially exposed people identified from memory by COVID-19 infected individuals are too time-consuming and erratic to be effective and begin the campaign to shift the United States to digital surveillance, South Korean-style or worse.

It would be unlike anything ever seen or contemplated in this country. "Traced" individuals all would be required to quarantine for at least fourteen days, creating huge disruptions in the workforce and every other aspect of life. It is estimated that at least 100,000 contact tracers would be required; I think the number necessarily would be much higher. Hundreds of new testing facilities also would have to be built and staffed, not to mention the production of test kits and other materials needed to take samples and analyze results.

For Progressives, it would be a dream come true. Every authoritarian government covets the ability to monitor the populations it controls. It is the key to quelling dissent and shutting down criticism and resistance. The right to be free of warrantless surveillance by our government and to have our privacy protected are among the most important civil rights guaranteed by the Constitution. They are rights Americans have fought and died to protect since our founding and with good reason. To have people now surrender those rights voluntarily and unwittingly on the panicked hope doing so will protect them from COVID-19 would provide Progressives with perhaps the most unanticipated victory of all in their war against American democracy.

The simple truth is, contact tracing works most effectively with pathogens like Ebola that can be detected easily and early and infected individuals isolated quickly before they come into contact with large numbers of people. It does not work well with a contagion like COVID-19, which spreads rapidly, widely, and surreptitiously, particularly after the pathogen already is established in the population. If the virus is as contagious as experts currently claim, then one person walking through a mall, a subway station, or an airport may be able to infect dozens. And for anyone to suggest contact tracing can be done effectively without jeopardizing our liberties has something other than the preservation of democracy in mind.

It should be obvious why more modest levels of testing cannot possibly be effective in containing the spread of COVID-19. Using Virginia as an example, to date the state has barely managed to test 160,000 people during the entirety of the pandemic. Testing 100,000 people a day, or even 500,000, in a state of 8.5 million, assuming those levels of testing could be achieved, provides no information about the health of the 8 million not tested. Even for those tested, all you know is whether or not at the moment of the test an individual is positive for COVID-19, and it is unlikely that test results would be available for 2 or 3 days. If the tested individual did not self-isolate in the interim, they could be infected, or infect others, in the next hour, the next day, and certainly by the time test results are received To be of any true value as a containment strategy, testing has to encompass entire populations, if not daily, at least over a very short time period—two or three days at the most— and test results have to be available more or less in real-time.

The testing also must be continuous; this is not a "one and done" proposition. Whether the test protocol calls for a test every day or every three days, the cycle must be continued, uninterrupted, for as long as it takes to develop an effective vaccine. A test every nine days, useful only if implemented in conjunction with contact tracing, would mean every American would need to be tested forty times a year. Everyone in the country would have to be tested 120 times a year if contact tracing is not utilized.

Progressive state governors know the impracticability of testing every American forty times a year, much less one hundred and twenty times, but by insisting that testing is key to containing the virus, they keep open options too valuable to cede. Some already have been mentioned, including the easy means the testing narrative provides for criticizing the President. People who do not understand the infeasibility and unconstitutionality of doing what would be necessary for testing to serve as an effective containment strategy are easy marks for claims that the COVID-19 testing done by the US, despite being the most by any country in the world, is "inadequate," a major flaw in our defense against the spread of the virus, and the "fault" of the Trump administration.

The same state governors also understand the value of conditioning Americans to accept government surveillance. While most Americans instinctively recoil from allowing their governments, state or national, to spy on them, they have been frightened into accepting contact tracing, a massive government encroachment on the privacy rights that underlie most constitutional protections against government abuse and over-reach, as nothing more than benign government effort to protect their health, safety, and welfare. The same people undoubtedly allow their insurance companies to track and monitor their driving habits if it saves fifty dollars in insurance premiums. We are a naïve nation.

The "more tests are needed" narrative, however, is just as important for another reason: it allows governors to keep their states closed for as long as they wish simply by maintaining that unless and until "adequate" testing is available, non-essential businesses must remain at least partially shut down, people cannot be allowed to gather in public places, and similar impositions on basic liberties and freedoms. The more restive people become and the more damage that is done to the economy, the better Progressive's chances are in November, the less the President can accomplish between now and then, and the more people will grow dependent on government.

To be fair, in individual cases testing can provide doctors with valuable diagnostic information. It also can provide researchers with data that may help them develop treatments and protocols for dealing with the virus more effectively down the road. But neither of these observations is the point. The testing currently being done, or that practically could be done, has limited effect on *containing* the virus, the supposed goal of Progressive governors clamoring for more testing.

Researchers one day may develop tests that can be used easily and widely with large populations. Work already is underway, for example, to develop oral test strips that would provide immediate indications of a COVID-19 infection. It is similar to home pregnancy or HIV screening tests.[379] Rapid response "antigen" tests are another possibility, although the results are not immediately available. Nevertheless, both types of tests, if widely accessible at a reasonable cost, could help weed out COVID 19 infected individuals for such purposes as determining who could attend spectator events or participate in sporting events and other group activities. As containment strategies, however, even these approaches would require everyone in the country to diligently test every day or every two or three days and self-report positive results. As always, some people would not test at all, and others, particularly those with important events on their schedules, illegally in the country, or adverse to the prospect of quarantine, would not report infections. Because only portions of the population would be participating, the need for additional testing, contact tracing, or both would not go away.

I am not arguing against these or any other testing technologies. The more tools we have to combat COVID-19, the better. Cheap, reliable, easily available tests with immediately available or nearly immediately available results would do away with many of the excuses governors are using to keep their states shut down But the testing technologies available at the moment are not particularly useful for containment purposes, and they are not inexpensive.

It is important to keep in mind that even with a vaccine, good test and treatment options, and a level of naturally developed herd immunity, people will continue to get sick from COVID-19. The virus is endemic and will be with us for many years to come. Some will die every year, perhaps many, just as they do from flu. Is the country willing to accept as many as 60,000 deaths annually from COVID-19, the same as flu, without having a complete societal meltdown with each return of the virus? I am not confident.

I know this. What I said when I first started this chapter has not changed. We cannot close the country again for the coronavirus. We do not shut down our economy for anything else, and if we cannot maintain our wits and sensibilities in dealing with this pathogen, those trying to send us back to the caves will get their wish sooner than expected. It's the reason Alexandra-Ocasio Cortez and other Progressives celebrated the economic shutdown caused by the coronavirus; it resembles the type of economy they envision for America once the Green New Deal is implemented. It also satisfies their peculiar sense of "social justice"—everyone suffers equally. If you like what you see, vote for them.

CHAPTER 20

UNIVERSITY OF VIRGINIA

I end this book with a chapter that gives me no pleasure to write. It will be brief because I have no desire to dwell on an episode that demonstrates too grimly the state of disunity that exists in America today.

The victory of the University of Virginia basketball team for the national title in 2019 represented one of the greatest stories of redemption in team sports. From a crushing and humiliating defeat as the number one team in the country in the 2018 NCAA tournament at the hands of a feisty University of Maryland, Baltimore County team, a number sixteen seed—the first time a number one seed ever had lost in the NCAA tournament to a number sixteen seed—to national champion a year later was a true story of fortitude, perseverance, and courage by a remarkable group of young athletes. Three times the Cavaliers essentially were beaten in the 2019 tournament, trailing with only seconds remaining, but refused to lose, going to overtime in two of the victories. Although favored over a great team from Texas Tech in the Championship game, more than a few doubted Virginia's ability to match up physically with a team that had eliminated several of college basketball's true "blue bloods" en route to the finals. The fact Virginia prevailed was a testament to the character and unflappability of a veteran team and its celebrated coach, Tony Bennett.

As a graduate of its law school, I have been a long-time, avid Virginia sports fan, enduring years of disappointments along with countless other long-suffering fans as the football team, and until Tony Bennett arrived, the basketball team, struggled. The basketball team's victory in the national championship was one of the most satisfying nights I have experienced in sports. But it now comes with an asterisk. Invited to the White House to share its victory with the nation, the Virginia basketball team declined, citing "difficulties" with scheduling, allegedly because of the number of team members who were leaving school to go into the NBA draft.

The excuse for declining the White House visit was transparent from the beginning, but it might have sufficed if not for a tweet by De'Andre Hunter, one of the stars of the team and its best NBA prospect. The tweet said, "No thanks, Trump," and was annotated with double, smiling emoji faces. Although it was later deleted, the tweet seemed to confirm the declination of the President's invitation had little to do with scheduling.

Sports are supposed to be one of the unifying and surpassing activities in America, a retreat where politics can be set aside and Americans of all persuasions can come together to enjoy competition at levels both high and low. The American amateur sports scene is unique in the world, particularly at the college level. Nowhere else do millions annually fill hundreds of stadiums and arenas across the country to watch amateur players compete in football, basketball, and an enormous variety of other sports. Successful college sports programs build alumni support and pride, increase applications, and raise millions of dollars for colleges and universities. While fans and supporters are fiercely loyal to their alma maters or favored teams, in the main they respect their rivals and their rivals' supporters. It is called "sportsmanship," and the experience bonds Americans in ways few other things can.

Invitations to the White House for college and professional teams that win national championships have long been a tradition in this country. It is a form of national celebration and tribute that even defeated opponents can acknowledge and salute. Shaking hands and affirming those who are the best among us is a time-honored catharsis for mind and spirit.

The University of Virginia was established by Thomas Jefferson, one of the nation's founding fathers and a staunch advocate of education as a bulwark of democracy. The University of Virginia is one of our most prestigious public universities and purports to be a champion of diversity, inclusiveness, and tolerance, as well as an elite center of learning and scholarship. So how was such an obvious "teaching moment" missed? I can understand young athletes not fully comprehending the opportunity they had to embrace something larger than themselves, to show the country that despite what may divide us, we are Americans first with respect for our institutions and traditions and willing to share successes. But how could Tony Bennett and the university have missed it? Visiting the White House after winning a national championship is not an endorsement of the occupant, but a simple acknowledgment that what has been accomplished is something for all Americans to reflect on, celebrate, and enjoy.

I do not know Tony Bennett. From all I have read and heard, however, he is an extraordinary man, a gifted teacher and leader of young men, selfless in attitude and inclination. I also do not know his political leanings, nor do I care. But if there ever was an opportunity to teach obligation to things bigger than self, to show the young men he coaches the value of respecting history, country, and office, I do not know what it could have been. However great a leader of young men he may be, in this instance he missed the opportunity to teach responsibility, tolerance, true inclusiveness, and the importance of civil engagement. He missed the opportunity to drive home the point that as national champions the UVA players were champions of a nation, not a political philosophy. If we cannot come together to honor a college sports team celebrating a national championship, how can we possibly engage on anything at any level? On a more macro basis, I am disappointed in the university which, despite its claims, appears to be interested in teaching and practicing tolerance and inclusiveness only for ideas, viewpoints, and individuals with which and with whom it agrees.

Perhaps Tony Bennett and the university did their best to teach these lessons to the Virginia players but were unsuccessful. Maybe. Perhaps De'Andre Hunter's tweet reflected only his personal views, the posting a youthful indiscretion, and scheduling was, in fact, an insurmountable problem for the team. While I hope that was the case, I doubt it. Certainly, there were no apologies, no expressions of disappointment for not being able to visit, no contrition, and no indications that efforts had been made to make the visit possible.

I contrast the actions of the Virginia basketball team with those of Rodney Robinson from Richmond, Virginia, voted "teacher of the year," who accepted an invitation to meet with the President at nearly the same time. Rodney described the meeting as a "very pleasant experience."[380] I have no idea whether Rodney, a Black man, supports the President, but he clearly understood the importance of the meeting for expanding appreciation for teaching and its value in promoting education. He recognized, in other words, that as Teacher of the Year, he had responsibilities that transcended his personal views and circumstances and was representing a profession made up of individuals with many different interests, viewpoints, and political convictions.

Teachers of the year from some other states chose to boycott the meeting. It raises the question of how people can be entrusted with the education of our children who are so politically radicalized and out of step with what it means to be a teacher they are unwilling to engage those with whom they disagree. What does "inclusiveness" represent when those claiming to be "teachers" refuse to meet with those whose views they oppose, even to share and celebrate an award with the rest of the nation? Are there any "adults" left in the room or has the radicalization of the educational system finally brought us to the point where our schools have become the equivalent of the fundamentalist Madrasas of Islam, teaching an orthodoxy designed to limit independent thought and channel decision-making into narrow parameters?[381]

At the very least, public school teachers boycotting the White House highlights my concerns with the state of education in America. *Inclusiveness* is a meaningless concept when only certain political thought is welcome. *Education* itself is meaningless when teachers abandon any pretext of providing balanced content and perspective and become committed to teaching from a singular viewpoint. It is one thing for young basketball players not to understand that some matters are larger than self and beyond politics, quite another for those pretending to be "teachers" to subordinate educational mission to political militancy. Parents should be gravely concerned about what these petty partisans, who shame the rich traditions of the profession they claim to be a part of, are teaching their children.

I am not placing Tony Bennett in that category. He is a basketball coach who missed an opportunity. There is no reason to believe it was anything more. As to the Virginia basketball team and university, Thomas Jefferson would not be proud. I am not proud. It's a shame that what arguably was

470

the grandest moment of Virginia's long sports history has been stigmatized by a lost teaching moment.

ENDNOTES

1   Zieger, Hans (2008) "Educating Citizens: Have We Kept the Founders' Ideals for Higher Education?," *Pepperdine Policy Review:* Vol. 1 , Article 3. (2008), https://digitalcommons.pepperdine.edu/ppr/vol1/iss1/3/

2   Brown, Susan Stamper, Is Progressivism the New Communism? *New Haven Register,* April, 17, 2012 At 12:00 am, EDT, https://www.nhregister.com/news/article/SUSAN-STAMPER-BROWN-Is-Progressivism-the-new-11526345.php

3   *Id.*

4   Burns, Alexander, "On Health Care, 2020 Democrats Find Their First Real Fault Lines," February 20, 2019, *New York Times,* https://www.nytimes.com/2019/02/20/us/politics/bernie-sanders-socialism-democrats.html.

5   Sweden, Norway and Denmark typically are considered "Scandinavia," Finland, Norway, Sweden, Denmark and Iceland, together with the autonomous territories connected to these countries, the Faroe Island, Greenland and Aland, make up the Nordic region. *See e.g.* Kronval, Alf, Facts about the Nordic countries, *Nordic Co-operation, https://www.norden.org/en/information/facts-about-nordic-countries*

6   Sanandaji, N., Scandanavian Unexceptionalism: Culture, Markets and The Failure of Third-Way Socialism, *The Institute of Economic Affairs,* (2015), https://iea.org.uk/wp-content/uploads/2016/07/Sanandajinima-interactive.pdf

7   Sanandaji, N., Rethinking the Scandinavian Model, *New Geography,* August 4, 2015, ; ;https://www.newgeography.com/content/005012-rethinking-scandinavian-model *see also,* Sanandaji, N.,

Scandavanian Unexceptionalism: Culture, Markets and the Failure of Third-Way Socialism, *supra..n. 6*

8   *Id.*

9   For another view of the "unexceptional" outcomes produced by the "Scandinavian miracle," *see* Boothe, Michael, "Dark Lands: the grim truth behind the 'Scandinavian miracle," *The Guardian,* January 27, 2014, https://www.theguardian.com/world/2014/jan/27/scandinavian-miracle-brutal-truth-denmark-norway-sweden

10   Sanandaj, N., Scandanavian Unexceptionlism, *supra* n. 6

11   *Id.*

12   Vyshinsky, Kirill, *Sweden Faces Brain Drain, Entrepreneur Exodus, Researcher Warns,* Sputniknews.com, December 18, 2018, 8:33 GMT, https://sputniknews.com/europe/201812181070782804-sweden-brain-drain-emigration/; *see also,* Korhonen, Juho, Finland's brain drain: what happens to small countries when the talent leaves, *Independent,* July 3, 2017, 11:36, https://www.independent.co.uk/news/long_reads/finland-s-brain-drain-what-happens-to-small-countries-when-the-talent-leaves-a7812686.html

13   Huang, Yiping, China: a sixty-year experiment with free markets, *EASTASIAFORUM,* October 4, 2009, https://www.eastasiaforum.org/2009/10/04/china-a-sixty-year-experiment-with-free-markets/

14   Liptak, Adam, *Update 2: Compare the treatment of the accused in China and America in two crime stories* originally published in the *New York Times,* lfslessonsasia.com, March 21, 2012

15   Huang, Cary, *No sign of change in China's deeply flawed criminal justice system,* South China Morning Post, December 14, 2016, 3:06 pm, https://www.scmp.com/comment/insight-opinion/article/2054456/no-sign-change-chinas-deeply-flawed-criminal-justice-system

16   Chow, Eugene K., *China's War on Poverty Could Hurt the Poor Most,* foreignpolicy.com, January 8, 2018, 11:45 AM, https://foreignpolicy.com/2018/01/08/chinas-war-on-poverty-could-hurt-the-poor-most/

17   How does water security affect China's development? *China Power,* https://chinapower.csis.org/china-water-security/

18 https://www.worldbank.org/en/country/china/overview

19 *How well-off is China's middle class?*, April 26, 2017, updated May 29, 2019, https://chinapower.csis.org/china-middle-class/#:~:text=-Most%20of%20China's%20middle%2Dclass,its%20lower%20and%20 upper%20echelons.

20 Novak, Michael, "Social Justice: Not What You Think It Is," *Heritage Foundation,* December 29, 2009, https://www.heritage.org/ poverty-and-inequality/report/social-justice-not-what-you-think-it

21 DeMint, Jim, Heritage Mourns Michael Novak, *The Heritage Foundation,* February 17, 2017, https://www.heritage.org/conservatism/impact/ heritage-mourns-michael-novak

22 *Novak,* Social Justice, *supra,* n. 20

23 See e.g. Sowell, Thomas, *Wealth, Poverty and Politics, Revised and Enlarged Edition,* Basic Books, NY (2016).

24 *Id.*

25 Reed, Lawrence W., The XYZ's of Socialism, *Foundation for Economic Education,* Atlanta, April 5, 2018, https://fee.org/resources/ the-xyz-s-of-socialism/

26 Strategy and Tactics of the Proletarian Revolution, p. 7, *International Publishers Co., Inc.,* New York (1936)

27 Mutsaka, Farai, *Zimbabwe's capital runs dry as taps cut off for 2M people,* apnews.com, September 24, 2019, 7:23 AM, https://www.dai-lyherald.com/article/20190924/news/309249951

28 Main, Douglas, *Slavery Reparations Could Cost Up To $14 Trillion, According To New Calculation,* Newsweek.com, August 19, 2015, 12:12 PM EDT, https://www.newsweek.com/slavery-repara-tions-could-cost-14-trillion-according-new-calculation-364141

29 See e.g. Wilkie, Christina, *"Donald Trump Attacks Alexandria-Ocasio-Cortez's Green New Deal in a preview of things to come for the 2020 election,* cnbc.com, Feb. 12, 2019, 11:51 AM EST, updated 4:19 PM EST, https://www.cnbc.com/2019/02/12/trump-targets-alexandria-ocasio-cortez-green-new-deal-in-campaign-speech.html

30 See Sperry, Paul, *Trump-Russia 2.0: Dossier-Tied Firm Pitching Media Daily On 'Collusion,"* March 20, 2019, https://www.realclearinves-tigations.com/articles/2019/03/11/trump-russia_20_dossier-tied_firm_sending_dc_journalists_daily_collusion_briefings.html; *see also,* Vadum, Mathew, Origins of Antifa, *Capital Research Center,* April 16, 2018, https://capitalresearch.org/article/origins-of-antifa/

31 Parisi, Peter, Al Gore's Carbon Footprint Hypocrisy, *The Dailey Signal,* August 15, 2017, https://www.dailysignal.com/2017/08/15/al-gores-carbon-footprint-hypocrisy/; Goldstein, Lorrie, Al Gore's hypoc-risy 'breathtaking, Toronto Sun, July 29, 2017, updated 6:14 PM EDT, https://torontosun.com/2017/07/29/al-gores-hypocrisy-breathtaking/wcm/f586dad0–668c-4a14-bf7c-206e2a92da43

32 Evidence for The Unpopular Mr. Lincoln, *American Battlefield Trust,* https://www.battlefields.org/learn/articles/evidence-unpopular-mr-lincoln

33 *Id.*

34 See e.g. Willams, Walter E., Walter Williams: We accept and expect lower standards from blacks, *nwfdailynews.com,* April 19, 2017, 2:00 AM, https://www.nwfdailynews.com/news/20170419/walter-wil-liams-we-accept-and-expect-lower-standards-from-blacks; Williams, Walter E., Black Unemployment, April 10, 2013, http://walterewilliams.com/black-unemployment/; Williams, Walt, Blacks Must Confront Reality, *Washington Examiner,* August 25, 2014, 6:56 PM, https://www.washingtonexaminer.com/blacks-must-confront-reality;, Walter E., Black Americans and Liberty, walterewilliams.com, 2010, http://walterewilliams.com/black-americans-and-liberty/

35 Blake, Aaron, "Elizabeth Warren and Donna Brazile both now agree that the 2016 Democratic primary was rigged," *The Washington Post,* November 2, 2017, 5:04 pm, EDT, https://www.washingtonpost.com/news/the-fix/wp/2017/11/02/ex-dnc-chair-goes-at-the-clintons-al-leging-hillarys-campaign-hijacked-dnc-during-primary-with-ber-nie-sanders/

36 Brady, Jeff, Ludden, Jennifer ,"Skipping School Around the World to Push for Action on Climate Change," *National Public Radio,* March 14, 2019, 5:10 PM ET, https://www.npr.org/2019/03/14/703461293/skipping-school-to-protest-climate-change

37   Burnett, Craig M. and Kogan, Vladamir, "Ballot (and Voter) 'Exhaustion' Under Instant Runoff Voting: An Examination of Four Ranked-Choice Elections," *Electoral Studies*, Vol. 37, March, 2015, pp. 41–49, https://www.centralmaine.com/2018/05/27/another-view-one-person-one-vote-at-risk-if-ranked-choice-voting-approved/

38   Weil, Gordon, "Another View: 'one person, one vote' at risk if ranked-choice voting approved," centralmaine.com, May 27, 2018, https://www.centralmaine.com/2018/05/27/another-view-one-person-one-vote-at-risk-if-ranked-choice-voting-approved/

39   *Id.*

40   Rogers, Adam, "Elections Don't Work At All. You Can Blame The Math," Wired.com, June 6, 2018, 8:44 PM,

https://www.wired.com/story/elections-dont-work-at-all-you-can-blame-the-math/

41   von Spakovsky, Hans A., Adams J., Ranked Choice Voting Is a Bad Choice, *The Heritage Foundation*, https://www.heritage.org/election-integrity/report/ranked-choice-voting-bad-choice, August 23, 2029.

42   Gomez, Luis, "What Is 'Ballot Harvesting' and How Was It Used in California Elections?" *The Baltimore Sun,* December 10, 2018, 2:25 PM, https://www.baltimoresun.com/sd-what-is-ballot-harvesting-in-california-election-code-20181204-htmlstory.html

43   A typical procedure for absentee or mail-in ballots is to include two envelopes. The marked ballot is put into a "security" envelope and sealed. That envelope is then placed in a second envelope, which is addressed and signed by the voter, attesting that they are a "registered voter." While in theory the signature, or signatures if more than one is required, can be verified, it is not something that is easily done.

44   Groening, Chad and Brown, Jody, "'Ballot harvesting'—a sure-fire way for Dems to win," *NE News Now*, December 3, 2018, https://onenewsnow.com/politics-govt/2018/12/03/ballot-harvesting-a-sure-fire-way-for-dems-to-win

45   Eggers, Eric, "How Ballot-Harvesting Became The New Way To Steal An Election," *The Federalist,* December 14, 2018, https://www.centralmaine.com/2018/05/27/

another-view-one-person-one-vote-at-risk-if-ranked-choice-voting-approved/

46   Davis, Victor Hanson, "California has become America's cannibal state," *Chicago Tribune*, April 11, 2019, 9:20 AM, https://www.chicagotribune.com/sns-201904101001—tms—vdhansonctn-vh-a20190411–20190411-column.html

47   Wright, Robin, "Will Trump Give Away Too Much To North Korea—And Get Too Little?" *The New Yorker*, February 25, 2019, https://www.newyorker.com/news/news-desk/will-trump-give-away-too-much-to-north-korea-and-get-too-little

48   French, David, "A Trip Down Memory Lane: In 2015 The Obama Administration Said the Iran Deal Wasn't Even a 'Signed Document,'" *National Review*, May 10, 2018, 6:08 PM, https://www.nationalreview.com/corner/iran-nuclear-deal-not-signed-document-not-binding/

49   Wright, *supra.* n. 47

50   Vinograd, Samantha, "Hanoi Summit Fails Because Trump Refuses To Prep," *Dailey Beast*, February 28, 2019, 10:37 AM ET, updated 2:00 PM ET, https://www.thedailybeast.com/after-the-hanoi-fail-heres-a-textbook-for-trump-summiting-for-dummies

51   "Talks were held at Justice Department about removing Trump, former acting FBI director says," *CNN Newsource*, February 14, 2019, https://www.fox4now.com/news/national/talks-were-held-at-justice-department-about-removing-trump-former-acting-fbi-director-says

52   *See e.g.* Report, Review of Four FISA Applications and Other Aspects of the FBI's Crossfire Hurricane Investigation, *Office of the Inspector General, U.S. Department of Justice*, December, 2019 (Revised), Executive Summary, p. iv, https://www.justice.gov/storage/120919-examination.pdf

53   Solomon, John, "Memos detail FBI's 'Hurry the F Up Pressure' to probe Trump campaign," *The Hill*, July 6, 2018, https://thehill.com/hilltv/rising/395776-memos-detail-fbis-hurry-the-f-up-pressure-to-probe-trump-campaign

54   Statement by FBI Director James B. Comey on the Investigation of Secretary Hillary Clinton's Use of a Personal E-Mail System, July 5, 2016,

https://www.fbi.gov/news/pressrel/press-releases/statement-by-fbi-director-james-b-comey-on-the-investigation-of-secretary-hillary-clinton2019s-use-of-a-personal-e-mail-system

55   Hanson, Victor Davis, "Is Trump the only adult in the room?" *Richmond Times-Dispatch*, December 12, 2019, https://richmond.com/opinion/columnists/victor-davis-hanson-column-is-trump-the-only-adult-in-the-room/article_ddd9a75a-21d0–513b-aef6-bdff53a5dac9.html

56   Goodman, Alana, "John Kerry's son cuts business ties with Hunter Biden over Ukrainian oil deal," *Washington Examiner*, August 27, 2019, 6:30 AM, https://www.washingtonexaminer.com/politics/john-kerrys-son-cut-business-ties-with-hunter-biden-over-ukrainian-oil-deal

57   Sweizer, Peter, "How five members of Joe Biden's family got rich through his connections," *New York Post*, January 18, 2020, 3:02 pm, https://nypost.com/2020/01/18/how-five-members-of-joe-bidens-family-got-rich-through-his-connections/; *see also,* McCaughey, Betsy, "Joe Biden Must Explain His Ukraine Dealings," RealClear Politics, January 29, 2020, https://www.realclearpolitics.com/articles/2020/01/29/joe_biden_must_explain_his_ukraine_dealings_142255.html

58   " Many who met with Clinton as secretary of state donated to foundation," *CNBC,* August 23, 2016, https://www.cnbc.com/2016/08/23/most-of-those-who-met-with-clinton-as-secretary-of-state-donated-to-foundation.html at 5:19 pm EDT.

59   Hitt, Caitlyn, "Prince Harry and Megan Markle Face Criticism Over Name of New Foundation," *Popculture.com,* July 18, 2019, 7:53 pm EDT, https://popculture.com/celebrity/news/prince-harry-meghan-markle-criticism-name-new-foundation/

60   Massoglia, A. and Yu, Y., "Clinton Foundation donations continue to drop years after 2016 election loss," *OpenSecrets*, November 18, 2019, 10:31 am, https://www.opensecrets.org/news/2019/11/clinton-foundation-cash-flow-drop/

61   "Many who met with Clinton as secretary of state donated to foundation," *supra* n. 58

62   See generally, Kinkopf, Neil J. and. Whittington, Keith E., Article II, Section 4, *National Constitution Center,* https://constitutioncenter.org/interactive-constitution/interpretation/article-ii/clauses/349 ;

The Heritage Guide to the Constitution, https://www.heritage.org/constitution ; "Impeachment," *United States House of Representatives History, Arts & Archives,* https://history.house.gov/

63   Nash, Charlie, "Nancy Pelosi Said in March That She Would Only Consider Impeachment With Bipartisan Support," *Mediaite,* October 31, 2019, 3:48 pm, https://www.mediaite.com/politics/nancy-pelosi-said-in-march-she-would-only-consider-impeachment-with-bipartisan-support/

64   Leonor, Mel, Spanberger says she will vote to impeach Trump, *Richmond Times-Dispatch,* December 16, 2019, https://richmond.com/news/virginia/spanberger-says-she-will-vote-to-impeach-trump/article_138baa75–6507–5d16–829c-c5f18960f997.html

65   Dibble, Madison, "'We can impeach again: Democratic congressman suggests continuous impeachment effort," *Washington Examiner,* December 5, 2019, 11:39 AM, https://www.washingtonexaminer.com/news/we-can-impeach-again-democratic-congressman-suggests-continuous-impeachment-effort

66   I discuss the so-called Biden Rules in the chapter entitled *News Media.* Essentially, they suggest that the Senate should not confirm, absent compelling circumstance, a presidential nominee for the Supreme Court during an election year. The idea is to prevent a form of "court packing," by having older justices resign in the last year of a presidential term so that younger justices can be appointed by the incumbent president before leaving office. *See also,* n. 296 *infra*

67   Bills of attainder, part of the English common law until the late 18th century, but prohibited by Article I, section 9, paragraph 3 of the Constitution, were legislative acts that declared groups or individuals guilty of crimes and punished them without a trial or protection of their civil rights. Their use in England resulted in numerous atrocities, including the execution of many historical figures.

68   Dibble, Madison, "De Blasio haunted by weeks-old tweet urging people to 'get out on the town despite coronavirus," *Washington Examiner,* March 25, 2020, 10:28 AM, https://www.washingtonexaminer.com/news/de-blasio-haunted-by-weeks-old-tweet-urging-people-to-get-out-on-the-town-despite-coronavirus

69 Mastrangelo, Dominick, "Pelosi encouraged public gatherings in late February, weeks after Trump's China travel ban," *Washington Examiner*, March 30, 2020, 4:49 PM, https://www.washingtonexaminer.com/news/pelosi-encouraged-public-gatherings-in-late-february-weeks-after-trumps-china-travel-ban

70 "The Great Fire of Rome, Background," May 29, 2014, https://www.pbs.org/wnet/secrets/great-fire-rome-background/1446/

71 *See* Valerie Jarrett—Obama's Rasputin, *Investor's Business Daily*, September 25, 2012, 6:47 PM ET, https://www.investors.com/politics/editorials/valerie-jarrett-rasputin-to-barack-obamabarack-obama-valerie-jarrett-wields-rasputinlike-power-and-influence-over-the-president-and-his-administrations-decisions/

72 Orwell, George, *1984*, New York, Signet Classic, 1977.

73 *See* The Trustworthy Encyclopedia, *Conservapedia.com/The Democracy Integrity Project*, March 28, 2019 at 15:02, updated July 4, 2019 at 15:55, https://www.conservapedia.com/The_Democracy_Integrity_Project

74 Ross, Chuck, Firms Tied to Christopher Steele, Fusion GPS Were Paid $3.8 Million by Soros-Backed Group, *The Dailey Caller News Foundation*, April 1, 2019, https://stream.org/firms-tied-fusion-gps-christopher-steele-paid-3–8-million-soros-backed-group/

75 *See* Brown, Is Progressivism the New Communism, *supra* n 2

76 Bowden, John, Breitbart editor: Biden's son inked deal with Chinese government days after vice president's trip, *The Hill*, March 15, 2018, 2:49 PM EDT, https://thehill.com/blogs/blog-briefing-room/news/378629-breitbart-editor-biden-and-kerrys-sons-inked-deal-with-chinese

77 Beck, Glenn, Biden part Deux: the China connection, *glennbeck.com*, April 15, 2019, https://www.glennbeck.com/glenn-beck/biden-part-deux-the-china-connection

78 Sweizer, Peter, How five members of Joe Biden's family got rich through his connections, *Washington Examiner*, *supra* n. 57

79 Woody, Paul, "Coaches and teachers were heroes in Florida, but will the government help keep them safe?" *Richmond Times-Dispatch*,

February 16, 2018, https://richmond.com/sports/high-school/woody-coaches-and-teachers-were-heroes-in-florida-but-will-the-government-help-keep-them/article_9f8688ff-3f49–53d4-b852-f7818aa2a6c1.html

80 Kelly, Steve, *Richmond Times-Dispatch* (editorial page), February 19, 2018.

81 Nicodemo, Allie and Petronio, Lia, Schools are safer than they were in the 1990s, and school shootings are not more common than they used to be, researchers say, *News@ Northeastern*, February 26, 2018. https://news.northeastern.edu/2018/02/26/schools-are-still-one-of-the-safest-places-for-children-researcher-says/

82 Teen Drivers: Get the Facts, *CDC, Motor Vehicle Safety*, https://www.cdc.gov/motorvehiclesafety/teen_drivers/teendrivers_factsheet.html#:~:text=The%20risk%20of%20motor%20vehicle,be%20in%20a%20fatal%20crash.cdc.gov/motorvehiclesafety/teen_drivers

83 Homicide and knife crime rates up in England and Wales, BBC News, 27 April 2017, https://www.bbc.com/news/uk-39729601

84 One dead, at least nine wounded in France after suspected knife attack, *Reuters,* August 31, 2019 at 12:25 p.m. EDT, https://www.reuters.com/article/uk-france-crime/one-dead-six-wounded-in-france-after-suspected-knife-attack-idUSKCN1VL0KN#:~:text=One%20dead%2C%20nine%20wounded%20in%20France%20after%20suspected%20knife%20attack,-1%20Min%20Read&text=LYON%2C%20France%20(Reuters)%20%2D,a%20police%20source%20told%20Reuters

85 Miles, Frank, London Mayor Sadiq Khan targets knives as murder rate spikes: 'There is never a reason to carry a knife,' *Fox News,* April 8, 2018, https://www.foxnews.com/world/london-mayor-sadiq-khan-targets-knives-as-murder-rate-spikes-there-is-never-a-reason-to-carry-a-knife

86 Juristat, *Canadian Centre for Justice Statistics, Statistics Canada— Catalogue,* No. 85–002—XPE, Vol. 17 No. 7.

87 Mathews, Dylan, Here's how gun control works in Canada, *Vox*, October 24, 2014, 8:50am EDT, https://www.vox.com/2014/10/24/7047547/canada-gun-law-us-comparison

88   Trudeau's Gun Policy: Forward into the Past, *NRA-ILA*, February, 3, 2020, https://www.nraila.org/articles/20200203/trudeau-s-gun-policy-forward-into-the-past

89   Kwong, Matt, "Calgary Stabbings: How knife crime in Canada can cause 'moral panic,'" *CBS News*, April 16, 2014, 5:00 AM ET, https://www.cbc.ca/news/canada/calgary-stabbings-how-knife-crime-in-canada-can-cause-moral-panic-1.2611698

90   Cohen, Stanley, Folk Devils and Moral Panics: The Creation of the Mods and Rockers, New York, St. Martin's Press, 1980.

91   See e.g. Davies, Stephen, The Anatomy of a Moral Panic, *American Institute for Economic Research*, February 12, 2019, https://www.aier.org/article/the-anatomy-of-a-moral-panic/#.XGLICIhFcO0.facebook

92   For a list of political leaders who suspended the constitution, *see Wikipedia*, April 12, 2019 at 19:55 (UTC), last updated, May 12, 2020 at 2:10 (UTC), https://en.wikipedia.org/wiki/List_of_political_leaders_who_suspended_the_constitution

93   *See* Gramlich, John, Schaeffer, Katherine, 7 facts about guns in the U.S., *Pew Research Center*, December 27, 2018, https://www.pewresearch.org/fact-tank/2019/10/22/facts-about-guns-in-united-states/

94   Elder, Larry, How Many Lives Are Saved by Guns—and Why Don't Gun Controllers Care, *Capitalism*, April 6, 2019, 10:08 AM, https://www.newbernsj.com/opinion/20180303/larry-elder-how-many-lives-are-saved-by-guns——and-why-dont-gun-controllers-care

95   , "Drunk Driving," *NTSA*, https://www.nhtsa.gov/risky-driving/drunk-driving#; "Impaired Driving: Get the Facts," *CDC*, https://www.cdc.gov/motorvehiclesafety/impaired_driving/impaired-drv_factsheet.html.

96   Masters, Jacob, Texting While Driving vs. Drunk Driving: Which Is More Dangerous? *Brain Injury Society*, October 27, 2013, http://www.bisociety.org/texting-while-driviing-vs-drunk-driving-which-is-more-dangerous/

97   Fatality Facts 2018: Teenagers, *IIHS-HLDI*, https://www.iihs.org/topics/fatality-statistics/detail/teenagers#:h

98   Tanner, Lindsey, Trump focus on mental health after Parkland school shooting denounced, *The Florida Times-Union*, February 19,

2018 at 3:48 pm, updated 9:12 pm, https://www.jacksonville.com/news/20180219/trump-focus-on-mental-health-after-parkland-school-shooting-denounced

99 Bacon, John and Hughes, Kevin, Students walk out of Colorado school shooting vigil, saying their trauma was being politicized, *usatoday.com*, May 9, 2019 at 8:36 am ET, updated 3:23 pm ET, https://www.usatoday.com/story/news/nation/2019/05/09/colorado-school-shooting-vigil-students-walk-out-protest/1150282001/

100 Fox, Kara, How U.S. gun culture compares with the rest of the world, *CNN*, August 6, 2019, updated 6:58 PM ET, https://www.cnn.com/2017/07/19/world/us-gun-crime-police-shooting-statistics/index.html

101 Gramlich, John, What the data says about gun deaths in the U.S., *Fact Tank, Pew Research Center*, August 16, 2019, https://www.pewresearch.org/fact-tank/2019/08/16/what-the-data-says-about-gun-deaths-in-the-u-s/

102 Mercer, Marsha, "Divide on gun laws sets stage for 2020," *Richmond Times Dispatch*, May 2, 2019, https://richmond.com/opinion/columnists/marsha-mercer-column-divide-on-gun-laws-sets-stage-for-2020/article_20ef1c94-f6ec-5344-b73d-33ab2d0e0e67.html

103 *See* McWorter, John, *Racist* Is a Tough Little Word, *The Atlantic*, July 24, 2019, https://www.theatlantic.com/ideas/archive/2019/07/racism-concept-change/594526/

104 *Id.*

105 *Id.*

106 *Id.*

107 *Id.*

108 *Id.*

109 Hinson, Sandra, Healey, Richard Weisenberg, Nathaniel, Race, Power and Policy: Dismantling Structural Racism, *Grassroots Policy Project*, https://www.racialequitytools.org/resourcefiles/race_power_policy_workbook.pdf.

110 Beinart, Peter, Republican Is Not a Synonym for Racist, *The Atlantic*, December, 2017 issue, https://www.theatlantic.com/magazine/archive/2017/12/conservatism-without-bigotry/544128/

111 Migrant caravan members reject offer to stay in Mexico, *Associated Press*, October 27, 2018, 1:03 AM EDT, https://www.nbcnews.com/news/world/migrant-caravan-members-reject-offer-stay-mexico-n925171 ; Izaguirre, Anthony, Caravan inches closer to border as many reject Mexican asylum, *New York Post*, October 27, 2018, 8:44 pm, https://nypost.com/2018/10/27/caravan-inches-closer-to-border-as-many-reject-mexican-asylum/

112 Walker, Alice, *In Search of Our Mothers' Gardens*, Harcourt Brace Jovanovich, New York (1983)

113 *Id.*

114 Leonor, Mel, First Lady Pam Northam under fire for handing out piece of cotton during tour of Executive Mansion slave quarters, *Richmond Times-Dispatch*, February 27, 2019, https://richmond.com/news/local/government-politics/first-lady-pam-northam-under-fire-for-handing-out-piece-of-cotton-during-tour-of/article_08bc3182-c2cd-5e04-b6a3–88165857edf3.html

115 *Id.*

116 *Id*

117 *Id.*

118 https://president.yale.edu/sites/default/files/files/CEPR_FINAL_12–2-16.pdf

119 Wikipedia 2020, "Great Soviet Encyclopedia," last modified June 22, 2020 at 10:15 (UTC), https://en.wikipedia.org/wiki/Great_Soviet_Encyclopedia

120 163 U.S.537 (1896)

121 410 U.S. 113 (1973)

122 Serwer, Adam, A Nation of Snowflakes, *The Atlantic*, September 26, 2017, https://www.theatlantic.com/politics/archive/2017/09/it-takes-a-nation-of-snowflakes/541050/

123 Hanson, Victor Davis, The Regrettable Decline of Higher Learning, *National Review,* February 4, 2016 at 5:00 AM, https://www.nationalreview.com/2016/02/college-campus-safe-spaces-speech-codes-decline/

124 UC Admissions Still Getting Harder for Asians From CA, *Flex College Prep,* May 16, 2018, https://flexcollegeprep.com/uc-admission-still-getting-harder-for-asians-from-ca/#gref; Lifson, Thomas, Move Over Harvard, University of California sued on Asian-American admission data, *American Thinker.com,* November 18, 2018, https://www.americanthinker.com/blog/2018/11/move_over_harvard_university_of_california_sued_on_asian_american_admissions_date.htmlhttps://www.americanthinker.com/blog/2018/11/move_over_harvard_university_of_california_sued_on_asian_american_admissions_date.html

125 Koseff, Alexei, The next battle over affirmative action is about discrimination against Asian-Americans, *The Sacramento Bee,* January 23, 2018, 12:00 AM, updated 3:47 PM, https://www.sacbee.com/news/politics-government/capitol-alert/article196035824.html

126 Scheuer, Jeffrey, Critical Thinking and the Liberal Arts, *American Association of University Professors,* November-December 2015, https://www.aaup.org/article/critical-thinking-and-liberal-arts#.X3c0e2hKiUk

127 Sakuma, Amanda, Dianne Feinstein gets into feisty exchange with schoolkids over the Green New Deal, *Vox,* February 23, 2019, 11:10am EST, https://www.vox.com/2019/2/23/18237410/dianne-feinstein-children-green-new-deal

128 Bryant, Nick, Barack Obama legacy: did he improve US race relations? *BBC News,* January 10, 2017. https://www.bbc.com/news/world-us-canada-38536668

129 Fernandez, Manny, *et al.,* Five Dallas Police Officers Were Killed as Payback, Police Chief Says, *The New York Times,* July 8, 2016, https://www.nytimes.com/2016/07/09/us/dallas-police-shooting.html

130 Schaper, David, Obama's Links to Ex-Radical Examined, *npr.org,* October 6, 2008 at 4:00 pm ET. https://www.npr.org/templates/story/story.php?storyId=95442902

131 Kincaid, Cliff, Obama's Communist Mentor, *Accuracy in Media*, February 18, 2008, https://www.aim.org/aim-column/obamas-communist-mentor/

132 Ross, Brian *et al.*, Obama's Pastor: God Damn America, US to Blame for 9/11, *ABCNews*, May 7, 2008, 2:34 PM, https://abcnews.go.com/Blotter/DemocraticDebate/story?id=4443788&page=1

133 See von Spakovsky, Hans A., Strobel, Grant, Obama's Legacy is a Weaker and More Divided America, *The Daily Signal*, January, 19, 2017, https://www.dailysignal.com/2017/01/19/obamas-legacy-is-a-weaker-and-more-divided-america/

134 Re, Greg, Green New Deal would cost up to $93 trillion, or 600G per household, study says, *Fox News*, February 25, 2019, https://www.foxnews.com/politics/green-new-deal-would-cost-93-trillion-or-600g-per-household-study-says

135 Williams, Walter, Walter Williams: We expect and accept lower standards from blacks, *nwfdailynews.com, supra* n. 34

136 *Id.*

137 In the chapter entitled "Racism and Bigotry," I address the changing definitions of words like *racism* and *racist* and how the evolving definitions are being used to stifle debate about issues and policies affecting minorities. For a more detailed analysis of the evolving standards for racism, *see*, McWorter, John, Racist Is a Tough Little Word, *supra* n. 103

138 Understanding Racial and Ethnic Differences in Health in Late Life, *The National Academies of Sciences, Engineering, Medicine*, ch. 7, 2004, https://www.nap.edu/catalog/11036/understanding-racial-and-ethnic-differences-in-health-in-late-life

139 Perper, Rosie, China and the NBA are coming to blows over a pro-Hong Kong tweet. Here's why, *Business Insider*, October 22, 2019, 10:47 pm, https://www.businessinsider.com/nba-china-feud-timeline-daryl-morey-tweet-hong-kong-protests-2019–10

140 Will, George, China extends its reign of random fear, Editorial Page, section D, p. D3, *Richmond Times-Dispatch*, July 5, 2020

141 Sheriff, Lucy, "Burn It Down: Black Lives Matter leader threatens to 'burn down the system if they don't get want they want,'" *The U.S. Sun*, https://www.the-sun.com/news/1037853/black-lives-matter-leader-hawk-newsome-burn-it-down/, June 25, 2020 at 15:07 ET

142 McDonald, Heather, There is no epidemic of fatal police shooting against unarmed Black Americans, *USA Today*, https://www.usatoday.com/story/opinion/2020/07/03/police-black-killings-homicide-rates-race-injustice-column/3235072001/, July 3, 2020 at 3:15 am ET

143 Davis, Elizabeth, et al., Contacts Between Police And The Public, 2015, *Bureau of Justice Statistics*, October, 2018, https://www.bjs.gov/content/pub/pdf/cpp15.pdf

144 Johnson, Richard R., PhD, Dispelling the Myths Surrounding Police Use of Lethal Force, *Dolan Consulting Group*, pp. 12–13, July, 2016, https://www.dolanconsultinggroup.com/wp-content/uploads/2019/02/Dispelling-the-Myths-Surrounding-Police-Use-of-Lethal-Force.pdf

145 *Id.*

146 Brooks C., Cesario, J., The Truth Behind Racial Disparities in Fatal Police Shootings, *MSUToday*, July 22, 2019,3:00 pm EDT, https://www.newswise.com/articles/the-truth-behind-racial-disparities-in-fatal-police-shootings

147 *See, e.g.* sources cited in Johnson, Dispelling the Myths Surrounding Police Use of Lethal Force, *supra* n. 144, at pp. 11–12

148 *See,* Brooks C., Cesario, J., The Truth Behind Racial Disparities in Fatal Police Shootings, *supra.* n. 146

149 Dobuzinskis, Alex, More racial diversity in U.S. police departments unlikely to reduce shootings: study, *Reuters*, July 22, 2019, 8:26 pm EDT, https://wkzo.com/news/articles/2019/jul/23/more-racial-diversity-in-us-police-departments-unlikely-to-reduce-shootings-study/920401/

150 Hand, L., The "Spirit of Liberty" Speech, 1944, Taken from Our Nation's Archives: The History of the United States in Documents, edited by Erik Bruun and Jay Crosby, Black Dog & Levanthal Publishers, Inc. 1999, https://www.btboces.org/Downloads/1

151 Black Public Officials by Office, 1970-2002, and State, 2002, https://www2.census.gov/library/publications/2010/compendia/ statab/130ed/tables/11s0413.pdf; Major African American Office Holders Since 1641, *Black Past*, https://www.blackpast.org/ special-features/major-african-american-office-holders/

152 Dionne T. Powe, 300 In Black: A Look Back At Black Mayors In America, *The New Orleans Tribune.com*, June 16, 2020, https://theneworleans-tribune.com/300-in-black-a-look-back-at-black-mayors-in-america/;

153 Williams, William Julius, *The Declining Significance of Race*, first edition, The University of Chicago Press Books, 1978

154 Hinson, Sandra, *et al*, Race, Power and Policy: Dismantling Structural Racism, *supra*. n. 109

155 Karnowski, Steve, Attorneys: 2 ex-cops charged in Floyd's death were rookies, *StarTribune.com*, June 4, 2020, 7:00 pm, https://www.star-tribune.com/judge-750k-bail-for-3-ex-officers-accused-in-floyd-s-death/571020052/

156 Police departments confront 'epidemic' in officer sui-cides, *pbs.org/newshour/nation/police*, August 15, 2019 6:21 pm EDT, https://www.pbs.org/newshour/nation/ police-departments-confront-epidemic-in-officer-suicides

157 Johnson, Richard, PhD, Dispelling the Myths Surrounding Police Use of Lethal Force, *supra*, n. 144, at p. 5

158 *Id. at p. 4.*

159 *Id.*

160 *Id.*

161 *Id.*

162 *Id.*

163 *Id.*

164 *Id.*

165 *Id. at p. 2*

166 *Id.*

167 *Id.* at P. 9

168 *Id. at p. 4*

169 *Id.*

170 *Id.*

171 Id. at p. 13

172 *Id.* at p.7

173 *Id.*

174 T. Winter, A. Blankstein, J. Dienst, NYDP's Terrorism Official Says Unnamed Groups Planned Protest Violence In Advance, *nbcnewyork. com*, May 31, 2020, updated June 1, 2020 at 9:05 am., ,https://www.nbcnewyork.com/news/local/nypds-terrorism-chief-says-unnamed-groups-planned-protest-violence-in-advance/2440722/

175 Isaiah 11:6.

176 Jeremiah 11:19.

177 Eder Campuzano, Portland superintendent says he's 'discontinuing' presence of armed police officers in schools, *The Oregonian, oregon-live.com*, June 4, 2020, updated June 5, 2020, https://www.oregonlive.com/education/2020/06/portland-superintendent-says-hes-discon-tinuing-school-resource-officer-program.html

178 *Id.*

179 Burkeman, Oliver, What drives the 'moral grandstanding' that has infected our politics, *The Guardian*, January 3, 2020 at 10:00 EST, https://www.theguardian.com/lifeandstyle/2020/jan/03/moral-grandstanding-politics-emotional-needs-oliver-burkeman

180 Growing Concerns, Opinions, *Richmond Times-Dispatch*, April 8, 2019

181 Baker, Sam, "Vitals," Editorial: The American health care crisis, *Axios*, April 7, 2019, https://www.richmond.com/opinion/editorial/edito-rial-the-american-health-care-crisis/article_07bfeb3b-a907–563a-bd5b-48c53de412cf.html

182 Dreyfuss, Emily, Want To Make A Lie Seem True? Say It Again. And Again. And Again, *Wired.com*, February 11, 2017, 7:00 AM, https://www.wired.com/2017/02/dont-believe-lies-just-people-repeat/

183 *Id.*

184 Scott, Ellen, If you repeat a lie often enough, people think it's true, *Metro News*, December 1, 2015, 10"37 AM, https://metro.co.uk/2015/12/01/if-you-repeat-a-lie-enough-people-think-its-true-5536488/

185 Dreyfuss, Emily, Want To Make A Lie Seem True? Say It Again. And Again. And Again, supra n. *182*

186 See Bloom, Linda and Charles, The Bandwagon Effect, *Psychology Today*, August 11, 2017, https://www.psychologytoday.com/us/blog/stronger-the-broken-places/201708/the-bandwagon-effect#:~:-text=The%20bandwagon%20effect%20is%20a,they%20may%20ignore%20or%20override.&text=The%20bandwagon%20effect%20has%20wider%20implications%20outside%20of%20politics%20and%20buying%20behaviors.

187 Schmitt-Beck, Reudiger, "Bandwagon Effect," *The International Encyclopedia of Political Communications*, First Edition (2015), Wiley Online Library, https://onlinelibrary.wiley.com/doi/full/10.1002/9781118541555.wbiepc015

188 *Id.*

189 *Id.*

190 Wehner, Peter, Why people are wired to believe what they want to believe, *Trust, Media & Democracy*, March 13, 2018, https://medium.com/trust-media-and-democracy/why-people-are-wired-to-believe-what-they-want-to-believe-4d9b4e161eb5

191 *Id.*

192 Samuelson, Roger J., America's cycle of disappointment, *Richmond Times-Dispatch*, July 16, 2019, https://richmond.com/opinion/columnists/roger-j-samuelson-column-americas-cycle-of-disappointment/article_6fd7d392–3ba4–5bb7-a9e6–12df45384e2e.html

193 Wealth Tax: Sen. Warren's Latest Bad Idea Will Slow Growth and Kill Jobs, *Investor's Business Daily,* January 25, 2019, 4:37 PM ET, https://www.investors.com/politics/editorials/wealth-tax-sen-warren-envy/

194 Will, George F., The Democrats and the 1919 World Series were both trying to lose, *Richmond Times-Dispatch,* August 1, 2019, https://richmond.com/opinion/columnists/george-will-column-the-democrats-and-the-1919-world-series/article_7475cf8f-1dbf-52a7-b321–45411daa3b95.html

195 Mathews, Dylan, Modern Monetary Theory, explained, *Vox,* April 16, 2019, 1:00 pm EDT, https://www.vox.com/future-perfect/2019/4/16/18251646/modern-monetary-theory-new-moment-explained

196 See e.g. Aladangady, A., et al., The Effects of Sales-Tax Holidays on Consumer Spending, *FEDS Notes,* March 24, 2017, https://www.federalreserve.gov/econres/notes/feds-notes/effect-of-sales-tax-holidays-on-consumer-spending-20170324.htm

197 Einav, L., et al., Consumer behavior in on-line shopping is affected by sales tax, *LSE Research Online,*, January 14, 2014, http://eprints.lse.ac.uk/58453/

198 Thorne, Ashley, U.S. Founding Fathers on Education in Their Own Words, *National Association of Scholars,* July 2, 2010, https://www.nas.org/blogs/article/u_s_founding_fathers_on_education_in_their_own_words

199 Akadjian, David, 7 things our founders believed about public education, *Daily Kos,* January 27, 2015, 12:50 PM EST, https://www.dailykos.com/stories/2015/1/27/1360440/-7-things-our-founders-believed-about-public-education

200 *Id.*

201 American Council of Trustees and Alumni, *What Will They Learn?* 2018–19, Foreword, https://www.goacta.org/wp-content/uploads/ee/download/what-will-they-learn-2018–19.pdf

202 *Id.* at p. 1, Introduction.

203 American Council of Trustees and Alumni, *supra.* n. 201

204 American Council of Trustees and Alumni, What Will They Learn? 2010, https://www.goacta.org/wp-content/uploads/ee/download/what_will_they_learn_2010–11.pdf; *See also,* Letter from Former Harvard Dean Harry Lewis contained in: *What Will They Learn,* https://www.whatwilltheylearn.com/about

205 Kopel, David B., "The American Revolution against British Gun Control," *Administrative and Regulatory Laws News* (American Bar Association), Vol. 37, no. 4, Summer 2012, http://www.davekopel.org/2A/LawRev/american-revolution-against-british-gun-control.html

206 *Id.*

207 Ganim, Sarah, et al., "UNC report finds 18 years of academic fraud to keep athletes playing," *CNN,* October 23, 2014, 10:28 AM ET, https://www.cnn.com/2014/10/22/us/unc-report-academic-fraud/index.html

208 See e.g. Fain, Paul, Average Loan Debt for Graduates of Four-Year Colleges: $28,650, *Inside Higher Ed.* September 20, 2018, https://www.insidehighered.com/quicktakes/2018/09/20/average-loan-debt-graduates-four-year-colleges-28650

209 Kelly Blue Book, *PRnewswire.com,* October 2, 2018, https://www.prnewswire.com/news-releases/average-new-car-prices-rise-2-percent-year-over-year-according-to-kelley-blue-book-300722416.html

210 Konish, Lorie, U.S. median household income climbs to new high of $61,372, *MSNBC,* September, 12, 2018, updated September 14, 2018, 11:36 AM EDT, updated September 14, 2018, 5:31 PM EDT, https://www.cnbc.com/2018/09/12/median-household-income-climbs-to-new-high-of-61372.html

211 Baum, Sandy, "The Evolution of Student Debt in the U.S: An Overview," *The Urban Institute, George Washington Graduate School of Education and Human Development,* October, 2013, http://www.upjohn.org/stuloanconf/Baum.pdf

212 Bruffey, Wade, Cost of a Car in the Year You Were Born, *Cars & Trucks,* April 19, 2016, 4:13, https://blog.chron.com/carsandtrucks/2016/04/cost-of-a-car-in-the-year-you-were-born/

213 United States Census Bureau, Median Family Income Up in 1970 *(Advance Data from March 1971 Current Population Survey)*, May 20, 1971, https://www.census.gov/library/publications/1971/demo/p60–78.html#:~:text=The%20median%20money%20income%20of,the%201969%20figure%20of%20%249%2C430.

214 Rampell, Catherine, Warren's free-college-and-debt-forgiveness plan might be liberal, but it isn't progressive, *Richmond Times-Dispatch*, April 29, 2019, https://richmond.com/opinion/columnists/catherine-rampell-column-free-college-and-debt-forgiveness-plan-may-be-liberal-but-it-isnt/article_6a75d89c-e468–589e-b565–65924f56e544.html

215 Baum, Sandy "The Evolution of Student Debt in the U.S: An Overview," *supra* n. 211

216 Friedman, Zack, Student Debt Loan Statistics in 2019: A $1.5 Trillion Crisis, *Forbes*, February 25, 2019, 6:51 pm, EST, https://www.forbes.com/sites/zackfriedman/2020/02/03/student-loan-debt-statistics/#3088c27a281f

217 Wilson, Reid, Census: More Americans have college degree than ever before, *The Hill*, April 3, 2017, 11:56 AM, EDT, https://thehill.com/homenews/state-watch/326995-census-more-americans-have-college-degrees-than-ever-before

218 O'Shaughnessy, Lynn, Federal Government Publishes More Complete Graduation Rate Data, *Cappex*, https://www.cappex.com/articles/blog/government-publishes-graduation-rate-data

219 *Id.*

220 *Id.*

221 Kiersz, Andy, The 15 US states with the lowest college graduation rates, *Business Insider*, June 7, 2019, 2:29 IST, https://www.businessinsider.in/the-15-us-states-with-the-lowest-college-graduation-rates/articleshow/69697552.cms

222 Cooper, Preston, Betsy DeVos Is Wrong about the Government Takeover of Student Loans, *Forbes*, November 30, 2018, November 30, 2018, 2:30 am EST, https://www.forbes.com/sites/prestoncooper2/2018/11/30/betsy-devos-is-wrong-about-the-government-takeover-of-student-loans/#67ac69f84990

223 Richardson, Valerie, Oops: Maxine Waters grills banks on student loan crisis even though feds took over in 2010, *The Washington Times*, April 10, 2019, https://www.washingtontimes.com/news/2019/apr/10/maxine-waters-goofs-grilling-banks-student-loans/

224 *See generally*, Cooper, Preston, Betsy DeVos Is Wrong about the Government Takeover of Student Loans, *supra* n. 222

225 Connley, Courtney, Google, Apple and 12 other companies that no longer require employees to have a college degree, *cnbc.com*, October 8, 2018, 12:51 PM EDT, updated 12:51 PM EDT, https://www.cnbc.com/2018/08/16/15-companies-that-no-longer-require-employees-to-have-a-college-degree.html

226 Koncz, Andrea, Salary Trends Through Salary Survey: A Historical Perspective on Starting Salaries for New College Graduates, *NACE*, August 2, 2016, https://www.naceweb.org/job-market/compensation/salary-trends-through-salary-survey-a-historical-perspective-on-starting-salaries-for-new-college-graduates/; *see also*, Nace Salary Survey Winter 2019, https://www.utdallas.edu/career/docs/about/NACESalary2019.pdf

227 Richardson, Valerie, Project Veritas: Sanders staffer says 'cities burn' if Trump re-elected, predicts violence at DNC, *The Washington Times*, January 14, 2020, https://www.washingtontimes.com/news/2020/jan/14/project-veritas-sanders-staffer-says-cities-burn-i/; *see also*, Sheriff, Lucy, "Burn It Down: Black Lives Matter leader threatens to 'burn down the system if they don't get want they want,'" *supra* n. 141

228 McCarthy, Niall, The Countries with the Most People Living in Slavery, *Forbes.com*, May 31, 2016 at 8:20 am, https://www.forbes.com/sites/niallmccarthy/2016/05/31/the-countries-with-the-most-people-living-in-slavery-infographic/#3994817b1b12

229 Williams, Walt, Blacks Must Confront Reality, *supra* n. 34; Williams, Walt, The Welfare State's Legacy, *nwfdaileynews.com*, September 20, 2017, 5:00 AM https://www.nwfdailynews.com/news/20170920/walter-e-williams-welfare-states-legacy

230 Williams, Walt, Walter E. Williams: Welfare state holding back African-Americans, *Charleston Gazette-Mail*, April 19, 2017, updated November 21, 2017, https://www.wvgazettemail.com/opinion/

walter-e-williams-welfare-state-holding-back-african-americans-dai-ly-mail/article_31249047–5ac2–501a-8140–7f42ec325fe3.html

231 *Id.*

232 Holding a Four Year College Degree Brings Blacks Close to Parity With Whites, *The Journal of Blacks in Higher Education,* July 16, 2020, http://www.jbhe.com/news_views/47_four-year_collegedegrees.html

233 *Id.*

234 *Id.*

235 Williams, Walt, Walt Williams: Black Americans and Liberty, *supra* n. 34

236 Williams, Walt, Dirty College Secrets, *The Patriot Post,* January 10, 2018,

https://patriotpost.us/opinion/53321-dirty-college-secrets-2018–01–10

237 *Id.*

238 Monroe, Rob, The History of the Keeling Curve, *Scripps Institution of Oceanography*, April 3, 2013, https://scripps.ucsd.edu/programs/keelingcurve/2013/04/03/the-history-of-the-keeling-curve/

239 Geggel, Laura, How Often Do Ice Ages Happen? *Livescience.com,* March 25, 2017,https://www.livescience.com/58407-how-often-do-ice-ages-happen.html#:~:text=The%20five%20major%20ice%20ages,to%20260%20million%20years%20ago) ; Ross, Rachel, What Are the Milankovitch Cycles, *Livescience.com,* February 20, 2019, https://www.livescience.com/64813-milankovitch-cycles.html

240 Sustainable nuclear energy, *SCK.CEN, Belgium Nuclear Research Centre*, 2019, https://www.sckcen.be/en/expertises/technology/new-reactors-and-fuels

241 , Generation IV Nuclear Reactors, *World Nuclear Association*, December, 2017, updated May, 2019, https://www.world-nuclear.org/information-library/nuclear-fuel-cycle/nuclear-power-reactors/generation-iv-nuclear-reactors.aspx

242 Moore, Stephen, Why The Greens Hate Nuclear Power, *The Heritage Foundation*, July 14, 2017, https://www.heritage.org/nuclear-energy/commentary/why-the-greens-hate-nuclear-power

243 *Id.*

244 *Id.*

245 *Id.*

246 Nuclear Power in China, *World Nuclear Association,* March, 2019, updated, April, 2020, https://www.world-nuclear.org/information-library/country-profiles/countries-a-f/china-nuclear-power.aspx#:~:text=Mainland%20China%20has%20about%2045,30%20GWe%20more%20under%20construction.

247 Johnson, Scott K., Last time the Earth was this warm, sea level was a whole lot higher, *Ars Technica*, January 23, 2017. 6:15 PM, https://arstechnica.com/science/2017/01/last-time-the-earth-was-this-warm-sea-level-was-a-whole-lot-higher/

248 Williams, Walt, Environmental doom? Grossly wrong predictions, *Richmond Times-Dispatch*, October 10, 2019. P. 11A

249 Moore, Stephen, Why The Greens Hate Nuclear Power, *supra*. n. 242

250 Thorne, Ashley, U.S. Founding Fathers on Education, in Their Own Words, *supra* n. 198

251 *Id.*

252 297 U.S. 1 (1936).

253 317 U.S. (1942).

254 *343 U.S. 549* (1952).

255 Huxley, Aldous, *Brave New World,* Chatto & Windus, London, 1932

256 Roy, Avik, ACA Architect: The Stupidity of the American Voter Led Us to Hide Obamacare's True Costs from the Public, *Forbes.com*, November 10, 2014 at 5:32 pm, https://www.forbes.com/sites/theapothecary/2014/11/10/

aca-architect-the-stupidity-of-the-american-voter-led-us-to-hide-obamacares-tax-hikes-and-subsidies-from-the-public/#467d36ff7c05

257　See Garfield, Rachel, et al., Estimates of Eligibility for ACS Coverage Among the Uninsured in 2016, *The Henry J. Kaiser Family Foundation*, January, 2016, http://files.kff.org/attachment/data-note-new-esti-mates-of-eligibility-for-aca-coverage-among-the-uninsured; *see also*, Syrop, Jackie, Neaerly 12 Million People Are Uninsured but Eligible for ACA Financial Help, *AJMC.com*, November 1, 2016, https://www.ajmc.com/newsroom/nearly-12-million-people-are-uninsured-but-eligible-for-aca-financial-help

258　See Roy, Avik, ACA Architect: The Stupidity of the American Voter Led Us to Hide Obamacare's True Costs from the Public, *supra* n. 256

259　See e.g. Smith, Aarron, Record shares of Americans now own smart-phones, have home broadband, *FactTank, Pew Research Center*, January 12, 2017, https://www.pewresearch.org/fact-tank/2017/01/12/evolution-of-technology/

260　Associated Press, Medicare will become insolvent in 2026, U.S. government says, *Los Angeles Times*, June 5, 2018 at 12:50 PM, https://www.latimes.com/nation/nationnow/la-na-pol-medi-care-finances-20180605-story.html#:~:text=The%20report%20from%20program%20trustees,years%20earlier%20than%20previ-ously%20forecast.&text=%E2%80%9CLackluster%20economic%20growth%20in%20previous,both%20Social%20Security%20and%20Medicare.%E2%80%9D

261　Freeman, Robert A. and D. Wayne Taylor, Be wary of Canada's drug price controls and lack of IP protections, *thehill.com*, March 19, 2018 at 2:00 p.m., https://thehill.com/opinion/healthcare/378686-be-wary-of-canadas-drug-price-controls-and-lack-of-ip-protections

262　*See,* Jacobson, Louis, How Expensive Would a Single Payer System Be, *Politifact*, July 21, 2017, https://www.tampabay.com/news/perspective/politifact-how-expensive-would-a-single-payer-system-be/2331631/

263　Reich, Robert, "How blue states help red states," *Richmond Times-Dispatch*, Wednesday, November 14, 2018

264 Boaz, David, "Davy Crockett's Lesson for Congress," *Cato Institute*, March 18, 2010, 5:07 PM, https://www.cato.org/blog/davy-crocketts-lesson-congress

265 Frohnen, Bruce, Beer Jeremy, Nelson, Jeffrey O., *American Conservatism: An Encyclopedia*, ISI Books, p. 865,Wilmington, De, 2006, citing article entitled, "Totalitarianism," by Mark C. Henrie.

266 Krayden, David, Biden Says He's the 'Most Progressive' Democrat as He Almost Announces His 2020 Candidacy, *The Dailey Caller*, March 17, 2019, 10:02 AM ET, https://dailycaller.com/2019/03/17/biden-most-progressive-democrat-2020/

267 Sherman, Amy, Allen West says about 80 House Democrats are members of the Communist Party, *PolitiFact Florida*, April 11, 2012, https://www.politifact.com/factchecks/2012/apr/11/allen-west/allen-west-says-about-80-house-democrats-are-membe/

268 Valerie Jarrett—Obama's Rasputin, *Investor's Business Daily*, September 25, 2012, 6:47 PM ET, https://www.investors.com/politics/editorials/valerie-jarrett-rasputin-to-barack-obamabarack-obama-valerie-jarrett-wields-rasputinlike-power-and-influence-over-the-president-and-his-administrations-decisions/

269 *Id.*

270 *Id.*

271 *Id.*

272 *Id. See also,* Klein, Edward, *The Amateur,* Regnery Publishing, Washington, D.C., 2012.

273 Miniter, Richard, *Leading from Behind: The Reluctant President and the Advisors Who Decide for Him,* St. Martin's Press, (August, 2012).

274 *See also,* Scheiber, Noam, The Obama Whisperer, *The New Republic*, November 9, 2014, https://newrepublic.com/article/120170/valerie-jarrett-obama-whisperer

275 Galioto, Katy, Second woman accuses Biden of inappropriate touching, *Politico*, April 1, 2019, 4:26 PM EDT, https://www.politico.com/story/2019/04/01/joe-biden-second-woman-touching-1246875

276 Hains, Tim, Gates Stands by Statement That Biden Has Been Wrong on Nearly Every Major Foreign Policy Issue, *Real Clear Politics,* May 13, 2019, https://www.realclearpolitics.com/video/2019/05/13/gates_stands_by_statement_that_biden_has_been_wrong_on_nearly_every_major_foreign_policy_question.html

277 See e.g. Selby Gardner,W., Beto O'Rourke arrested in 1990 for burglary and DWI, *Poynter Institute, Politifact.com,* August 23, 2018, https://www.politifact.com/factchecks/2018/aug/22/silvestre-reyes/beto-orourke-arrested-1990s-burglary-and-dwi/ ; Menn, Joseph, Beto O'Rourke's secret membership in America's oldest hacking group, *Reuters*, March 15, 2019, 3:30 pm GMT, https://www.reuters.com/investigates/special-report/usa-politics-beto-orourke/; *Wikipedia*, Beto O'Rourke, updated July 18, 2020, 14:00 (UTC), https://en.wikipedia.org/wiki/Beto_O%27Rourke

278 Robbins, James S., End of Elizabeth Warren's presidential campaign? New claim of 'American Indian' heritage, *USA Today*, February 7, 2019, 1:42 pm ET, https://www.usatoday.com/story/opinion/2019/02/07/elizabeth-warren-dna-results-percentage-cherokee-nation-native-american-column/2799968002/

279 Vesoulis Abby, This Presidential Candidate Wants to Give Every Adult $1,000 a Month, *Time*, February 13, 2019, 4:10 PM EST, https://time.com/5528621/andrew-yang-universal-basic-income/

280 Amadeo, Kimberly, Anderson, Somer G., US Federal Government Tax Revenue, *the balance,* updated July 1, 2020, https://www.thebalance.com/current-u-s-federal-government-tax-revenue-3305762

281 See Safir, Ibn, Florida Mayor and Former FSU Wide Receiver Wayne Messam Announces 2020 Bid, *The Root*, March 28, 2019. 9:25 PM, https://www.theroot.com/florida-mayor-and-former-fsu-wide-receiver-wayne-messam-1833655516

282 *See* https://www.politico.com/2020-election/candidates-views-on-the-issues/, updated March 5, 2020

283 Schneider, Katy, The Best Books for Understanding Socialism, According to Experts, *The Strategist*, March 8, 2019, https://nymag.com/strategist/article/best-socialism-books.html

284 *See* Santayana, George, *The Life of Reason* (Hudson River ed.), Scribner Book Company, New York, 1981

285 Will, George F., The Democrats and the 1919 World Series were both trying to lose, *supra* n. 194

286 President Daniels to graduates: Your choices, not chance, will help you achieve great things, *Purdue University News*, May 13, 2016, https://www.purdue.edu/newsroom/releases/2016/Q2/president-daniels-to-graduates-never-forget-those-who-helped,-but-your-successes,-failures-are-your-own.html

287 See e.g. Paul, James, Wanner, Lindsey, The Self-Fulfilling Prophesy of Low Expectations, *Commonwealth Foundation*, December 19, 2014, https://www.commonwealthfoundation.org/policyblog/detail/the-self-fulfilling-prophecy-of-low-expectations

288 Rosenthal, R. and Jacobson, L., *Pygmalion in the classroom: Teacher expectations and students' intellectual development.* Holt, Rinehart & Winston, New York (1968); Babad, E. Y., Inbar, J., Rosenthal, R., Pygmalion, Galatea, and the Golem: Investigations of biased and unbiased teachers, *Journal of Educational Psychology*, 1982, https://psycnet.apa.org/record/1983–01891–001

289 *See*, Williams, Walter E. Williams: Welfare State holding back African-Americans, *supra* n. 230

290 Cole, Devan, *et al.*, Klobuchar lays out 'bold, trillion-dollar' infrastructure plan, *CNN Politics*, March 28, 2019, 9:58 PM ET, https://www.cnn.com/2019/03/28/politics/amy-klobuchar-infrastructure-plan/index.html

291 Crowe, Jack, Blasey Ford's Lawyer Admits Client Wants 'Asterisk' Next To Kavanaugh's Name When He Rules On Roe, *National Review*, September 4, 2019, 1:12 PM, https://www.nationalreview.com/news/christine-blasey-fords-lawyer-admits-client-wants-asterisk-next-to-kavanaughs-name-when-he-rules-on-roe/

292 What is the Purpose of Journalism, *American Press Institute*, (2018), https://www.americanpressinstitute.org/journalism-essentials/what-is-journalism/purpose-journalism/

293 Pitts, Leonard, Do we really need to 'understand" Trump supporters, *Richmond Times Dispatch,* May 6, 2018. Although I have not been able to confirm it, an even more strident version of this article called, *"No need to understand Trump supporters,"* may have been published. *See e.g.* Herman Birdsong, COD, May 11, 2018: Pitts is guilty of his own accusations, *Richmond Times-Dispatch*, editorial page, May 11, 2018.

294 Bouie, Jamelle, There's No Such Thing as a Good Trump Voter, *slate.com,* November 15, 2016 at 12:00 PM, https://slate.com/news-and-politics/2016/11/there-is-no-such-thing-as-a-good-trump-voter.html

295 *Id.*

296 Grassley, Sen. Chuck, *Supreme Court Vacancies in Presidential Election Years: "The Biden Rules,"* Prepared Floor Statement of Senator Chuck Grassely of Iowa, Chairman Senate Judiciary Committee, Monday, February 22, 2016, https://www.grassley.senate.gov/news/news-releases/grassley-floor-statement-politicizing-court

297 Kertscher, Tom, *What Ruth Bader Ginsburg said about Donald Trump,* Politifact, July 13, 2016 at 2:36 PM, https://www.politifact.com/article/2016/jul/13/what-ruth-bader-ginsburg-said-about-donald-trump/

298 Hsu, Charlotte, How media 'fluff' helped Hitler rise to power, *University of Buffalo News Center*, http://www.buffalo.edu/news/releases/2015/08/034.html, August, 2015.

299 Thomas, Cal, Victory for the pro-choice side, *Richmond Times Dispatch*, June 2, 2018.

300 410 U.S. 113 (1973).

301 Merelli, Annalisa, The arguments against "late-term abortion" are based on a mistrust of women, *Quartz*, January 31, 2019, updated January 21, 2020, https://qz.com/1539219/what-are-late-term-abortions-and-who-gets-them/

302 *U.S. Abortion Statistics*, Abort73.com, February 18, 2019, https://abort73.com/abortion_facts/us_abortion_statistics/

303 *Id.*

304 https://www.guttmacher.org/united-states/abortion

305 See e.g., Elliott, Ian A., Zoophilic and pedophilic advocacy groups: Political bedfellows? Wordpress.com, https://ianaelliott.wordpress.com/2012/12/03/zoophilic-and-pedophilic-advocacy-groups-political-bedfellows/

306 381 U.S. 479 (1965).

307 428 U.S. 52 (1976)

308 505 U.S. 833 (1992)

309 See e.g. Samanta-Laughton Dr. Manjir, Was Mary Magdalene just a vessel for the Holy Blood? *Paradigm Revolution*, February 23, 2018, https://www.paradigmrevolution.com/was-mary-magdalene-just-a-vessel-for-the-holy-blood/

310 Lasch, Christopher, *The Culture of Narcissism: American Life in an Age of Diminishing Expectations*, W.W. Norton & Company, New York, 1978, reissue 2018

311 Gabler, Neal, *Winchell: Gossip, Power and the Culture of Celebrity,* 1st edition, Vintage Books, a Division of Random House, Inc., New York (October, 1995)

312 Richardson, Valerie, George Soros funded network drives anti-Kavanaugh activism, *The Washington Times,* October 8, 2018, https://www.washingtontimes.com/news/2018/oct/8/george-soros-funded-groups-deny-paying-protesters/

313 Barrett, Ted, McConnel blasts Hillary Clinton for preaching no civility with GOP, *CNN Politics*, October , 2018 at 5:53 pm ET, https://www.cnn.com/2018/10/09/politics/mitch-mcconnell-hillary-clinton-civility/index.html

314 Burke, Michael, Eric Holder: When Republicans go low,' we kick them,' *The Hill*, October, 10, 2018 at 2:31 pm, EDT, https://thehill.com/business-a-lobbying/410801-eric-holder-when-republicans-go-low-we-kick-them

315 O'Reilly, Andrew, Trump officials hounded and harassed as protestor tactics take a turn, *Fox News*, June 25, 2018, https://www.foxnews.

com/politics/trump-officials-hounded-and-harassed-as-protester-tac-
tics-take-a-turn

316 The rioting following George Floyd's death in Minneapolis, of course,
is the most recent and widespread manifestation of the violence
Progressives are fomenting against America. I have dedicated a separate chapter of this book to the repercussions resulting from Mr.
Floyd's death.

317 11 Facts About Global Poverty, *dosomething.org*, https://www.
dosomething.org/us/facts/11-facts-about-global-poverty

318 Rector, Dr. Robert and Sheffield, Rachel, Understanding Poverty In the
United States: Surprising Facts About America's Poor, http: //tinyurl.
com/448flj8); *see also* Williams, Walter E., Dependency, Not Poverty,
Creators.com, February, 12, 2014, https://www.creators.com/read/
walter-williams/02/14/dependency-not-poverty

319 Camaroto, Steven A., Immigration's Effect on the Redistribution of
House Seats, *Center for Immigration Studies*, August 1, 1998, https://
cis.org/Press-Release/Immigrations-Effect-Redistribution-House-Seats,

320 See e.g., Thornton, Bruce, Melting Pots and Salad Bowls, *Hoover
Digest*, 2012 No. 4, October 26, 2012, https://www.hoover.org/
research/melting-pots-and-salad-bowls

321 *Id.*

322 *Id.*

323 Cadman, Dan, No-Go Zones and Assimilation, *Center for
Immigration Studies*, March 5, 2018, https://cis.org/Cadman/
NoGo-Zones-and-Assimilation

324 Weaver, Matthew, et. al., Angela Merkel: German multiculturism has 'utterly failed,' *The Guardian*, October 17, 2010,
6:58 EDT, https://www.theguardian.com/world/2010/oct/17/
angela-merkel-german-multiculturalism-failed

325 *Id.*

326 *See, e.g.,* Rappaport, Nolan, Bizarro world: Pelosi angry over
Trump plan to send illegal crossers to sanctuary cities, *The Hill*,
April 13, 2019 at 10:30 AM EDT, https://thehill.com/opinion/

immigration/438742-trump-proposes-transporting-illegal-cross-ers-to-sanctuary-cities-and

327 Camarota, Steven A., Enforcing Immigration Law Is Cost Effective, *Center for Immigration Studies*, October 28, 2018, https://cis.org/Camarota/Enforcing-Immigration-Law-Cost-Effective

328 American College of Emergency Physicians, *EMTLA (Emergency Medical Treatment and Labor Act)*, newsroom.acep.org/2009–01–04-emalta-fact-sheet, https://www.acep.org/life-as-a-physician/ethics—legal/emtala/emtala-fact-sheet/#:~:text=The%20Emergency%20Medical%20Treatment%20and,has%20remained%20an%20unfunded%20mandate.

329 Malkin, Michelle, Fake Illegal Alien Families, *National Review*, May 8, 2019, 6:30 AM, https://www.nationalreview.com/2019/05/border-crisis-illegal-immigrants-use-fake-family-members/

330 Joyce, Kathyrn, The Crime of Parenting While Poor, *The New Republic*, February 25, 2019, https://newrepublic.com/article/153062/crime-parenting-poor-new-york-city-child-welfare-agency-refor

331 See Vannorsdall, Joan, A gift for Governor Northam, *Richmond Times-Dispatch*, May 29, 2019 https://richmond.com/opinion/columnists/joan-vannorsdall-column-a-gift-for-gov-ralph-northam/article_7970d956-dc6d-51ee-985b-c0d6a4124aeb.html,

332 *Id*

333 Jacobson, Louis, Viral post gets it wrong about extent of slavery in 1860, *PolitiFact*, August 24, 2017, https://www.politifact.com/factchecks/2017/aug/24/viral-image/viral-post-gets-it-wrong-extent-slavery-1860/

334 Gates, Jr., Henry Louis, Did Black People Own Slaves, *theroot.com*, March 4, 2013 @ 12:03 AM, https://www.theroot.com/did-black-people-own-slaves-1790895436

335 Jacobson, Louis, Viral post gets it wrong about extent of slavery in 1860, *supra*, n. 333

336 See generally, History Detectives, Causes of the Civil War, *pbs.org*, https://www.pbs.org/opb/historydetectives/video/1479848529/;

Pierce, John, The Reasons for Secession, *American Battlefield Trust,* https://www.battlefields.org/learn/articles/reasons-secession ; Causes of the Civil War, *America's Civil War, (HistoryNet),* September, 2010, https://www.historynet.com/causes-of-the-civil-war.

337   Edwards, Lee, What Americans Must Know About Socialism, *The Heritage Foundation*, December 3, 2018, https://www.heritage.org/progressivism/commentary/ what-americans-must-know-about-socialism

338   Darrah, Nicole, Thank U, Next, Controversial columnist Karen Attiah says Texas Rangers must change name now that Washington's NFL team retired Redskins, *The Sun*, July 14, 2020, updated 16:54, https://www.thesun.co.uk/news/12122724/ texas-rangers-mlb-washington-redskins-name-change-team/

339   Zito, Salena, Madonna of the Trail defies statue-toppling culture, *Opinions, Richmond Times-Dispatch*, July 1, 2020, p. A15, https:// richmond.com/opinion/columnists/salena-zito-column-madonna-of- the-trail-defies-statue-toppling-culture/article_2364c2c6-f012–50ff- b43b-3f381cb9c897.html

340 Severino, Carrie, Justice delayed: Anti-conservative bias kept Clarence Thomas from black history museum, *thehill.com*, September 29, 2017 at 8:00 am EDT, https://thehill.com/opinion/judiciary/353035-jus- tice-delayed-black-history-museum-finally-recognizes-justice-clarence

341 Report outlines principles for renaming campus buildings, *Yale News*, December 2, 2016, https://news.yale.edu/2016/12/02/ report-outlines-principles-renaming-campus-buildings

342 The :Famous Five," *United States Senate,* https://www.senate.gov/ artandhistory/history/minute/The_Famous_Five.htm

343 Report, *supra* n. 341 at p. 18

344 *Id.* at p.19

345 *Id.*at p.20

346 *Id.*

347 *Id.* at p. 19

348 *Id.* at p.18

349 *Id.* at p. 2

350 *Id.*

351 *Id.* at p. 20

352 *Id.* at p.2

353 *Id.*

354 *Id.* at p. 22

355 *See* n. 119, *supra*

356 Managing Epidemics: Key facts about deadly diseases, Part I, p 18, 2018, *World Health Organization,* https://www.who.int/emergencies/diseases/managing-epidemics-interactive.pdf

357 *Id.*

358 Allen-Ebrahimian, Bethany, Timeline: The early days of China's coronavirus outbreak and cover-up, *Axios.com,* March 18, 2020, https://www.axios.com/timeline-the-early-days-of-chinas-coronavirus-outbreak-and-cover-up-ee65211a-afb6–4641–97b8–353718a5faab.html

359 Pappert Tom, Flashback: Biden Called Trump's Coronavirus Travel Ban 'Xenophobia,' *National File,* March 12, 2020, https://nationalfile.com/flashback-biden-opposed-trumps-covid19-travel-ban-as-xenophobia/

360 Hamblin, James, You're Likely to Get the Coronavirus, *The Atlantic,* February, 24, 2020, https://www.theatlantic.com/author/james-hamblin/

361 *Id.*

362 *Id.*

363 Fleming, Michaela, US Flu Cases Hit 29 Million: Have We Hit Peak Season? *ContagionLive,* February 27, 2020, https://www.contagionlive.com/news/us-flu-cases-reach-29-million-have-we-hit-peak-season

364 Gardner, Jennifer, Swine flu and coronavirus: Are these pandemics different? *wkrn.com,* March 16, 2020, 7:58 PM EDT,

updated 7:59 PM EDT, https://www.news10.com/news/comparing-swine-flu-and-coronavirus/

365 Klaiman, Tamar, *et al.*, Variability in school closure decisions in response to 2009 H1N1: a qualitative systems improvement analysis, *BMC Public Health,* February 1, 2011, https://bmcpublichealth.biomedcentral.com/articles/10.1186/1471–2458–11–73

366 Patton, Mike, How Stocks Reacted During Past Flu Pandemics and Steps You Can Take to Minimize Losses, *Forbes.com,* February 28, 2020, 3:45 pm EST, https://www.forbes.com/sites/mikepatton/2020/02/28/how-stocks-reacted-during-past-flu-pandemics-and-steps-you-can-take-to-minimize-losses/#691dfabc448d

367 Managing Epidemics: Key facts about deadly diseases, *World Health Organization, supra.* n. 356, Part I, p. 24.

368 Managing Epidemics: Key facts about deadly diseases, *World Health Organization, supra,* n. 356, Part I, p. 14.

369 Pike, Brian L., et al., The Origin and Prevention of Pandemics, *Clin Infect Dis,* June 15, 2010, https://europepmc.org/article/pmc/pmc2874076

370 Nguyen, Hein H., MD, *et al.,* Influenza, *Medscape,* January 8, 2020, https://emedicine.medscape.com/article/219557-overview

371 Final Flu Season Numbers 2020, *Rochester Regional Health,* June 2, 2020, https://www.rochesterregional.org/news/2020/01/flu-season-2020

372 Gerson, Michael, Jerry Falwell Jr.'s coronavirus response shows his staggering level of ignorance, *Washington Post,* March 30, 2020, https://www.washingtonpost.com/

373 Krugman, Paul, Krugman: This land of denial and death, *The Philadelphia Tribune,* April 4, 2020, https://www.phillytrib.com/news/health/coronavirus/krugman-this-land-of-denial-and-death/article_af23b22d-7788–5755–8bd0–4dac011aa01c.html

374 Bedard, Paul, Liberty University, wrongly declared a virus disaster, now the 'model' to follow: Jerry Falwell, *Washington Examiner,* May 11, 2020, 3:41 PM, https://www.washingtonexaminer.com/

washington-secrets/liberty-university-wrongly-declared-a-virus-di-saster-now-the-model-to-follow-falwell

375 Walker, Molly, Study: Masks Fail to Filter Virus in Coughing COVID-19 Patients, *MedPage Today*, April 6, 2020; Brosseau, Lisa and Margaret Sietsema, Commentary: Masks-for-all for COVID-19 not based on sound data, *CIDRAP, University of Minnesota*, April 1, 2020, https://www.medpagetoday.com/infectiousdisease/covid19/85814

376 See e.g. Schneider, Katy, The Best Books for Understanding Socialism, According to Experts,, *supra* n. 283

377 Irfan, Umair, The case for ending the Covid-19 pandemic with mass testing, *Vox.com*, April 13, 2020, 3:20 pm EDT, https://www.vox.com/2020/4/13/21215133/coronavirus-testing-covid-19-tests-screening

378 Case Investigation and Contact Tracing: Part of a Multipronged Approach to Fight the COVID-19 Pandemic, *CDC,* updated April 29, 2020, https://www.cdc.gov/coronavirus/2019-ncov/php/princi-ples-contact-tracing.html

379 Chen, Angus, To Speed Coronavirus Treatment Some Mass. Scientists Are Designing Faster Tests, *wbur*, February 28, 2020, https://www.wbur.org/commonhealth/2020/02/28/coronavirus-diagnostic-testing

380 Gaudiano, Nicole, Teacher of the year gets to meet with Trump after all, *Politico*, April 29, 2019, 6:50 PM EDT, updated 8:10 PM EDT, https://www.politico.com/story/2019/04/29/trump-teacher-of-the-year-1393506

381 See e.g. Templin, James D., Religious Education of Pakistan's Deobandi Madaris and Radicalisation, *Counter Terrorist Trends and Anlayses,* Vol. 7, No. 5, (June, 2015),

https://www.jstor.org/stable/26351354?seq=1#metadata_info_tab_contents

CPSIA information can be obtained
at www.ICGtesting.com
Printed in the USA
BVHW031135200122
626624BV00001B/36